THE DAWN OF A NEW ERA 1250-1453

the text of this book is printed on 100% recycled paper

THE RISE OF MODERN EUROPE

Edited by **WILLIAM L. LANGER**
Harvard University

Edward P. Cheyney	THE DAWN OF A NEW ERA, 1250-1453. HR/3002
Myron P. Gilmore	THE WORLD OF HUMANISM, 1453-1517. HR/3003
E. Harris Harbison	THE PROTESTANT REVOLT, 1516-1560.*
Philip Hughes	THE CATHOLIC REFORMATION, 1560-1610.*
Carl J. Friedrich	THE AGE OF THE BAROQUE, 1610-1660. HR/3004
Frederick L. Nussbaum	THE TRIUMPH OF SCIENCE AND REASON, 1660-1685. HR/3009
John B. Wolf	THE EMERGENCE OF THE GREAT POWERS, 1685-1715. HR/3010
Penfield Roberts	THE QUEST FOR SECURITY, 1715-1740. HR/3016
Walter L. Dorn	COMPETITION FOR EMPIRE, 1740-1763. HR/3032
Leo Gershoy	FROM DESPOTISM TO REVOLUTION, 1763-1789. HR/3017
Crane Brinton	A DECADE OF REVOLUTION, 1789-1799. HR/3018
Geoffrey Bruun	EUROPE AND THE FRENCH IMPERIUM, 1799-1814. HR/3033
Frederick B. Artz	REACTION AND REVOLUTION, 1814-1832. HR/3034
William L. Langer	POLITICAL AND SOCIAL UPHEAVAL, 1832-1852, HR/1455
Robert C. Binkley	REALISM AND NATIONALISM, 1852-1871. HR/3038
Carlton J. H. Hayes	A GENERATION OF MATERIALISM, 1871-1900. HR/3039
Oron J. Hale	THE GREAT ILLUSION, 1900-1914.*
Bernadotte Schmitt	THE WORLD IN THE CRUCIBLE, 1914-1919.*
Raymond Sontag	REVOLT AGAINST THE OLD ORDER, 1919-1939.*
Gordon Wright	THE ORDEAL OF TOTAL WAR, 1939-1945, HR/1408

**** In preparation***

THE DAWN OF A NEW ERA

1250-1453

BY EDWARD P. CHEYNEY

HARPER TORCHBOOKS
Harper & Row, Publishers
New York, Evanston, San Francisco, London

THE DAWN OF A NEW ERA, 1250-1453

Printed in the United States of America

This book was originally published in 1936 by Harper & Brothers in The Rise of Modern Europe series edited by William L. Langer.

First HARPER TORCHBOOK edition published 1962, by
Harper & Row, Publishers, Incorporated
New York & Evanston.

TABLE OF CONTENTS

LIST OF ILLUSTRATIONS

The illustrations, grouped in a separate section, will be found following page 210.

INTRODUCTION

Our age of specialization produces an almost incredible amount of monographic research in all fields of human knowledge. So great is the mass of this material that even the professional scholar cannot keep abreast of the contributions in anything but a restricted part of his general subject. In all branches of learning the need for intelligent synthesis is now more urgent than ever before, and this need is felt by the layman even more acutely than by the scholar. He cannot hope to read the products of microscopic research or to keep up with the changing interpretations of experts, unless new knowledge and new viewpoints are made accessible to him by those who make it their business to be informed and who are competent to speak with authority.

These volumes, published under the general title of *The Rise of Modern Europe* are designed primarily to give the general reader and student a reliable survey of European history written by experts in various branches of that vast subject. In consonance with the current broad conceptions of the scope of history, they attempt to go beyond a merely political-military narrative, and to lay stress upon social, economic, religious, scientific and artistic developments. The minutely detailed, chronological approach is to some extent sacrificed in the effort to emphasize the dominant factors and to set forth their interrelationships. At the same time the division of European history into national histories has been abandoned and wherever possible attention has been focussed upon larger forces common to the whole of European civilization. These are the broad lines on which this history as a whole has been laid out. The individual volumes are integral parts of the larger scheme, but they are intended also to stand as independent units, each the work of a scholar well qualified to treat the period covered by his book. Each volume contains about fifty illustrations selected from the mass of contemporary pictorial material. All non-contemporary illustrations have been excluded on principle. The bibliographical note appended to each volume is designed to facilitate further study of special aspects touched upon in the text. In general every effort has been made to give the reader a clear idea of the main movements in European history, to embody the monographic contributions of research workers, and to present the material in a forceful and vivid manner.

. . . . . .

It seemed advisable, in planning this series, to provide for an introductory volume, sketching in broad lines the background of some of the outstanding movements and characteristics of the modern era. The difficult task of selecting the salient points in the development of two centuries has been undertaken by Professor Cheyney, a dean of the historical profession in America and a scholar well known through his previous writings. Professor Cheyney has very wisely eschewed any attempt to present a complete or exhaustive account of this long and involved period. He has, instead, kept constantly in mind the requirement that he write an introductory volume. His stress throughout has been placed on those factors and developments of the so-called later middle ages which were to have a future. In other words, he has consistently directed his glance forward rather than backward, and he has tried, not to be inclusive, but to select typical phenomena to illustrate general tendencies. Considering the European scene as a whole, he has written at some length of the development of trade and communications, of the rise of capitalism, of the emergence of the middle class. He has considered also the repercussions of these factors, such as the appearance of representative government, the growth of popular unrest, the rise of national feeling, the transformation of the Church and the new movements in literature and art. Quite apart from the function of this volume in the general series, the reader should find this book a stimulating account and appraisal of the historical origins of some of the outstanding traits of the modern world.

William L. Langer

PREFACE

If the merit of this book were in proportion to the time it has taken to write it; if the vistas of human history through this period of endings and beginnings that have disclosed themselves to the writer would open out to the reader; if the hundreds of famous men and women that crowded the stage during these two hundred years could have been given speaking parts, no reader or reviewer could, probably, speak too highly of the book. There is no lack of richness and variety of material in its subject. But I fear its long chapters lie lifeless and vapid. The performers necessarily come on the stage and go off again uncharacterized and often even unnamed. The difficulty lies not in the abundance and variety of the events, the personality of the people, or the interest and significance of the institutions of the period; but in the difficulty of narrating and describing them, in the inspiration that would be necessary to give them life. The imagination of the reader will have to fill out the deficiencies of the writer. Moreover this volume is intended as an introduction to a long series. Something of contemporary interest has necessarily, therefore, been sacrificed to the prospective of its outlook.

It is obvious that so many aspects of so long a period could not have been studied or written altogether from contemporary sources. I can only say that the material has been drawn from the best and most scholarly works I know, that I have had the constant and invaluable criticism of the editor and of other academic friends, that here and there this study represents old fields of original research, and that some of it has been subjected to the best of all tests, the interest of my students.

Edward P. Cheyney

Springfield, Pa.
September, 1935.

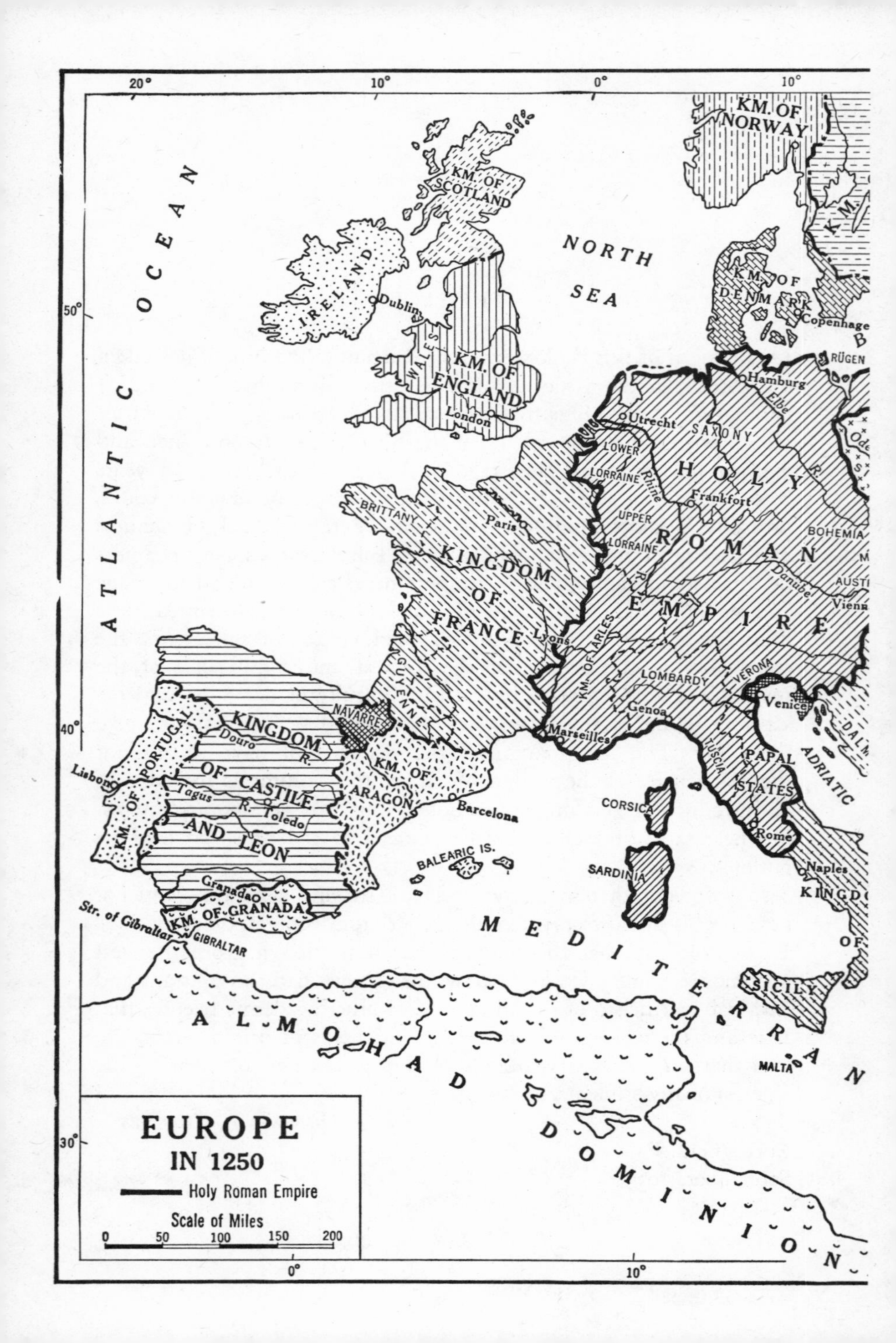

EUROPE
IN 1250
Holy Roman Empire
Scale of Miles
0 50 100 150 200
ATLANTIC OCEAN
NORTH SEA
KM. OF NORWAY
KM. OF SCOTLAND
IRELAND
Dublin
WALES
KM. OF ENGLAND
London
KM. OF DENMARK
Copenhagen
RÜGEN
Hamburg
Elbe
Utrecht
SAXONY
LOWER LORRAINE
Rhine
UPPER LORRAINE
HOLY ROMAN EMPIRE
Frankfort
BOHEMIA
Danube
Vienna
BRITTANY
Paris
KINGDOM OF FRANCE
Lyons
KM. OF ARLES
GUYENNE
LOMBARDY
VERONA
Venice
Genoa
Marseilles
NAVARRE
KINGDOM OF CASTILE AND LEON
Douro R.
Tagus R.
Toledo
KM. OF PORTUGAL
Lisbon
KM. OF ARAGON
Barcelona
Granada
KM. OF GRANADA
Str. of Gibraltar
GIBRALTAR
BALEARIC IS.
CORSICA
SARDINIA
PAPAL STATES
Rome
ADRIATIC
Naples
SICILY
MALTA
MEDITERRANEAN
ALMOHAD DOMINION

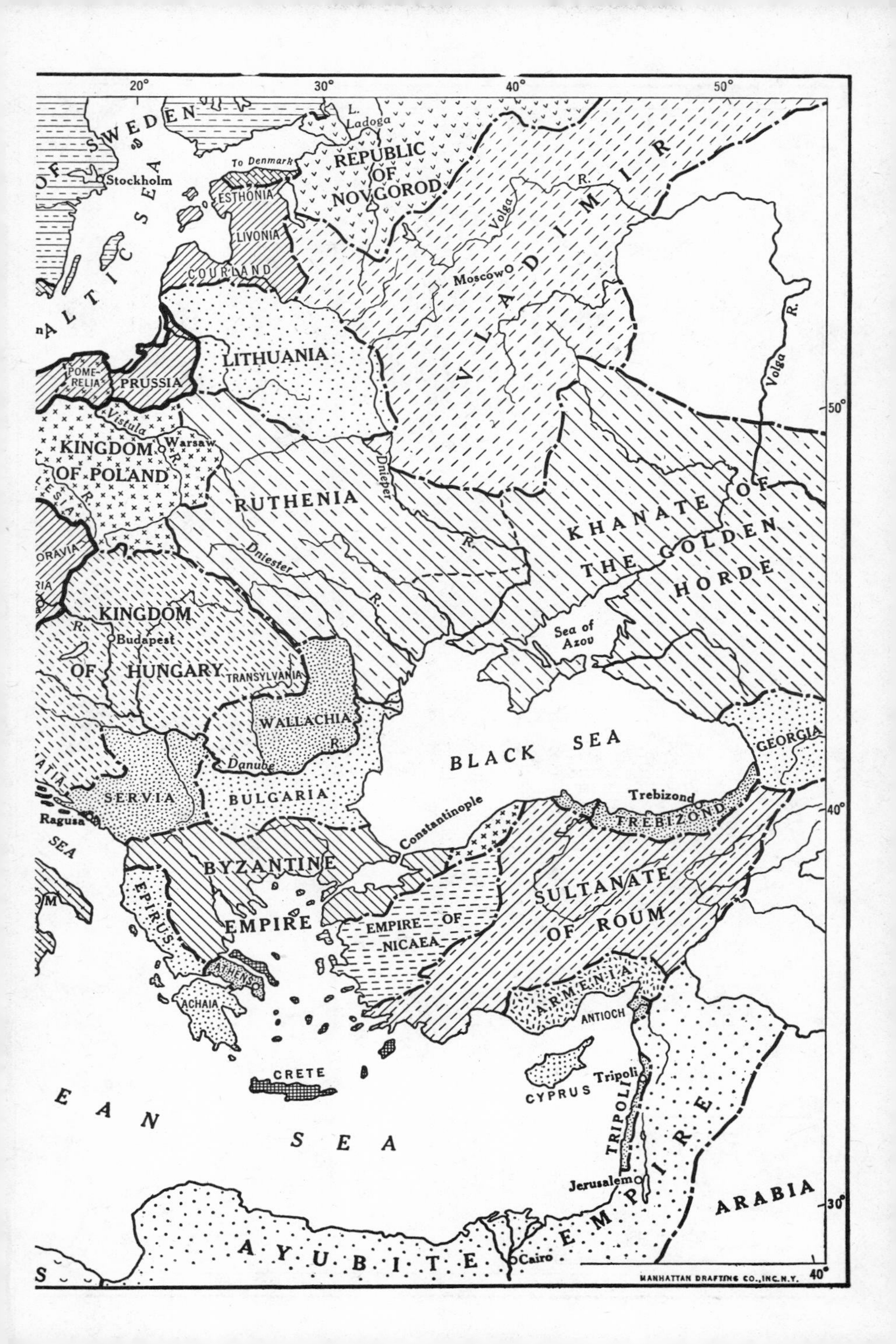
20°
30°
40°
50°
SWEDEN
L. Ladoga
REPUBLIC OF NOVGOROD
To Denmark
Stockholm
ESTHONIA
LIVONIA
COURLAND
BALTIC SEA
VLADIMIR
Volga R.
Moscow
LITHUANIA
POMERELIA
PRUSSIA
Vistula
KINGDOM OF POLAND
Warsaw
RUTHENIA
Dnieper
Dniester
KHANATE OF THE GOLDEN HORDE
KINGDOM OF HUNGARY
Budapest
TRANSYLVANIA
WALLACHIA
Danube
Sea of Azov
BLACK SEA
GEORGIA
SERVIA
BULGARIA
Ragusa
Constantinople
Trebizond
TREBIZOND
BYZANTINE EMPIRE
EPIRUS
ATHENS
ACHAIA
EMPIRE OF NICAEA
SULTANATE OF ROUM
ARMENIA
ANTIOCH
CYPRUS
Tripoli
TRIPOLI
CRETE
SEA
Jerusalem
ARABIA
AYUBITE EMPIRE
Cairo
MANHATTAN DRAFTING CO., INC. N.Y.

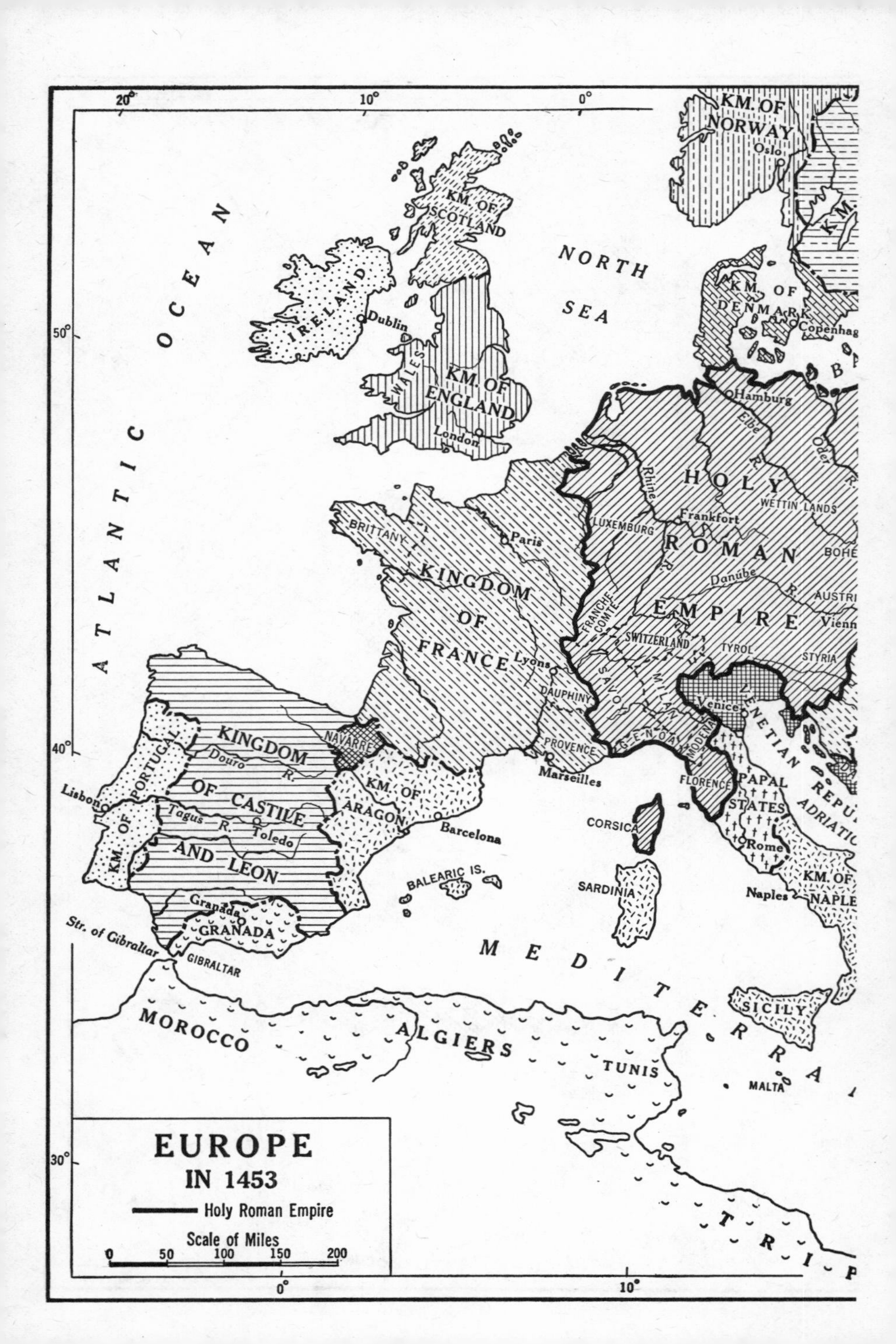
EUROPE
IN 1453
Holy Roman Empire
Scale of Miles
0
50
100
150
200
ATLANTIC OCEAN
NORTH SEA
KM. OF NORWAY
Oslo
KM. OF SCOTLAND
IRELAND
Dublin
WALES
KM. OF ENGLAND
London
KM. OF DENMARK
Copenhag
Hamburg
Elbe R.
Oder R.
HOLY ROMAN EMPIRE
WETTIN LANDS
Rhine R.
Frankfort
LUXEMBURG
BOHE
Danube R.
AUSTRI
Vienn
TYROL
STYRIA
BRITTANY
Paris
KINGDOM OF FRANCE
Lyons
FRANCHE COMTE
SWITZERLAND
SAVOY
MILAN
DAUPHINY
PROVENCE
GENOA
MODENA
Venice
VENETIAN REPU
Marseilles
FLORENCE
PAPAL STATES
Rome
ADRIATIC
NAVARRE
KINGDOM OF CASTILE AND LEON
Douro R.
Tagus R.
Toledo
KM. OF PORTUGAL
Lisbon
KM. OF ARAGON
Barcelona
CORSICA
SARDINIA
BALEARIC IS.
Naples
KM. OF NAPLE
Granada
GRANADA
Str. of Gibraltar
GIBRALTAR
MEDITERRA
SICILY
MALTA
MOROCCO
ALGIERS
TUNIS
TRIP
20°
10°
0°
50°
40°
30°
0°
10°

OF SWEDEN
Stockholm
BALTIC SEA
ESTHONIA
LIVONIA
Riga
COURLAND
SAMOGITIA
Königsberg
D. OF PRUSSIA
Danzig
Vistula
Warsaw
POLAND
SILESIA
Ladoga
REPUBLIC OF NOVGOROD
GRAND PRINCIPALITY OF MOSCOW
Moscow
KHANATE OF THE GOLDEN HORDE
Volga R.
Don R.
GRAND PRINCIPALITY OF LITHUANIA
Kiev
Dnieper R.
Dniester R.
KHANATE OF THE CRIMEA
Sea of Azov
KHANATE OF ASTRAKHAN
GEORGIA
KINGDOM OF HUNGARY
Budapest
PRINC. OF MOLDAVIA
PRINC. OF WALLACHIA
Danube R.
BLACK SEA
KM. OF BOSNIA
KM. OF SERVIA
MONTE NEGRO
Durazzo (Ven.)
ALBANIA
Constantinople
TREBIZOND
ARMENIA
OTTOMAN EMPIRE
KARAMAN
Athens
MOREA
CRETE
CYPRUS
AEGEAN SEA
DOMINIONS OF THE MAMELUKES
Cairo
ARABIA
20°
40°
50°
30°
MANHATTAN DRAFTING CO., INC. N.Y.

Chapter One

THE EXPANSION OF TRADE AND THE INCREASE OF WEALTH

I. INTRODUCTION

IT IS AN EXPERIENCE, not so common perhaps as it should be, but not unknown to some of us, to watch the increasing glow of the early morning spread over the landscape. Few of the objects disclosed are new, but all appear in an altered and constantly changing light. It is the dawn of a new day. The scene is set for a series of new occurrences. So it was with the coming on of modern times. No thoughtful student of history will now think of the middle ages, as he might have a generation ago, as a period of darkness. They had their own interest, their own culture, their own greatness. It is not in a contrast between darkness and light that the distinction between the middle ages and modern times is to be found, but in a difference of environment. The more the sources of our knowledge of the early modern centuries are studied the more do they disclose a new age. It is in a very real sense the dawn of a new era.

The tendency of scholarship has been to push the beginning of the modern period further and further back. As we obtain a clearer perspective, it becomes increasingly evident that by the middle of the thirteenth century the real middle ages were over. A great era had passed away, its special characteristics outlived, its work accomplished. Those institutions which were destined to permanency had been placed on durable foundations. The Catholic church had been organized and its doctrines formulated, the basic systems of law had been elaborated, the universities had been founded, the older towns had been chartered, the chief lines of commerce had been marked out. On the other hand those institutions which were to disappear were obviously already in decay: feudalism was losing its universal sway; the Crusades were over; in the very year with which this volume begins Frederick II, the last of the medieval emperors claiming universal dominion, died and the long struggle between empire and papacy gradually ceased to interest their respective proponents. Little that was specifically medieval survived in any vigor the middle of the thirteenth century.

There was no sudden change. Birth and death of institutions as of populations nearly balanced one another. Most periods of history —and this is no exception—are marked by the simultaneous fading away of old institutions and the rise of new.[1] From the middle of the thirteenth century onward, through the remainder of that century, in the active hundred years that followed and as the fifteenth century progressed, old institutions sank into insignificance, much that was new appeared. In these 200 years trade, industry and finance, under the influence of a nascent capitalism, superseded agriculture as the main economic basis of European society; town life grew in importance; the middle classes became more influential, the lower classes more restive; freedom took the place of serfdom among the rural masses; signs of the awakening of a national spirit became visible; boundaries of states were more settled. New dynasties took advantage of these conditions to build centralized monarchical states; the art of war was more highly developed; the church, weakened from within and without, lost its authority; new knowledge and new habits of thought were acquired. By some such date as 1450 a new age had arrived, and on the stage of a new Europe the drama of modern history was to be played. The present volume is the prologue of the play. It is an account of the principal developments in the history of Europe from 1250 to 1450, or perhaps to 1453, to include the last dying gasp of the old Eastern Empire.

II. THE SPREAD OF COMMERCE

The most fundamental of the changes that marked the passage from medieval to modern times was the increase of wealth, and the principal cause of the increase of wealth was the extension of commerce. The exchange of goods has been of great significance in the advance of civilization. Even the chaffering of the local market-place

[1] J. Huizinga, in his suggestive book *The Waning of the Middle Ages* (London, 1924), contends that this period looks backward rather than forward, but he fails to consider the merchant, the banker, the explorer, or the religious reformer.

breaks the stolid inertia of mere domestic production and consumption. Distant trade exerts a more profound influence. The trails along which merchants have carried goods for sale are older and better worn than the routes by which tribes have migrated or armies have marched. Articles of Asiatic jade found along the wayside in western Russia, the Arabic coins collected along the Baltic coasts and now in Swedish museums, Roman coins picked up on obscure Alpine passes, these are but chance evidences of the distant journeyings of early merchants.[2] Along these trading routes, across frontiers of climate and race have come men of different nationalities and stages of culture, bringing objects of need or desire and luxuries which soon became necessities. Imports enriched the life of the lands to which they came and furnished an incentive to the production, for purposes of exchange, of things in demand elsewhere. The very name "goods," common to so many languages, indicates the desirability of objects of trade and the satisfaction men have felt in obtaining them.

Nor is the process of trade merely an economic one. Commerce has built bridges across which ideas as well as men and goods have passed. The foreign costume, customs and language of merchants have stirred the sluggish minds of backward nations. Traders from the Mediterranean brought in their packs to the northern and western barbarians objects of art, pictures, manuscripts and other such marvels, as well as coarser necessary goods. In like fashion the products of barbarous lands have always intrigued the imagination of civilized peoples. Trade destroys isolation. Provincialism cannot long survive the arrival and departure of ships and caravans, the intercourse of merchants at markets and fairs. The exchange of goods, in early times, was the most influential of economic processes.

It is not, however, with this primitive and seminal trade that we are now engaged, nor indeed with that body of widespread commerce that existed through the whole middle ages, but rather with the extension and development of trade, amounting almost to a transformation, that characterized the period now under discussion.

[2] See, e.g. E. J. Arne, *La Suède et l'Orient* (Uppsala, 1914); R. Hennig, "Zur Verkehrsgeschichte Ost- und Nordeuropas im 8ten bis 12ten Jahrhundert," *Historische Zeitschrift,* CXV (1915), 1-30; J. E. Tyler, *The Alpine Passes in the Middle Ages, 962-1250* (Oxford, 1890), chap. xv.

During these years commerce became Europe-wide, just as a century later it was to become world-wide. New routes by land and river and along the coasts were opened up. Old cities with roots deep in the past, if they were favorably situated for trade, grew in population, wealth and influence. Towns formerly insignificant, if they were similarly situated, became rich and powerful. Some, especially in France, were deliberately founded.[3] Capital came to be extensively used, notwithstanding religious opposition, and increased in volume. Commerce was the foundation of the policy of some states and one of the leading motives for public action in all. This is reflected in the surviving records. If a calculation of the number of written documents of all kinds could be made from the statute books, city memorandum books, correspondence and diplomatic collections of that time, it would probably show more items connected with trade than with either the state or the church. Men engaged in purchasing goods for export or import, in transporting them by ship, boat, wagon or pack, in traveling or sojourning in foreign cities, in financing them and those served by them are the great constituency back of these records. In general literature the merchant becomes almost as familiar as the knight, the monk or the minstrel. Even in Chaucer's varied company of pilgrims

> "A merchant was there with a forked beard,
> In motley, and high on horse he sat,
> Upon his head a Flemish beaver hat."

III. THE MATERIALS OF COMMERCE

There was no lack of materials for trade. The oldest and still probably the largest in amount were those natural productions and commodities which, in demand everywhere, could only be produced easily in certain places. An instance was that simple necessity of all life, salt. It was one of the oldest objects of trade and even in our day caravans still cross the desert to Timbuctoo burdened with

[3] The best single study of the rôle of the towns is H. Pirenne, *Medieval Cities: their Origins and the Revival of Trade* (Princeton, 1925); but see also A. Luchaire, *Les Communes Françaises à l'époque des Capétiens Directs* (new edit., Paris, 1911); G. Schmoller, *Deutsches Städtewesen in älterer Zeit* (Bonn, 1922); A. Luchaire, *Les Démocraties Italiennes* (Paris, 1915).

it, while modern steamers bring it from Spain to the cod-fisheries of Nova Scotia. In the early modern centuries, when rising populations created a growing demand and when many nearby sources of supply were still undiscovered, it was especially familiar.[4] It was evaporated by the sun in the artificial salt pools on the islands surrounding Venice and in the natural lagoons on the Bay of Biscay, or pumped from the salt wells of Lüneburg, or hewn from the mines of Salzburg, and was then carried in great quantities to other regions.[5] Long lines of packhorses came down to the Istrian and Dalmatian shores of the Adriatic to obtain the salt brought over in boats from Venice and to carry it inland through Serbia, Croatia and Hungary. One of the largest convoys of vessels sailing from North Germany was the salt fleet, going to the coast of France to bring back the requirements for salting the herring of the Baltic and the stockfish of the Scandinavian coast. English vessels regularly frequented the same source of supply. One of the busiest scenes of the early modern world was that described by a fourteenth century traveler sailing through the Sound between Denmark and Sweden. For fifty miles along the shores of Scania, while the shoals of herring were passing from the North Sea into the Baltic in early autumn, he saw thousands of boats engaged in catching, salting, packing and shipping fish. A whole population of coopers, ropemakers, blacksmiths and other artisans as well as purveyors of food and drink, 300,000 men, the traveler thought, were established in a temporary city of huts along the shore.[6]

Wine was in demand by the well-to-do in all countries, but it could be produced only where a southern sun ripened the grapes. There was therefore a wine-trade between the south and the north along all available routes, and as wealth became greater and luxury more widespread this trade came to play a larger and larger part. Gascony and Guienne were the most famous wine growing regions in Europe. The purchase and sale of wine gave the fairs of central

[4] See the highly interesting essay of Henri Hauser, "Le Sel dans l'Histoire," *Revue Économique Internationale*, III (1927), 270-9.

[5] Hermann Heineken, *Der Salzhandel Lüneburgs mit Lübeck bis zum Anfang des 15 Jahrhunderts* (Berlin, 1908), esp. the introduction; and Heinrich Ritter von Srbik, *Studien zur Geschichte des Oesterreichischen Salzwesens* (Innsbruck, 1917), 114-26.

[6] Philippe de Mézières, "Le Songe du Vieil Pèlerin," *Académie des Inscriptions*, XVI, 226; XVII, 491; L. F. Salzman, *English Trade in the Middle Ages* (Oxford, 1931), 372-5.

France much of their activity, while in the south wine was the staple commodity, and the great city of Bordeaux lived largely on the profits of its export. In England duties on its import were one of the principal sources of royal income. The struggle for the possession of this trade was among the causes of the Hundred Years War, and Gascony was for its sake the last of the English possessions in France to be surrendered.[7]

The wines of Burgundy and other parts of France made up a considerable part of the trade of Bruges; the great wine-house of the German merchants near the Thames in London testified to the popularity of the wines shipped from Cologne, Mainz and Strassburg; the sweet wines of Italy, Greece and Crete were known and favored everywhere in Europe. Wine was the principal constituent of the brisk trade between France and Ireland as iron was in Irish-Spanish commerce before "Ireland's undoing."[8]

The list of such simple products, each with its supply, its demand, its transportation, its contribution to the increasing bulk of commerce, could be extended almost indefinitely. Lumber was already running short in many shipbuilding regions; the shores of the lagoons of the northern Adriatic and the coast lands of the Mediterranean islands had been denuded of their forests, and oak, larch and fir had to be brought to Venetian, Ragusan and other shipyards from farther and farther inland or from the Black Sea.[9] The word "spruce" still testifies to its introduction into England from Prussia on the Baltic. The Dutch were already bringing shipbuilding materials from the same shores. Pitch, so necessary for treating vessels and cordage, had to be brought from regions naturally producing resinous trees. The furs worn by noble, prelate and wealthy burgher, except for the commonest kinds, were brought from the north and east.[10]

[7] See A. L. Simon, *The History of the Wine Trade in England* (London, 1906), I, passim; H. Pirenne, "Un Grand Commerce d'Exportation au Moyen Age: Les Vins de France," *Annales d'Histoire Économique et Sociale,* V (1933), 225-43.

[8] Salzman, op. cit., chap. xviii; Alice S. Green, *The Making of Ireland and Its Undoing* (London, 1908), 13-14, 18-25, 28-9.

[9] F. C. Lane, "Venetian Shipping during the Commercial Revolution," *American Historical Review,* XXXVIII (1933), 224-6.

[10] The 2,764 ermine skins used for a robe, the 2,741 for one dressing-gown and 1,762 for another, for the Duke of Orleans, all in one year, would themselves have made a good pack-horse load brought from some distant fair or market. Charles VII of France spent in one year, 1404, 4,200 livres for furs.

So hides, leather, tallow, hemp, honey, wax and grain to supplement deficient harvests were carried from region to region. Iron, lead, copper and tin, silver and gold were produced in very restricted areas but were in universal demand. Lead was used to cover the roofs of churches, castles and town halls; tin, produced almost exclusively in England, was mixed with lead to make the pewter work of English and Continental craftsmen, and with copper to make the bronze for casting fourteenth and fifteenth century cannon and other masterpieces of the new founders' art of Italy.

Wool played perhaps the largest part of any of these material products. Sheep were of course raised everywhere, and there was in many places a considerable local trade in wool and sheepskins between the town and the surrounding country-side. But not every country was orderly enough to enable the manor, the castle or the abbey to keep its large flocks safe from predatory hands till they could be shorn. Besides, climate, herbage and established breeds made the wool of some regions better or cheaper or more suited to certain purposes than that of others, so that hundreds of thousands of bales and sacks were transported yearly from favored wool growing areas to the centers of textile industry. Eastern England and northern Spain were regions famous for their wool. From the English moors it was carried across the Channel to the manufacturing towns of Flanders and northern France. Much was carried by sea to Florence and Pisa and by land across the Alps to northern Italy, and especially to Venice for manufacture or for export. One Italian company, the Scotti of Piacenza, in 1273 shipped wool worth 14,266 pounds, the equivalent in buying power of more than three-quarters of a million dollars of our money. The export duty on wool made up approximately one-third the ordinary income of the English crown. In 1273 the total export of wool from England was worth some $9,000,000 in modern value, for which the government received about $200,000 in taxes.[11] The duty on wool was offered

[11] A. Schaube, "Die Wollausfuhr Englands", *Vierteljahrschrift für Sozial und Wirtschaftsgeschichte,* VI (1908) 52-56, 68, 183. Exact equivalents in modern value of sums of money named in early records are almost impossible to obtain. In order to give some impression of reality to such figures, however, each sum has been changed into its modern bullion equivalent, then multiplied by ten as an approximation to the ratio of fourteenth to twentieth century prices. These amounts therefore must be considered suggestive rather than accurate.

as security for the large sums borrowed by the English kings from the bankers, and the bills of lading drawn against cargoes exported were one of the principal forms of international finance. The power to specify the staple town to which all wool from England had to be sent was, during the first half of the fourteenth century, one of the chief weapons of her diplomacy.[12]

England was late in developing manufactures, and continued to export wool and other raw materials to the very close of this period, but on the Continent one of the most marked changes of the thirteenth and fourteenth centuries was the specialization which made handicrafts rather than trade the characteristic occupation of many towns. The Flemish cities, Ghent, Ypres, Courtrai and others, bought their food supply from the surrounding country and from England and wool for their manufactures from England and Spain. In turn they exported fine woolen, linen and even cotton and silk cloths woven from imported materials. This shift from trade to handicraft worked a profound transformation in their economic and social, and indeed in their political, organization. This will be discussed later; here we need only note that it made Flanders rich and increased her political and commercial significance.[13]

Much the same was true of several Italian towns, notably Florence, which became famous for fine weaving and dyeing, importing the wool for her manufactures directly by land and, through Pisa and Livorno, by sea. By the close of the fourteenth century a whole list of towns, Bourges and Roussillon, Augsburg and Ulm, Barcelona and Beauvais and many others, were producers of woolen goods and other textiles for home use and for export. Other cities gained a reputation for special manufactures and based their trade upon them. Milan, Bordeaux, Nürnberg and Marseilles were noted for products of iron and steel, armor, swords, firearms and cutlery; Lucca and Paris for silk; Venice for iron, glass, goldsmith's work, bronze and silver bells; other cities and districts for leather goods,

[12] A. L. Jenckes, *The Origin, the Organization and Location of the Staple of England* (Philadelphia, 1908); E. E. Rich, "The Mayors of the Staples," *Cambridge Historical Journal,* IV (1933), 120-42; Salzman, op. cit., 285-320.

[13] G. Espinas, *La Draperie dans la Flandre française au Moyen Age,* two vols. (Paris, 1923), is the basic study, but see also H. Pirenne, "The Place of the Netherlands in the Economic History of Medieval Europe," *Economic History Review,* II (1929), 20-40.

objects of art in gold, silver, carved wood, iron and bone, statuary, gloves, fine productions of wool, linen and silk, illuminated manuscripts and musical instruments.

Some of these manufactures have perpetuated the names of their place of special origin; Cambric from Cambrai, lawn from Laon, diapered cloth from Ypres, hangings from Arras, the lace of that name from Valenciennes, Brussels carpet and lace from that Netherland city. Others came from farther away, muslin from Mosul, calico from Calicut, damask from Damascus, buckram from Bokhara.

It is not to be considered, therefore, that the trade in gross commodities, notwithstanding their volume, was the principal material of commerce. Indeed, as the period progressed, the number, variety and value of fine products, especially manufactures, became greater and greater. A fifteenth century versifier gives long lists of goods customarily brought into England.[14] Of all the commodities he enumerates,—from Spain, dates, raisins, licorice, iron, Castile soap, wax, quicksilver; from Flanders, cloth and cartwheels; from Prussia, beer and bacon, copper, silver, and bowstaves, pitch, canvas and flax; from Ireland, woolen and linen cloth and otter skins, and from other countries scores of other products—there are none on which he dilates more and, it must be acknowledged, with greater disapproval than those with which

> "The great galleys of Venice and Florence
> Be wel ladene with things of complacence."

The "spicerye and other grocers' ware," the "sweet wynes," the "nifles, trifles, that litell have availed," the "apes and japes and marmusettes tayled," and the other things with which they "cleverly blear the eyes" of the innocent Englishmen, are typical products of the Levant trade, one of the lines of early commerce of the greatest interest. This trade included not only the products of the Levant proper, that is of the shores and islands of the eastern Mediterranean, but also the products of the Far East which reached Europe for the most part through the Levant. From the islands of

[14] "The Libelle of Englysche Polycye", written 1436, in *Political Poems and Songs relating to English History* (Rolls Series) II, 160, 169, 171, 172 (new edition, Oxford 1926).

Cyprus and Crete, from Phocea with its rich deposits of alum, and from Chios with its groves of mastic, from the mainlands of Asia Minor and Greece, and from many of the islands, came olives, nuts, dyes, wine, certain fine leathers and cotton.

But nature's treasure-house for a whole group of objects which have always been keenly desired by men lay still further east. From Persia, India, Ceylon, Java, Sumatra, the Moluccas and even from as far away as China, came drugs, perfumes, musk and civet, medicines, camphor, indigo and other dyes, fragrant and polished woods, fine silks, cottons and other woven goods, ivory, porcelain, and all known precious stones—diamonds, rubies, emeralds, sapphires, turquoise, onyx, jade, pearls. From the same regions came all the edible spices of the world, pepper, cloves, nutmeg, cinnamon, mace, allspice.

The growing wealth of Europe could almost be measured by its increased demand for these luxuries. Attractive, precious, compact, these Far Eastern goods were traded in throughout the East and made their way westward along various routes and by various conveyances. There were land and river routes by which they reached Europe, across the Caspian and up the Volga to the far north, across the Black Sea through Poland or up the Danube to central Europe, but in the main they were brought by more southern routes to the ports of Asia Minor, Syria and Egypt. Here they became a part of the varied commerce of the Mediterranean.[15]

IV. THE FLANDERS FLEET OF VENICE

A map of the trade routes of Europe at this time shows a maze of lines.[16] Every navigable river was a highway, every protected bay a harbor, every practicable pass across the mountains a road by which

[15] W. von Heyd, *Histoire du Commerce du Levant au Moyen-Age* (Leipzig, 1885-6), II, 563-711; E. P. Cheyney, *European Background of American History* (New York, 1904), chaps. i and ii; G. J. Bratianu, *Recherches sur le Commerce Génois dans la Mer Noire au XIIIe Siècle* (Paris, 1929). G. Bens, *Der Deutsche Warenfernhandel in Mittelalter* (Breslau, 1926), gives an excellent catalogue of articles of trade and their provenance.

[16] An excellent map of the principal trade routes is in J. W. Thompson, *Economic and Social History of Europe in the Later Middle Ages, 1300-1530* (New York, 1931), opp. p. 4, with many detailed maps scattered through the volume; other suggestive maps are in Clive Day, *History of Commerce* (New York, 1908), and in *Putnam's Historical Atlas, Medieval and Modern,* edited by Ramsay Muir and others (sixth edition, New York and London, 1927).

raw materials could be imported or goods be taken to some market. There were, besides, some roads across open country. The tentacles of commerce reached from Novgorod in Russia in the northeast to Toledo in Spain in the southwest, from the Slavic, German and Scandinavian coasts of the Baltic in the north, to the African shores of the Mediterranean in the south, to the Levant in the southeast, and even beyond these limits. It is no more possible in a few paragraphs to describe even the main routes in detail than it has been to enumerate all the materials of early modern commerce. All that can be done is to sketch two or three developments that were especially characteristic of this period.

No one can look at a map of the trade routes without being struck by the favorable location of Venice. Built up on her traditional sixty islands, as a coral reef is lifted above the surface of the sea, she was surrounded by navigable waters and yet protected from attack by the Lido and her marshes. She was almost in the geographical centre of Europe. Of all the greater western cities she was nearest to the East and of all cities in contact with the East she had the easiest access to the West. The Adriatic was her natural outlet to both the eastern and western Mediterranean. The valleys of the Po and the Adige facilitated intercourse with the wealthy cities of northern Italy—Padua, Verona, Brescia, Milan, Ferrara, Mantua. Through the eastern passes of the Alps she had direct connection with the cities of southern Germany, and through the western passes more indirectly with Constance, Zurich, Lucerne and Geneva, and so with central Europe. This position of commercial advantage she had utilized to the full. Her whole spirit and organization corresponded to her geographical and commercial position. The government was that of a joint-stock trading company, the Doge its president, the Senate its board of directors, the populace its shareholders. The policy of Venice was consistently that which would best subserve the demands of her commercial interests. From the outset that policy had been carried out with intelligence, enterprise and unscrupulousness. It had given her great power and wealth. Her commerce was already old and far-flung throughout the Mediterranean and all the waters connected with it at the time we take up the story.

Shortly after the beginning of our period Venice advanced her commerce by two innovations: one the introduction between 1290 and 1300 of a new type of merchant vessel, the "great galley"; the other the establishment, in 1317, of an all-water trading route to England and Flanders. In Venice, as elsewhere in the Mediterranean, there had been in use from time immemorial two types of vessel, the short, broad, high-built sailing ships, and the lower, longer, narrower and swifter vessels propelled largely by oars—descendants of the old Roman trireme. They can both be seen in any Renaissance view of any Mediterranean harbor.[17] In both types there were new developments at this time, but with the "round" ships we have little to do, as they were not of great importance till late in the fifteenth century and even then affected private trading more than government enterprises, with which we are here concerned. The "argosies with portly sail" of the *Merchant of Venice* were doubtless of this build. The word "argosy" was derived from Ragusa, their supposed place of origin.

But the partial replacement of the light galleys of the middle ages by the "great galleys" which were introduced at the close of the thirteenth century was of great and immediate importance. The new vessels, from 120 to 150 feet in length, carried a crew of 100 to 200 or even more. At first they relied largely on their oars, though provided with one or two masts and sails that could be used in open water when the wind was favorable. They had twenty-five to thirty benches on each side, either two or three banks of oars, with one man at each oar; they were shallow and had but a single deck. Nevertheless there was room for a considerable cargo. This was the type of vessel used by the Venetians for their long voyages during the period from 1290 to the middle of the sixteenth century, when the galleys were superseded by the larger and more developed "round" or purely sailing ships.[18]

In the meantime, as the fourteenth century progressed, less and less reliance was placed on the oars of the galleys and more and

[17] E.g. Pompeo Molmenti, *Venice* (London, 1906-1908), I, i, 28, 34, 68, 115-431, 204, 215.

[18] "F. C. Lane, "Venetian Shipping during the Commercial Revolution," *American Historical Review,* XXXVIII (1933), 209-31; there is much of interest on the methods of shipping in E. H. Byrne, *Genoese Shipping in the Twelfth and Thirteenth Centuries* (Cambridge, 1930).

more on the sails, till the former came to be used only to overcome that greatest navigating difficulty of early times, getting into and out of harbors, or to meet an emergency. It is to be remembered that the galleys were also war ships, armed to protect themselves while on mercantile voyages, and to act as a navy in time of war. They had become by the end of our period swift, low-built sailing vessels, provided with auxiliary oars. Some forty or fifty such galleys, requiring 11,000 men for their crews, were usually in commission, in addition to the multitude of smaller vessels of various rigs belonging to Venetian merchants or to the government.[19] The oarsmen were generally free men, often immigrants from Slavonia or other part of the mainland, hired for each voyage. Later we hear of the use of prisoners taken in war, condemned felons and even slaves bought in the east. Slaves were still a constituent of Venetian trade with the Black Sea and with Egypt, although the slave trade was officially frowned upon.[20] A special guard of twenty or thirty bowmen was provided for each galley; upon occasion the rowers, too, must fight and weapons were carried along for their use if needed.

Shortly after the introduction of these galleys, in 1299, their organization into fleets was initiated. The commanding officer was elected by the Senate and strict regulations were established for their use. They were given the monopoly of the import and export of silks, spices and light and precious wares generally. After about 1350 the galleys were generally the property of the government, merely rented to the merchants, who paid the expenses and reaped the profits of their voyages.[21]

It was with such fleets that the sea trade with England and the Netherlands was opened up in the fourteenth and fifteenth centuries. The Genoese had already, according to tradition, sailed out through the Straits of Gibraltar in 1270 and 1291 into that open ocean which was later to become so familiar to them, and by way of which one of their fellow countrymen was ultimately to make

[19] Statement of the Doge Mocenigo, A.D. 1423 (Muratori, *Rerum Italicarum Scriptores,* xxii, 942, 959-60).

[20] Heyd, *Commerce du Levant,* II, 555-83; Molmenti, *Venice* I, i, 124-6.

[21] F. C. Lane, *Venetian Ships and Shipping of the Renaissance* (Baltimore, 1934), chap. i.

the discovery of a new world. But Genoa's commercial ventures were ill-supported from home; these expeditions came to nothing, and her carracks, if they passed outside the Straits at all, continued long to hug the shore and seldom to venture to the south or the north.

Venice on the other hand habitually gave to her trade direction and support. When, in the later years of the thirteenth century, a quarrel broke out between the Venetian and French governments which made difficult the land traffic across the Alps to the fairs of Champagne and the Netherlands, the sea route was resorted to. In 1317 a fleet of galleys passed boldly through the Straits, skirted the coast of Spain and Portugal, crossed the Bay of Biscay, rounded Cape Finisterre and made its way to England and the Netherlands, something over 2500 miles, the longest voyage undertaken by European trading vessels since antiquity. Almost every year thereafter a fleet was sent to England and Flanders.[22] To distinguish it from the four or five fleets sent more or less regularly to different points in the Mediterranean (the Tana Fleet, the Syrian Fleet, the Egyptian Fleet) this was known as the Flanders Fleet. It had a long, varied and interesting history, extending well into the sixteenth century.

In January or February or at latest in March the Senate ordered the equipment of one to six galleys, appointed a captain and a vice-captain of the fleet from one or other of the 200 noble Venetian families—a Dandolo, a Bembo, a Zeno, a Morosini, a Loredano; arranged for the protection of each galley by a company of archers made up of young members of the aristocracy, and then proceeded to auction off freight space to merchants who had goods to export or wished to order goods for the return voyage. Even the masters of the individual galleys were usually members of the aristocracy—Trevisani, Contarini, Giustiniani. This however signifies little, since almost all Venetians, even the highest, were merchants and most saw sea-service at one time or another in their lives. The captain of the fleet had to live with some display. At one time he was

[22] See especially A. Schaube, "Die Anfänge der Venezianischen Galeerenfahrten nach der Nordsee," *Historische Zeitschrift,* CI (1908), 28-89.

required to take with him two trumpeters, two fifers, a notary public, a physician, and a group of clerks.[23]

The fleet sailed usually in the early spring. It made its way down the Adriatic, passed to the south of Sicily or between the island and the mainland, crossed the Tyrrhenian Sea to Corsica, then to the Balearic Islands and the southern coast of Spain, and so out through the Straits and up the coast of Spain and Portugal. A bold dash across the Bay of Biscay and into the Channel brought it to Southampton or Dover, whence some of the galleys went to Sandwich or up the Thames to London; the larger part crossed to Sluys, the seaport of Bruges in Flanders, or to Middelburg in Holland or Antwerp in Brabant. Stops were made on the way and merchants and mariners went ashore to set up small, temporary markets in the Mediterranean ports or in Lisbon, but bulk was not really broken till the fleet reached the Flemish or English ports.

Galley Wharf on the Thames is thought by some to indicate the traditional landing-place of the Venetians in London. A less doubtful survival of their visits is a tablet in the little village church of Stoneham near Southampton, carved with the Imperial double eagle and with the inscription *Sepultura di Schola dei Schiavoni*, doubtless the burial place of members of the gild of Slavonian rowers of the Venetian galleys who died in port at Southampton or near enough to shore to be buried in consecrated ground.[24] The fleet during the thirty, forty, or fifty days it was allowed by local regulation to remain in Flanders or England, disposed of the sugar, spices, currants, dates, wine, alum, dyes, drapery, cotton, silk, armor, paper, glass, books and other fine goods that made up the greater part of its cargo, and loaded for the return voyage wool, cloth, hides, leather, iron, lead, tin and pewter from England; serges, caps, cutlery, brass and bowstrings from Bruges, and similar gleanings from the fairs and market-places which were in reach of the stopping-places of the fleet.[25]

Return cargoes were assembled in advance by resident Venetian

[23] *Calendar of State Papers, Venetian,* I. 42, 53.

[24] *Victoria History of the Counties of England; Hampshire and the Isle of Wight,* W. Page, ed., III, 480.

[25] The preface of the *Calendar of State Papers, Venetian,* by Rawdon Brown, gives an excellent account of Venetian commerce with England.

merchants. In the fifteenth century there were regularly established settlements, "factories" or communities of Venetian merchants in Bruges and in London. Lists of the consuls and vice-consuls and of the merchants who acted as their counsellors still exist. There is extant also an abundant correspondence between them and the home government. The Venetian Senate never relaxed its control over its subjects. When, in 1402, the captain of the fleet, Ser Lorenzo Contarini, asked to be allowed to fulfil a vow by visiting the shrine of St. Thomas of Canterbury, he was granted permission, but only on condition that he go ashore, make his pilgrimage and return within the one day, not sleeping off his galley. As little independence was left to the merchants in these outlying residences as to the officers of the fleet. Letters and presents for the king, courtiers and other persons of influence were provided by the Senate, and instructions were constantly being sent to resident Venetian merchants in the Netherlands and England. A courier was sent overland monthly with communications to and from the government and for the convenience of the merchants, who defrayed his expenses. By a resolution of the Senate, not more than £2 sterling could be spent by the merchants in England in celebrating the festival of St. Mark, and not more than £20 yearly could be given in bribes to the English customhouse officers to induce them to put a low valuation on goods. Although the export duties paid on goods shipped from Venice to London were estimated at a sum equivalent to some $80,000 in modern money, the salaries of the consul and vice-consul were fixed at a low figure. By order of the Senate and by grant of the English and various Flemish town governments, disputes among Venetian merchants could be settled before their own consuls, without appeal to local authorities. Extra-territoriality was a familiar practice in the fifteenth century.

Foreign traders, and especially sailors, seldom come into alien communities without becoming involved in occasional strife. The whole history of this period was punctuated with conflicts between foreigners and natives, even in time of peace when the foreigner was supposed to enjoy the protection of royal favor and local tolerance. In 1319 Nicoleta Basadona, agent for a Venetian merchant, sold in London 10,000 pounds of sugar and 1000 pounds of candy, invested the money in wool at Boston fair, loaded his goods on two English vessels and sailed for Flanders. On the way the English crew murdered him and seized the wool, or else he died and they stole it, took it to Bruges and sold it. This was pure piracy, so after a long dispute the king apparently made recompense. Scarcely was this matter settled when in 1322 a brawl occurred at Southampton between the crews of five Venetian galleys and a crowd on the wharves. Several Englishmen lost their lives and some property was destroyed. The masters of the galleys acknowledged their responsibility and agreed to make payment to the parties aggrieved. In the meantime, two Venetian ships of the next year's fleet were plundered by the English in retaliation. But the king valued his import and export duties and deprecated the violence, so after various payments had been made all prosecutions were withdrawn. The king issued a pardon and promised the Venetians protection and continued freedom of trade. There were more disputes in 1370 and 1374, this time concerning certain Venetian goods seized by Englishmen. On these occasions the officers of the fleet found it advisable to deny the oarsmen shore-leave in order to avoid "affrays and other mischief."[26]

Causes of conflict were various. Three English ships, asserting England's "command of the sea," ordered a fleet of galleys between Antwerp and Southampton to strike their sails and, when they refused, tried to board them. The Venetian captain called his troops to quarters and in a running fight killed eighteen English sailors with the loss of but two of his own men. The king, not wanting to enter upon a dispute, made light of the matter, declared that sailors who of their own accord entered into a fight must bear their own losses, and suggested that the whole matter be settled over a friendly pot of wine. The Venetians, along with other foreigners, suffered also from the popular rising of 1381 and from Jack Cade's rebellion of 1456. They were so harshly treated at this time and "insulted," to use their word, that all Venetians, Genoese, Florentines and Luccans quit London and established themselves for a time at

[26] Rymer, *Foedera,* II, pt. 1, 514, 546, 568, 593. H. S. Rawlinson, "The Flanders Galleys", *The Mariner's Mirror,* XII (1926), 150-1 154-6, 157.

Winchester, agreeing that none of their number would buy or sell in London.[27]

It will be observed that in all these disputes, however unpopular the foreigners may have been with the populace, the government favored them. This was natural. In addition to the import and export duties they paid to the crown and the attractive commodities they brought to England, the Venetian merchants, like others, were from time to time induced by the king to lend him money.[28] When he asked for the loan of galleys, however, he was put off on various pretexts. Edward III, Henry VI and Edward IV successively asked and were refused. The Venetian government was always close-fisted with its ships. The galleys were apt to be away from Venice on a northern voyage for six or eight months, and the Doge and Senate were always restive till the ships were again safely behind the Lido. Letters were constantly being sent ordering the captain of the fleet to hasten his departure from Bruges or London, or to assemble his fleet promptly at Southampton for the journey back.

Our period closes with the career of the Flanders Fleet in full progress. At no time were its arrivals and departures more regular, or the commodities it brought in and took out of England and the Netherlands more varied and valuable. Its decline lies in the next century, though the total amount of Venetian trade rose for a time after 1450 and only gradually changed in character.[29] What was its average or total volume during the fourteenth and early fifteenth centuries or what was the increase of wealth of Venice during that period we have no means of calculating exactly. Of its great extent there is no doubt. The wealth of Venice was one of the marvels of the time. It approached the age-long acquisitions of Constantinople. Certainly the funds in its city treasury and the private fortunes of its merchants were sufficient, notwithstanding consuming wars and expensive diplomacy, to erect great churches and public buildings, to carry on public works, to collect treasures of art, to build the palaces we still admire, most of which were erected in this period,

[27] *Calendar of State Papers, Venetian,* I, 84-5.

[28] W. E. Rhodes, "The Italian Bankers in England and their Loans to Edward I and Edward II", *Owens College Essays,* Manchester (1902).

[29] Lane, "Venetian Shipping during the Commercial Revolution," 219, etc.

and to make Venice a leader in the artistic and intellectual Renaissance.

V. THE HANSEATIC LEAGUE

Any attempt to describe in brief terms other lines of commerce in the Mediterranean and in central Europe, or to discuss the evidence of its extension in those regions and the consequent increase of the wealth of Europe, must necessarily be futile. Genoa, Pisa, Florence, Marseilles, Barcelona and a score of other cities had each a history comparable to that of Venice. It may be worth while, however, to call attention to a field of maritime trade, not very different from that of the Mediterranean, in the far north of Europe, which rose, came to its culmination and began to decline within the limits of this period. This was the trade carried on by an organized group of cities in northern Germany, the well-known Hanseatic League.[30]

Confederations of towns, familiar elsewhere in this period of active city life, were especially characteristic of Germany. The loose organization of the Empire left the numerous and growing cities semi-independent but subject to many dangers; they took refuge in combination. The weakness of the central government left their merchants exposed to exorbitant tolls on rivers and roads—there were at one time sixty-two custom-house frontiers on the Rhine alone—to the tyranny of the great and the violence of the petty nobles, and to the depredations of pirates and highwaymen. Their destructive competition with one another was scarcely less injurious. It was, besides, only the combined influence of a group of cities that could bid for or wrest privileges of trade in foreign parts. There were earlier confederations, the Westphalian, the Swabian, three successive Rhenish leagues and others, which included from five or six to eighty or ninety towns. These were mostly in southern and central Germany, seeking for the most part political strength in the Reichstag and in the government of the country.

[30] Among recent treatments see E. Daenell, *Geschichte der deutschen Hanse in der zweiten Hälfte des 14ten Jahrhunderts* (Leipzig, 1897); Idem, *Die Blütezeit der deutschen Hanse*. Two volumes (Berlin, 1905-1906); and the survey of later literature by Carl Brinkmann, "The Hanseatic League," *Journal of Economic and Business History*, II (1930) 585-602. The popular account by E. G. Nash, *The Hansa, its History and Romance* (New York, 1929), is well illustrated, but not otherwise useful.

Meanwhile the great northern confederation, based on purely commercial foundations, was taking shape. Imperial control over these cities was even slighter than over those of the centre and south of Germany. The shadowy powers of the emperor did little to limit their independence and less to assist their commercial ambitions. On the other hand their mercantile enterprise seemed boundless; small towns favorably situated on harbors or deep rivers, like Lübeck, Hamburg and Rostock, became great by developing new lines of trade, by capturing the commerce of others, like that of the Slavonic traders along the shores of the Baltic or the old Scandinavian trade with the German settlers at Wisby on the island of Gothland, or by gaining their share of the international trade with Novgorod in the east and with Bruges in the west. Mere villages on the river systems of northern Germany grew in the thirteenth century from agriculture and serfdom into commerce, freedom and self-government.[31]

In this process of expansion the advantages of union showed themselves in a score of ways. In the early thirteenth century agreements for reciprocal privileges of trade and protection were entered into frequently by pairs or small groups of towns. Sometimes these newly formed alliances were used to obtain local privileges in other cities, more often to secure rights in other countries. Indeed, common privileges won by German merchants of different towns in some foreign city frequently became the basis of a closer union among those towns at home, already feeling the tendency of the time toward combination. Sometimes it is hard to say whether the drawing together of German towns was a result of the comradeship of their merchants abroad, or whether their common action abroad resulted from the alliances of their home governments. Whichever influence was the stronger, in the second half of the thirteenth century these German cities and groups of cities coalesced in a larger unity. They developed a habit of common action which became stronger and stronger until a veritable confederation of eighty or more cities and towns came into existence. This was the Hanse of the North German cities or the Hanseatic League.

[31] H. Pirenne, *Medieval Cities, their Origins and the Revival of Trade* (Princeton, 1925), goes to the twelfth century and deals largely with Flemish towns. See also Paul Sander, *Geschichte des deutschen Städtewesens* (Bonn, 1922), a convenient digest.

The League was rather a natural growth than an artificial creation, so it is hardly to be expected that a definite date can be given for its origin. But its history is practically coterminous with the period with which we are concerned. The year 1252, when Lübeck and Hamburg obtained common rights in the Flemish city of Bruges, may be taken as the beginning of deliberate joint action abroad, although there are instances of the possession of common privileges in the Netherlands earlier in the century and in England still earlier. Joint action at home soon became usual. The search for security against depredators was reflected in the agreement between Lübeck, Rostock and Wismar in 1259, specifying that any of these cities which allowed known pirates or robbers to dispose of their goods in it should be proscribed and held by the other member cities as equally guilty with the outlaws.[32] Within the next decade there were a number of similar agreements for joint protection of merchants against robbers, bandits, pirates and feudal lords. The year 1265, when a group of North German towns agreed to be subject to one code, "the law of Lübeck," marks the beginning of a further process of internal coherence which gained such momentum that in 1293 the representatives of twenty-six towns in assembly at Rostock adhered to this agreement. By 1300 there was such a network of town agreements and such frequent gatherings of a varying number of cities that the foundations of a general league had evidently already been laid.

At the same time the trade of these towns was being extended more and more widely. It was principally a maritime commerce, although in that region of rivers the smaller towns flourished on a boat trade that hardly reached salt water at all. Those cities which lay on the Baltic or on the large rivers soon secured all the old trade between the German, Scandinavian and Slavonic shores, as far as Reval to the east, the island of Gothland to the north and England, Norway and Iceland to the west. By the time the Venetian ships were regularly sailing out of the Mediterranean through the Straits of Gibraltar on their long voyages, the ships of the Hanseatic cities were similarly making their way out of the Baltic through the Sound

[32] See Fritz Endres, editor, *Geschichte der Freien und Hansestadt Lübeck* (Lübeck, 1926), which contains an admirable chapter on medieval Lübeck by Fritz Rörig, the leading authority.

and northward, westward and southward. The commerce of the south and the north met and overlapped in London, Bruges, Rouen and other west European cities. Hanse ships imported salt from western France and local southern products from Lisbon and Oporto, from Seville and Cadiz, as well as wool and tin from England.[33] At the fairs and in the market-places of England, Flanders, France and Spain merchants bringing Levantine and Mediterranean goods from Italy met traders from Germany with the coarser products of the north.

By 1360, the date of the earliest known membership list, the League included fifty-two towns. At the time of its greatest development there were seventy or eighty. The number was never fixed. Some towns were included at one time, not included at another; sometimes recalcitrant cities were expelled; others, as in the case of a later League of Nations, deliberately withdrew; new towns were occasionally admitted. Ninety-six seem at one time or another to have been members.[34] The League's ambitions grew with its power. In 1367 it first took united military action. After a series of disputes with the king of Denmark, who had recently brought under his power several of the Hanse towns and had secured control of certain other regions in which the League had trading privileges, a conference of the representatives of the cities was called at Cologne and decided to make war upon him. Although only twelve cities were represented, the conference undertook to speak in the name of the full number. It was agreed that each town should furnish certain military forces, supplies or money, and that any which failed to join in the common action should be excluded from all trade with the others, and with all places where they had joint privileges. The League was successful in its naval and military operations, captured Copenhagen and most of the towns and fortresses of Denmark and Norway, and in 1370 dictated the Treaty of Stralsund, by which it obtained all the commercial privileges it desired in the region of the Baltic and a considerable degree of political influence in the north generally. In 1375 the Emperor Charles IV visited Lübeck

[33] A. Agats, *Der Hansische Baienhandel* (Heidelberg, 1904), studies the activities of the Hanse in Spain and Portugal.

[34] See F. Frensdorff, "Die Hanse zu Ausgang des Mittelalters," *Hansische Geschichtsblätter*, VII (1894), 75-104.

and in his address gave formal recognition to the union of the northern cities.

From this time forward the Hanseatic League became one of the great powers of Europe. Like other states it had varied success and failure, but until after the end of this period it retained an organization that enabled it to obtain and preserve valuable advantages in other countries and to control much of the internal policy of its members. Frequent meetings of a larger or smaller number of the cities gave opportunity for the creation of precedents, the adoption of ordinances binding on the members, the regulation of commerce and the exclusion of interlopers from their fields of trade. The League possessed its own flag, sent diplomatic representatives abroad, and made treaties with the Scandinavian kingdoms, with England and with Poland, like any independent power.

Five hundred years later, in the nineteenth century, when the German empire embarked on a policy of sea power and colonial expansion, a warm historical interest was awakened in this, the only earlier German experience of maritime activity. In response to this interest scholars drew up the record of meetings of the League in a long series of stately volumes, the *Hanserecessen*. A patriotic historical society has for many years published a monthly journal devoted to its history,[35] and a whole library has grown up about the League. From the *Recessen* it appears that between 1363 and 1400 there were some twenty-four full diets or meetings of delegates of the cities of the League; between 1400 and 1450 there were fourteen. Later they became less frequent. Larger cities often represented groups of smaller. In 1447, at the largest recorded gathering, the deputies of thirty-nine towns attended. In addition, there were many gatherings of small groups of towns to consider special interests of their own. The full meetings, which were held with great formality, usually in the great gild hall at Lübeck, although they dealt to some extent with political, military or diplomatic matters, were concerned principally with the commercial interests of the cities. They provided for the protection of merchants and their merchandise at sea and on the roads, and for the improvement of rivers and harbors; they established common weights, measures

[35] *Hansische Geschichtsblätter*, published since 1871.

and coinage; they arranged for the settlement of disputes among merchants at home and abroad; they secured new privileges and opened up new lines of trade; they drew up a *Seebuch* or almanac showing the harbors, lighthouses, buoys and other indications useful to navigators from Riga to Lisbon.[36]

The cities were in the main aristocratic in their government, and the older towns contained a large patrician class of property owners and office holders. On the other hand the commercial interests of the populations extended down to the middle and even to the lower classes. Ships, although frequently owned entirely by rich burghers, were as often the property of the chamber of commerce of the town, or were commonly owned jointly by quite small people. As in the Italian and French towns they were a favorite form of investment, and we hear of ownership of a thirty-second or even of a sixty-fourth part of a ship. The captain, master and sailors were often large or small shareholders. The vessels used in the early period were, like the early Venetian "round" ships, mostly small, of but forty tons burden or thereabouts; later the "hulks" or "cogs" which made the longer voyages were of 200 to 250 tons burden, drawing about twelve feet of water, broad and heavy, with one to three masts, high at bow and stern, and manned by a numerous crew and carrying some twenty or more armed men as protection from pirates or hostile merchantmen. At times they sailed in fleets accompanied by a convoy. Few statistics of Hanse trade are available. We hear of 392 vessels leaving Danzig for London in 1392 with cargoes of grain, honey, salt, potash, furs and beer, and at another time of a fleet of 40 Hanse salt ships sailing from the mouth of the Loire for the North.

Of the cities of the League, some of the largest and most influential were Lübeck, Hamburg, Danzig, Bremen, Dortmund, Cologne, Hanover, Grönigen, Magdeburg. All lay within the German Empire, the kingdom of Poland, or in the territory of the Teutonic Knights, but merchants of the League were established in settlements and enjoyed trade privileges, landed property and an organized life of their own in many towns of France, England, the

[36] Ernst Daenell, "The Hanse and the Mercantile Marine," *American Historical Review,* XV (1909), 48-52.

Scandinavian kingdoms and Russia. Of these outlying settlements four were of unusual extent and importance. They were known as foreign "factories" or "Kontoren" of the League, and were located at Bruges, Bergen, Novgorod and London. A short description may be given of each.

Bruges in the thirteenth and fourteenth centuries was the most important commercial city in Europe outside the Mediterranean.[37] Lying where the north and south and east and west lines of commerce crossed, Bruges became the exchange center for a greater variety of products than were handled in any other city. Located at the head of navigation back of the heavy dykes which separated the Swyn river from the sea, it had a harbor and it developed a civic and commercial organization to meet these needs and possibilities. There was no line of trade in the fourteenth century that did not connect in some way with Bruges. The Hanseatic settlement, dating from 1252, with its warehouses and dwelling-places and its 200 to 500 resident merchants, stretched along the harbor and was the most conspicuous of the fifteen settlements of foreigners in that city. The colony was highly organized, with six aldermen, a council of eighteen, its own courts, and a body of ordinances governing its members and defining its relations with the city.[38]

The "Court of St. Peter" at the Russian free city of Novgorod, with its German church, its palisaded courtyard, its dwellings, brewhouse, bakery, hospital and warehouses, with its group of merchants living under the rule of their alderman and the protection of grants from the city-government, had been, from its settlement in 1272, the resort of German merchants who formed a link in the long trade routes from the east and south.[39]

Bergen in Norway was not only the location of an outlying settlement of the League, but was completely in its power. In this city the Hanse had obtained at an early date a practical monopoly of all exchangeable products of the northernmost regions of Europe—

[37] R. Häpke, *Brügges Entwickelung zum mittelalterlichen Weltmarkt* (Berlin, 1908).

[38] W. Stein, *Die Genossenschaft der deutschen Kaufleute zu Brügge in Flandern* (Berlin, 1889), 10, 19, 31, etc.; K. Bahr, *Handel und Verkehr der deutschen Hanse in Flandern* (Leipzig, 1911).

[39] C. R. Beazley, *The Dawn of Modern Geography* (London, 1897-1906), III, 493; F. Keutgen, *Die Beziehungen der Hanse zu England* (Giessen, 1890), 55; A. Winkler, *Die Deutsche Hanse in Russland* (Berlin, 1886).

fish of all kinds and salt for curing them, whale-oil, rosin and pitch, eiderdown for pillows, and many rough commodities the trade in which, though it belonged naturally to the region, was beyond the enterprise of the native Norwegians. At the height of its prosperity the League had in Bergen twenty-two separate "yards," or blocks of buildings, each with storing and shipping facilities and each with dwellings for merchants and their employees. The German colony is reputed to have numbered at one time 3000 members, representing fifty-eight Hanse towns. It was governed by two aldermen, eighteen members of a council and a secretary, who was always a doctor of laws. There was a deputy governor for each yard. The Hanse went to every length to retain its monopoly in Bergen. When some English merchants from Lynn tried to break its monopoly at the beginning of the fifteenth century and establish a settlement, their houses were broken into, they were beaten and their goods were seized by the Germans. In 1406 ninety-six Englishmen were captured while fishing off the coast and were thrown overboard to drown, their hands and feet tied together.[40]

VI. THE STEELYARD IN LONDON

The "Steelyard" in London was the best-known of these outlying agencies of the Hanseatic League. Like the others it was a small island of foreign life in the midst of a native community. Just above London Bridge, on the edge of the river, the settlement grew up on the basis of concessions by the king and by the city government. The German merchants bought land and during the thirteenth and fourteenth centuries covered it with dwellings, warehouses, the great council hall, a kitchen, offices, gardens, a strong building for treasure and records, a storage house for wine, a great wharf with weighing beam and crane, all closed in with outer gates, making it almost a fortification. In the later fourteenth and fifteenth centuries they added to the original settlement a number of houses in the vicinity which they rented from the owners. The origin of the name is a provocative but an unsolved problem. It is practically the same in German as in English, *Stahlhof*. Early German traders

[40] Helen Zimmern, *The Hansa Towns* (New York, 1889); J. H. Wylie, *England under Henry IV* (London, 1884-98), IV, 11.

may have landed their steel here; or the great weighing beam, steelyard, or "stilliard," being the most conspicuous feature, may have given it its name; or it may have been a contraction of "stapleyard" or *stapelhof*, but no guess has received general acceptance, and we have no knowledge of its origin.[41]

Here, from at least 1250 when King Henry III gave or confirmed letters of protection to the "merchants of Germany," during a period of more than 300 years merchants representing at one time or another some sixty German cities lived and carried on their trading activities. With their journeymen, apprentices, servants and clerks, coming and going, they made up a community of perhaps 200 or 300 persons. The colony was governed by its alderman, who was elected anew each year. A certain Arnold, son of Thedmar, a merchant of Bremen, was apparently the first of the long line, holding office as an alderman both of London and of the Steelyard from 1250 to 1260. A city grant of 1262 confirmed the merchants' right to have their own alderman, who by right was supposed to have first attained citizenship in the city. Royal grants corroborated this privilege. Somewhat later, as the community became more numerous and varied, two assistants of the alderman and nine counsellors were appointed yearly. Elections for these twelve officers were held on New Year's Eve, and there was much rivalry for office among merchants from the various German cities. The election was a formal and complicated process, and the chosen rulers of the settlement had to take a solemn oath not only to support the customs of the Steelyard merchants and to do justice among them, but to respect the laws and the customs of the city of London. There was also, after 1400, a clerk of the Steelyard who exercised much influence and ultimately came to carry on most of the intercourse of the merchants with the municipal and national governments. This official was sometimes a clergyman and regularly trained in the Roman law.[42]

Within their walls the merchants and their employees lived a

[41] K. Kunze, "Das erste Jahrhundert der deutschen Hanse in England," *Hansische Geschichtsblätter*, XVIII (1891), 129-54; K. Höhlbaum and others, editors, *Hansisches Urkundenbuch* (Halle, 1876), I, 540, 552; Wylie, *England under Henry IV*, II, 72-5; John Stow, *Survey of London*, edited by C. L. Kingsford (Oxford 1908).

[42] F. Schulz, *Die Hanse und England* (Berlin, 1911), 177-84, 189-90.

closely regulated life; no one was allowed outside after nine o'clock at night; there were to be no women in the establishment; each person had to have his armor and weapons ready for use in case of riot and to do his part in defending the city against enemies. Outside the settlement the German merchants bought and sold in the fairs and town markets. In the church of All Saints, the parish in which the Steelyard lay, they attended regular services and on the 5th of December, their gild-day, they held special services before adjourning to a sumptuous feast in the great hall. The Steelyard and its occupants are a familiar matter of mention in the English records. Similar "steelyards" existed on a smaller scale in Yarmouth, Boston, Lynn and other towns in the east of England, but they were of relatively little importance.[43]

VII. OTHER TRADING SETTLEMENTS

The outlying settlements of the Hanseatic League in Bruges, Novgorod, Bergen and London were typical of the organization of early modern commerce. For the most part trade was carried on not by individuals, under general international law or national commercial treaties, but by merchants living as a group in a foreign city under special privileges granted by national, feudal or municipal governments.

These rights were not hard to obtain. The merchants were always welcome to rulers and to the nobles and clergy. To the government the activity of merchants meant an opportunity to levy import and export duties; to the upper classes generally it meant opportunity to obtain articles of beauty, convenience or luxury. It was, as has been pointed out, the importers of wine and the exporters of wool who made the contributions to the treasury of the king which enabled England to play a great part on the Continent. Moreover the merchants could often be induced to lend money. The Venetian Senate was provided with enough funds for its expensive foreign policy by its very moderate impositions upon the Levant and Mediterranean goods that passed through its warehouses. The hand-

[43] Schulz, op. cit., 166-70; Reinhold Pauli, *Pictures of Old England* (London, 1861), Essay vi.

somest garments of nobleman, courtier and fine lady in most countries were the product of foreign looms. This was because some countries were ahead of others in industry, and because all were dependent on others for some of their luxuries. The "wine and spices, velvet and camlet furred with grise," which John Ball described as the portion of the nobility, were imported goods, while the "poor cloth, the drawing out of the chaff and water to drink" were as native as "the pain and travail, rain and wind in the fields," which were the portion of the common people. For the period we are describing the foreign merchant invariably found a ready welcome from princes and almost as generally from city governments.

The late thirteenth century marked a series of grants of trading privileges to foreigners throughout Europe. In 1259 the king of England accorded commercial rights to the Genoese. In 1260, as has been noted, he extended to the merchants of all North German cities the permission to trade which previously had been given only to those of Cologne and Lübeck. Edward I, who repeatedly gave evidence of his desire for the entrance of foreign traders and even artisans into his dominions, in 1303 issued an invitation so general and so liberal in its terms that it may be considered the type of all such privileges. It has come down to us in its full text and with its contemporary name of *Carta Mercatoria*, the "Merchants' Charter." Freedom of entry into England with their goods, residence there, and departure with such goods as they may have bought from Englishmen or other foreigners in any town, fair or market, was offered to all merchants of Germany, France, Spain, Portugal, Navarre, Lombardy, Florence, Provence, Catalonia, Flanders, Brabant, "and of all other foreine countries and places by what name soever they be called." Disputes with native merchants were to be settled by the "Law merchant," promptly and before mixed juries composed one half of countrymen of the merchant, if so many could be found. Standard weights and measures were to be openly displayed and were to be uniform throughout all England. Goods might be imported and, if not sold, exported again, except wine, which was too much in demand to be allowed to leave the country.

If the wine or anything else was taken by the king it was to be at a negotiated, not at an imposed price.[44]

It is true, these privileges were not given for nothing. But certain favored foreigners like the Genoese, Venetians and Hansards were required to pay only the same duties as Englishmen, and other groups were from time to time admitted to like privileges. This open-door policy continued to be the practice of the English government for almost 200 years, though the pressure from native merchants and towns with special charters was strong enough to force modifications in special cases. Similar invitations or favorable responses to requests for permission to trade were made by other rulers and city governments.[45]

Merchants living in an alien community, even under protection and with the favor of the local government, could seldom be safe unless they stood together. Besides, there were manifest advantages in community life, satisfaction to themselves and sometimes to the government under which they were temporarily living. Therefore there were established during this period, in most of the larger and in some of the smaller cities, privileged settlements or colonies, or "quarters," *fondachi*,[46] "houses," "factories," "halls" or "consulates," as they were variously known. Merchants from Lucca, for instance, had settlements in at least nine cities: Paris, London, Bruges, Rome, Naples, Venice, Genoa, Avignon and Montpellier, each with its charter of privileges and its group of officials, and some with dwellings and warehouses.[47] Lübeck had special privileges, besides those enjoyed by the Hanse generally. The Venetians had quarters in Alexandria, Constantinople, London, Bruges and Nicopolis. Around the Venetian consulate in London, in the fifteenth century, were gathered the merchants who made ready for the coming of the great fleet, or who remained behind to dispose of its wares, or came and went on independent voyages.

[44] Richard Hakluyt, *Principal Voyages*, twelve volumes (Glasgow, 1903-1906), I, 319-38.

[45] In general, see Levin Goldschmidt, *Universalgeschichte des Handelsrechts*, vol. I (Stuttgart, 1891).

[46] *Fondaco*, like so many other commercial terms of the time, is Arabic, from *funduk*, a shop.

[47] Léon Mirot, *Études Lucquoises* (Paris, 1930) gives an excellent account of the Luccan settlement in Paris in the 14th and 15th centuries and of the ramifications of three important firms.

In Venice itself there were settlements of Germans, Luccans and many other foreigners. The fine old building of the *Fondaco dei Tedeschi*, the settlement of the Germans at Venice, with its fifty-six rooms, was situated on the Canal near the Rialto bridge.[48] In the flourishing period of the city the German merchants who came across the Alps to trade in Venice had to dwell there, where they were under the supervision and regulation of Venetian officials. From the few surviving records and from the testimony of their burial places on the island of Murano, it is obvious that although the supervision was close there was in the settlement much opportunity for social life and for some less formal intercourse with Venetian citizens. These German merchants with their long trains of horses and mules crossed the Brenner pass, stopping at Innsbruck, Botzen and Trent. They came principally from Regensburg, Augsburg, Ulm, Munich and other South German cities. On their return to Germany they must have been broadened by their residence, even if only temporary, in a city of older civilization, in contact, as it always was, with the East. Indeed the influence of Venice on the culture and art of the cities of South Germany was then and has always since been conspicuous.

Similar settlements might be found, then, in almost all commercial cities, as they are still to be found in the Far East. The single, unsupported merchant carrying on business in a foreign city was almost unknown, at least in the early part of this period, though as time passed men who did business on a large enough scale to act independently or as members of a small partnership came, as will be seen, to be more numerous.

VIII. THE SPREAD OF MARITIME AND COMMERCIAL LAW

The extension of commerce was much aided by, indeed it must have been to a certain degree dependent upon the spread of that body of maritime and commercial law which was so strikingly alike in countries which differed widely in other forms of law and custom. This uniformity of maritime law along all the coasts of Europe was doubtless due, in the first place, to its reflection of customs

[48] See the basic account of Henry Simonsfeld, *Der Fondaco dei Tedeschi in Venedig und die deutsch-venezianischen Handelsbeziehungen* (two volumes, Stuttgart, 1897).

which must necessarily be much the same for all those who go down to the sea in ships and traffic in the great waters. But it was due secondly to the large extent to which medieval and indeed modern maritime law was derived from the old Roman sea-law. The Rhodian and Basilican codes of the later Roman Empire were well known in the early middle ages to the Italian maritime towns, and the conquerors of those regions willingly left undisturbed the practices for which they had no substitutes.[49] Rules governing the sharing of losses from collision, shipwreck, or piracy, salvage, liability for the payment of freight, wages of mariners, joint ownership, charter party and a vast number of other customs, including even marine insurance, go back largely to classical times. Except for the gradual changes due to the slowly changing conditions and to the slightly varying decisions of local magistrates, they appear in much the same form wherever early medieval trade existed. They reappear in the later middle ages in the sea laws of Trani, Amalfi, Pisa, Venice, Ancona, Genoa and other Italian cities.[50] From Italy the custom of formulating codes of sea law and much of the material of that law spread to France, Spain and northward.

These early codes borrowed from one another to such an extent that it was almost a matter of chance which gained the greater recognition. Among them all it was probably the "Rolls" or "Laws" or "Judgments" of Oléron that came early to be the best known and most influential.[51] The date or occasion of their origin is unknown, and it is impossible to say why the decisions of the local judges of this little island trading-town on the west coast of France achieved so wide an acceptance. They were well known in the thirteenth, perhaps in the twelfth, possibly in the eleventh century. In their earliest known form they consisted of twenty-four articles, but these were added to in many successive recensions. More author-

[49] F. R. Sanborn, *Origins of the Early English Maritime and Commercial Law* (New York, 1930), 1-4; W. Ashburner, *The Rhodian Sea Law* (Oxford, 1909).

[50] See André Sayous, "Les Transformations des Méthodes Commerciales dans l'Italie Mediévale," *Annales d'Histoire Économique et Sociale,* I (1929), 161-76; Idem, "Le Commerce Terrestre de Marseilles au XIIIe Siècle," *Revue Historique,* CLXIII (1930), 27-50.

[51] See T. Kisselbach, "Der Ursprung der Rôles d'Oléron und des Seerechts von Damme," *Hansische Geschichtsblätter,* XXXIII (1906), 1-60; P. Boissonade, "La Renaissance et l'Essor de la Vie et du Commerce Maritimes en Poitou, Aunis et Saintonge du Xe au XVe Siècle," *Revue d'Histoire Économique et Sociale,* XII (1924), 259-325.

ity may have been given to them by the influence of the powerful duke of Aquitaine, in whose dominions Oléron lay, or by Henry II of England when he inherited that duchy. Or it may have been their simple and lucid form, their practical spirit and inclusiveness that commended them to magistrates in various countries dealing with maritime cases.[52]

They became familiar or were deliberately adopted as a satisfactory and even as an authoritative statement of maritime law in Brittany, Normandy, England and the Netherlands, where the same code appears under the name of the "Sea Laws of Flanders." Even where other codes were used, the Rolls of Oléron were known and respected. In the Baltic the "Town Laws of Wisby" and the "Law of Lübeck" rivalled them. The latter became the basis of the whole system of sea-law of the Hanseatic League. Somewhat later another code, the "Consulate of the Sea," emanating from Barcelona, spread among the seacoast cities all the way from the Mediterranean to the Baltic. There were few questions of dispute likely to come up in trading by sea that could not be settled on familiar principles in whatever port they might arise.[53]

Much the same was true of commercial law, as it grew up about trade on land, at fairs and in city markets. Contracts, security of purchases and responsibility for payment, partnerships, powers and charges of brokers, trademarks, bills of lading and of exchange and a dozen other subjects related to buying and selling, were the interest of special courts and were decided by appropriate law. There was in this perhaps a larger body of local custom than in maritime law, and even where it was generalized it included basic elements of Germanic as well as of Roman law. Nevertheless the legal problems arising in trade were much the same everywhere, and so commercial law also tended to become clear and uniform. "Consuls of the Merchants" or officials known by similar titles had been established in the Italian cities for the purpose of trying cases arising among visiting or native merchants, certainly as early as the twelfth century. In other places gild courts fulfilled the same

[52] Sanborn, op. cit., 63-75; T. Twiss, *Black Book of the Admiralty* (Rolls Series), I, 88, Vols. III, IV.

[53] R. G. Marsden, *Select Pleas in the Court of Admiralty*, Selden Society, (London, 1892), I, introduction.

functions; in still others the "pie powder" courts of the towns and fairs.[54] Under one name or another in all trading cities and at fairs jurisdiction was exercised and a "law merchant" grew up that was practically uniform through all Europe.[55]

Most of this legal development had been accomplished before the beginning of our period. It was truly medieval. By 1250 there already existed a body of maritime and commercial law that was essentially cosmopolitan. It was the first form of law to approach the status of international law. There is therefore little to record of its history during the period 1250 to 1450. Nevertheless its spread, clarification and development must be noted as a recognizable phenomenon, the natural result of the great extension of commerce. In all countries of Europe where foreign trade developed, the earlier medieval codes were adopted in amplified form. In 1254 the Senate of Lübeck sent to the master of the Teutonic Order a collection of their sea laws now extending to 250 articles. From 1360 onward the Admiralty in England developed more and more its jurisdictional side. In its "Black Book," compiled about 1460, it included a copy of the Rolls of Oléron, together with a series of much more specialized rules for commercial jurisdiction.

The "Consulate of the Sea" became better and better known at Barcelona, the place of its origin, and was used more widely and elaborated more extensively elsewhere through the whole fourteenth century. Ultimately it comprised no less than 334 chapters. To pass for a moment beyond the limits of this volume, it may be observed that most of the maritime codes and much of the *lex mercatoria* were among the first matters put into print when the great invention was made that closes our period and opens the next.[56]

IX. THE INCREASE OF WEALTH

No adequate statistics are available by which to measure the increase of wealth in Europe between 1250 and 1450. Indeed, as one reads the contemporary records of destruction by war, riot and

[54] The standard account is P. Huvelin, *Essai Historique sur le Droit des Marchés et des Foires* (Paris, 1897). Charles Gross, "The Court of Piepowder", *Quarterly Journal of Economics,* XX (1906), 231 ff.

[55] F. R. Sanborn, op. cit., 125-261; C. Gross, *Select Cases Concerning the Law Merchant,* Selden Society, (London, 1908), introduction.

[56] Sanborn, op. cit., 77-86.

waste one would think that the productive powers of man were sufficiently taxed in replacing by his industry what was destroyed by his passion. Nature herself joined in devastation. The Black Death swept across Europe in the middle of the fourteenth century, leaving neglected fields, abandoned houses, a reduced population and depressed spirits; and it returned repeatedly, as if to complete its destructive task. The influence of this catastrophe on the church, on learning, on architecture, on serfdom, on social life has been variously estimated by different authors, and it may well be that, like other catastrophic occurrences in history, its effects were less important than the workings of more silent and persistent forces. Still, the immediate loss of man-power, capital and industrial organization must have been great, even though it was accompanied by a gain in freedom.[57]

Losses by war and by the hand of God had to be made up by the labors of but a part of the population. The whole feudal and clerical castes were relatively valueless from the point of view of creating or restoring wealth. A certain number of noblemen and lords of manors did some service in encouraging agriculture and other forms of industry and in protecting those engaged in them. A part of the work of the church was the development of productive land and patronage of some of the higher forms of wealth. But compared with the vast indolence, the disorderliness and the wastefulness of the noble, seigneurial and clerical classes and the destructiveness of royal military ambitions, what they did for the creation of any kind of value was nil. All saving of capital and all production of utilities fell upon the merchant, the farmer and the artisan.

Nevertheless out of this balance between destruction and production emerged in the middle of the fifteenth century a Europe much richer and far better equipped for attaining a higher civilization and engaging in more ambitious projects than she had been in the middle of the thirteenth. If it were possible to watch this process, even on its commercial side; if a man could picture in his mind all the vast activity of the time in transport, exchange, the

[57] F. A. Gasquet, *The Black Death of 1348 and 1349* (London, 1908). See also R. Hoeniger, *Der Schwarze Tod in Deutschland* (Berlin, 1882), and many studies of its incidence and effects in individual localities.

purchase and sale of goods; if one could, like Piers Plowman on Malvern Hills, look down on the busy traders of Europe as on a "fair field full of folk"; if he could see the packhorses and wagons on the roads, toiling on their long journeys across country or creeping over mountain passes, the fleets of vessels sailing from port to port or loading and unloading their cargoes at the wharves, the strangely clad foreigners and busy natives buying and selling at the fairs or in the market-places of the towns; if the depth of the residuum of wealth left on the soil of trading regions, like the deposits left on its overflowed banks by the Nile, could be in some way measured; if the lordly houses of the rich merchants and the long rows of humble dwellings of poorer participants in the trade of hundreds of cities of Italy, France, the Netherlands, Germany, England and all Europe could be seen and valued, we would have the best of all backgrounds against which to draw the picture of government and diplomacy, of the wars, the travels, the labors, the ambitions and the jealousies of the church, of the literature and of all the varied life of the time. But this cannot be; all we can get is a partial view, at most suggestive. We can, however, follow somewhat further the thread of economic development in the field of finance and observe the fortunes of certain individual men or groups of men whose lives can be read in the records of their business dealings.

Chapter Two

MERCHANT PRINCES AND BANKERS

I. MERCHANT MONEY-LENDERS

THE GREAT MAJORITY of those who by trade, handicraft and the transportation of goods were giving Europe the material means of a higher civilization have necessarily remained nameless. Contemporary chroniclers were more interested in the court and the church, in the picturesque scenes of war, in lay and ecclesiastical diplomacy, and in the personal careers of princes, nobles and prelates. On the other hand, town records and certain government documents, when examined, disclose a restless, active, enterprising group of merchants, local landowners and artisans, carrying on a busy life of earning and spending and reflecting all the human interests that gather around those processes. The wealth of a few score, or perhaps a few hundred of these, their intercourse with kings and popes or their connection with great movements have lifted them from obscurity and made their names as well known as those of men of the older and superior classes.[1]

Some of them were merchants pure and simple. What they did not spend for comfortable or luxurious living or for religious, charitable or civic purposes they used as capital for more extensive trading ventures. Capitalism entered into the life of Europe earlier than is commonly realized and there were few regions where its fructifying and disturbing influence was not already felt. There were numerous places, especially Italian and Flemish cities, where

[1] The number of these names and personalities rescued from oblivion by the modern interest in economic and social history is increasing daily through the study, and in many cases through the publication, of the records of towns, mercantile companies and the financial departments of governments. Some of these are listed in the Bibliography, but see in general: Gino Luzzatto, "The Study of Medieval Economic History in Italy," *Journal of Economic and Business History,* IV (1932), 708-27, who surveys a huge mass of Italian monographic material, and M. Postan, "Medieval Capitalism," *Economic History Review,* IV (1933), 212-27, who reviews the outstanding recent contributions. Interesting also is N. L. B. Gras, "The Rise of Big Business," *Journal of Economic and Business History,* IV (1932), 381-408.

manufacturing was carried on on a large enough scale to utilize considerable capital. But there were at this time few rich merchants or manufacturers who were not also something of money-lenders. In earlier times successful merchants invested their money in landed property in the growing towns and became a patrician class living on their rents and on the gains of civic office. They were the oldest element of the bourgeoisie.[2] In later times trade and banking became quite separate. But in the period we are discussing, the line between the merchant and the money-lender was an indistinct one. The fortune of the merchant-banker was founded on trade, but it grew great by lending money to kings, nobles, clerics and to any others who needed immediate funds and could give some promise of repayment. It was this function, rather than their activity as merchants, that has preserved to us their names and their actions.[3]

Instances are numerous; a few may be named. Among the Germans bringing goods from the Rhine region to England to exchange for wool and other English products, was a certain Tiedemann of Limburg. He carried on an extensive business, had a house of his own on Thames street, besides his membership in the Steelyard, and during his long stay in England from 1346 to 1360 became wealthy. Tiedemann was one of a syndicate of German merchants, Kleppings, von dem Walde, von Menden, Sudermann and others, who lent money on a small scale to English nobles, citizens and occasionally to the crown. Later he became, on his own account, one of the moneyed men who lent large sums to Edward III, at one time £600, equalling perhaps $30,000 in present value, later even more. He farmed certain of the taxes and took over the administration of the royal tin mines. His name runs through the records in connection with imports and exports, loans, law-suits, repayments and assignments, and he seems to have left England under suspicion of connection with an obscure crime.[4]

Tiedemann's trouble in England does not seem to have shadowed

[2] Henri Pirenne, "The Stages in the Social History of Capitalism," *American Historical Review,* XIX (1913) 506-9; Jacob Strieder, "Origin and Evolution of early European Capitalism," *Journal of Economic and Business History,* II (1929), 1-19.

[3] See J. Kulischer, "Warenhändler und Geldausleiher im Mittelalter," *Zeitschrift für Volkswirtschaft,* XVII (1908), 29 ff., 201 ff.

[4] Alice Beardwood, *Alien Merchants in England, 1350-1377* (Cambridge, Mass., 1931), 17-19.

his reputation, for he later built a fine house in Cologne, in the present Hochstrasse, and there carried on a wholesale wine business. Ultimately he became the wealthiest property holder in Cologne, and acquired land also in Andernach. In 1360 he engaged again in banking operations, transmitting the collections made by the papal agent in Germany to the Alberti, the papal bankers at Bruges. He seems to have been on good terms with the Pope, for he received from him a special dispensation to take with him on his travels a portable altar, a privilege usually accorded only to noblemen. In his later years he prepared for himself a magnificent tomb in the Augustinian convent near his home, and presented to that church a silver-gilt cross weighing 70 pounds, with a reliquary, a masterpiece of the goldsmith's art of which a copy still exists in the convent museum. The cross itself remained an object of admiration and veneration till 1802 when, on the dissolution of the monastery, it was removed to a neighboring church and later melted down. Tiedemann died in 1386 and was buried in the tomb he had built, "wrapped in balsam and aromatic spices," as the record of the convent states, with an epitaph of twenty lines of laudatory Latin. He made other bequests to Cologne and to his native city of Limburg.[5]

In a similar position was a Nicholas Bartholomew of Lucca, who was in London about the same time as Tiedemann. He, too, was an exporter of wool, importing in exchange silk and other fine wares from his native city, which was at that time the most famous silk manufacturing center in Europe. Bartholomew carried on a business sufficiently large to pay at one time a tax of £300, at another to be fined £1000 for smuggling, and to arouse the violent antagonism of the native English mercers. Like Tiedemann and many other foreign and native merchants he loaned money to Edward III to meet the diplomatic and military expenses of the early campaigns of the Hundred Years war.[6]

Successive mayors of London, like Sir John Pultney, the cloth merchant who was mayor four times between 1331 and 1337, ad-

[5] Joseph Hansen, "Der Englische Staatscredit unter Eduard III," *Hansische Geschichtsblätter,* XVI (1910), 325, 349, 350-62, 402-7; F. Schulz, *Die Hanse und England,* 7-9.

[6] Alice Beardwood, op. cit., 10, 74.

vanced money to the king. By way of compensation Pultney was allowed to export wool during an embargo without paying duty. He acquired much landed property in both the city and country, and built himself a magnificent house in the parish of St. Lawrence. Later in the century Sir John Philpot, an importer of spices, sugar and such wares, was able to lend the king £10,000, the equivalent of perhaps half a million dollars in modern purchasing power, and to fit out at his own expense a squadron with 1000 men to drive a predatory French fleet away from the English shore.[7]

The best example of London merchant money-lenders was Sir Richard Whittington, "that famos marchant and mercer," as he is called by a chronicler of the same century; "the sonne of marchaundy, that lode-sterr and chefe chosen floure," as a contemporary ballad calls him; *flos mercatorum,* as his epitaph describes him. Lord mayor in 1398, 1406 and 1419, he was, like most such men, a son of a country gentleman, and came to London to make his fortune. This he accomplished by importing, among other things, silks, velvets and damasks to supply the household of the Earl of Derby, afterward Henry IV, and later by furnishing cloth of gold and other mercery for the bridal outfits of Henry's daughters.[8]

He frequently made loans to the crown. When Richard II was deposed he owed Whittington some £600. Later he advanced money to both Henry IV and Henry V, frequently as much as £1000 at a time, once £2800, at another time £6400,—all which sums were, it is recorded, duly repaid. In his life-time and by bequest Whittington provided for the erection of many public buildings and established a hospital and a college which survived to the Reformation. He had charge of the rebuilding of the present nave of Westminster Abbey, though the expense was met by the king.

Much exaggerated tradition grew up about the wealth of these merchant princes, but Whittington was the only one to become, long afterward, the subject of a whole literature of drama, chapbook and ballad. He was the "Dick Whittington" of nursery story who sent the cat which he had bought for a penny to kill the rats in his garret and which was his only possession, as his investment in

[7] Gregory's *Chronicle,* 156.

[8] Wylie, *England under Henry IV,* I, 64, 252; II, 442, 448; III, 65, 256; IV, 103, 162-3.

the cargo of his master's good ship *Unicorn*, on a voyage to Barbary. The sale of the cat to a potentate who was plagued by rats and mice for more than all the rest of the cargo together, the Bow Bells that rang, "turn again, turn again, Whittington" with their prophecy of his three mayoralties of London; and, when he became rich, his fine gesture of burning the bonds that showed the king's debts to him, all date only from the seventeenth century and have unfortunately no more connection with the real fifteenth century merchant than has the Shakespearean "Old Sir John of the Castle" with the real Lollard knight, or, for that matter, than has Joan of Arc as she is travestied in English chronicle and drama with the real Maid of Orleans.

The rich merchant meets us everywhere. Early in the fourteenth century Regnault d'Auriac of Montpellier in France extended his business so widely that he had branch offices in Figeac, Paris and Bruges, and left to his heirs 30,000 livres, which may equal three quarters of a million dollars in modern value. We shall later meet one of his agents at Paris, Pierre Gilles, an importer of sugar and other Mediterranean goods, who with a jeweler, Pierre Barres, supported Etienne Marcel, himself the richest merchant of his time in France, in the rising of the bourgeoisie of Paris against the Dauphin in 1357-8. Gilles had his day of wealth and power but fell with Marcel and was beheaded at the Halles in the reaction of 1358. Somewhat later Liutfried Muntprat of Constance, said to be the richest man in south Germany left a fortune of 71,400 pounds, probably equal to $3,000,000. So scores might be named.[9]

II. THE BANKERS

The superabundant wealth of merchants undoubtedly provided much of the money borrowed by kings and others. But there already existed a class of genuine bankers, whose funds were either lent outright, or, if used in trade, served to facilitate financial arrangements. Modern banking seems to have sprung from four roots: first, from the excess profits of trade; secondly, from the business of the money-changers who bartered coin of one country

[9] S. Luce, *La France pendant la Guerre de Cent Ans* (Paris, 1890); Bruno Gebhardt, *Handbuch der Deutschen Geschichte* (seventh edition, Stuttgart, 1930), 516.

for that of another; thirdly, from the transfer for a consideration of money from place to place, or its safe-keeping for a certain time; lastly, from the needs or desires of kings, popes and others for ready money to carry on campaigns or for other uses.

The word "table," in its Italian form *tavola* so generally used for a syndicate lending money, arose no doubt from the table used by money changers everywhere and at all times. It was an indispensable accompaniment of financial operations wherever coins from different mints or of different values were offered in trade. Just as there were tables of money-changers in the Temple at Jerusalem, so there were tables along the Rialto and in the Piazza of St. Mark at Venice and in the Old Market at Genoa. It is said that in 1422 there were seventy-two exchanges along a gallery that surrounded the New Market at Florence and one of the city gilds was the *arte del cambio* of the money changers.[10]

In England foreign merchants acted as money-changers under royal license, though they were constantly under suspicion and were not infrequently expelled for a time or subjected to extortion. When the government in 1299 issued a new and more drastic requirement that no English money should be taken abroad, it established a government "table" or exchange where foreign coins might be obtained for export and the English retained in the country. In France, at least in the royal domain, all exchanges belonged to the government.[11]

At every fair and every point of international trade the establishments of money-changers existed. From them more extensive enterprises easily developed. The *Taula di Cambi* at Barcelona was the first known bank of deposit in Europe. The *Gran Tavola* was a group of Sienese bankers who lent money to the pope, to cardinals and to others throughout Europe.[12] In this general banking business Italy had precedence in time and long retained preeminence. This was no doubt due partly to her early economic development,

[10] J. W. Thompson, *Economic and Social History of the Middle Ages, 300-1300* (New York, 1928), 459, with references.

[11] R. Ruding, *Annals of the Coinage of Great Britain,* (London, 1840), II, 56, 185, 191, 196, 200-1, 208, 211, etc. *Statues of the Realm,* I, 322.

[12] F. Schevill, *Siena, the Story of a Medieval Commune* (New York, 1909), 112-3; Abbott P. Usher, "Deposit Banking in Barcelona, 1300-1700," *Journal of Economic and Business History,* IV (1931), 121-55; Idem. "The Origins of Banking. The Primitive Bank of Deposit, 1200-1600." *Economic History Review,* IV (1934), 399-427.

partly to the mental activity of her people, but certainly in large measure also to the location of the papal court at Rome. The pope had claims to Peter's Pence, annates and numerous other payments, some regular, some occasional, from various countries. These could be better secured through the mediation of bankers than by direct collection and transfer. Like other sovereigns he had also political and military ambitions which required ready money. For these and similar purposes the popes needed and early obtained the services of men who possessed and dealt in money.[13]

About the middle of the thirteenth century two brothers, Orlando and Bonifazio Buonsignori, established at Siena a business of money lending which gradually drew in associates and was carried on by them and their descendants for more than a half century. They were said to have had in 1289 a capital of their own amounting to 35,000 gold florins besides what was deposited with them. They became regular bankers to the Holy See in the time of Innocent IV and remained in that service through six pontificates. They collected foreign income, advanced money for the papal expenses connected with the expedition of Charles of Anjou to Naples and for many other purposes. They held papal funds on deposit and made loans to cardinals and other prelates, from whom they also received money on deposit. In the later years of the century there were rumors of their insolvency. They complained that all their creditors were claiming reimbursement at the same time. They had "frozen assets" in distant enterprises and their funds were otherwise unavailable; although they had recently paid to their creditors some 200,000 florins they were in much difficulty and feared they would have to suspend payments. They appealed to Pope Boniface VIII to use his influence for their sake and to protect his own deposits. Boniface with his usual vigor came to their rescue for the time, but in 1307 the catastrophe came; they closed their doors. Philip the Fair of France claimed that the agents of the Buonsignori had fled from France owing him 54,000 livres and, according to the practice of the time, seized the property of all Sienese merchants

[13] Giovanni Villani, *Chroniche Fiorentine,* Trans. by P. H. Wicksteed and Ross E. Selfe, (London, 1906), 308, 351, 427, etc.; W. E. Lunt, "The Financial System of the Medieval Papacy," *Quarterly Journal of Economics,* XXXIII (1909), 251-95. See also L. Nina, *Le Finanze Pontifiche nel Medio Evo* (two volumes, Milan, 1929-30).

in France to recoup himself for his losses. Clement V, now pope, sequestered their possessions wherever he could get control of them, and for many years, certainly till 1344, papal officials were still trying to close out their accounts. The effect of this failure on the city of Siena itself was most disastrous.[14]

The Buonsignori were only one of the banking firms which looked after the financial affairs of the popes. The Tolomei, also of Siena, the Ricciardi of Lucca, the Chiarenti and Ammanati of Pistoia, and above all a group of Florentine banking houses were in their service. In 1277 Pope Nicholas III borrowed 200,000 gold florins from Pistoian and Florentine bankers to equip the expedition of Rudolph II of Hapsburg against Ottokar of Bohemia. Rudolph's victory on the Marchfeld led to the establishment of the House of Hapsburg in the Austrian dominions. Over and over again during these centuries important political movements were influenced, often made possible, only by loans from the rising class of bankers.[15]

During the later years of the thirteenth century Rome teemed with representatives of financial firms. At least twenty were named in the papal registers, rising and falling in prominence, uniting and separating, being utilized for various purposes, reflecting the fortunes of their home cities and the preferences of successive popes. They were for the most part family businesses, though some banks combined the capital of several families and only took their name from the most prominent or oldest constituent of the group, much like the Barings, the Rothschilds, the Drexels and the Morgans of modern times.

III. FLORENCE AS A BANKING CITY

Florence excelled all other Italian cities as a money market. Ill-situated compared with Venice, Genoa, Pisa and even many inland cities like Milan and Verona, for purposes of commerce, the city

[14] E. Jordan, "La Faillite des Buonsignori," in *Mélanges Paul Fabre* (Paris, 1902), 416-35. See also Q. Senigaglia, "Le Compagnie Bancarie Senesi nei secoli XIII e XIV," *Studi Senesi,* XXIV-XXV (1907-1908); G. Arias, *La Compagnia Bancaria dei Buonsignori* (Florence, 1902).

[15] S. L. Peruzzi, *Storia del Commercio e dei Banchieri di Firenze del 1200 al 1343* (Florence, 1867); G. Schneider, *Die Finanziellen Beziehungen der Florentinischen Bankiers zur Kirche* (Leipzig, 1899); A. Fliniaux, "La Faillite des Ammanati de Pistoie et le Saint-Siège," *Revue d'Histoire de Droit Français et Étranger,* III (1924), 436-72.

on the Arno was yet endowed with vigor, enterprise and business capacity that raised it quite to their economic level. Wool manufactures first made it rich,[16] and neither the disorders of the old noble families of Tuscany, who had their town houses there, nor the turbulence of a particularly restless populace prevented the growth of a group of new families who made banking their principal if not their sole avocation. Their names were soon as well known through Europe as those of the Florentine artists and poets of a somewhat later generation. Beyond the Arno were the great half-fortified dwellings of a whole group of allied banking families, the Mozzi, Peruzzi and Bardi. The towered house of the Frescobaldi was at the south end of the bridge of Santa Trinita, which was built largely at their expense. A painting by Ghirlandaijo now hanging in the neighboring church of Santa Trinita shows the palace of the Spini, the scene of a miracle performed by St. Francis on a child of that family. The houses of the Scali, Pulci and Abbati were further in the heart of the city, while the Cerchi, early known as one of the greatest banking families, were rich neighbors of Dante's family, the Alighieri. The Falconieri, the Alfani, the Alberti and other Florentine families followed the same business.[17]

One of the principal functions performed by the agents of these bankers at Rome was the collection of the papal dues referred to above. At one time the house of Spini had charge of collections in Germany, the Alfani in Hungary, Poland, Slavonia, Norway and Sweden, the Chiarenti in Spain, and six other Florentine companies in England.[18] The garnering of the harvest of papal dues in foreign lands was a difficult task, and the carriage of the precious metals by land or sea was dangerous. When Philip IV took with him into Flanders four horses loaded with boxes of gold and silver coin, intending to use them to bribe the emperor, he evidently relied on his troops for their protection. The Templars, being armed knights, were often entrusted with the conveyance of money. They not only

[16] A. Doren, *Die Florentiner Wollentuchindustrie vom XIV-ten bis zum XVIten Jahrhundert* (Stuttgart, 1901); R. Davidsohn, "Blüte und Niedergang der Florentinischen Tuchindustrie", *Zeitschrift für die gesamte Staatswissenschaft,* LXXXV (1928), 225-55.

[17] Schneider, op. cit., 8-9; Villani, *Chroniche,* 160; there is an admirable discussion of Florentine banking in Robert Davidsohn, *Geschichte von Florenz* (Berlin, 1896-), IV.

[18] See Emilio Re, "La Compagnia dei Riccardi in Inghilterra," *Archivo della R. Società Romana di Storia Patria,* XXXVII (1914).

carried the large amounts of specie belonging to the Order itself from one of their commanderies to another and for deposit in the Temples in Paris and London,[19] but they were also engaged by kings and private persons to guard shipments of money. Not only violence, but legal obstruction had to be guarded against. In those times of shortage of bullion, governments frequently forbade the export of gold and silver; goods only, not money or plate, could be carried out of most countries.

It was in this service that the Italian bankers played, in the early period at least, the most conspicuous part. In the case of England the transmission of the papal dues or their equivalent was much facilitated by the demand for English wool in Italy. Taking advantage of this, the collectors, usually clerics, deposited with Italian bankers in England the proceeds of their collection, often very considerable sums of coined money, and received from them a primitive form of bill of exchange which could be sent by messenger to Rome, where it was payable in cash or credit. In the meantime the agents of the bankers in England would invest the money in wool or other native produce and ship it to Flanders, France or Italy to be sold, often at a second profit. Everywhere, at fairs and town markets, at religious houses and manors, perhaps among wool raisers themselves, these merchant-bankers were constantly buying wool to be shipped abroad in payment of the bills of exchange held in Italy. As many as twenty banking firms from Siena, Lucca, Florence or Rome itself were carrying on such operations in England at one time. Long lists of monasteries where wool could be bought, the relative excellence and probable price at each, and other data still exist in Italian city records, drawn up by these companies.[20]

The transfer of the papal residence from Rome to Avignon in 1309 brought about a great change in the relations between the bankers and the papal treasury. Much the same work had to be

[19] L. Delisle, *Les Opérations Financières des Templiers* (Paris, 1889).

[20] William Cunningham, *Growth of English Industry and Commerce* (fourth edition, London, 1905-1907), I, 628-641; see also E. Dixon, "The Florentine Wool Trade in the Middle Ages," *Royal Historical Society, Transactions,* XII (1908), 151-79; and especially G. Bigwood, "Un Marché de Matières Premières; Laines d'Angleterre et Marchands Italiens vers la fin du XIIIe Siècle", *Annales d'Histoire Économique et Sociale,* II (1930), 193-211.

performed, but new practices were introduced and one set of bankers gradually yielded to another. By this time, however, the main profits of the banking companies were being secured through other connections. Kings had even more insistent need for ready money than had the popes for they had to finance the national wars which were then beginning. Papal funds often lay in the banks and accumulated for considerable periods, but kings were always in need of money; they were seldom in a position to await the slow processes of tax collection, and at times of crisis required larger sums than taxes alone would produce. These sums were supplied by the professional bankers, with great profit to themselves.

About 1290 three brothers, Muschiato, Biccio and Nicolo Guidi, left Florence for France to enter the service of Philip the Fair. The oldest brother became receiver of taxes and treasurer, and all three acted as financial agents. Through their connections with the Florentine banking houses they were able to lend the king money and to negotiate many of his financial operations. They were with him in Flanders in 1295, advancing money to bribe Guy de Dampierre, the Duke of Brabant and the Count of Holland to take Philip's side and thus break off their alliance with England. They were instrumental in seizing the money deposited by the Bishop of Winchester in the abbeys of St. Denis and St. Genevieve at Paris. Through the company of the Peruzzi they engaged the services of Raynaldo de Supino and his mercenary band for 10,000 florins, to carry out for King Philip the brutal attack on Pope Boniface at Anagni. They assisted in the seizure and transfer to the king's coffers of the treasure of the Templars. They were reimbursed by liens on the taxes, a share in the profits of the royal exchanges and doubtless in other ways.[21]

The coast was more clear for money-lenders and banking companies in these later days of the thirteenth century than it had ever been before. The Jews, after having been for centuries exploited, taxed, tallaged, held to ransom, driven from town to town, oppressed and persecuted, and having at best been protected by the king while they amassed wealth which was later extorted from them, or

[21] Kervyn de Lettenhove, "Les Argentiers Florentins," *Bulletin de l'Académie Royal des Lettres. . . . de Belgique,* second series, XII (1861), 123-42.

permitted to make doubtful loans to university students at usury, had at last, in 1252, been expelled from France and in 1290 from England.[22] Even the small money-lenders, the Caursians and Lombards, at least as that name was then generally applied,—Piers Plowman's

"Lombardes of Lucques that liven by lone as Jews"

had ceased to be of sufficient importance to the kings to command their protection. Therefore, like the Jews, "Lombards" were, nominally at least, expelled successively from both England and France, though they usually bought their way back again.[22] Even the banking families found their occupation a speculative one and endured a series of depression periods. Within the first quarter of the fourteenth century eighteen banking houses either failed or allowed themselves to be absorbed by others. The Buonsignori, the Franzeni, the Mozzi, the Pulci, the Rimbertini, the Cerchi and others, dropped out of active business, some of them permanently, others for a time. In 1311 the Frescobaldi were banished from England through the influence of the Lords Ordainers and soon afterward they failed.[22]

This left the two houses of the Bardi and Peruzzi almost alone in England, except for the rising class of native capitalists, to enjoy the profits and dangers of money lending to an ambitious and none too conscientious government. Some lesser Italian firms appeared from time to time, like the Albertini and the Pulci, and no doubt others had money invested with the Bardi and Peruzzi. These two houses were veritable international bankers. The Peruzzi, for instance, had agencies in sixteen cities scattered through five countries. Boccaccio the elder was a representative of the Bardi in Paris when he became the father of the novelist, and Giovanni

[22] R. Ruding, *Annals of the Coinage,* 187; Cunningham, *Growth of English Industry and Commerce,* I, 285-7. Decrees of expulsion of the Lombards from France were issued in 1269, 1274, 1277, 1291 and from England in 1295. Thompson, op. cit., 3; see C. Pitou, *Les Lombards en France et à Paris* (two volumes, Paris, 1891-1892); W. Stubbs, *Constitutional History of England* (fourth edition, Oxford, 1896), II, 245; Armando Sapori, *Le Crisi delle Campagnie mercantili dei Bardi e dei Peruzzi* (Florence, 1926), 29-31; this is a basic account of the activities of Italian bankers in England, but see also W. E. Rhodes, "The Italian Bankers in England and the Loans to Edward I and Edward II," *Owens College Essays,* Manchester (1902); R. J. Whitwell, "Italian Bankers and the English Crown," *Royal Historical Society, Transactions,* XVII (1903), 173-233.

Boccaccio himself was sent as a boy to Naples to learn the banking business in the branch house there. The chronicler Villani was in the employ of the Bardi. At one time the chamberlain of the King of Naples was Arnold Peruzzi, a member of the Peruzzi firm. Both the Bardi and the Peruzzi repeatedly made loans to the Neapolitan kings of the House of Anjou for their war-like operations and for the support of their brilliant and expensive court until the king and the banking houses were alike deeply involved.[23] They also financed the Italian *condottieri* and the new ducal families which were building up their power in the cities of Italy. They made loans at the same time to the King of France and to French nobles and prelates.

As the extensive plans of Edward III for sending an overwhelming force against the King of France took shape in 1337, 1338 and 1339, he was forced to borrow in all directions. While he and his envoys were in the Netherlands he borrowed from three citizens of Mechlin 54,000 gold florins, giving in return a document which was practically a short-term government bond, since it was signed by the king, promised repayment in three months and was payable to the lenders, their representatives or any bearer. The wording of this and similar documents gives a clue to one means by which lenders, notwithstanding the fact that all interest was regarded as usury and forbidden by canon law, found their operations profitable. The agreement entitled the lender, in case of default, to fifty florins a day in addition to all other expenses of collections, so long as the debt remained unpaid. This netted the lenders, after the first three months, interest at the rate of 25 per cent a year. Edward borrowed from the Archbishop of Trèves 25,500 florins, pledging his "great crown" for their repayment, and from citizens of Cologne a smaller sum, leaving with them the crown of Queen Philippa and "a certain small crown" as security. His keeper of the wardrobe pawned the crown jewels at Bruges for a loan of 16,000 florins. These and other foreign loans were ultimately taken over by the English agents of the Bardi and Peruzzi so that the crowns and royal jewels might be brought home and the king's envoys themselves enabled to

[23] G. Yver, *Le Commerce et les Marchands dans l'Italie Méridionale au XIIIe et au XIVe Siècle* (Paris, 1903).

return, for they had bound themselves not to leave the Continent till the loans were repaid.[24]

The bankers were in a difficult position when the Hundred Years War began, for they had made loans to the kings of both countries and had deposits in both kingdoms. In 1338 Philip seized the property of their agents in France on suspicion of their favoring England. Although the pope, as their protector, interceded and pointed out that the interests of bankers were for peace rather than for war, they regained their property only after making large payments.[25]

In England their advances continued in ever increasing amounts as the expenses of the war grew and it became evident that the war could not be made to pay for itself. In one year the Peruzzi, on the expectation of a parliamentary grant, advanced a sum that would equal about a million and a half dollars in modern value. As the war progressed Edward became more and more remiss in his repayment of loans. On the other hand the banking companies were debtors as well as creditors. They were bound to those who had invested money with them and they even owed the king on certain accounts, though far less than he owed them. In the administration of the customs and other operations in England and in their commitments abroad they were behindhand with their payments and dependent on collections from the royal treasury that could not always be made. They were evidently in a dangerous position.

In 1341 a war broke out between Florence and Pisa which created complications for the bankers at home. In the same year the King of Naples was forced to repudiate a debt of some 200,000 gold florins owed to the Bardi and Peruzzi. There were still other losses. The Peruzzi were not able to stand the strain. In 1343 they failed, carrying down with them another weak company. The Bardi soon followed. Edward was not able to meet his payments and the company suspended in December 1344. The exact state of the accounts is still a matter of controversy. The large sums named by the contemporary chronicler Villani are no longer accepted. According to the latest calculation the king was in debt to the Bardi to the extent

[24] Rymer, *Foedera* (Ed. 1821), II, ii, pp. 1081-2, 1085, 1124.
[25] *Calendar of Papal Registers*, II, 572.

of 500,000 to 900,000 gold florins or in modern values perhaps four and a half to eight million dollars. It appears that the loans of the two companies to the crown between the beginning of these operations in England in 1290 and the failure in 1343 and 1345 amounted to somewhat over £400,000 sterling or twenty million dollars in modern value. Of course much of this was repaid and reloaned, some of it repeatedly. During the next half-century the king repaid to the Bardi some £20,000 and in 1391 all the old accounts were settled by a payment to a representative of the company, who gave a receipt in full.[26]

It was at the time of the failure of the great Italian companies that the king turned, as already recounted, to the German merchants for loans, and to certain lesser Italian banking companies. But in the main both in England and on the Continent the governments relied for loans more and more on their own capitalists, such wealthy merchants as the mayors of London, the three generations of the Pole family of Hull or Sturmys of Bristol in England, and similar capitalists in other countries. Before long the English government turned again from the great capitalists to the small and borrowed several thousand pounds from sixty-eight towns, seventy-eight ecclesiastical bodies and forty-seven noblemen and gentry. The changing appeal for mercantile and banking credits from the foreigner to the native is one of the many instances of the advance of nationalism as this period progressed.[27]

IV. JACQUES COEUR

The most conspicuous instance of this change was the famous French merchant-banker Jacques Coeur. Almost every element of dramatic interest marked his career. Charles VII of France, Joan of Arc, Queen Marie of Anjou, the beautiful Agnes Sorel, the group of princes and nobles who first betrayed and then saved France, and finally the English rulers of Aquitaine are the characters who surrounded him; the Levant, the Mediterranean, Italy, the commercial cities and war-torn provinces of France were the scenes of his activity. His was one of the traditional instances in

[26] Sapori, op. cit., 158-182; Beardwood, *Alien Merchants in England,* 3-9, 122-33.

[27] A. Anderson, *Origin of Commerce* (London, 1764), I, 210, 213; II, 222-3; William Cunningham, *Growth of English Industry and Commerce,* I, 385.

history of the rapid rise and sudden fall of human fortunes, and the great house he built and adorned for himself at Bourges still stands, except perhaps for the Ca d'Oro of Marino Contarini at Venice, as the finest example of the wealthy domestic architecture of that age.

Jacques Coeur was born of a merchant family of no great wealth or pretensions at Bourges, an old city, famous for its cloth trade. It was, so long as the English occupied Paris, Normandy and the south, the residence city of the disinherited dauphin.[28] Coeur began his commercial career in 1427 with a voyage to the Levant, where he went as far inland as Damascus. On the return voyage he seems to have visited many of the famous islands and cities of the eastern Mediterranean and Italy, with which he later established trade connections. He soon entered upon an extensive and profitable commercial career, using the city of Montpellier as a base. That city enjoyed a papal dispensation from the standing prohibition of traffic with the infidels. It was allowed to send six ships a year to Alexandria.

Coeur proceeded to deal in Mediterranean goods and to build up a domestic business. He handled silks, armor, feathers, spices, furs and, according to a statement of the time, "every class of merchandise, especially that required by the king, the dauphin and the nobles." The profits of successful voyages were so great that capital for new expeditions could soon be amassed, but there are many evidences that Coeur possessed besides unusual commercial and financial abilities. He soon owned four large galleys and three smaller vessels and doubtless had freight on many others. In 1448 he was able to equip at short notice and at his own expense eleven ships for the relief of an endangered French possession, and some at least of these ships were his own.

Coeur sent his vessels as far as Egypt and Syria and did commercial work for the Knights Hospitallers at Rhodes. When a truce intervened in the long war between France and England he

[28] The basic account of Jacques Coeur's career is Pierre Clément, *Jacques Coeur et Charles VII* (Paris, 1886), a work of more than ordinary carefulness in referring to the sources. Of recent studies see Heinrich Prutz, *Jacques Coeur* (Berlin, 1911), and R. Bouvier, *Un Financier Colonial au XVe Siècle: Jacques Coeur* (Paris, 1928), an excellent and well-illustrated account, emphasizing Coeur's great accomplishment in opening the Oriental trade to French enterprise.

shipped fine goods across the channel. He established warehouses at Tours, Marseilles, Paris, Perpignan, Narbonne, Beaucaire and many other French cities, and is said to have had 300 agents in his service. He was a bold builder; some of his warehouses were handsome dwellings as well. In Paris a bust and tablet in the Rue Rambuteau mark the location of one of them; another was on the site of the present Palais Royal. He made additions to the cathedral at Bourges and founded a chapel and charitable establishment in the Rue St. Honoré in Paris. Above all he began the erection and the ingenious adornment of his great house at Bourges. The interpretation of its curious allegorical carvings is still a matter of speculation. He received a special personal permit from Pope Eugenius in 1446 to carry on trade with the Saracens, and by a fortunate mission to Turkey, supported by the king, he was able to secure for French trade in the dominions of the Sultan the favored position which it did not lose for centuries.

Nearer home Coeur worked silver, copper and lead mines near Lyons under a royal grant, and purchased from reckless or impoverished representatives of old noble families thirty or more seigneuries in the center and south of France.

Thus in the critical years when Joan of Arc was playing her part in the drama of French history, and the dauphin was being transformed by her services into a king of France, Jacques Coeur was becoming the richest man of his age. No satisfactory estimate of his fortune or income can now be made, but it was princely. It was based for the most part on his commercial operations, which were made more profitable by the constant favor of the king. His loans to the court and to others must also have shown a handsome return. In 1440 he became *argentier* to the king, that is, steward or paymaster of the household, and subsequently he entered more and more completely into the royal service. He was made a member of the council and was given a patent of nobility. Later he became master of the mint both of Bourges and of Paris, and was in a position to advance the fortunes of his relatives and friends. One of his daughters married the son of the Vicomte de Bourges. His brother was appointed Bishop of Luçon, one of his sons became Archbishop of Bourges, although only twenty-five years old, and another was made Dean of Limoges. He himself was sent on one mission after another, to the republic of Genoa, to the Count of Savoy, to the Pope. He was commissioner for the king at the meetings of the estates of Languedoc for eight successive years, wringing from them reluctant grants of taxes, but receiving also from them yearly personal allowances, probably for not being still harder upon them. To the end he lived a double life, partly as a merchant with many business interests, partly as councillor following the king and the court as best he might.

More and more he became the recourse of all in need of ready money. The queen borrowed from him, giving a pearl at one time, a Bible at another as security; one of the king's daughters borrowed eighty livres "from Jacques Coeur for a robe"; the wife of the dauphin, Margaret of Scotland, borrowed 2000 livres for silk and skins of sable for her wardrobe. Little by little the list of his creditors grew, the Count of Maine, Dunois, the admiral, the Count of Foix, Biron, Louis de Beauveau, Adam de Cambrai, Maupas, Boucicault, La Tremouille, all owed him money. It was a dangerous list. A money-lender is not loved in proportion to the favors he has granted. When he loaned his royal master 20,600 crowns to buy back the jewels he had formerly given to one mistress in order that he might present them to another, he was exposing himself to still more imminent peril.

He made, however, some loans of quite another class, which have placed him high among French patriots. Since the relief of Orleans, the coronation of the dauphin, the treaty of Arras, the recapture of Paris and the army reforms of 1445, the spirit of France had asserted itself, her military fortunes had risen and the hold of England had been severely shaken. A bold campaign in Normandy might expel them from the whole north. But the money for immediate service was lacking. Coeur came to the rescue; he loaned 200,000 crowns for military purposes in one year and 60,000 crowns for the expense of the siege of Cherbourg the next. During the campaign he accompanied the king, and when the royal cavalcade made its victorious entry into Rouen in November 1449, he was one of the group of French seigneurs whose gorgeous robes made this a famous scene of chivalry.

This was the height of the fortunes of the great merchant; all that followed was an anticlimax. There is no doubt that among his debtors jealousy, fear of being called on to repay their loans and hatred of the rich upstart and royal favorite were rising higher and higher until a pretext was found to attack him. Agnes Sorel, the beautiful mistress of the king, died in childbirth. As so often, the rumor spread that she had been poisoned, and, absurd as it was, the murder was charged to Jacques Coeur. He was arrested; other offenses were discovered with which he was charged; he was tried, subjected to torture till he made a garbled confession of all except the poisoning, and threw himself on the mercy of the king. The mercy of the king was no more tender than in other cases where royal advantage might be reaped from its refusal. The fallen minister was ordered to pay the king a fine of 100,000 crowns for his offense and 300,000 as indemnity for the king's losses. His property was confiscated and he was ordered to be banished from France. Long imprisonment, escape by the aid of some of his former employees, refuge with the pope, another voyage to the Levant, this time as captain of a papal expedition against the Turks, death and burial on the island of Chios brought his life to a close in 1456. It may be an alleviation to the crass injustice of the proscription of the last great merchant of this age, that the 100,000 crowns which the king realized immediately from the sale of his property was used to pay the expenses of the expedition which captured Bordeaux and completed the expulsion of the English from France. The rest of his wealth, except for some concealments by his agents and some minor restorations to his descendants in better times, was scattered and wasted among courtiers, mistresses and lawyers.

V. THE ORIGIN OF MODERN BANKING

It may be of interest to notice that among the most obscure of the bankers of this period were the predecessors of the most famous of the next. When the principal Florentine companies failed in the middle of the fourteenth century, the business of the Medici, too obscure to be seriously affected by the crisis, survived. In the persons of Giovanni de Medici and his two sons, Cosimo and the elder

Lorenzo, the family had already, by the middle of the fifteenth century, entered upon its career of greatness.[29]

In Augsburg old Johannes Fugger was a linen weaver, of country stock; his son Johannes became a dealer in linen fabrics, a merchant and burgher of standing who, when he died in 1409, bequeathed a fortune of 3000 gold florins to his two sons. One of these bought a patent of nobility, married a lady of quality and drifted away from the bourgeoisie into the rural gentry. The other established a banking business and on his death in 1460 left in the hands of his seven sons what was perhaps the most powerful financial concern that has ever existed. Such seems to have been the natural evolution of the early capitalist, from peasant to artisan, from artisan to merchant, from merchant either to noble or to banker, to the old or the new aristocracy.[30]

More important than the continuance of the old system of private banking houses was the beginning of a more familiar modern form, the government-chartered bank. We need not trace here the early growth of modern banking. It played no significant part in the general history of the thirteenth and fourteenth or even of the fifteenth century. It is true nevertheless that at Venice there were not only merchant bankers, the Pisani, the Priuli and others, but also persons who loaned money to the government, received public financial privileges and were known as *banchieri*. There was some kind of bank of deposit at Rome about 1400, and at Barcelona there was founded in 1401 the "Taula" or municipal bank. In 1407 there was established at Genoa the bank of St. George, an institution destined to have financial influence for centuries, whose noble building still stands in the Piazza Caricamento.[31]

VI. THE INFLUENCE OF COINED MONEY

It is to be noted that, notwithstanding the progress made in these early modern centuries in the use of instruments of credit, the vast amount of business—hiring, buying and selling, borrowing, lend-

[29] See O. Meltzing, *Das Bankhaus der Medici und seine Vorläufer* (Jena, 1907).

[30] Max Jensen, *Jakob Fugger der Reiche* (Leipzig, 1920); Richard Ehrenberg, *Das Zeitalter der Fugger* (two volumes, Jena, 1896).

[31] See J. G. van Dillen, "De Girobanken van Genua, Venetie en Hamburg" *Tijdschrift voor Geschiedenis* (1927), and the beautifully illustrated monograph by E. Marengo, C. Manfroni and G. Pessagno, *Il Banco di San Giorgio* (Genoa, 1911).

ing and repaying, importing and exporting—was based on the use of actual coined money. The acknowledgments which the English king gave the bankers who loaned him money were careful to state that the actual pieces had been counted out and handed over. Money meant coin. In 1242, for instance, Henry III took with him to Poitou for the expenses of the expedition of that year thirty barrels of money, 160,000 silver pennies in each barrel.[32] The English pound was literally a pound weight of silver, coined into 240 pennies or into a corresponding number of half-pennies and farthings. After 1248, possibly somewhat earlier, groats, or four-penny pieces, were coined; there were no sixpences or shillings till long after this time. Similarly on the Continent money meant visible, tangible pieces of definite weight of one or other of the precious metals.

The growth of wealth and its economic and social effects were therefore largely conditioned by the increase of silver and gold mined and minted. Notwithstanding the general shortage of the precious metals previous to the discovery and conquest of America, the amounts produced in Europe and coined in the mints were considerable. There were mines in Italy, in southern France, in Spain, in Germany, in the southeastern mountainous parts of Europe, Silesia, Austria, Hungary and Bohemia, and in England. None were rich and the technical skill with which they were worked was slight, so that some had been exhausted by the end of the fourteenth century. Yet production was large enough to make gold and silver bullion one of the regular objects of use and of commerce, and to supply the mints of kings as well as of nobles and cities which had the privilege of coinage.

Between 1294 and 1300 an average of some 500 pounds of silver was annually brought to the English mint from the mines of Devonshire. For a while these mines were so productive that additional workers were brought from Derbyshire and lodged at government expense. In 1296 more than 700 pounds was produced. Governments were always on the lookout for mines of the precious metals and offered many inducements to prospectors. There was also some dabbling in alchemy in the hope of increasing the supply. In times of crisis holders of gold and silver plate were required to

[32] Holinshed, *Chronicle*, II, 229, 337; Ruding, *Annals of the Coinage*, I, 183.

dispose of a certain proportion of it at the mint for purposes of coinage.[33]

The money of other countries brought into England was also from time to time ordered to be brought to the mint for recoinage. But in the main the English mint had to rely on the importation of bar silver and gold, which were bought like other commodities. In the year the English mines sent to the mint 709 pounds of silver 1063 pounds was obtained from other sources. At times large amounts were obtained; in one year 6,000 pounds, in another 18,000 pounds. In still another, 30,000 pounds of silver was available for coinage. It has been estimated that in the thirty-five years of the reign of Edward III, nearly a million pounds of silver coins and bars were imported into England. Somewhat later 2000 pounds of gold was brought to the mint in one year, 3500 pounds in another. There is reason to believe that in 1307 about £1,600,000 was in circulation in England.[34]

Conditions in other countries which had no large native supply were much the same. In view of the drain of commerce, the anxiety of governments for larger incomes, the constant demand for precious metals for ornament and the relatively small production of bullion, practically all countries found it necessary to forbid the export of their own money, and to seize and recoin all foreign money imported. Foreign money was usually paid for by the export of goods, not in coin. Various devices were used to bring in money or bullion. Exporters of goods were required to give bonds that they would bring back at least part of the proceeds of their sale in silver or gold.[35] By these methods the mints were enabled to turn out a relatively steady and abundant supply of coined money. In England all the mints belonged to the government, though they were frequently sublet. In France twenty-nine feudal lords had the right of coining money, in addition to the royal mints. Many cities also by virtue of their charters or by usurpation coined their own money.[36]

There are few better indications of the larger part trade and

[33] Ruding, op. cit., 60-65.
[34] Ruding, op. cit., 65.
[35] *Rotuli Parliamentorum,* II, 137; Ruding, op. cit., 215.
[36] E. Boutaric, *La France sous Philippe le Bel* (Paris, 1861), 324.

finance were coming to play in European affairs than the sudden and almost simultaneous introduction of gold into the coinage of so many different countries. Up to the middle of the thirteenth century the money of western Europe, except for a few gold bezants introduced from the Eastern Empire, had been exclusively of silver. Not since the time of Charlemagne had gold money been coined west of the Adriatic. Now within a half-century gold was adopted for coinage in a dozen different states. Just before the middle of the thirteenth century Frederick II had struck his Sicilian *augustales*, a tentative gold coinage that was not continued by his imperial successors. But in 1252 Florence began the issue of its famous gold florins.[37] In 1257 Henry III of England coined a gold penny, twice the weight and twenty times the value of the old silver penny or sterling. The Venetian ducat appeared in 1284 and before the end of the century Philip the Fair was minting gold coins in France. By the middle of the fourteenth century the English noble was in common use and various other gold coins were being issued from many mints.

The most famous and the earliest of these gold coins was the Florentine gold florin, the *fiorino d'oro*, the "golden flower," so called because it bore the arms of the city, the lily, on one face, while the figure of John the Baptist, patron saint of the city and its "Florentia," were on the other. The coin was a beautiful one, of pure gold, weighing 54 grains, about twice the weight of the American gold dollar of 1932. It was a bold exercise of independence for a city, acting without imperial or royal authorization, to coin money, especially of gold, which in the nature of things was designed for external rather than domestic use. But Florence, like many other cities, had already usurped the right to coin silver money, a right which in Italy belonged to the Emperor, who neglected it. The coinage of gold was simply one more assertion of Florentine independence. Once it was begun, the issue increased rapidly till it averaged 300,000 or 400,000 coins a year. By 1300 there were estimated to be 2,000,000 in existence. One of the reasons for

[37] See Marc Bloch, "Le Problème de l'Or au Moyen Age," *Annales d'Histoire Économique et Sociale,* V (1933), 1-34; W. A. Shaw, *The History of Currency, 1252-1894* (New York, 1896), chap. i; W. W. Carlile, *Evolution of Modern Money* (London, 1901), chaps. iii-v.

the prominence and success of the Florentine banking companies was the excellence and abundance of the coinage issued by the city's mint.[38]

No coin ever captured the confidence or aroused the imitation of the world more quickly. Within a few years florins were in wide circulation. They were used at the fairs of Champagne, they were lent by Italian bankers to the pope and by Flemish merchants to the King of England; they were paid by Edward III to his mercenaries and allies in the Netherlands and were circulated among small cities in Germany. Soon coins of the same name and of approximately the same value were issued by many sovereigns and cities. Lucca, Perugia, Genoa coined florins; so did the mints of Hungary, Bohemia and the pope, to say nothing of various Rhenish and Netherland cities. The English gold pennies were not popular, and were not long in use. When gold coins were again minted, in 1344, they were at first called florins, though they were double the weight of the Florentine coin. Soon afterward they were increased still further in size and called nobles; as such they were the characteristic English gold coin during the next century. An ingenious investigator has counted up forty-eight mints that at one time or another and in one form or another issued coins called florins, and the name is in use for some of these even today.[39]

The high reputation of their gold coin and outside competition with it led the Florentines to exercise special care in preserving its weight, purity and excellence of workmanship. The mint was a well defended building near the palace of the signory on the site later occupied by the Loggia dei Lanzi. It was under the charge of important officials chosen anew each year. Florentine coiners were famous and were put in charge of the mints of England, France and other countries at various periods. In the Old and the New Market and in other places in the city and suburbs of Florence "weighers of florins" were stationed to settle all disputes as to genuineness and weight. Questionable coins were withdrawn from

[38] Davidsohn, *Geschichte von Florenz,* IV, 139; G. Schneider, *Die Finanziellen Beziehungen der Florentinischen Bankiers zur Kirche,* 8.

[39] Davidsohn, *op. cit.,* IV, 138-40; Thomas Snelling, *View of the Gold Coinage of Great Britain* (London, 1762), 1-3.

circulation and their holders were paid only the value of the pure gold they contained.[40]

The Venetian ducats were scarcely less well known and ultimately became more so. But their range of circulation was rather eastward, throughout Italy, the Mediterranean lands and the Orient, where they became familiar under the later name of sequins. By 1400 the Venetian mint coined annually a million ducats.[41]

Notwithstanding the prevalence of gold coins, they can have played but a small part in the actual work of buying and selling. Commercial transactions were still carried on in silver and often in very small units. The "nimble sixpence" of modern times does but slight service compared with the humble silver penny that corresponded to it in the fourteenth and fifteenth centuries. Difficult as it is to trace the course of coined money from the mints through the arteries of daily trade and to follow its actual circulation, it cannot be doubted that its increasing supply was one of the most potent forces of the time. We have seen some of the larger work it was doing. But it must be remembered it also seeped out beyond bankers and great merchants into the hands of the mass of the common people. This obscure process of dissemination of money among the lower classes has unfortunately left but little record and it must therefore remain largely a matter of inference if not of guesswork. Not only the silver penny, but the great number of half-pence and farthings that were coined at the English mints—almost 3,000 pounds of silver were turned into 2,217,600 halfpence and farthings, in the one year 1281, for instance[42]—must have been intended for the use of people whose expenditures were on the smallest scale, for a loaf of bread, a quart of beer, church dues, a half day's wages or a petty purchase from a peddler.

There is little difficulty in picturing the spread of money in the towns, the natural sphere of exchange of services and goods. But how did the money reach the country? The tables of wages in the statutes of laborers that followed the Black Death and other records leave no doubt that the wages of artisans were paid in money, even in the country, and the manorial records so generally state the

[40] Davidsohn, op. cit., IV, 139.
[41] Molmenti, *Venice*, I, Pt. i, 153-162.
[42] Ruding, *Annals of the Coinage*, I, 84.

value of agricultural services in terms of money—pence, halfpence and farthings—that there must have been many cases in which actual money wages were paid to the peasantry by lords, their stewards or well-to-do farmers. These in turn were in a position to sell their surplus products at the fair or market and so get money in their purse.

A "money economy" is traceable even in the thirteenth century and even in the lowest ranks of society. In the manor courts fines and amerciaments were already fixed in terms of money. The rebellious peasants of 1381 demanded among other things that rent of land should never exceed fourpence per acre, and that tolls, which were payable in money, should not be increased. We know that in some regions, certainly in Burgundy and southern France, the Caursians and other money-lenders carried on their usurious trade, speculated in grain and farmed the tolls even in country villages. Doubtless discharged soldiers, wandering minstrels, students, friars and even beggars dispersed as well as collected petty coins. Whatever the process, an appreciable amount of money was, from the middle of the thirteenth century, being disseminated in the country and was exercising a subversive effect on old conditions. For one thing, the villain who in the fourteenth century negotiated with the steward of the lord to pay three pence a week instead of working as many days on the land was nearer the status of a free man because of this money relationship. The gradual fading away of serfdom in France, England, Spain, the Netherlands and the lands along the Rhine, so hard to trace and so inadequately explained by any sudden or specific provisions of law, was certainly closely connected with the possession of money by the peasantry.[43]

Thus money, banking, wealth, trade, capitalism did their work of attrition upon the agricultural, feudal, custom-controlled middle ages. Agricultural life, feudal institutions, chivalric ideals, still subsisted and dominated large regions of Europe and whole classes of society, but alongside of them, interpenetrating them, was this other set of influences, transforming their own age and creating the conditions for still further change.

[43] E. P. Cheyney, "The Disappearance of English Serfdom," *English Historical Review*, XV (1900), pp. 20-37.

It is time to turn from economic interests to those of a less material nature, though it will be impossible to leave them quite aside from any satisfactory explanation of this period. It is one of the characteristics of our own time that it has not only raised economic considerations to an unwonted importance in society, but has opened our eyes to their significance in all earlier ages.

Chapter Three

THE RISE OF THE MIDDLE CLASS: THE DEVELOPMENT OF REPRESENTATIVE GOVERNMENT

I. THE TOWNS

THE ATTAINMENT of political recognition by the middle class was one of the principal characteristics of this period. Alongside the feudal noble, strong in the support of his military and feudal tenants, and the prelate, endowed with religious prestige as well as land, appears on the political scene the townsman, the merchant, wealthy, industrious, intelligent, trained to take part in government under the charter of his town. We have already noted the rise to prominence of many merchants and financiers, and we shall have to add to the list lawyers, scholars, soldiers, statesmen and travelers, who, though they sprang from the unprivileged classes, nevertheless reached eminence and exercised great influence. But in addition to the success of individuals we have to consider the rise of the burghers as a class. The towns were the milestones in the progress of Europe from the dark ages to modern times. It is true that the increase of freedom and prosperity had created in some large villages, among the free landholders in England, Scandinavia and elsewhere, and among the artisans of the countryside of Flanders, the south of France, and northern Italy, a rural middle class that must be counted with. But it was the populous, walled, self-governing cities and towns that were the embodiment of the power of the middle classes. There were no extensive regions of Europe, except perhaps in the east, without such cities.

In the history of Spain during the middle ages cities had played a large part. The centuries-long crusade by which the Moors were driven southward into their last stronghold of Granada, where they were ensconced at the beginning of this period and where they remained until the very end of the fifteenth century, had required the establishment of walled cities as outposts of the Christian conquerors. To the inhabitants of these communities the kings of Leon and Castile had found it desirable to grant *fueros* or charters endowing them with extensive privileges.[1] The popular councils created in these cities were the oldest in Europe, except perhaps those of Italy. Their independence of action, their governmental system and the strength of their local spirit became famous and were imitated long afterward in Spanish America and in the Far East.[2]

As the reconquest extended southward into regions long the domain of the wealthy and cultured Moorish civilization, more blest by nature, older, richer and more highly developed, a new group of cities were added to those of the rugged north and midlands. Cordova was acquired in 1236, Murcia in 1241, Seville in 1248, Medina Sidonia in 1253, Cadiz in 1262, Tarifa in 1292, Algeciras, where Chaucer's "parfit knight" had fought, in 1344. The export of Spanish wool and hides from the midlands, of olive oil, fruit and fine manufactures from the south, became the basis of a foreign trade which supplemented the older local exchange. Gilds were organized in the towns, industries flourished, population grew, till there were in the dominions under the Castilian crown approximately a hundred such cities. From Burgos, Valladolid, Madrid and Toledo in the north and centre to Jaen, Seville and Cartagena in the south, Castile was dotted with these large, self-governing towns, many of them surrounded with dependent villages or extensive stretches of populated country under their civic control.

Aragon, more rugged and more feudal than Castile, was less a land of cities. Nevertheless Saragasso, Huesca, Lerida and other inland towns, originally Gothic or Moorish strongholds, had by this time taken on much the same characteristics. Catalonia, distinguished from Aragon though under the same crown, was marked by the supremacy of Barcelona, one of the largest, proudest and most advanced cities of Europe. Two successive charters granted at the very beginning of our period by the king in 1247 and 1258,

[1] Ramon Carande, *Sevilla Fortaleza y Mercado* (Madrid, 1925), gives an excellent picture of the development of a Spanish town, economically and institutionally.

[2] Ulick R. Burke, *History of Spain, from the Earliest Time to the Death of Ferdinand the Catholic* (second edition, London, 1900), I, 366.

endowed it with astonishingly large powers of self-government. We have already had occasion to notice its influence in all Mediterranean commerce. It was the location of the first bank of deposit in Europe and the focus of dissemination of the most widespread system of sea law used in the fourteenth century. Valencia was a typical Moorish city, a late conquest of the king of Aragon.[3]

Of all the great countries of Europe France was the richest in cities. The preceding two centuries had been filled with the reverberations of their struggle for self-government, or at least for civic freedom.[4] At the beginning of our period this process was approximately complete, and the cities and towns were approaching what proved to be the summit of their power and prosperity. Their increasing populations were overflowing their limits and spreading out into new suburbs. Trade was enriching the inhabitants and handicraft was making the population more numerous and more varied. Before the blight of the Hundred Years War fell upon one city and one region after another, there was rapidly increasing wealth.

This growing opulence and population enhanced the desire for freedom from overlords, royal, abbatial, episcopal, feudal. So there came into existence the "communes" and the "good towns," of every size and degree of self-government or chartered privilege, from practically independent republics, like Marseilles, Narbonne, Toulouse, Montpellier, to places hardly distinguishable from those rural villages which were still only half-emancipated from serfdom. The cities of the south, especially, whose life and trade had hardly been interrupted since the days of the Roman Empire, and whose prosperity revived early, on the basis of commerce and local independence, formed a score and more of rich and cultured communities. Equally rich and populous and almost equally early in the attainment of the degree of self-government indicated by the name commune were a number of cities in the northeast, St. Quentin, Arras, Beauvais, Amiens, Lille, Noyons and others in Flanders, Artois, Picardy, Burgundy and adjacent provinces. In the centre of

[3] Burke, op. cit., I, 213-18, 252-4.

[4] See the brilliant chapter on the emancipation of the towns by A. Giry and André Réville, in E. Lavisse and A. Rambaud, *Histoire Générale* (third edition, Paris, 1925), II, chap. viii.

France, the king, sometimes forced by insurrection, sometimes influenced by a money payment, sometimes moved by the desire to encourage the prosperity of the inhabitants, enfranchised the growing towns of his direct domain, Orleans, Mantes, Clermont, Melun, Paris itself and many others. In his own interest he aided also the towns in the domains of his great vassals which had demanded charters of liberties from their overlords.

It was a principle asserted by the kings' legal advisers, men learned in the Roman law, that each city on becoming a commune came under the direct administration of the king, no matter in the domain of what lay or ecclesiastical lord it might lie. Indeed, the greater civic communities were in many ways treated as though they were feudal holdings-in-chief, paying to the king acknowledgments in money and military service, possessing certain rights of jurisdiction and of peace and war, and in turn granting out fiefs to dependent knights, towns and villages. The town wall, the belfry which summoned its inhabitants to its defense, the prison and the trained bands of the towns were not without political significance in an age still largely feudal.

Certain cities set the model on which the self-government of many others was patterned. Such was the "establishment" of Rouen, granted in the first place by Henry II of England. This was later extended to the other cities of Normandy and to Angoulême, Poitiers, Cognac and other holdings of the English king, and was retained by them when they came under the direct rule of the King of France.

Some new towns were established in the twelfth and thirteenth centuries by bishops, abbots and lay lords and by the king, with the idea of making their territories more valuable. They offered advantages of self-government to settlers, and a new population of merchants, artisans and others grew up in them much as they grew up in Spain on the lands conquered from the Moors. Such, either by actual origin or by chartered increase in importance, were Bayonne, La Rochelle, Montauban, Beaumont. In these newer towns the city government seems to have been more democratic. The conditions of their origin led to a diffusion of control among all the inhabitants. But the usual type of town government was highly aristocratic. Generally speaking, hereditary office-holders, the owners of the land, well-to-do merchants, the artisans in the higher industries, and in many cases members of a traditional group of families, controlled the policy of the city and appointed its officers and representatives.

The names that have been mentioned are but a few among the 400, according to a traditional calculation, cities and chartered towns of France. Chronicles, fiscal records, court rolls and even the town archives themselves give us but a formal and vague knowledge of life in these cities, but there is quite enough to let us know that they were, by the end of the thirteenth century, crowded hives, buzzing with trade and industry, filled with a population relatively rich, enterprising and enlightened.

The rise of the towns in England had been much like that of the French towns, though they were, generally speaking, neither so numerous nor so large, nor so wealthy, and but few English cities attained self-government as complete as that of the communes of France or the cities of Spain. Certainly none were so nearly independent republics as were many in Germany and Italy.[5] The hundred or more named in Domesday Book had increased in number by the thirteenth century, by growth from mere village status and by new foundations, to 150 or more. The distinction between cities, places which possessed a cathedral and were the location of a bishop's see, and boroughs, which included all other recognized municipalities, had no relation to size or wealth. Nevertheless, on one occasion 110 cities and boroughs were considered of sufficient importance to be represented in a national assembly; at one time or another about half as many more were named. Some, like London, Bristol, York, Hull, Yarmouth and the towns along the south coast, were old sea or river ports and felt the invigorating effects of the growing commerce. Others were county towns, fortified centres,

[5] See the vivid, if somewhat antiquated chapter on the rise of the towns in J. R. Green, *History of the English People* (four volumes, London, 1877-1880). There is much on the subject in Mrs. J. R. Green, *English Town Life in the Fifteenth Century* (London, 1894), chaps. iv-xi. There is a remarkable paucity of works on the English cities as a whole. H. A. Merewether and A. J. Stephens, *The History of the Boroughs and Municipal Corporations of the United Kingdom* (three volumes, London, 1835), is almost the only general work.

places enriched by the concourse of buyers at nearby fairs or of pilgrims to local shrines.

Like Spanish and French cities the liberties of an English chartered town often extended over surrounding villages and open country. As in Spain and France, also, the charters of certain English cities served as models for a whole group. London served as the prototype for Norwich, Lincoln, Northampton and others; York for Beverley and Scarborough, Winchester for Wallingford, Andover, Salisbury, Wilton, Portsmouth, and these in turn were models for privileges of later chartered towns. There were even cases in which the charters of some town on the continent served as pattern for an English city or borough, which in turn was copied by others.[6] The extent to which the chartered towns and boroughs were self-governed cannot be exactly stated, since they differed from one another by an infinity of gradations. But the powers of the king had been, ever since the Conquest, so great that the towns themselves never attained, and the abbots, bishops or nobles on whose domains towns grew up never claimed to grant, more than a very limited political independence. A certain amount of judicial, administrative and financial autonomy and some responsibility for military service measure the rights and powers of the town governments in the political sphere. All other activities of the citizens were devoted to their trade, their industries and such cultural life as they may have developed.

At the opposite pole from those of England, so far as control by the central government goes, were the old and famous cities of Germany. Along the Rhine were cities like Constance, Coblentz, Mainz and Cologne, whose names still testify to their survival from Roman times. The great cities of south Germany, Augsburg, Regensburg, Nürnberg, Ulm, Munich, Vienna and many others we have already noted as growing populous and rich from the north and south lines of trade just as the member towns of the Hanseatic League grew great on the east and west trade. Many German cities had been founded or had grown up farther eastward on the edge of or well within the regions of the Slavs, who were

[6] William Stubbs, *Constitutional History of England* (third edition, London, 1891), I, 667-76.

less inclined to city life than the Germans. It is hardly necessary to mention the existence of cities in Italy. Italy was a land of cities. They dominated her history as markedly as they do her landscape.

In the far east of Europe, in Poland, in Bohemia, in Hungary and in the southeast, cities were less numerous and less close to one another, though hardly less important. So much of the incident of medieval and early modern history gathers around Thorn, Warsaw, Kovno, Grodno, Lemberg, Cracow, Budapest, Belgrade, Kiev, Moscow, Nicopolis and a score of other eastern cities that they rise into almost equal prominence with those of the west notwithstanding the vast stretches of open country that lie between them.

II. CONFEDERATIONS OF CITIES

It was in Germany that one of the characteristic town practices of the age became most widespread. This was the formation of leagues or confederations of towns. Under a distant elective ruler, poorly provided with the powers of a central administration and constantly turned aside from the further development of his powers by reminiscences of antiquity and by schemes for the extension of his authority beyond practicable limits, the feudal princes and nobles, the great prelates and the cities all alike acted largely in disregard of the German King and Emperor and often in opposition to him. The Hanseatic League has already been discussed. Less firmly founded on an economic basis but scarcely less drawn into combination by general disorder and local violence were the leagues of cities already adverted to, such as the Rhenish League of 1254, acknowledged by King William in 1255 and reorganized from time to time afterwards. The Swabian League, 1379-1388, included at one time as many as seventy towns and was in a position to enrol 10,000 men in a war on the emperor and on the territorial princes.[7]

In Spain similar leagues were known as *hermandades*, "brotherhoods," which played a large part in the struggle between the forces of order and disorder in the thirteenth and fourteenth centuries.[8] They were for the most part temporary unions, formed during the

[7] See Bruno Gebhardt, *Handbuch der Deutschen Geschichte* (seventh edition, Stuttgart, 1930), 379, 395, 488, 491-3, and the references there given.

[8] See J. Puyol y Alonso, *Las Hermandades de Castilla y Leon* (Madrid, 1913).

minorities of kings or at other times of confusion, for protection against the nobles or outlaws and for the preservation of good order and the enforcement of the law. Great as was the interest from an intellectual and scientific point of view of the long reign of Alfonso X, the Wise, which fills the early years of our period, from 1252 to 1285, little was then done to place the royal government on a strong foundation.[9]

The next king, Sancho IV, gave an example of crime and rapine instead of repressing them, and his successor, Ferdinand IV, was a child. On his accession in 1295 thirty-four cities of Castile sent representatives to Burgos and there entered into a solemn brotherhood. They drew up a formal act, reciting the evils of the time and declaring their intention of protecting their members from all attacks, and of supporting the royal authority. They organized an armed force, adopted a common seal, promulgated regulations for good order, appointed deputies to meet from time to time and proceeded to inflict punishments and to issue warnings, which often proved effective, to offenders. This body received the approval of the queen regent but was attacked by the king, when he reached his majority, and so passed out of existence.[10] In 1315, under Alfonso XI, who was also a child, a new *hermandad*, this time including 100 cities of Castile, Leon and Galicia, was formed at Valladolid and accomplished something toward keeping the country in order. Others, varying in extent and in duration, were formed during the next half-century. Sometimes they reflected more ambitious plans, such as the brotherhood formed among the towns on the Biscayan coast, which made commercial arrangements with inland towns and even with foreign countries. Similar *juntas*, as they were there called, were formed during the same period in Aragon, though there the power of the nobles was so great that the cities more frequently entered along with them into "Unions" or "General Privileges" against the crown for common advantages or against intrusion of the king upon their independence.[11]

Such leagues or unions of towns, though especially characteristic

[9] See the interesting chapter on his reign in Burke, op. cit., chap. xxv.

[10] Roger B. Merriman, *The Rise of the Spanish Empire in the Old World and in the New* (New York, 1918-1934), I, 191-4; Burke, op. cit., I, 317-18.

[11] Merriman, op. cit., I, 192-5, 432-7.

of Germany and of Spain, were by no means unknown in other countries. The cities of Lombardy, municipalities continuously from Roman times, repeatedly formed themselves into leagues, as in the time of Frederick Barbarossa, and again when Frederick II drew them together.[12] Just before our period a number of the Italian cities bade fair to join themselves into two or more rival confederations. Florence, Orvieto, Viterbo, Assisi and Perugia opposed Spoleto, Gubbio, Foligno, Cremona, Bergamo, Parma, Modena and Verona. But the unions of towns in the thirteenth and fourteenth centuries were usually temporary attachments to emperor or pope in some military adventure, as during the invasion by Henry VII, or the result of the reduction of some to dependency on others. Florence subjected Pistoia, Pisa and ultimately all Tuscany; Milan reduced Pavia and Cremona; Venice made the cities on the adjacent mainland her dependencies, till all Italy was reduced by the end of this period to few more than five states and groups of cities. But Italy was as exceptional as she was precocious and the parallelism between her history and that of other countries is hard to discern. Moreover, the tyrants early suspended all city liberties, including that of voluntary combination.[13]

In France the cities of the south frequently united for common defense or common aggression. Toulouse, Marseilles, Avignon, Périgueux and Narbonne at one time united in an offensive and defensive league; in 1247 Arles, Avignon and Marseilles formed a league which it was agreed should last fifty years. Each town was to furnish 100 men in time of war, fifty in time of peace, and to keep ten vessels in commission for two months each year to protect their harvest on the lands along the sea and river shore. In the north of France unions were less usual and everywhere were deprecated by the king. In Flanders, however, which was a French province, unions of towns were formed over and over again, sometimes in preparation for rebellion, sometimes as a more normal system.[14]

In England instances are few but not unknown. The Cinque Ports on the southeast coast were an ancient confederation of the

[12] W. F. Butler, *The Lombard Communes* (New York, 1906).
[13] A good general account may be found in F. Gianani, *I Communi* (Milan, 1909).
[14] Lavisse et Rambaud, *Histoire Générale,* II, 449-51.

seaport towns of Hastings, Sandwich, Dover, Romney and Hythe. To them, as sharers in their privileges and burdens, had gradually been added others till there were in actuality fifteen members of the group with twenty-four unincorporated towns or dependent villages. Their customs were ancient and peculiar, and much valued by them; they included some degree of political independence from Parliament, the courts and even from the crown. All the towns along the south coast, from Southampton to the mouth of the Thames which faced a similar line of towns on the north coast of France, formed an agreement with the Cinque Ports and with the inhabitants of the French ports opposite to regulate possible captures and subsequent settlements.[15]

III. THE CORTES OF CASTILE AND LEON

These leagues or confederations were obviously attempts to gain for townsmen acting in a larger group power or influence beyond what each town possessed separately. They were instinctive efforts to attain something like equal power with other classes. There was, however, coming into existence, probably quite unrealized by them and intended originally for quite a different object, another practice much better adapted to their attainment of such power. This was the summons by kings of representatives of the towns to the meetings of the old national councils—the addition of a "third estate," the commons, to the two already existent.[16]

Chronologically speaking, Spain is "the mother of parliaments," if by a parliament is meant a national body in which the middle classes are represented, as contrasted with an old feudal council to which only nobles and churchmen were called. In all the kingdoms of the Spanish peninsula, in Leon, Castile, Aragon, Catalonia and Valencia there were already in the twelfth century occasional meetings or cortes to which representatives of towns were called. Such was the cortes summoned by Alfonso IX of Castile to meet at Burgos in 1189, in which fifty-eight cities and towns are said to have been represented. Of this and of other assemblies of that early

[15] *Historical Manuscripts Commission*, IV, i, 434; v. 537-8; Mrs. J. R. Green, *Town Life in the Fifteenth Century* (London, 1894), I, chap. xii.

[16] C. H. McIlwain, in the *Cambridge Medieval History* (London, 1911-), VII, chap. xxiii; D. Pasquet, *Essai sur les Origines de le Chambre des Communes* (Paris, 1914), 38-43 (English translation, London, 1925).

period we know little beyond the fact of such representation. They corresponded to those sporadic summons of representatives of the cities of the kingdom of Naples in 1232 and 1234 by Frederick II, or of the counties of England in 1213, and perhaps at other times, by John and Henry III in England. The cortes of 1250, held at Seville, was a joint cortes of the two kingdoms of Castile and Leon, and this practice of combining the cortes of those two kingdoms, which always had the same sovereign, gradually became an invariable one.[17]

The inclusion of the "third estate" in the great national assemblies of Castile was, however, by no means a uniform custom. It occurred only some eighteen times before the end of the thirteenth century. The enlightenment of Alfonso the Wise (1252-84), his scholarship, his interest in mathematics, in the national chronicles and literature, his codification and promulgation of the great code of national law, the *Siete Partidas*, and even his diplomatic efforts to be elected emperor, made him less interested in those warlike expeditions which were so likely to require new taxation and therefore the convocation of a national assembly in which the cities should be represented. For it was evident that access to the wealth of the towns was the leading, in many cases the sole, motive that led the kings to summon these representatives of the moneyed middle classes to their assemblies. Once summoned, however, the third estate had its opportunity to grant taxes only on certain conditions, and thus to secure legislation favorable to its interests or ambitions. So from 1295, a historic date in the history of the English parliament also, the representatives of the cities came to be invariably included in the cortes. Through the fourteenth century they asserted constantly higher claims. It was no longer a cortes unless they were included. A cortes sat in every year from 1295 to 1313 and there was seldom, for more than 150 years, a period of more than three years in which such a gathering of the Castilian estates did not take place. It is a long and interesting series.[18]

In the cortes of Valladolid of 1295 the deputies of the towns in-

[17] The two names were, however, still retained.

[18] The records of sixty meetings of the cortes between 1295 and 1450 are printed in *Cortes de los antiguos Reinos de Leon y de Castilla*, edited by M. Colmeiro (five volumes, Madrid, 1861-1906), I and II.

sisted on acting separately from the nobles and prelates, thus introducing an embryonic bicameral system. The cortes of Cuellar in 1297 was memorable for having secured from the king the regular appointment of representatives of the cities to sit in the royal council in the intervals between meetings of the cortes. This provision was often disregarded and its renewal often insisted upon, till almost a century later it was confirmed by John I in a decree providing that the royal council should always consist of four nobles, four prelates and four citizens. At the cortes of Medina del Campo in 1305 "Don Mahomet Abenazar, rey de Grenada, vassalo del Rey," a fugitive pretender to the Moorish throne, sat among the nobles much as Alexander, King of Scotland, sat in the parliament of Edward I in 1279. At Valladolid in 1313 it was agreed that a cortes should be held every two years, but, as has been indicated, no such regularity was attained. The cortes of 1351, like the English parliament of the same year, established the wages of laborers, which had shown a tendency to rise above their traditional level as a result of the pestilence of the immediately preceding years. The cortes of 1358 regulated the expenditures of the king's household as the English parliament did in 1381.[19]

When Henry of Trastamare in 1370 returned victorious from the battle of Montiel he assembled a cortes at Toro and induced it to pay to Bertrand du Guesclin, his French ally, the price of his aid, 120,000 doblas. The representatives of the towns took this occasion to press upon the king the expulsion of the Jews, whom, largely for financial considerations, he was inclined to favor, but the townsmen secured only a general regulation requiring Jews to live in their own Ghetto, apart from the Christians, in each city; to wear a mark of distinction on their clothes, and to refrain from dressing richly and from riding on horse or mule back. At the same cortes an ordinance was also passed regulating the church courts and the rights of the clergy in general. At the cortes of Guadalajara in 1390 King John showed himself willing to agree to almost any demands, especially those of the third estate, the source of supply of funds. So in response to their complaints of the increasing bur-

[19] M. Colmeiro, *Cortes de los antiguos Reinos de Leon y de Castilla* (two volumes, Madrid, 1883-4). This is the introduction to the records of the cortes, and the standard account.

den of taxation he accepted a set sum as the total income of the crown, approved their organization of the military system of the country and their establishment of a fixed number of soldiers and their wages and equipment. The same cortes, like the parliament of England of the next year, urged the king to check the growing papal practice of appointing foreigners to local ecclesiastical offices.[20]

The death of the king occurring shortly after the dissolution of this cortes and much dissatisfaction being felt with the membership of the council of regents he had appointed for his minor son, a cortes was immediately summoned in the name of the young king, Henry III. It met at Madrid later in the same year. This was attended by 126 deputies, representing fifty towns. Opened with a speech in the name of the king by the Archbishop of Toledo, the assembly proceeded to take things into their hands by naming ten nobles and fourteen representatives of the third estate to act as a council of regency till the new king should be sixteen years of age. They imposed upon the councillors an oath not to increase the size of the standing army, not to go to war without the consent of the cortes, not to denounce existing alliances or form new ones without the same consent, not to levy or collect any taxes except those granted by the same body, and not to execute or banish anyone except after judicial trial. The young king was thereupon brought before them and took his oath to preserve to all individuals, classes and corporations in the kingdom all franchises and good usages they had possessed in the time of his father. These meetings of the cortes at Guadalajara and Madrid in the year 1390 represent the high-water mark of the power of the third estate in Castile. Although cortes continued to be held frequently in the reigns of Henry III and John II and their successors till after the end of our period, it may be well to suspend the narrative in order to give a more systematic statement of the organization, powers and practices of these parliamentary bodies, which have the distinction of being the earliest in modern Europe.

There was no certain place or time at which the cortes of Castile met. In sending out the summons the king consulted his own convenience or necessity. The relative frequency of meetings at

[20] Burke, *History of Spain*, I, 370 note.

Burgos and Valladolid probably reflects the need of the king to be frequently in that turbulent northern region. The same is true of time as of place. The decision whether to call a cortes or not and if so, when, rested entirely with the king, though the pressure of circumstances must often have forced his hand, and nominally they should have been called yearly. Three estates were clearly recognized, though the selection of the actual representatives in each estate was again largely in the control of the king. The clergy were regularly represented by the masters of the four great military orders, the archbishops, bishops and, until well into the fourteenth century, the abbots, but the individuals summoned varied from cortes to cortes. The Castilian nobility was of most diverse origin and status and no holder of any particular title seems to have had a prescriptive right to appear at the cortes; he came, in fact he had to come, if he was summoned, otherwise he could not come. Therefore individual dukes, marquises, counts, viscounts, knights, squires and those *hidalgos* who can perhaps only be described by the English word gentry, were summoned by name, as the king or his officers specified them.

The first two estates were exempt from the payment of taxes, so in financial matters they were largely disregarded. What gave these early modern cortes their real significance, as against the feudal councils of earlier times and the personal councils of the more autocratic kings of a later period, was the presence of the representatives of the cities, the third estate. There was great diversity in the lists of towns sending representatives. The number itself varied from ninety, as at the cortes of Burgos in 1315, down to a score. The number of *procuradores* or deputies from each town was also indefinite until fixed at two by a law passed by the cortes of Madrid in 1429-30. The delegates of the towns were provided by the authorities of their cities with written *poderes* or strict instructions, from which they could not deviate. The choice of representatives seems to have depended on the provisions of individual city charters. We have little knowledge of the position or ideas of those who attended. The names, for instance, of the 125 representatives of the forty-eight towns sent as delegates to the cortes at Madrid in 1390, names like Diego Alvarez, Gonzalo Garcia, Alvar

Nunez, John Sandeval, Alonzo Ruiz, throw little light on their social or economic position, though, as elsewhere, it was evidently the well-to-do merchants and officers of the towns who controlled the appointments.

The meetings were occasions of much ceremony. The opening session was attended by the king and all who had been summoned. The appointment and instructions of the representatives of the towns were read, a speech from the throne indicated the reason for the convocation and replies were made to it by a representative of the house of Lara as chief of the nobility, by the Archbishop of Toledo for the clergy and by one of the delegates from the city of Burgos—often challenged by a delegate from Toledo—on behalf of the third estate. The petitions to the crown from each of the three estates were drawn up and presented. These *cuadernos* or petitions, with the king's replies to them, prepared and circulated after the cortes was over, were made the bases for statutes or royal proclamations. They have been preserved in great fullness and published with pious care by the Spanish Society of History, and it is from them that most of our knowledge of the Castilian cortes is drawn. There is no indication that the cortes of Castile ever took steps, as did the English parliament and the cortes of Aragon, to have the answers to their petitions given while they were still in session. Each estate seems to have sat separately and all enjoyed freedom of speech and exemption from arrest. Representatives were paid until the very close of this period by the bodies that sent them.[21]

The right of the cortes to grant or deny special taxes demanded by the king was asserted and conceded at an early date. The opportunity to ask for such a grant was one of the earliest and most potent incentives to the king to call a meeting of the cortes, especially of the third estate, and the right to refuse it, except on their own conditions, was one of the first uses that estate made of their membership in a national assembly. Already in the thirteenth century this right was recognized. It was formulated at the cortes of Valladolid in 1307 and confirmed in the cortes of Madrid of

[21] R. B. Merriman, "The Cortes of the Spanish Kingdoms," *American Historical Review,* XVI (1911), 479-83.

1329, and successively in later gatherings. At the time of the greatest authority of the cortes it was extended to the right to appropriate the grants to specific objects and to audit expenditures, and even, in one case, to appoint treasurers to whom the proceeds of the taxes should be paid and on whose order alone they could be expended. This financial control was weakened, as in other countries similarly situated, by the possession by the crown of considerable wealth, by the power of the king to borrow from the Jews, from Italian bankers and from wealthy native merchants, and by the early use of indirect taxes, such as the familiar Spanish *alcabala* or sales tax, which were not under the same restrictions.

IV. THE CORTES OF ARAGON, CATALONIA AND VALENCIA

The separateness of the countries of the Spanish peninsula during these centuries makes it necessary that any account of their history and institutions should be separately given, but there is no need to repeat that which is common to them. The beginning of representation of the cities of Aragon goes back, as in Castile, to the twelfth century, Queen Petronilla in 1162 having called a cortes at Huesca at which prelates, great nobles, knights and representatives of towns and villages were present. James the Conqueror, the famous King of Aragon who reigned from 1213 to 1276, almost exactly contemporaneously with Henry III of England and St. Louis of France, called cortes at one time or another in each of his three kingdoms, Aragon, Catalonia and Valencia; at Lerida, at Huesca, at Tarragona, at Tortosa, at Barcelona and elsewhere. His financial needs, if no other cause, required the inclusion of representatives of the towns.[22] The reign of Peter III, the son of James, who postponed his coronation till he could put the crown on his own head in a full cortes at Saragossa, in 1276, may be considered the period in which the cortes of Aragon became a regularly established institution.

The independence of the cortes of Aragon was remarkable. The

[22] *Documentos ineditos,* XIV, 555; there is much material on the early cortes of Aragon in V. de la Fuente, *Estudios Criticos sobre la Historia y el Dereche de Aragón* (three volumes, Madrid, 1884-86). The records may be found in *Cortes de los Antiguos Reinos de Aragon y de Valencia y Principado de Cataluna* (vols. I-XXIV, Madrid, 1896-1918).

proud formula *Yo el Rey*, "I, the King," affixed to official documents gives an erroneous impression of royal freedom of action. There was no such liberty on the part of the king to choose the individual members of each cortes as existed in Castile. Any noble or churchman whose office or lineage had once been recognized as justifying a summons had a right always afterward to be included. A city that had once been called retained a claim always to send delegates.

The special preeminence of the nobility in the cortes of Aragon is attested by the fact that it formed two estates of the realm, the grandees or *ricos hombres*,[23] a few of the most exalted nobles of the realm, and the *caballeros*, or lesser nobility. With the clergy and the townsmen, therefore, Aragon had four estates, the only instance of such an arrangement in Europe, except for two or three of the almost cityless countries of eastern Europe, where the nobility was similarly divided into two ranks, and certain Scandinavian states where the free peasantry formed a separate estate. Instead of the English, or rather the French term "estates," which has come to be generally applied to the separate political classes represented in national assemblies, the word *brazos* or "arms" was used in the cortes of Aragon. The high nobility, the lesser nobility, the clergy and the deputies of the towns are constantly spoken of as the four *brazos*.

The cortes should have met every year, according to the "Privilege" of 1283, every two years according to a law passed in 1307. But in Aragon as in Castile there was frequency rather than regularity of meetings. It is evident, however, that representation in the cortes early came to be looked upon by the towns as an opportunity to secure advantages rather than merely as a royal requirement preliminary to a demand for taxes.

Meetings of the cortes were formal to the limits of pedantry. Three prorogations of four days each were provided so that no one who started should fail to arrive at the first meeting. After the summons was read and the session opened by the king each estate appointed a committee to examine the qualifications and the instructions of its members. Each then appointed a *tratador* or inter-

[23] *Ricos* is from the same root as *Reich*, or the last syllable of *bishopric*, or the Latin word *regere*. *Ricos hombres* means men of the ruling class, not rich men.

mediary to communicate with the king and with the other estates. Decisions were by law to be unanimous, but this requirement was generally disregarded, or else its difficulties were overcome by the practice of choosing a working committee free from this restriction, to transact business either separately for each *brazo* or in common.

The most significant difference between the cortes of Aragon and of Castile was the *solio* or full meeting of the king and the four estates just before the end of the session. At this meeting, and not, as in Castile, after the dispersion of the cortes, all the agreements of the session were repeated, proclaimed and sworn to, thus ensuring a common understanding and giving a guarantee of the fulfilment of royal promises. Still further control over the course of events, so far as the power of the cortes extended, was exercised through the appointment of a committee of the four estates, the *Diputacion*, usually composed of two members from each, to oversee the observance of the laws, the administration of the public revenue and the preservation of the peace during the interval between meetings of the national assembly.[24]

The cortes had practically complete control of legislation and of the collection and use of funds appropriated by it. It received the oath of the king on his accession and claimed that he could not legally exercise his powers until its recognition had been expressed. It granted naturalization, shared in the declaration of war and the making of peace and in the appointment and instruction of ambassadors. It had an unrestricted right, frequently exercised, to investigate and provide for the correction of grievances brought to its attention by deputies or others. Of all the parliamentary bodies of European countries that of Aragon occupied the most independent, influential and well established position. It is true that many of the interests of the sovereigns of Aragon lay outside that realm and were therefore not under the control of its cortes. The period was one of conquest by sea and land, and popular assemblies could exercise but little control on the water or on the battle-field. But so far as the authority of the cortes extended its powers were coordinate with, in some respects superior to, those of the king.

[24] R. B. Merriman, "The Cortes of the Spanish Kingdom," loc. cit., 489.

The cortes of Catalonia was similar in much of its organization and analogous in most of its powers to that of Aragon. There were but three *brazos* instead of four, although there were some late and ineffective attempts to organize an additional estate of the lesser nobility. The equality of the third estate corresponded to the more commercial and maritime interests of the country. It was on the Catalonian cortes that the kings of Aragon relied to support their adventures in the Balearic Islands, in Sardinia and in Sicily, and the voluminous records of its proceedings give little indication of opposition to the royal ambitions.[25]

The cortes of Valencia was not sufficiently distinctive to require detailed analysis here, though it had a long and influential history. It remains to note that there was occasionally a joint meeting of the estates of the three countries of the Aragonese crown, usually held at Lerida or some other place near the borders. Any account of the cortes of Navarre belongs rather with the history of France than of Spain, and Portugal from the beginning of this period had a separate and characteristic history of its own.

The cortes of the Spanish countries continued to flourish until well into the fifteenth century, but by the end of the period covered by this volume as an institution it showed signs of decadence. It met less frequently and showed less self-assertion as against the growing power and authority of the king with his appointed ministries. The same decadence occurred, as will appear, in most countries of Europe. The monarchy which shared its authority with the nobles, the clergy and the representatives of the middle classes was superseded by absolute monarchy. This transition was much facilitated by the financial support, the patriotic spirit and the prestige that the entrance of the middle classes into partnership with it had given to the monarchy as a form of government. This increased strength it now used for its own ends, personal and national. In Spain under Henry IV of Castile and John II of Aragon, from the middle of the century till 1479, and still more conclusively under Ferdinand and Isabella, in the infrequent meetings of the cortes the middle classes ceased to exercise much control over the course

[25] Twenty-six large volumes are required to give in printed form its proceedings, down to 1479.

of events. Their influence may be detected in the added income, the centralization of government and the national spirit which they placed at the disposal of the crown. But these are the marks of the history of Spain in the next period, not in this.

V. THE ESTATES GENERAL OF FRANCE

A narrative of the dispute between Philip the Fair of France and Pope Boniface VIII which filled the years from 1298 to 1303 with clamor belongs properly to another chapter of this book, that of the decline of the Church. But it must be mentioned here as it was the occasion for the first entrance of the representatives of the middle classes upon the political stage of France, where they were to play so large a part in the next three centuries. Councils had been called by the French kings from time immemorial, but they were feudal assemblages and included only nobles and great churchmen, the magnates of the kingdom. Now, suddenly, in connection with the dispute with Boniface, representatives of the middle classes were included in the summons to such an assembly.[26]

This appearance of suddenness is somewhat deceptive. Men of the middle class, acting as advisers to the king, as his bankers, as his mentors in the Roman law, as officials at court and in the provinces, had long exercised an influence in government. Even as communities the towns had occasionally been consulted on matters of an economic nature. An ordinance issued in 1263 by Louis IX, defining the respective limits of circulation of the money of the king and of the great nobles, states that the arrangement had been assented to by citizens of Paris, Provins, Orleans, Sens and Laon. The king repeatedly consulted the towns on matters of coinage and weights and measures. Quite through the thirteenth century representatives of the towns in the south attended local assemblies when matters of taxation were under discussion. In 1290 an embassy sent by Philip to the pope was composed of "deputies of the nobility and of the communes of France."

There are other indications that the population of the cities was

[26] Good general accounts of the French estates may be found in E. Lavisse, *Histoire de France* (Paris, 1900-11), III and IV (by C. Langlois and A. Coville); see also standard works like R. Holtzmann, *Französische Verfassungsgeschichte* (Munich, 1910); J. Declareuil, *Histoire Générale du Droit Français* (Paris, 1925); and E. Chénon, *Histoire Générale du Droit Français public et privé* (two volumes, Paris, 1926-1929).

on the brink of recognition as a power in the state. Indeed, the king could hardly fail to recognize and eventually to utilize the force inherent in the mass of his subjects living in the large and numerous cities under his sovereignty. The nobles were conspicuous and powerful, the church was well-organized and well-endowed, but the cities were rich, populous and intelligent.

To strengthen his position in the controversy with the pope the king now for the first time formally drew upon this force. In March, 1302, after forbidding the collection of the taxes demanded by the pope and after prohibiting the departure of the prelates to Rome, whither Boniface had summoned them for conference, Philip sent letters to the principal dukes, counts, viscounts and other nobles and to the archbishops, bishops, abbots and other ecclesiastics of the kingdom, convoking them to Paris in April to take council with him. At the same time letters were addressed from the royal chancery to the bailiffs and stewards who exercised authority in the king's name over the twenty-eight administrative divisions of the country, ordering them to send delegates from the towns in their bailiwicks to meet the king at the same time and place.

We have no list of the persons sent in answer to this summons or of the places from which they came, or what instructions they carried, if any. The real significance of the event is the formal recognition of the representatives of the towns, the "Third Estate," as they came to be called, as a distinct political class, called to take its share in the settlement of national questions. This comes out clearly in the brief surviving records of the assembly. It met at Notre Dame in Paris April 10, 1302, and completed its labors in the one day. It was opened by the chancellor, Pierre de Flotte, in a long address arguing against the pope's claim to superiority over sovereigns and appealing to the three estates to give the king, "as their lord and friend," their counsel and aid. The king himself then spoke. There was general acclamation from the nobles and townsmen; some demur, as might be expected, from the clergy.

The nobles and deputies of the towns then went to separate rooms where each agreed to the despatch of a letter, drawn up no doubt in the king's chancery, to the college of cardinals at Rome, asserting in strong terms the independence of France from papal intrusion. The clergy, who had remained in their seats in the nave of the cathedral hesitating between the authority of the pope and the king, overawed, as they acknowledged, by the union of "our lord the king and the common people of the kingdom," finally drew up a letter to the pope assuring him of their fidelity, explaining the difficulty of their position, deploring his quarrel with Philip and begging him to spare them from going to Rome against the king's will. The estates were then dismissed by the king.[27] This first meeting of the Estates General has always been considered, and rightly, an occasion of crucial importance in French history. It was, with all its inadequacy as a representative assembly and all its royal dictation, an appeal, the first appeal of the French government to all France. There was always after this the precedent of an embodiment of the whole people in a solemn assembly.

In 1308 the Estates General were formally summoned for the second time, on this occasion to support the king in his attack on the Templars. This meeting, like the first, was intended to bring pressure to bear upon the pope. In 1308 the new pope, Clement V, on whose election Philip had exerted much influence, was still evading the king's demand for aid in the destruction of the great Order. Philip desired to bring to bear the united pressure of the whole French nation to overcome this resistance and he secured this, as he had in 1302, by a united vote of all three orders. This assembly is of special interest because of the very wide representation of the estates. It included, apparently, the whole town population of France; delegates came not only from the communes, the chartered cities and the larger places, but, in some provinces at least, from every town that had a fair or market. From Champagne, for instance, there were deputies from more than forty towns, some of them little more than villages. Two hundred and twenty-six towns, at least, sent delegates, and there were probably others of which we have no record. The other estates were as widely represented. We hear of more than 500 persons present at Tours, the scene of the gathering. The king seems to have wished to impress

[27] R. Jallifier, *Histoire des États Généraux* (Paris, 1885), 17-23.

the pope by the large numbers. The records of this meeting also disclose much of the procedure of the Estates General.[28]

The next Estates, those of 1314, were for the natural and legitimate, if as yet unfamiliar, purpose of the grant of a tax. So far it had been their moral pressure that was desired, now it was their money. The king was engaged in an expensive war in Flanders and, since the resources of feudal dues, loans and money obtained by coercion were exhausted, he now sought some new source of income. In the Estates he made his appeal especially to the townsmen, there being no expectation at this time of laying any new burden on the nobility or clergy, who were already required to make many payments. The meeting was in the courtyard of the palace in Paris. The superintendent of the finances made a long speech and transmitted the king's request for an aid. No mention was made of its object and no amount was named. Popular control of taxation was evidently still in an embryonic state. The leaders of the bourgeoisie gave a favorable but equally indefinite answer. The king thanked them, the estates were dissolved and the treasury officials proceeded to announce and collect a sales-tax, which proved to be singularly unpopular and called forth much protest. It helped build up such hatred against Enguerrand de Marigny, the finance minister who was held responsible for it, that in the next reign he fell from power, was tried for extortion and executed.

Estates General were called repeatedly, though irregularly, during the remainder of the first half of the fourteenth century. The "Salic Law," invented by the nobles and the lawyers to exclude women from the throne, was accepted and thus given greater authority by a meeting of all the Estates in 1317; the claims of Edward III to the crown of France are said to have been rejected in a similar gathering; more than once grants of money to the king were approved; common weights and measures were adopted for the whole kingdom by the Estates held at Pontoise in 1321; the

[28] E. Boutaric, *La France sous Philippe le Bel* (Paris, 1861), 459-60. A valuable list of the towns represented at this meeting is given in an appendix to this somewhat old-fashioned work. A list of all the nobles, clerical establishments and towns represented in the first seven Estates General, with many illustrative documents, is printed in Henri Hervieu, *Recherches sur les Premiers États Généraux* (Paris, 1879), 236-311.

coinage was regulated at Orleans in 1343. But there was little clear recognition of functions, much less any extension of powers.

This procrastination in what would seem the normal development of the organization and powers of the Estates General was in large part due to the existence and use of other means of communication between the king and the middle classes of the people. In 1303 and again in 1309 and 1314 a number of "the good people of the good towns of the kingdom" were convoked without the other two estates for purposes which interested them more than the nobles and clergy. At the meeting of 1314 citizens from forty-one of the principal towns were summoned. These meetings were characteristic of the age. The fourteenth century was a period of many assemblages. There was constant traveling and foregathering. The roads were full not only of merchants and pilgrims but of messengers, clergy and laymen, obeying summons to attend some council or journey to reach some place of assembly. Gatherings of all classes except the very lowest were frequent. Churchmen were apt to be called to five different kinds of councils, apart from voluntary journeys to Rome or to a university or some shrine. It was a restless assembly-loving age. At the request of the king individual towns as well as nobles and clergy from time to time sent in their assurances of support. We hear of assemblies of the citizens in Limoges, Compiègne, Beauvais, Amiens, Montreuil, Bapaume and elsewhere voting their approval of the king's policy and sending messengers to notify him of their assent to his purposes. National councils of the nobles and of the clergy, separately and together, with and without the representatives of the towns, were also called. Only when all three were summoned at the same time was it a veritable Estates General.

These varied forms of assembly, so far as they involved the recognition and influence of the middle class, were gradually reduced to a more consistent practice. Instead of Estates General of all France, two separate bodies were sometimes called at the same time, the estates of Languedoc and those of Langue d'Oil. The former was the group of five provinces south of the Garonne and the Dourance rivers, the lands where Provençal and Catalan were the prevailing languages. The twenty-three provinces of the Langue d'Oil were the north of France. Sometimes the estates of both regions were called at the same time, though separately, sometimes of one and not of the other. In 1346 for instance the estates of Languedoc were gathered at Toulouse, those of Langue d'Oil simultaneously at Paris. Again, the estates of separate provinces were sometimes convoked—of Normandy, of Orleans, of Berry, of Champagne—corresponding rather to the administrative divisions recently created by the crown than to the ancient feudal divisions of France. It was a not unusual practice to obtain the general consent of the Estates General to a tax or levy, then through royal commissioners to call provincial estates together to obtain the actual grant of payment. This was done after the Estates General of 1351, when it was necessary for the king to appeal to the estates of each province to obtain the aid promised by the more general body. Sometimes indeed, with the same object of seeking aid in his necessities, the king had recourse to individual towns.[29]

VI. THE SUPREMACY OF THE THIRD ESTATE IN FRANCE

Participation of the middle classes in government had by the middle of the fourteenth century become well established. But it was always passive, casual, uncertain in opportunity, indefinite in extent, a mere concession on the part of the king, used largely for his own ends. Then, with a suddenness that rivalled their first summons, the Estates General, especially the Third Estate, asserted and for a while exercised powers beyond those of any corresponding bodies in other countries, and even, in principle, challenged the supremacy of the king. This bid for power was a direct result of the bad progress of the Hundred Years War. The invasions of the English and the civil wars which the invasions had encouraged did much to impair the wealth of the country and the prestige of the crown. Sluys and Crécy had been fought, Calais captured. The loose hold of the king on Brittany and Gascony had been weakened, Picardy and much of Normandy and Guienne had been repeatedly overrun. Heavier and heavier taxes were collected and spent and there seemed no end to waste and loss. The years 1354 and 1355 were years of successive ravagings by the English, largely unop-

[29] Georges Piest, *Histoire des États Généraux* (Paris, 1872), introduction.

posed. Much of Languedoc was devastated. Estates General and Provincial protested against the incapacity, wastefulness and corruption of the king and his ministers, but without apparent result. When, at the king's despairing summons, the Estates of the Langue d'Oil met at Paris in December 1355, they took the bit in their teeth and proceeded to govern France. The Estates of Languedoc were called at the same time at Toulouse, but they played only a minor part, following at a distance and with but little enthusiasm the rapid strides of the Estates at Paris.

The Third Estate from the beginning took the lead. Its members were for the most part, as usual, magistrates, prominent merchants or other notables of the towns, typical representatives of the bourgeoisie. There was among them no lack of experience in government. Their presiding officer was Stephen Marcel, "provost of the merchants," that is to say the head of the group of merchant and artisan companies whose officers governed the city of Paris. He was a draper previously unmentioned but from this time destined to take the leadership of the whole movement.[30]

Each estate deliberated separately on the king's appeal, then jointly, and after a few days they laid before him the offer of a grant for a year of 3,000,000 Parisian livres—enough to send to the army 30,000 men. This grant, however, was made with four conditions: that the tax be paid equally by persons of all classes, that it be collected and expended by officers appointed by the Estates, that the whole financial administration be placed for the time under the control of nine superintendents appointed by the Estates, and that the Estates meet again three months later, in March, to examine into the collection and expenditure of the grant, and a year later, in November, to take up the question of a possible future grant.

Two of these provisions, equality of taxation and unanimity of action of the Estates, were intended to be permanent. Even the temporary provisions, the control of the finances and the appointment of the time and place of the next meetings, should have prepared the way for a rapid and steady growth of participation

[30] See François Perrens, *Étienne Marcel, Prévot des Marchands* (Paris, 1875); Yves Le Tebore, *Étienne Marcel et le Paris des Marchands au XIVe Siècle* (Paris, 1927). There is an excellent treatment of this stormy period in R. Delachenal, *Histoire de Charles V* (Paris, 1909-1928), I and II.

of the Estates in the government. The meeting appointed for March and an adjourned meeting in May, though occupied with modification of the unpopular sales-tax and gabelle on salt, imposed by the Estates to secure the 3,000,000 livres promised to the crown, still showed only a moderate degree of influence exerted by the Estates.

Before the meeting appointed for November 1356, however, a great catastrophe had fallen upon France, the battle of Poitiers. In September, 1356, the French army was cut to pieces by the English, the greater part of the noblesse was killed, taken captive or driven into flight. The king was carried prisoner to Bordeaux and then to England. The government of the country was without funds or morale, and guided only by the dauphin, a youth of unknown abilities, advised by a discredited and unpopular council. The Estates General were the only possible recourse, and the dauphin, acting as regent for his father, immediately summoned them to meet in October, a month earlier than the date they had already appointed for themselves. It was a notable assembly. The nobility were few, for their numbers were depleted and their spirit dampened by their losses and their dishonor on the field of battle. The clergy was numerously represented but, under the leadership of Jean de Craon, Archbishop of Rheims, and Robert Lecoq, Bishop of Laon, both reformers, was inclined to follow the lead of the Third Estate, to which more than 400 of the deputies belonged. The commoners were again led by Marcel, whose reputation and influence had been enhanced since the preceding year by his activity in strengthening the defenses and organizing the military force of Paris in the weeks after Poitiers. At first, the Estates sat as three separate bodies, but they soon elected a group of eighty to represent, speak and act for the assembly as a whole.

Two problems faced them: making head against the foreign enemy and general reform of the administration. The first of these was met by offering the dauphin, as in the previous year, means to pay 30,000 men, for which the deputies voted a tax the collection and expenditure of which was, as before, to be under the charge of their own appointees. With a view to the second they demanded the arrest and trial of eight of the king's officers, one of whom, the chancellor, Pierre de la Forêt, they charged with corruption, betrayal of the king and disregard of the interests of the people. They demanded also the appointment of a royal council of twenty-eight, to consist of four members elected by the clergy, twelve by the nobility and twelve by the commons, without whose agreement no action was to be taken. They proposed that the deputies on their return home should, under the name of "reformers," look into and report on the actions of the royal officials in their provinces. There should be another meeting of the Estates at Easter.

This was not reform but revolution. The dauphin, shrewd and determined to an unsuspected degree, was unwilling to let the reins of government pass so completely out of his hands. He procrastinated, promised, then withdrew his promise, protested against their demands, went to Metz to visit his uncle, the Emperor Charles IV, and sought from his imprisoned father support in resistance to the Estates' proposals. He obtained voluntary subsidies from some provincial estates, though he was refused by others. So he wore away the winter without a settlement and, after promising them an early recall, adjourned the Estates, but not before their leaders had read aloud before him at a concluding session twenty-one articles of proposed reform.

It was only delay, not freedom of action, that the dauphin had gained. Marcel held Paris in leash, but threatened any day to meet the procrastination of the dauphin with revolt. Large concessions were offered but in vain; finally Charles yielded. In December he recalled the Estates for the early spring. Three successive assemblies were held in the year 1357, in February, April and November. During the early days of the first session the resolutions of the former Estates were hastily brought before the provincial estates, discussed and approved by them, drawn up in a long series of provisions and again read publicly before the dauphin, the Estates General and a great concourse of the people. The dauphin, confronted with what seemed the united demand of the French people, was powerless to resist. He accepted the proposals and issued them the next month, in a statute always since known as the "Great Ordinance."[31]

[31] Printed in the *Ordonnances des Rois français.*

This remarkable document can be fairly contrasted with John's "Great Charter," to measure alike the changes that had passed over Europe in the century and a half between 1215 and 1357 and to note some of the fundamental differences between England and France. The two documents are, curiously enough, of almost exactly the same length, the Ordinance having sixty-one, the Charter sixty-three articles. But whereas Magna Carta was a feudal scheme, forced upon the king by his barons, the Great Ordinance was a middle-class, almost a democratic measure, forced upon the king by the Third Estate, a class that had come into existence, politically speaking, in all countries since the grant of the Charter.

The Ordinance makes no mention of feudal powers except to restrict hunting rights and to guarantee to the great feudatories in their domains, as to the king in his, the right to summon their own vassals for military service. The Third Estate had no intention of bearing all the military burdens. At the same time the Ordinance prohibits private warfare and forbids the taking of feudal forces out of the country. It was a natural result of its origin that the Ordinance was positive rather than negative; filled with definite requirements for what the authors considered good government, rather than with the catalogue of restrictions on the actions of the king which make up so large a part of the Great Charter.

The restrictions on the powers of the king were in the interests of orderly government rather than of baronial privilege. Supervision was to be exercised, not by a group of elected barons, as provided by the Great Charter, but by the Estates General, meeting whenever and wherever it should seem best to themselves. Restriction was not, however, the main characteristic of the Ordinance. It touched constructively almost every phase of government, establishing an appointed council, financial responsibility, a graduated judicial system. Magna Carta is a constitutional document only in the sense that it clears the way for the growth of a limited monarchy. The Great Ordinance comes nearer a written constitution than anything proposed anywhere in Europe before the seventeenth century or than anything France was to have till the work was taken up by the national assembly in 1789.

Quite as striking was the contrast of language. Magna Carta

appears in sonorous Latin, not in the spoken language of the barons; the Ordinance was in the vernacular, the spoken French of its authors. Just who were its authors is not known, though Marcel and Lecoq certainly shared in its composition and approved it. It was essentially a city-man's, a lawyer's plan of good government. It represented the best political ideas of the middle classes.

The Estates proceeded in accordance with the spirit of the Ordinance to elect a temporary commission of thirty-six, twelve from each of the three estates, which was for the time at least to take over control of all state functions and functionaries. The government was practically in the hands of this body.

This was the high-water mark of what was practically a revolution. But France was not yet ready for a revolution. The tide soon turned. The thirty-six not infrequently used their unlimited powers without discretion and so created antagonism. The Estates, meeting so frequently, in March, May and October 1356, in February, April and November 1357, in January and February, 1358, became commonplace. The attendance diminished, the nobles and the clergy were more and more poorly represented, many towns neglected to send their delegates. The meetings became more and more representative of the Third Estate alone and almost of Paris alone. Jealousy awoke and neglect developed opposition. There was no effective carrying out of the Great Ordinance. Several of the ministers who had been assailed slipped away from the city and from the country. The dauphin avoided giving any support to the new system, and used his powers of personal charm to build up for himself a party. There was an epidemic of appeals to the populace for and against the course of affairs. In this age of popular preaching not only the dauphin, but Charles the Bad of Navarre, and Marcel himself delivered sermons to the people of Paris on Biblical texts supporting their respective claims.[32]

The inactivity of the English invaders for the time being removed the overwhelming need for unity; yet the efforts to collect the subsidies kept the people dissatisfied. Marcel, in order to preserve

[32] R. Jallifier, *Histoire des États Généraux,* 34-62; A. Coville, in Lavisse, *Histoire de France,* IV, pt. i, 123-29.

his power, adopted a more and more radical policy. In March, 1358 he led a Parisian mob to the Louvre and into the very presence of the dauphin. He there ordered the assassination of two noblemen of the court. The blood of the Marshal of Champagne spattered the clothes of the dauphin, who was himself forced, like his successor four centuries later, to put on the red and blue Parisian cap. "Fear nothing, what is being done is being done by the will of the people," Marcel cried to him. The "will of the people" was a new cry in the fourteenth century, but for awhile it bade fair to become dominant in France, if that will was fairly represented by the populace of Paris. The dauphin was forced to take as his sole counsellors Marcel, Charles Toussac, and Jean de l'Isle, three officials of the city of Paris, the Bishop of Laon and the small surviving group of the thirty-six who had been given charge of the government by the Estates General in 1357.

The Estates were by this time suffering as much from their own party as from those who might be considered hostile to them. The high idealism of the Great Ordinance had degenerated into a dictatorship of Stephen Marcel, based on the doubtful support of the Parisian populace. Outside of Paris all interest in the government seemed to have ceased; inside it was still at white heat. In March, 1358, the dauphin escaped from his virtual captivity in the Louvre and slipped away from Paris by night in a river-boat. He went to Senlis, where the Estates of Picardy were sitting, and to Provins, where those of Champagne were gathered; finding widespread hostility to Paris in other cities and sympathy for the crown, he ventured to issue orders that the Estates General which had been summoned to meet in Paris on the first day of May should instead meet him at Compiègne. In much of France the order was obeyed, and the Estates which assembled there, though few in number, gave the dauphin an aide and also approved a subsidy for the support of the captive king.

The government at Paris, deprived of all legality by the absence of the Estates, lost its hold on even the populace of the city. Marcel and his party were suspected of planning to make common cause with the Jacquerie, in revolt in the open country, and to admit Charles of Navarre to the city to make him king of France. At midnight on the 31st of July, Jean Maillart, an old supporter of the Estates, but now a partisan of the dauphin, met Marcel at one of the gates, "the keys of the city in his hand. 'Stephen, Stephen, what are you doing here at this hour?' 'Jean, why do you ask? I am here taking care of the city of which I have the government.' 'By God,' replied Maillart, turning to those with him, 'he is a traitor. See his keys; he is about to betray the city.' 'You lie,' cried Marcel. 'Nay, but you lie, traitor; death to him and all those with him, for they are traitors,' cried Maillart. And so Marcel and six of those with him were struck down." In these words the closing scenes of Marcel's power and of the effort to govern France by the Estates General are described by the contemporary chronicler. Their short-lived supremacy was over.[33]

Adherents of the dauphin invited him to return. When he reentered the city he was received with joy by the inhabitants. He was able the next year, in May, 1359, to convoke in Paris a loyal Estates General, which, though it protested against royal misgovernment and insisted on many of the claims made by recent Estates, yet gave him full support in his rejection of the harsh treaty recently negotiated by the king with the English. The Estates encouraged the dauphin to renew the war and promised him sufficient subsidies to carry it on, a promise which the more favorable terms of the treaty signed at Calais in 1360 relieved them from fulfilling.

Three times within the next ten years the king called Estates General: once in 1367 at Chartres to take united action against the free companies, and twice at Paris in 1369, first to approve and then to provide means for renewing the war against the English. Other meetings were summoned at ever less frequent intervals, in 1380, 1413 and from time to time afterward. They made few claims to control the government. That quarrel had been fought out. The Great Ordinance was disavowed by the king from London in the very year of its adoption and, although it still remained on the statute book, nothing was heard of its enforcement.[34]

The gatherings traditionally reckoned as Estates General give

[33] Froissart, *Chronicles,* (Translated by T. Johnes, two volumes, London, 1855), I, 246.

[34] G. Picot, *Histoire des États Généraux,* I, 77-84.

small clue to popular influence on government. On the other hand, meetings of provincial estates, of separate estates of Languedoc and Langue d'Oil, of partisans of one or the other side in the civil wars, punctuate the records of the first half of the fifteenth century and give abundant evidence of connection between the crown and the middle classes of the people. Especially in the period of Jeanne d'Arc the rising national spirit was reflected by assemblies called to grant taxes or ratify treaties. The Estates General that met at Orleans in 1439 were of an importance probably not then realized, for it was there that the complaints and proposals were made which led to the ordinance of the next year establishing the standing army of France. At the same time the *taille* was granted which, under the interpretation given to it by the crown, relieved the king from future appeals to the Estates for funds, and eventually made possible the suspension of national assemblies for 175 years.[35]

VII. THE ENGLISH HOUSE OF COMMONS

There has been much discussion as to whether the English parliament is properly to be looked upon as a body of estates similar to those of the Spanish countries, of France and of the countries of the centre, east and north of Europe. This seems to be a discussion of terms rather than of realities. Parliament included much the same elements of the population as did the estates of France or the cortes of Spain. The middle classes were admitted to the old royal councils at much the same time and by almost identical summons and they fulfilled much the same functions. Its organization as it was developed followed much the same lines, and the powers of parliament declined contemporaneously with those of similar bodies on the Continent. The word *estates* had no exact legal definition or constitutional significance that would make it possible to give or to deny its application to any particular body. The *brazos* or *estamientos* of Spain, the *Stände* of Germany, the Lords Temporal and Spiritual and the Commons of England, the Estates General of France and their equivalents in other countries mean merely the well-established classes or representatives of certain classes in their respective national assemblies, from the beginning

[35] Jallifier, op. cit., 75-84; Picot, op. cit., I, 237-339.

of their recognition in these early modern centuries to the rise of the conception of popular sovereignty in the seventeenth and eighteenth centuries.[36]

The slow and often obscure process by which the English parliament obtained that secure position that enabled it to share in the national government in the fourteenth and fifteenth centuries, to withstand the adverse winds of the sixteenth and seventeenth, and to survive and play its great part in the history of its own country and of the world in more recent times, has long been the subject of careful study. Its main points are now familiar. Much of its history has little to do with the subject of this chapter which, it is to be remembered, is the attainment of political influence by the middle classes.

The first representatives of those classes, that is to say, of the well-to-do but non-noble and non-clerical portion of the population, to enter upon a political career were in England not the townsmen but the rural middle-class landholders. It is one of the peculiarities of the English system. More than once in the first half of the thirteenth century the king summoned "discreet men," "knights," chosen by the sheriffs or elected in the county courts to attend consultations and give their advice. The term "knight," *miles*, has been used with very different connotations in different connections. In official use at this time it had little of the military, the chivalrous or even the feudal sense. It meant ordinarily a man of moderate position whose living came from the land but who did not work with his own hands upon it; who could be called upon to pay a certain amount to the exchequer and to perform various public services. A "knight's fee," in the judgment of the treasury officials, was a holding of land of five hides, approximately 600 acres, an estate that would produce an income of some £20 to £40 or more a year, one that would in modern England perhaps bring in an annual income of $2000 to $5000 besides its value as a residence.

[36] A. F. Pollard, *The Evolution of Parliament* (London, 1920) devotes an interesting, ingenious and learned, but, as it seems to the writer, somewhat captious chapter to what he calls "The Myth of the Three Estates." The word is used more frequently but not more exactly on the continent than in England. See further C. Petit-Dutaillis, "Le Roi d'Angleterre et ses Parlements au Moyen Age," *Revue Historique*, CLIV (1927), 34-61: This article constitutes the introduction to the French translation of volume III of Stubbs, and is now translated in the author's *Studies and Notes Supplementary to Stubbs' Constitutional History* (three volumes, Manchester, 1908-29).

"Distraint of knighthood" was the requirement that every man, irrespective of birth or training, who possessed land worth £20, or later £40, must perform the services and make the payments proper to the status of a knight. He might or might not have been knighted in the chivalrous sense, he might or might not be related to one of the great noble families; he might be lord of a manor or he might be a tenant of a wealthier landholder—a noble, an ecclesiastical body or the king. The law *quia emptores* of 1290 was fast making all men direct tenants of the king, but the writs which brought the knights into parliament took no account of tenure. They were interested only in economic position. When the early writs, which in the thirteenth century specified knights, were changed in the fourteenth to include "others," it was not a new class but merely a broader choice that was intended. In 1311 the members from Rutlandshire were the *homines* Ralph of Bellafage and Nicholas of Burtin; in the Parliament of 1322 eight knights of the shire were described as *"valletti,"* a term hardly to be distinguished at that time from "yeomen." Most of the knights of the shire who filled the House of Commons from the fifteenth century onward were men like plain "John Stanley, Esquire" and "William Wiston, Gentleman," members from Surrey in 1447. A statute of 1445, when it was apparently felt that representation was becoming too plebeian, required that knights of the shire should be at least gentlemen born, and not yeomen or lower. That is to say they had to be men of leisure, so far as manual labor was concerned. In a word, the class of rural representatives that were thenceforth summoned to Parliament corresponded closely to the rural gentry or country squires of modern times.

Knights in this sense, with their leisure, their familiarity with local conditions, their social position, were the natural men-of-all-work for a central government expanding its activities and striving to control local conditions. They were assessors of subsidies, valuers of property under the assize of arms, members of the juries provided for in the new royal jurisdiction, holders of the minor judicial offices of coroner and justice of the peace. They assisted the sheriff in the collection of certain taxes and the king's judges when they came to their counties to hold the assize courts. Knights were appointed to inquire into and report on abuses charged on the king's officers in the Great Charter of 1215 and in the Provisions of Oxford of 1258. They had always been an active element in the ancient county court. Now they were summoned to share in more general duties, bringing with them authority to bind the county court by which they were chosen.

Their career as active participants in government goes back to the beginning of our period. In 1254 they were ordered to come, along with the representatives of the clergy, to Westminster to report what grant their constituents were willing to make to the king to meet the necessities of his war in Gascony. In the civil war that followed the failure of the Provisions of Oxford in 1261, each side summoned knights from the shires to consultations at St. Albans and London, and again the next year at London. The practice of including knights in the national assemblies either as a class, because of their numbers and means, or as representatives of the county courts, soon became well established.

In the year 1265 the towns appear on the parliamentary scene.[37] In that year, at the close of a period of civil war, the king, at the dictation of Earl Simon de Montfort, ordered the sheriffs to see that there were sent to the coming parliament at London not only the now familiar two knights from each county, but also two representatives from each considerable town. This innovation was repeated. Townsmen seem to have attended a parliament and to have agreed to a grant of taxes in 1267. Both knights of the shire and townsmen were summoned to the parliament of 1273 to recognize the accession of Edward I while he was still abroad, and again in 1275 to grant him a customs duty on wool and hides after he came home. Within the next twenty years there were instances of all the estates meeting together, but also of their meeting separately and in different combinations. In 1275 and 1278 knights of the shire but not townsmen were summoned with the barons and the clergy. In 1283 two meetings were held. At the first four knights from each shire and two men from each city, borough and market town were called together to make a grant for the Welsh war, in addi-

[37] See May McKisack, *The Parliamentary Representation of the English Boroughs during the Middle Ages.*

tion to the subsidy the king had just raised by negotiation with the shires separately. At the second two knights from each county and two representatives from each of twenty-one towns were convoked to a meeting with the barons at Shrewsbury, where they agreed to the changes in the law subsequently issued as the statute of merchants or of Acton Burnell.[38]

Thus far there was little regularity of recognition of either knights or burgesses. In the year 1295, however, there was a notable meeting which established the precedent for their invariable inclusion. Edward I was at war at once with France, Scotland and Wales. The King of France had seized Edward's ancestral lands in France and was threatening an invasion of England. In dire need of funds, Edward summoned the baronage, the prelates, representatives of all ranks of the lower clergy, knights of the shires and citizens of the towns to Westminster. It was a remarkable effort to draw together all classes of the English people. "What affects all should by all be approved; common dangers should be met by means provided in common," Edward or his chancery clerks quoted from the Roman law. In a writ to each sheriff the king explained that he intended to take counsel with the magnates of the kingdom concerning the dangers threatening from France and required him to send to Westminster at the same time two knights from his shire court and two townsmen from each city or borough in his county. These delegates were to be provided with full credentials to take part in the discussion and to agree to whatever should be settled upon.[39]

If all requirements had been conformed to the assembly would have included two archbishops, eighteen bishops, sixty-seven abbots, the heads of the Templars, Hospitallers and the Order of Sempringham, the deans or priors of the seventeen episcopal chapters, the archdeacons from each diocese, one representative from each cathedral chapter and two representatives of the parish clergy of each diocese, two knights from each of thirty-seven shires and two representatives from each of 110 cities and boroughs. This

[38] See G. O. Sayles, "The English Parliaments of Edward I," *Bulletin of the Institute of Historical Research,* V (1927-1928), 129-54.

[39] Translations of the parliamentary writs of 1295 are given in *Translations and Reprints* (University of Pennsylvania), 29-31, and elsewhere; in Latin in William Stubbs, *Select Charters* (Oxford, 1870), 474-76.

would have made an assemblage of some 500 persons. The Parliament of 1295 has been called the "Model Parliament." It was probably smaller in numbers and less clearly divided into political classes or estates than the summons would seem to suggest. Nevertheless both in intention and in fact it represented all classes of the English people above serfdom. Of these some seventy-five knights of the shire and 230 townsmen, if they all came, represented the middle, that is the non-noble and non-clerical class. It is of interest to note that the cortes of Castile and Leon which sat at Valladolid in the same year had the like universal character, as did the Estates General of France which met seven years later, in 1302.

The precedent of the Parliament of 1295 was not followed with absolute exactness; there are instances of meetings of the barons and prelates alone; the lower clergy attended very infrequently. But there were few parliaments or political assemblages of any kind to which the knights and burgesses were not summoned. The Parliament of 1305, for instance, of which we have especially full knowledge, was a repetition of that of 1295. It was composed of the same elements and sat for three weeks, and the full representation of the middle class was attained. Not only were the knights and townsmen regularly represented but the part taken by them increased steadily. The old mass of petitions from private persons or shires or individual towns, the presentation of which had kept early parliaments busy, was now relegated to the courts, the council or the chancery. This type of business gave way to discussion of the grant of money or to general petitions in which the whole body of knights or townsmen joined, and which when favorably answered by the king led to the enactment of new laws.

For a time the two middle-class groups, the knights of the shires representing the interests of the land-holding gentry and well-to-do landholders and the delegates of the towns representing trade, handicrafts, civic wealth and independence, seem to have acted separately. The rate of taxation granted was usually different. In 1296 the knights gave the same sum as the barons and the clergy, a twelfth of their possessions, while the burgesses gave an eighth; in 1306, again like the barons and clergy, the knights gave a thirtieth, the townsmen a twentieth. Even when in 1322 the knights and burgesses deliberated together they granted different amounts, the knights a fifteenth, the burgesses a tenth. Always the townsmen as the richer body, or at least the body with the larger supply of ready money, agreed to the higher rate; it was the period when income from land was yielding precedence to income from trade, commerce and finance.

On the other hand there was much to draw knights and townsmen together. Both were elected in the same county court, for although the actual selection of the delegates of the towns was doubtless made by the magistrates or the population of each town for itself, their summons came to the town through the sheriff, it was the sheriff who gave credentials to the burgesses, the county court that received the final report. In fact the sheriffs sometimes connived with towns desirous of avoiding the expense of sending representatives by testifying that there were no such boroughs in their counties.

Once elected the knights and the townsmen from the same shire had a long journey to make to Westminster, to York or Lincoln or Winchester; what more natural than that, with the sheriff or his deputy, they should make up a party to ride across country together, and what better opportunity to compare notes, to discuss local conditions and to agree on united action! Appearing in Parliament, the two groups were alike newcomers as compared with the older members of the great council. They both came in a representative capacity, and not as individuals, as did nobles and clergy. Both would be paid for their services, and they would alike be unprivileged, except as custom, in the frequent meetings of Parliament, gradually grew into privilege.

In some way the knights and the burgesses drew together into one body. The union was completed by the practice of sitting regularly together as one house. This process, like other parliamentary practices, developed gradually, but as early as the year 1332 there is mention of the lords spiritual and temporal sitting in one house, the "Commons" in another. After the opening exercises the "Commons" were ordered to withdraw to their own room. The chapter-house of the abbey became the regular meeting-place of the Commons whenever Parliament sat at Westminster, as was most generally the case. In 1375 it is already described as their ancient place of meeting.[40]

Thus the knights and burgesses, the representatives of the middle classes in counties and towns, coalesced into a single body, politically homogeneous and of almost undistinguishable origin. No observer has failed to recognize the strength of the Commons of England arising from this fusion of the rural gentry with the merchant aristocracy of the towns. That this was not entirely contrary to Continental practice has already been suggested and will appear more clearly later; nevertheless the completeness of the union of knights and townsmen, of rural and civic wealth, of social prestige and city enterprise, fitted the English House of Commons for an influential career and for ultimate survival. Its organization was completed by the regular appointment of a speaker, which dates from the third quarter of the fourteenth century.

The power of the House of Commons grew steadily during the fourteenth, the great century of estates, and more than held its own in that part of the fifteenth century which falls within the period of this volume. Its increase of power was favored by the wars in which the country was almost constantly engaged. They were, in the main, foreign wars, in which the English king took the offensive and had to come to Parliament for the means of carrying on the conflict. Over and over again various forms of taxation were utilized, the old feudal aids, taxes on personal property, subsidies, tenths of their possessions paid by the townsmen, fifteenths contributed by all other laymen, grants from both their temporalities and their spiritualities by the clergy, poll-taxes and customs; all except the first of these came to be dependent on a grant in Parliament in which the Commons joined and which ultimately they alone initiated.[41] Parliaments therefore had to be called frequently; forty-eight times in the fifty years from 1327 to 1377, sometimes twice, occasionally three times in a single year. It was established by law at an early date that Parliament should meet once a year,

[40] Pollard, *The Evolution of Parliament*, 122, and references there given; see also G. O. Sayles and M. G. Richardson, "The English Parliaments of Edward II", *Bulletin of the Institute of Historical Research*, VI (1928), 71-88.

[41] S. B. Terry, *The Financing of the Hundred Years War, 1337-1360* (London, 1914).

"oftener if need be"; but it was not this rule, it was rather the king's constant need for money that guaranteed regularity of recurrence.

In these frequent meetings customs grew up; concessions made by the king became "privileges of Parliament," privileges gradually became rights and so its powers continued to increase. Through its complaints and "common petitions" and the king's favorable replies to them Parliament became in all but form the sole source of legislation, as it had long been of taxation. Through its grants to the crown for the carrying on of the war Parliament possessed and occasionally used the opportunity to specify the purposes to which the amounts levied should be applied, and on more than one occasion provided, as the French Estates had in 1355, for the audit of the accounts of its expenditures.[42]

It was able in the same way to assert an influence over policy. Sometimes the king himself urged Parliament to give him advice, even upon foreign affairs, the favorite monopoly of the crown, and even upon royal marriages, a still more personal affair of the king. In 1333 the chancellor presented to Parliament the king's request for advice as to how to act in making peace with the French, and in 1369, he asked whether to resume war or not. In both cases advice was promptly given. In this growth of the powers of Parliament it was the House of Commons, representatives of the middle classes, that was intruding farther and farther into the field of government.

In the "Good Parliament" of 1376 the Commons took the full initiative. They asked, in the first place, for the renewal of the old statutes providing for a parliament every year, "for the correction of errors and falsities." They appealed for the exclusion of foreigners from retail trade in London and for the banishment of the Lombard bankers, for the prohibition of the export of grain and of yarn, for the regulation of fisheries, for the enforcement of the Statutes of Laborers, for the prevention of the grant of church preferments to aliens who lived in the "sinful city of Avignon." Their greatest assertion of influence, however, was their attack on

[42] There were instances under Edward III, in 1341 and 1376, under Richard II, in 1377, 1381 and 1399, and under Henry IV, in 1407.

the king's ministers. The years immediately preceding had been a period of foreign defeat and domestic misgovernment. The Commons now proceeded to make charges against a number of the king's officers: Richard Lyons, a member of his council, a merchant of London and controller of the customs; Lord Latimer, lord chamberlain and a member of the council, and various lesser officials, all of whom were removed from their offices, fined and imprisoned. Several of these judgments were reversed and much of the action of this parliament made void by the death of the king and the Black Prince and the accession of a new king with new advisers in the following year, but there emerged from it the precedent on which the whole practice of impeachment by the House of Commons was based.[43]

The first half of the fifteenth century saw Parliament at the fullness of its strength. The scene in the great hall at Westminster on September 30th, 1399, at the renunciation of the throne by Richard II, when the articles of accusation against him were read before Parliament and accepted by the Lords and Commons as sufficient grounds for his deposition; when Henry of Lancaster arose from his place and claimed the vacant throne and the Lords and Commons, asked their opinion, declared that it was their will that Henry should be king and Henry rose and thanked "all the estates of the land"—this scene represents Parliament, including the House of Commons, as the ultimate government of England.[44] During the next half-century that position was maintained and even strengthened. Parliament met almost yearly and took an active part in almost every phase of government. A lawyer of the time thus describes the relation of king and Parliament: The king "cannot by himself or his ministers lay taxes, subsidies or any imposition of what kind soever upon the subject, without the express consent of the whole kingdom in Parliament assembled." Its powers were not merely negative but positive. It asserted more than once its old claim to choose and control the counsellors of the king. The Parliament that met in 1404 obtained the royal consent to reorganize the council, and when Henry VI succeeded

[43] Stubbs, *Constitutional History* (fourth edition, Oxford, 1896), II, 448-58.

[44] J. H. Wylie, *History of England under Henry the Fourth* (four volumes, London, 1884-1898), I, 8-17; *Rotuli Parliamentorum*, III, 423.

to the throne in 1422 as a child of but nine months, Parliament appointed a council of regency and imposed upon it oaths and regulations.[45] Within the next twenty years the lower house made good its claim to initiate all money bills, to have freedom of speech in discussion, to have the king's answer to petitions for redress of grievances given before it made a grant of money, to regulate elections for the knights of the shire so that electors should, according to a law passed in 1430, be only free land-owners holding land amounting to perhaps a hundred acres. The middle classes clearly exercised a wide influence on the government of England.

VIII. THE GERMAN REICHSTAG

There are many characteristics of the history of Germany—its deep racial and political divisions, its elective monarchy, its union of kingdom and empire, the power of its city and princely confederations—which differentiate it from all other countries of Europe.[46] The history of its *Reichstage* or diets is, however, not radically different from that of the cortes of the Spanish countries, the Estates General of France, or the Parliament of England. The meticulous research of German historians has listed somewhat more than a hundred meetings of royal councils during the century and a quarter just preceding our period—the age of the Hohenstaufen emperors, from 1125 to 1247. But these assemblies, called at various imperial cities—Würzburg, Bamberg, Regensburg, Speyer, Worms or Mainz—contained only magnates, lay and spiritual, or at most nobles, lesser barons and knights. There is no instance of the summons or attendance of representatives of cities or of any other non-clerical and non-noble class previous to the middle of the thirteenth century. It was during the time of confusion known as the Interregnum, from 1254 to 1273, when there was no emperor and when all central government was at its weakest that such a summons was issued for the first time.

The political disorders of this period intensified many old diffi-

[45] Stubbs, *op. cit.*, III, 95-8.

[46] The two best treatments, supplementing each other, are those of Georg von Below, *Der Deutsche Staat des Mittelalters* (second edition, Berlin, 1925), and of F. Keutgen, with the same title (Jena, 1918). See also R. Schröder, *Lehrbuch der deutschen Rechtsgeschichte* (sixth edition, Leipzig, 1919), and A. Meister, *Deutsche Verfassungsgeschichte von den Anfängen bis ins 15te Jahrhundert* (third edition, Leipzig, 1922).

culties, the unsettledness of the coinage, the dangers of road and river traffic, the prevalence of banditry and other evils which bore with especial weight upon the merchant, the citizen, the man of the middle class. In the year 1255, therefore, William of Holland, lately elected king, called at Oppenheim a diet which was attended, according to the chronicle, not only by princes, counts and councillors, but by "the grave delegates of all the cities in the league for peace," that is by the cities of the Rhenish League. From this time forward cities were occasionally represented in the diet. Indeed, according to the strict historical definition of at least the older constitutional historians of Germany, no imperial assembly could after this time be called a diet or *Reichstag* unless it contained representatives of the Third Estate.[47] But the practice grew slowly. As a matter of fact the German cities were so strong, so wealthy, so firmly organized in their various leagues that they were rather a power coordinate with the emperor, the nobles and the great prelates than merely material for another estate of the realm. Their inclination, so far as they had the choice, was rather to seek to enforce order upon the country by their own power, than to expect it from the diets, where the ruling elements were so largely the very disturbers of peace and order, the makers of war and patrons of violence. It was primarily for this purpose that the city leagues were formed. On occasion, as has been observed, they opposed the emperor himself and when he demanded new taxes for warlike purposes, they closed their gates against him and his representatives.[48]

Yet as the imperial power was restored by the election in 1273 of Rudolf, Count of Hapsburg, the cities appeared in his first diet, that of 1274, in that held at Wurzburg in 1287 and in his last, at Speyer, in 1291.[49] The cities or some of them were now frequently called. Their delegates were in the diets of 1292 and 1298. Since the emperor summoned whom he chose from all the estates, the cities represented were a varying list. They were, however, all "free

[47] W. Arnold, *Verfassungsgeschichte der deutschen Freistädte,* II, 67.

[48] Bruno, Gebhardt, *Handbuch der deutschen Geschichte* (seventh edition, Stuttgart 1930) I, 433.

[49] See, for events of this reign, Oswald Redlich, *Rudolf von Habsburg* (Innsbruck, 1903).

and imperial cities," not cities belonging to bishops or abbots or directly under lay princes. Some fifty such cities were represented at one Reichstag or another in the century following their first appearance. The names of Nürnberg, Frankfurt, Rothenburg, Constance, Aachen, Ulm, Dortmund, Colmar, Mainz, Cologne, and others appear either as places represented or as cities in which the Reichstag sat.

The fullest recognition of the cities belongs here, as in other countries, to the fourteenth century. In the diet of Speyer of 1309, according to a contemporary chronicler, there were present "electors, princes and representatives of the cities." At the diet of Frankfurt the next year, called to make preparation for the journey of Henry VII to Italy, delegates of the cities were present to share in the arrangements.[50] In the second diet of the year 1338, at Frankfurt, there were representatives of ten imperial cities. In the diets of 1341 and 1344 townsmen appeared. In December, 1355, while in Paris the Estates General of France, under the leadership of Stephen Marcel, were drawing up reform measures, and the English Parliament at London was pressing for a stricter enforcement of the statutes of provisors and of laborers, a diet at Nürnberg including representatives of twenty cities was engaged in considering the early articles of the "Golden Bull," issued by the Emperor Charles IV the next year.[51] It is evident that by the middle of the fourteenth century delegates of the town made up a regular part, though it is true not a very large, conspicuous or influential part of the Reichstag. There were well established rules for their summons; they were required to bring full powers from the cities they represented and they had an established location and part in the ceremonial of the Reichstag meeting. They were, in short, one of its recognized *Stände* or estates.[52]

There were so many other ways in which the middle classes of Germany exercised an influence that the comparative lack of importance of their estate in the Reichstag at this time is not a

[50] F. Schneider, *Kaiser Heinrich VII* (two volumes, Greiz, 1924-1926).

[51] E. Werunsky, *Geschichte Kaiser Karls IV und seiner Zeit* (3 vols. Innsbruck, 1880-1892); K. Zeumer, *Die Goldene Bulle Kaiser Karls IV* (2 vols. Weimar, 1908).

[52] For the later history of the German Reichstag see A. Valen, *Der Deutsche Reichstag unter König Wenzel* (Leipzig, 1892); E. Zickel, *Der Deutsche Reichstag unter König Rupprecht von der Pfalz* (Frankfort, 1908), and H. Wendt, *Der Deutsche Reichstag unter König Sigmund* (Breslau, 1890).

measure of their real significance. There were, as in other countries, provincial estates, the *Landtage*. Mecklenburg, Bavaria, Württemberg, Pomerania and other almost independent states, including the great archbishoprics and bishoprics, like Salzburg, Trier, Liège, each had its separate body of estates, earlier organized and in many cases more fully developed than the general estates of the empire. In these the city populations, the knighthood or gentry, and even, in some cases, newly settled bodies of farmers exercised great influence. It is to be remembered that both in the diets and in the provincial assemblies the middle classes were represented in part through the delegates of the church. This was especially true of the representation of the abbeys, so numerous and so influential in Germany and so prominent in the Reichstag. Even the counts and lords of city territories must have acted largely as representatives of the populations from which they took their titles and received their income, and on whose prosperity and good will their prestige largely depended.

The systems of estates of the eastern and northern countries of Europe diverged from those of the more western countries and from one another. The crown of Bohemia was in a special position. Its connection with the remainder of the Empire was only through its king, who was one of the electors, and it sent no representatives to the imperial diets. Sometimes united diets were called at Prague or elsewhere for the whole kingdom. Sometimes the estates of each province, Bohemia proper, Moravia, Silesia and for a while the Lusatias were summoned separately. The estates were first the magnates, including the prelates, secondly the petty nobles or knights and only after the Hussite wars the burgesses of the towns. Moravia had the peculiarity of recognizing, like Aragon, four estates instead of three; the nobility being divided into two groups, the great nobles and the lesser nobles. Poland and Hungary were famous for their diets of large and turbulent membership.

Of the Scandinavian kingdoms the *Riksdag* of Sweden sprang into existence almost suddenly in January, 1435, in the midst of a national revolution led by the farmers of Dalecarlia, and bore a permanent impress of its origin in its inclusion of a fourth estate, the peasantry, in addition to the usual nobles, clergy and burgesses.

Chapter Four

POPULAR INSURRECTIONS

On the very threshold of this period we are met with the spectre of popular insurrection, which continues to haunt it to its end. Some of these risings were set on foot by leaders as part of their policy; more often they were, or appear to have been, purely spontaneous upheavals. Sometimes they led to far-reaching results; more often they were to all appearance purposeless and fruitless. They were always sudden, always obscure in origin and objective, always ruthless and shocking in their manifestations. They swept everything before them for awhile, then failed after a few days or weeks of triumph. Only in exceptional cases did it take years for the force of a popular rising to spend itself and reaction to restore approximately former conditions.

Popular revolts often begin leaderless, springing from some petty incident. They soon take on larger proportions and eventually some man arises with the qualities of leadership. He rides the storm for a few days or weeks, then falls a victim to the difficulties of his task, the dissatisfaction of his followers or the conservative forces of society. A long list of names are inscribed on the rolls of history made famous only by such brief and tragic authority. Watt Tyler, Cola di Rienzi, James van Artevelde, Stephen Marcel, Michele Lando, Jack Cade, drawing power for a time from the support of the populace, have played their part and have received from historians something like the attention that is given to kings and conquerors. Others more obscure have left a name and little more. Peter Koninck, Nicolas Zannequin, Guillaume Cale, the "Hungarian Master", Jacques Piet—all these were raised from obscurity only long enough to be named and then dropped again into the void of the unknown. The movements, too, of which these men were the momentary leaders, appeared suddenly and disappeared with but little reference to what preceded and what followed. The "Shepherds", the "Sicilian Vespers", the "Jacquerie", the Parisian "Maillotins", the English "Peasants", the "Ciompi" of Florence, the "Matins of Bruges" and successive risings in. Flanders were only a few of the most prominent of these sudden outbreaks. There is scarcely a country, a province, a city which does not have in its annals the record of some wild outburst of popular turbulence. They were as grim as they were sudden. The reprisals of those who claimed to represent law and order, or who at least had enough force in their possession to put down the risings, were hardly less barbarous than the most repulsive acts of the rebels. They have left a dark record of human rage, revenge, cruelty and futility.

What was the cause of this epidemic, so characteristic of the fourteenth and fifteenth centuries? What was there, if anything, common to all its manifestations? A study of their bare and obscure outlines gives but a vague and unsatisfactory answer to these questions. The records are inadequate, for the participants were for the most part inarticulate, and the contemporary chroniclers, members of another class, were invariably hostile. We know something of the occurrences, almost nothing of the motives behind them. These and their more remote causes and results must be largely a matter of inference.

I. THE INSURRECTION OF THE SHEPHERDS

The first to be noted, at the very beginning of the period, was one of those many echoes of the Crusades that simulated their appearance or reflected their distant influence long after their true age was past. In 1250 Louis IX of France was in Syria, disillusioned by his defeat at the hands of the Saracens, but still hopeful of succors from the west. He appealed by letter to his mother, the regent of France, to the pope and to other princes to come or send men and money to enable him to resume the struggle for the Holy Land. The lay and ecclesiastical powers, however, were otherwise employed, and, so far as the upper classes of society were concerned, the crusading spirit was gone. But among the mass of the people it still existed. In the spring of 1251 northern France was stirred by a series of restless movements especially among the shepherds and rural laborers in that populous agricultural and pastoral region.

They were going, the people said, to the Holy Land to rescue their abandoned king and the Holy Sepulchre. Thousands left their flocks and their farm-work, took to the roads, formed groups and wandered through the countryside. This was the rising of the "Shepherds."[1]

About Easter there appeared among them a leader, who, if he was not the originator, was at least the organizer of the movement. He was called by his contemporaries the "Master from Hungary." About sixty years of age, tall, meager, pale, with a long beard, he was well educated, used French, German and Latin, and was an eloquent speaker. He was said to be a Master of Arts from one of the universities, whence his popular name. He was evidently a mystic and a man with the personal fascination so often accompanying the unknown. One hand he kept continually closed, saying that it held a written commission from the Virgin, given him in a vision, ordering him to preach the crusade, not to the nobles, who had deserted it, nor to the clergy, who no longer preached it, but to the poorest and lowest of the people. He was said to have performed miracles, and greater ones were promised.[2] All sorts of rumors of his origin spread among the wonder-loving. He was, some believed, a saint, a veritable messenger from the Virgin, so they went on their knees to him. In the opinion of others he was an apostate, a Mahometan who had agreed to deliver a vast number of Christian Frenchmen into the hands of the Sultan of Egypt, leaving France denuded of its people so that it might easily be conquered by the Saracens. According to some of the chroniclers he was a necromancer, trained at Toledo in the shameful occult sciences of the Arabs. Others believed him a Manichæan, sworn to obtain revenge for the persecution of his fellow Albigenses of the south by deluding to their destruction the people of the north.

All tales disregarded, he was the leader of a constantly increasing number of poor countrymen of northeastern France. Groups appeared first in Picardy; then the rising spread to Flanders, to

[1] This and other agrarian movements are well discussed by G. Franz, *Die agrarischen Unruhen des ausgehenden Mittelalters* (Marburg, 1930).

[2] Matthew Paris, *Chronica Majora,* translated by J. A. Giles (London, 1852), V, 246-8, Rolls Series.

Brabant, to Lorraine, to Burgundy. They were said, doubtless with the usual medieval exaggeration, to number 20,000, then 60,000, then 100,000. Men, women and children made up the thronging masses. Many carried weapons—swords, axes, primitive arms, which they brandished and more and more frequently used. As they passed across the country in disorderly crowds they were joined by refugees and outlaws of all kinds.[3]

The most remarkable fact about these wanderers, and indeed about those who did not join but who were, at least in the beginning, sympathetic with them, was their outspoken hostility to the church. Notwithstanding the piety of their mission, while awaiting the beginning of their journey to the Holy Land they abused clergymen in the towns to which they came and pillaged monasteries throughout the country. Though not ordained, the leaders who arose among them took over priestly duties, preaching, performing irregular marriages, granting absolution, distributing crusaders' crosses, blessing religious banners, claiming to heal the sick and to give sight to the blind. The Master at one time put on a bishop's robe and mitre and preached to the people.

The first considerable city where they gathered was Amiens, where they were well treated and indeed welcomed. Then they flocked to Paris, where the queen mother, the famous Blanche of Castile, was acting as regent in the absence of the king.[4] Inspired perhaps by a superstitious belief in the mission of the insurgents, perhaps by a hope that in some way this horde might get to the east and provide her son with the forces he needed, the queen welcomed them, forbade any interference with their movements, and herself sent for the leader, whom she treated honorably and to whom she gave presents. He is said to have reported to his followers that he had bound the queen by his spells and that she would allow them to do what they would; they might therefore kill the priests and other clergy. However that may have been, conflicts did soon break out. There were bloody encounters at Paris with the university students and others; several were killed

[3] Ibid., V, 248-52.

[4] An admirable account of this movement, drawn from many contemporary sources, is to be found, somewhat unexpectedly, in Élie Berger, *Histoire de Blanche de Castile, Reine de France* (Paris, 1895), 393-401.

and their bodies thrown into the Seine; the bridges had to be closed to prevent further fighting.

On leaving Paris the "Shepherds," too numerous now to be fed in any one place, divided into several bodies, each with a leader, each carrying banners showing the Master's vision of the Virgin with a cross and the Lamb, each going in a different direction. By this time they had become, from their numbers and acts of violence, a terror to the quiet people. At Rouen they attacked the cathedral and archbishop's palace and drove out the clergy; at Orleans they quarreled with the university students. The Master announced that he would preach in the market-place, and the archbishop, to avoid scandal, ordered all clergymen to remain in their houses. But, as usual, some irrepressible students attended the service and one of the bolder ones charged the leader with deluding the people. He was struck on the head and killed by one of the marchers. Again fighting took place, with many dead on both sides. The bodies were thrown into the Loire. The crusaders plundered the synagogues and houses of the Jews, who were under the special protection of the crown. Notwithstanding the emblem on their banners some of them even mutilated a statue of the Virgin.

By this time their original object, whatever it may have been, was forgotten; they were mere brigands. Those who reached Tours fought with the clergy, while the townsmen looked on. Ultimately even lay opinion united against them, and orders at length came from the queen to repress them. When they entered the province of Berry, pillaging and murdering, twelve of their chiefs were taken and hanged. The citizens of Bourges offered aid to the royal officers, followed and caught up with the group under the Master himself, killed and hacked him to pieces, put others to death and chased away the rest "like mad dogs."[5] Another group made its way to Beaucaire, then into Provence and finally to Marseilles. But everywhere they were met, attacked and slaughtered. Those who reached English territory at Bordeaux were driven back by Simon de Montfort. The leader of the band tried to leave by sea, was recognized by the boatmen, and thrown into the Garonne,

[5] Matthew Paris, *Chronica Majora,* V, 252.

his hands and feet tied together. It was indeed a wide movement that saw the waters of the three largest rivers of France close over three of its leaders and many of their followers.

One group of the "Shepherds" with its leader made its way across the Channel to England, landing at Shoreham, where it gathered adherents from the neighboring country. Some 500 assembled on the same spot where 130 years later a group of the English peasant rebels gathered. When their leader undertook to preach, the bystanders attacked him and he was forced with his followers to take refuge in a near-by wood. On July 8, 1251, the king gave directions that they and all other riotous persons should leave England, and ordered the sheriffs to take action against them. Public opinion everywhere had turned from acceptance of the rebels as pilgrims or crusaders to condemnation of their irreligion and fear of their numbers and violence. They had become vagabonds and wherever they appeared there was rioting and bloodshed. After the deaths of the leaders many of those who were left threw away their unauthorized crusaders' badges and obtained new ones from the clergy, who alone had the right to bestow them. They then joined King Louis in Syria, or crept back as best they might to their homes.[6] Neither their nameless leader nor those under him have left us any statement of their objects or any defense of their actions. One credulous chronicler records that in the pack of one of the rebels was found money, a poisonous powder and a letter from the Sultan. But the passage of these wanderers across France and the Channel in April, May and June 1251, was a storm-wind of which, like any other, we know neither whence it cometh or whither it goeth.[7]

II. THE SICILIAN VESPERS

Late on the afternoon of March 31, 1282, the Tuesday after Easter, while the bells were ringing for vesper service at the church of Santo Spirito outside Palermo, some obscure incident set fire to fuel which had long been piling up. The Sicilian populace, which had gathered near the church for a festival, rose in wild and

[6] The entire wasting away of large groups, pilgrims or soldiers, far from their starting place, was not an unfamiliar phenomenon in medieval and early modern times.

[7] Matthew Paris, *Chronica Marjora*, V, 253-4.

murderous rage against the French soldiers, officials and merchants in their midst. It is said that 200 were killed in the first attack, almost before the vesper bells had ceased ringing. The storm of assassination spread into the city and then throughout Sicily. Palermo, then Corleone and then Messina set up popular governments and formed a league which gave some unity to later action. More than 2,000 men, women and children were killed the first night, and this slaughter continued till the French were practically exterminated. Monasteries and churches were invaded and clerics known to be French were dragged out and slain. Children at the breast were murdered along with their mothers, and there were miserable tales of the bodies of Sicilian women married to French husbands ripped open so that no French progeny should survive. Pits were dug where their bodies were buried without rites or memorials.[8]

In all this there is doubtless much exaggeration, but analogies are too numerous to allow one to be unduly sceptical, and the occurrence was terrible enough to send a thrill through Europe, to awaken the wild anger of the French king of Sicily, Charles of Anjou, and to make the "Sicilian Vespers" a tradition of popular savagery. As to the cause of the outbreak, it has long been a subject of learned controversy between Italian and French historians.[9] There is the usual story of the insult to a native woman by a French soldier, but this can hardly have been so unusual an occurrence in those days as to start so great a conflagration. A more adequate explanation is doubtless to be found in the forcible occupation of the island and the harsh administration of its affairs by the soldiers, officials and grantees of land of its French king. Foreign occupation is always unpopular. However, with the ultimate causes of the uprising, with the attempt of the king at revenge, and with its far-reaching effects in transferring the rule of Sicily from the French to the Spanish, we have nothing to do here. It is rather the abrupt appearance of the common people on the public scene, even more sudden than the rising of the "Shepherds";

[8] Michele Amari, *War of the Sicilian Vespers,* translated and edited by the Earl of Ellesmere, (three volumes, London, 1850), I, 180-86, 190-211; see also O. Cartellieri, *Peter von Aragon und die Sizilianische Vesper* (Heidelberg, 1904).

[9] Amari, op. cit., III, 301-47. In 1882 the 600th anniversary of the rising was celebrated in Sicily and gave occasion for a number of publications on its history.

it is their unexpected intrusion into the relatively orderly course of events, the unbridled license of their action, and its overwhelming if temporary success that attract the attention of the historian of the period. The prevalence of such occurrences is a characteristic of the time that can hardly be disregarded.

III. THE NETHERLANDS RISINGS

The Netherlands were more given to popular insurrections than any other part of Europe, excepting possibly Italy. There are instances of upheavals in 1255, 1267, 1275, 1280 and in other years of that half-century, in Liège, Utrecht, Valenciennes, Douai, Tournai, Ypres, Waesland.[10]

The prevalence of popular revolt in Flanders, the most restless part of the Netherlands, the heart of modern Belgium, justifies a short description of its political and social condition. Four parties contended for the control of its wealthy cities. Far away at Paris was their distant overlord, the King of France, watchful of every opportunity to extend his centralizing power to the utmost limits of his feudal territories. Immediate rule was exercised, so far as a feudal prince, himself a vassal, could exercise independent rule, by the Count of Flanders. Beneath him were the city governments of Ghent, Bruges, Ypres, Courtrai, Termonde, Oudenarde, Lille, Alost, Sluys, and some forty other towns, large and small. The region was then, as it is now, one of the most thickly settled parts of the world. In all the rest of the Netherlands together there were only some thirty-six cities of comparable size.[11] In these rich and populous towns the growth of commerce, the spread of manufactures, the increase of accumulated wealth and the progress of time had raised a group of families to the position of a rich and powerful patriciate. They were, at the beginning of this period, the ruling class within each city. They had by their intelligence and their persistence won the charters which gave them so nearly complete self-government as against the count and the king. By their wealth and their ability to use the services of others they had built the walls, erected the public buildings, bridges and parish

[10] P. J. Blok, *History of the People of the Netherlands,* translated by O. A. Bierstaat and Ruth Putnam (New York, 1898), I, 230-51.

[11] Henri Pirenne, *Les Anciennes Démocraties des Pays-Bas* (Paris, 1910).

churches, and had set ringing for municipal gatherings the bells in the belfries which are so characteristic a feature of that region. They formed a patrician class of merchants, manufacturers, capitalists, landowners and officials of the city, the count or the king.[12]

Far below them were the common people, small tradesmen, artisans, journeymen, members of the lesser gilds, working weavers, dyers, fullers, shearmen. Between these two classes there was a great gulf of economic interest, social position and sometimes of language, the upper classes frequently using French, the lower classes, except in the Walloon districts, always Flemish. The cities were much congested. At the beginning of the fourteenth century Ghent had 2,300 weavers. Bells rang for the noon hour and at one o'clock so that everybody else should leave the streets free for the coming and going of the workmen between their shops and their houses during the dinner hour. The upper classes ruled the cities in their own interest, and their control extended to economic as well as political affairs. In a country using large capital, importing raw material and manufacturing for export there was much suffering, the invariable accompaniment of capitalism, increased by disruption of business through political changes. The small gildsmen and workmen were more than elsewhere dependent on their economic superiors. Their whole existence was precarious; unemployment and consequent misery alternated with occupation during long hours and with irregular pay. No influence of the capitalist class over the life of the working classes in modern times approaches the minute, selfish and overwhelming control over the outward conditions of life and labor of the artisans of such cities as those of Flanders at the beginning of the fourteenth century. Disputes between these two classes and bitterness of spirit were therefore unending, and the lower class was always ready for an attempt to throw off the yoke of the upper.[13]

The "Matins of Bruges" of May 18, 1302, was, in reality, such an attempt, though it took the form of a rising against the French garrison. Nominally and normally the Flemish patricians felt them-

[12] Henri Pirenne, *Histoire de Belgique* (second edition, four volumes, Brussels, 1902-1911), I, 169-88, 355-62; II, 67-72.

[13] H. S. Lucas, *The Low Countries and the Hundred Years War* (Ann Arbor, 1929), 8-11; H. Pirenne, op. cit., *passim.*

selves bound to the king, the more distant of their lords and the least likely therefore to interfere with the self-government of their cities. Their party was therefore called the "Leliaerts," the party of the lily, the party of the French connection. The democracy were more closely tied to the Count of Flanders and therefore formed the "Klauwaerts," the party of the claw, that is of the rampant lion on the Flemish coat of arms.

In 1297 the count had allied himself with the English, thrown off his allegiance to the king, and angered the governing class of the towns by infringing their charters. The king had forced him to submission, had occupied the country and had favored the town rulers, but he had placed control, for the time at least, in the hands of a French governor, Jacques de Châtillon. A supporter of the city aristocracy, though himself a feudal noble with little sympathy for either party in the cities, Châtillon immediately antagonized the common people. Obscure movements began among the populace. A poor weaver of Bruges, Peter Koninck, or King, of whom we know nothing except that he was small of stature and with a natural gift for leadership, put himself at the head of the secret movement in that city and found support in a certain butcher, Johan Breydel and those whom he influenced. Châtillon entered Bruges with a body of troops on May 17, 1302. That night or early in the morning the people rose, strangled the French sentinels, attacked the soldiers in their sleep and beat large numbers to death, including some who tried to lose themselves in the crowd by joining in the native cry "Schild en Vriend," but betrayed themselves by their mispronunciation of the Flemish words. It was the "Matins of Bruges." Many of the aristocrats lost their lives at the same time. The rising spread rapidly to other towns and to the peasantry in the vicinity of the towns. Flanders was within a few days largely in the hands of the Klauwaerts.[14]

This rising of the democratic party, with its wide extension, infused with that spirit of nationalism which appears at so many unexpected points in this period, began a new epoch in Flemish history, the period of struggle for independence from France. The first fruits of nationalist and democratic enthusiasm was the battle

[14] Blok, *History of the People of the Netherlands,* I, 140-1.

fought two months afterward under the walls of Courtrai. It was a natural sequel to the popular rising at Bruges. The king of France could not leave unavenged the massacre of his troops and officials, even if the Leliaerts had been willing to accept the loss of so much of their power. The two armies, that of Châtillon, supported by a feudal array from the adjoining parts of France, by the aristocracy of the Flemish cities and by hired Genoese crossbowmen and German horsemen, met an army of weavers and other working-men and was overwhelmingly defeated. It was claimed that 20,000 were left dead in the field. Seven hundred gold spurs of the defeated chivalry were taken on the field after the battle, and the "Battle of the Spurs" it has remained since.[15]

It is true the townsmen were well led, the count himself, Guy de Dampierre, and some other knights of military experience providing skilled and gallant leadership. The region was seamed with canals, and to that extent unsuited to the use of French horsemen. The French suffered also from that insubordination and impatience in attack that drove so many of their armies to destruction in the fourteenth century. Nevertheless there was in the primitive, inexorable force with which the townsmen, mere mechanics, most of them, armed with the short heavy pike which was the weapon of the country, bore down the cavalry and drove them into helpless flight, something that reflected the spirit of national determination to defend their homes and their rights. The battle of Courtrai has remained a national and a democratic tradition among all Flemings.[16]

Revolution has always shown itself contagious and recurrent, so that it cannot be a matter of surprise that although the king and the aristocracy of Bruges and the other towns by steady pressure regained their control, revolts continued to occur through the succeeding decades. One of the most bitter and prolonged of these was the one which swept through the maritime regions, both urban and rural, between 1323 and 1328. It started among the peasants, some of them owners of land, others tenants of small holdings which they or their forefathers had rescued from the marshes and swamps

[15] Blok, op. cit., I, 141-2.
[16] Pirenne, *Histoire de Belgique,* I, 383-403.

of the seacoast. Their relation to their landlords and to the gentry and petty nobility of the region was not unlike that of the smaller gildsmen of the towns to their merchant aristocracy.

The disorders that broke out in west Flanders in 1323 under the leadership of a prosperous peasant, Nicolas Zannequin, apparently had some kind of a free rural democracy as their goal. But in 1324 the revolt became more fierce, and was more generally directed against the larger landowners, both lay and clerical. After December 1324 bands of rioters led by peasant captains spread through the country committing shocking atrocities. They drove out the officers of the count, pillaged and burned the country houses of the gentry, murdered those whom they caught and the members of their families. In addition to the usual narratives of the chroniclers and some testimony in legal documents we have for these occurrences a contemporary descriptive poem, the *Kerelslied*, evidently, like most contemporary literature, reflecting upper-class feeling. It breathes hatred and revenge toward the peasantry, prophesies the fate of all of them to be drawn on hurdles and hung. It represents no doubt the barbarism of the struggle between the classes. We get a rare, but unfortunately an obviously hostile glimpse of the peasant, his long beard, his ragged garments, his diet of cheese and curdled milk, his drunken arrogance when he has become for the time master in the land.[17]

Later the rising spread from the country to the town. Bruges, again under the control of its democracy, gave the rebels support. The populace of Ypres sent for Zannequin and his bands to help them drive out the patricians and to set up a government under the weavers and fullers. Attacks were made on the abbeys and churches. Leaders addressed the crowds in the churchyards, promising them a new world. There was much hostility to the church. A peasant named Jacques Piet declared that he would never again receive the offices of the church and hoped to see the last priest hung on the gallows.[18] An interdict laid on the country by the pope was disregarded and the priests were forced by the rebels to perform the most necessary rites. The rebels turned against their

[17] Henri Pirenne, *Le Soulèvement de la Flandre Maritime de 1323-28* (Brussels, 1900), xxiii-xxxiii.
[18] Ibid., p. xxvii.

count, Louis de Nevers, now no longer their natural ally but a courtier of the French king, seized him at Courtrai, murdered some of his counsellors before his eyes and imprisoned him in the cloth-hall at Bruges.

But, as usual, the powers of reaction were too strong and persistent for the endurance of the popular party. The end came when the king, appealed to by the count, the pope, the nobility and the town aristocracies, gathered an army of overwhelming strength, and at Cassel, August 1328, took revenge for Courtrai by cutting the army of the Flemish democracy to pieces. Zannequin and several thousand others were killed in the battle, and order was restored by October 1328. Other leaders and hundreds of common men who escaped from the battle were, in the course of the next ten years, hanged, beheaded or broken on the wheel; their property was confiscated. Some 1900 houses were listed as possessions of the rebels, and later seized. Further massacre of men, women and children and the burning of villages and towns as demanded by the local nobles, were prevented only by the unwillingness of the count and the king to allow the destruction of so valuable a part of their possessions.[19]

The most famous insurrection in Flanders in the fourteenth century, that connected with the name of Jacques van Artevelde, was the least characteristic as a popular rising. Van Artevelde of Ghent, "the greatest Fleming of all time," as he has been called by a modern biographer, held his position from the outbreak of the rising in 1337 to his murder by the mob, July 17, 1345, the longest period of control by any popular leader in ancient or modern times. His actions and character made a strong impression on contemporary chroniclers, and a whole library of modern writing has grown up about him. His life has been made the subject of biography, drama and patriotic appeal, and his period usually makes the longest chapter in any history of Belgium. But van Artevelde belonged to the upper rather than the lower classes. He was the leader of a Flemish national movement, not of an uprising of the lower classes. He made use of the mob of Ghent for his own pur-

[19] Ibid., pp. xxx-xxxii, 1-162.

poses and those of the existing government, not for the coercion of a ruling class. A history of the Flemish rising of 1337-1345 is in reality part of the record of the onset of the Hundred Years war and a description of it will be given in that connection.[20]

There remains to be mentioned one more effort of the lower classes to obtain some degree of control of the government before Flanders settled down under the strong rule of the house of Burgundy. This was the rising of 1381-1382 associated with the name of Philip van Artevelde. It need not be discussed in detail here, for, like the movement of 1337-1345, it was more a political than a social struggle and belongs to the general history of the efforts of Flanders to gain its independence from France.

IV. THE JACQUERIE AND THE RISING UNDER MARCEL

One of the most sudden, most brutal and most obscure series of events during these centuries was the "Jacquerie" of 1358.[21] The "marvelous trybulacion in the realme of France," as described by Froissart and his Elizabethan translator, Lord Berners, began when "certayne people of the common vyllages, without any head or ruler, assembled togyther in Beauvosyn. In the beginning they past not a hundred . . . they gathered togyder without any other counsayle, and without any armure, savyng with staves and knyves, and so went to the house of a knyght dwellyng therby, and brake up his house and slewe the knyght and the lady and all his chyldren, great and small, and brent his house. And than they went to another castel, and toke the knight therof and bounde hym fast to a stake, and than vyolated his wyfe and his doughter before his face and than slewe the lady and his doughter and all his other chyldren, and than slewe the knyght by great tourment and brent and beate downe the castell. And so they dyd to dyvers other castelles and good houses; and they multiplyed so that they were a six thousand. . . .

"These myschevous peple thus assembled without capitayne or armoure, robbed, brent and slewe all gentylmen that they coude lay handes on, and forced and ravysshed ladyes and damosels, and

[20] See Chap. v.; H. S. Lucas, op. cit.

[21] S. Luce, *Histoire de la Jacquerie* (new edition, Paris, 1894).

dyd suche shamefull dedes that no humayne creature ought to thynke on any suche, and he that dyd moost myschiefe was most preased with theym and greattest maister. I dare nat write the horryble dedes that they dyd to ladyes and damoselles; amonge other they slewe a knight and after dyd put hym on a broche and rosted hym at the fyre in the syght of the lady his wyfe and his chyldren; and after that the lady had ben enforced and ravisshed with a x. or xii. thei made her perforce to eate of her husband, and after made her to dy an yvell deth and all her chyldren."[22]

A comparison with other contemporary chronicles and even with the more matter-of-fact records of court proceedings does little to relieve this story of its stark horror and bestiality. At best these other records make more specific the statements and more obvious the general causes that led to the rising. We can understand the movement better than could the participants. "When they were demaunded why they did so yvell dedes they coude not tell." But we can easily imagine the demoralizing effect upon the people of twenty years of war and ravaging, of the barbarities of the "free companies," of the losses and sufferings of the Black Death, which swept across France in 1348 and 1349, of the extortions by the lords of money for the ransom of those captured at Poitiers in 1356, and we can picture the despair aroused by the order sent out from Paris, May 14, 1358, that all the castles and country houses of the nobility should be repaired and strengthened. This action of the Estates General of Compiègne was directed against the disorders of the free companies, and was ultimately conducive to good order, but to the common people of the time it meant forced labor, heavy taxes and the reconstruction of centres of petty tyranny, whether occupied by English brigands or feudal nobles.

The man who seems to have exercised the widest influence among the rebels was a certain Guillaume Cale, or Charles, as it appears in some of the records. The chronicles speak also of a mythical Jacques Bonhomme, a colloquial name for the peasant already familiar in poetry and romance, corresponding to Piers Plowman in England. Cale was said to have been a man of fine appearance,

[22] Froissart, *Chronicles,* chap. clxxxiii, Lord Berners' translation (Tudor Translations, London, 1901), I, 403-4.

natural eloquence and some education, received probably, as in the case of several of the lower class leaders, in a monastery school. He seems to have made some effort to check the barbarity of his fellows. During the few weeks of the rising he gathered around him a group of advisers who worked out a plan for the capture of certain cities and for a union with Marcel, then at the end of the resources of moderation at Paris and ready for reckless recruits. But Cale was captured in a battle between the peasantry and the local authorities which was fought against his advice. He was beheaded, along with a number of his principal followers, at Clermont. The rising, which had spread through twenty modern departments and touched more than 200 named places, was put down by officers and nobles, recovered from their early panic.[23]

An incident typical of the reaction was the attack on the rebels, who had been admitted by the citizens of Meaux and were established in the market-place, by a group of knights on their way home from a crusade against the heathen Prussians. Seeing the town in the hands of the rebels and certain noble ladies in danger they "anone wan the place and entered in amonge their ennemys and beate them downe by heapes and slew them lyke beestes and chased them all out of the towne and slew so many that they were wery. . . . And when these men of armes returned agayne to the towne, they sette fyre thereon and brende it clene and all the vilaynes of the towne that they coude close therein, bycause they tooke part with the Jaquez."[24]

At the battle, or rather the carnage near Clermont, where Cale was captured, 800 peasants were said to have been killed. We hear of 500 killed at one time, 1,000 at another and 300 burned in a monastery where they had taken refuge. Battles to put down rebels ran insensibly into reprisals against enemies. A number of troublesome tenants were hung by a count in Brie in front of their own cottages. Villages and farmhouses were burned, crops were destroyed, men, women and children in disturbed districts were slaughtered. All this was followed by executions and by pitiless confiscation of goods by the government. A few bought par-

[23] Luce, *Histoire de la Jacquerie*, 57-147.
[24] Froissart, *Chronicles* (Lord Berners' Translation), I, 407.

dons at crushing prices. *Effrois* is the contemporary term corresponding to the "frightfulness" of modern punitive warfare.[25]

While the *Jacquerie* was filling with horror many rural districts and some of the smaller cities of central France, Stephen Marcel, defeated in his efforts to reorganize the government of France under the Estates General with the approval of the dauphin, summoned from the back streets and courtyards of Paris the turbulent masses of the great city, with the object of putting still greater pressure on the royalist party. He is said even to have planned to change the succession to the crown, bringing in Charles of Navarre as a king more sympathetic with the people. It was the same design that was imputed to Jacques van Artevelde when he planned to make the Black Prince count of Flanders. A rising of the people followed, but it was not a spontaneous rising, like most of those we have to chronicle, but rather like those led by Jacques van Artevelde, Jack Cade and others, a rising fomented by a political leader for his own objects or those of his party. Paris was in the hands of Marcel and the populace for some months, but opposition to him was growing and dissension began in the ranks of the rebels themselves. It was apparently in an effort to communicate with the leaders of the *Jacquerie*, and perhaps to put a new and more popular monarch on the throne, that Marcel lost his supremacy and was assassinated at the gate of St. Antoine, as has been already described. The regent saw his body and those of some of the principal city leaders as they lay bleeding on the steps of the church of St. Catherine when he entered Paris the next day. During the next few weeks, executions, confiscations, and withdrawals of privileges obliterated the work of Marcel and the rebellious Parisian populace, leaving little more in the way of results than did the random excesses of the *Jacquerie*.[26]

V. ITALIAN RISINGS

Almost contemporaneous with the *Jacquerie* and the revolt of Paris was Rienzi's rising at Rome. How far this was a spontaneous movement that afterwards found its leader, how far Rienzi delib-

[25] Luce, op. cit., 57, 59-63.

[26] Luce, op. cit., 93-129; Henri Martin, *Histoire de France* (fourth edition, Paris, 1857), V, 208-13.

erately prepared the insurrection, is an old question that arises in this as in a score of other cases. It can seldom be answered from the material that remains. But that Italians more than other nations need a leader to embody their aspirations has been declared to be true from the time of Julius Caesar to that of Mussolini. Certainly the occurrences at Rome from 1347 to 1354, while bearing many marks of an independent popular insurrection, were largely guided by one man's ideas and actions.[27]

On May 20, 1347, Cola di Rienzi, accompanied by some leading conspirators and a great mob, took possession of Capitol Hill and announced a new, or rather a return to a simulacrum of the ancient government of Rome. This was declared to be the *buono stato*, the "good government." Rienzi was a low-born but a handsome, traveled, educated man, holder of the title of papal notary, a worshipper of the past and a compelling speaker. He took the title of "Tribune," and established a civic guard of cavalry and foot from each of the thirteen divisions of the city. All claims to authority of the old feudal families, the Orsini, the Colonni, the Savelli and others, who in the absence of the pope at Avignon were governing the city, were set aside; they were forbidden to fortify their houses or to arm their followers, and were ordered to take the oath of allegiance to the "good state." When they defied the new government their palaces were attacked by the populace; some fled, others yielded.

The new government lasted seven months. During that time Rienzi, relying on the support of the Roman populace, made higher and higher claims. In the troubled state of Europe the loss of prestige of both pope and emperor no doubt presented an opportunity for a bold stroke. But when Rienzi, intoxicated with the memories of old Rome and with the popular support of the new, summoned pope and cardinals to return, and bade the rival claimants to the imperial title bring their claims before him for settlement, he was living neither in old nor in modern Rome but in the realm of fantasy. When he arrested several of the Roman

[27] See Alain de Boüard, *Le Régime Politique et les Institutions de Rome au Moyen Age, 1252-1347* (Paris, 1920), the best study of the background. On Rienzi see Emmanuel Rodocanachi, *Cola di Rienzi, Histoire de Rome de 1342 à 1354* (Paris, 1888), and Konrad Burdach, *Der Briefwechsel des Cola di Rienzi und die geistige Wandlung seiner Zeit* (two volumes, Berlin, 1913-1928).

nobles on a charge of conspiracy and ordered their immediate execution, even though he pardoned them afterward, he was taking action that could be successful only if he had the continued united support of the great mass of the people. This he risked by his tone of increasing arrogance and by his magnificent mode of life. So opposition showed itself. The pope, angered by his disrespect, excommunicated him as a heretic, and on December 15, 1347, he abdicated his position in a panic and fled from Rome in disguise.[28]

The stir of the Roman people was, however, not yet over. In 1353, while Rienzi was in exile, they reasserted their control and restored the tribunate under a popular leader named Baroncelli. His leadership was unsuccessful and when in the intricacies of papal policy the pope found it desirable to reestablish Rienzi at Rome, the latter became again the trusted leader of the people. He now took the higher title of Senator. But the usual fate of leaders in class war soon overtook him. In a sudden access of suspicion of his plans he was put to death by the crowd on Capitol Hill on October 8, 1354, at the spot now marked by his monument. There have been few more complicated series of occurrences than those connected with Rienzi's rising, and, notwithstanding their appearance in literature and their discussion in serious history, the movement is still obscure and many of its incidents unexplained. Rienzi was the most declamatory but least understood of all the leaders of insurrection in the fourteenth century.[29]

However given to disorder the people of Rome and however numerous the conflicts in other cities, Florence was of all Italian towns the most torn by factions. Many of these struggles show little or no trace of class conflict. The party victory that drove Dante from Florence in 1302 involved no economic or social question. Guelfs and Ghibelins, Albizzi and Ricci, Whites and Blacks, even nobles and the richer citizens were not necessarily of different classes. The *popolo grasso* and *popolo minuto*, on the other hand, the great gilds and the lesser gilds, the aristocracy and democracy, were natural opponents, and the government of the republic was now in the hands of one, now of the other, or balanced in some

[28] See discussions and documents in F. Duncalf and A. C. Krey, *Parallel Source Problems in Medieval History* (New York, 1912), Problem V.

[29] The parallelism with certain aspects of the modern history of Italy is obvious.

temporary compromise.[30] Through the middle years of the fourteenth century it was coming more and more completely into the hands of the aristocracy.

But suddenly, in 1378, the *Ciompi* or common workmen of the city, lower in position even than the members of the smaller gilds who usually made up the democracy, rose in revolt.[31] The movement was initiated or soon came under the influence of a poor wool comber, Michele Lando, who was made *gonfalonier* or head of the city government by the populace. He proved to be a moderate and clear-sighted leader. Disorders were put down, new gilds were formed of those workmen who had never before been organized, and their representatives were added to the *signoria* alongside the older and richer organizations. Lando himself after two months of power resigned and furnished the traditional exception to the general rule. He was the only popular leader of the period who died in peace and obscurity. The revolutionary change lasted for four years after which the government was restored to its old form and 161 men prominent in the movement since the resignation of Lando were executed.

The period from 1378 to 1383 was in much of Europe a half-decade of revolt. The rising of the *Ciompi* in the first of those years and a revival of their activity in 1381, the English "Peasants' Rising" of the same year (the best known of popular insurrections of the fourteenth century) the "Maillotins" of Paris, the revival of revolt in Flanders, the "Harelle" of the city of Rouen in 1382 and others filled those five years with insurrection and bloody reprisals.[32] On St. Matthew's Day, February 24, 1382, the journeymen coppersmiths and drapers of Rouen rang the tocsin from the great bell, "Rouvel," in the city belfry, calling the populace into the streets; the mob pillaged the houses of the upper classes, opened the wine casks, attacked the ghetto, summoned the clergy of the cathedral to renounce their rents and tolls, and secured the agreement of

[30] G. Salvemini, *Magnati e Popolani in Firenze dal 1280 al 1295* (Florence, 1899); E. Staley, *The Guilds of Florence* (London, 1906); A. Doren, *Das Florentinische Zunftwesen vom XIVten bis zum XVIten Jahrhundert* (Stuttgart, 1908).

[31] C. Falletti-Fossati, *Il Tumulte dei Ciompi* (Florence, 1882); G. Scaramella, *Firenze allo Scappio del Tumulto dei Ciompi* (Pisa, 1914).

[32] L. Mirot, *Les Insurrections Urbaines au Début du Règne de Charles VI, 1380-1383* (Paris, 1906).

some of the richer merchants to the adoption of a new and more popular constitution for the city. But although "Rouvel" continued to ring day and night for three days, the excitement subsided. Another group of the citizens came into power and by the time the king arrived, but a month after the outbreak, the gate through which he entered was garnished with the heads of the leaders of the insurrection. There were many later executions, and the great bell, which had come to symbolize the revolt, was dismounted, a heavy fine was imposed on the city and many of its rights of self-government were taken away. It was a frequent occurrence that the putting down of an insurrection in this period of growing powers of the crown occasioned loss not only to the defeated rebels but to the higher class against whom they had risen.[33]

In Flanders the old struggle was renewed at Ghent in 1381 and soon came under the guidance of Philip van Artevelde, son of the famous leader of the rising of 1337. Philip's death was, like his father's, a violent one, though he died on the battlefield of Roosebeck, not on the streets of Ghent.[34]

In Paris, in 1382, as so often before and since, the hand of the government was forced and its policy dictated by a sudden popular uprising. Overpowering the ordinary guards the crowd rushed to the city hall and armed themselves with the leaden *mailles* or mallets prepared for use against the English if they should enter the city. The insurgents thus got the name of the *Maillotins* or "Malletmen." Barricades were thrown across the streets and they succeeded in extorting from the government repeal of the new sales-tax. Their success was short-lived. The young king Charles VI, victorious over Philip van Artevelde and the rebels in Flanders, came back to Paris, occupied the city with his troops and by a long series of executions and a withdrawal of many of the city liberties repressed for the time both the upper and the lower classes. The city remained restless and scarcely more than twenty years later, in 1413, occurred the rising led by Caboche, the butcher, in which the Bastille and the Louvre were captured by the mob and the enlightened, if ephemeral, *Ordonnance Cabochienne* was issued,

[33] Georges Lecarpentier, "La harelle, Revolte Rouennais de 1382," *Le Moyen Age,* second series, Tome VII (1903), pp. 12-32, 89-109.
[34] H. Pirenne, *Histoire de Belgique,* II, 200-12.

only to be withdrawn and the whole movement put down the next year with much bloodshed.[35]

VI. THE PEASANTS' INSURRECTION IN ENGLAND

The most famous of the risings of this period was the Peasants' Rebellion in England in 1381.[36] It has left in chronicles, court proceedings and statutes, in contemporary controversy and popular poetry, a mass of record that should enable us to learn at least in one instance the motives and objects of an insurrection of the common people. It was evident that trouble was brewing among the lower classes in England in the last quarter of the fourteenth century. In 1377 complaint was made in Parliament by both Lords and Commons that in various parts of the country the peasants "affirm them to be quit and utterly discharged of all manner of serfdom. They gather themselves together in great routs and do menace the servants of their lords, and will not suffer any distress or other judgment to be made upon them."[37]

Strange appeals were spreading through the country. We find them in rude English embedded in the Latin of the chroniclers:

"John Schep som tyme Seynt Marie prest of Yorke and now of Colchestre greteth welle Johan Nameles and Johan the Millere and Johan Cartere, and biddeth hem that thei . . . stondeth togiddir in Goddis name, and biddeth Peres Ploughman go to his werke and chastise welle Hobbe the robber and taketh with you Johan Trewman and all his felows.

Johan the Miller hath ygrownde smal, smal, smal;
The Kyngis sone of hevene shalle pay for alle."[38]

The same question was being asked in England as in Germany.

"Whanne Adam dalfe and Eve span,
Who was thanne a gentilman?"[39]

[35] M. H. Coville in Lavisse et Rambaud, *Histoire Générale*, Vol. III (Paris, 1922), chap. iii.

[36] Charles Oman, *The Great Revolt of 1381* (Oxford, 1906); André Réville, *Le Soulèvement des Travailleurs d'Angleterre en 1381* (Paris, 1898), Introduction by Charles Petit-Dutaillis.

[37] Richard II, c. 6, *Statutes of the Realm*, II, 2-3.

[38] Thomas Walsingham, *Historia Anglicana*, II, 33, Rolls Series.

[39] Henry Knighton, *Chronicon*, II, 138, Rolls Series. An old German distich ran

Als Adam hackt und Eva spann
Wer war da wol ein Edelmann?

After mass on Sundays, according to Froissart, a recreant priest named John Ball was accustomed to gather the people about him in the cloisters or the churchyards and say "Ah, ye good people, the matter goeth not well to pass in England, nor shall not do so till everything be common, and that there be no villains or gentlemen, but that we may be all united together and that the lords be no greater masters than we be. What have we deserved or why should we be thus kept in serfdom; we be all come from one father and one mother, Adam and Eve." It was the same text as that of a certain Johanes Quares who half a century before, in 1302, was put in prison in a Flemish town for declaring that "every man should possess as much as every other man." An equalitarian, almost a communistic thread ran through the popular revolts, as indeed it did through the heresies of the period. They were both rebellions of the common man against the powers of this world, economic, political and ecclesiastical.[40]

As the year 1381 came on there were not wanting actual instances of popular violence. In April the lower classes of the population of Cambridge intervened in one of the frequent conflicts between the university and the town. In May the inhabitants of two villages in Essex refused to pay their poll-tax and beat and drove out the tax collectors. Then suddenly, in June 1381, the storm broke. In various places in Kent and Essex the populace rose in riots. The Kentishmen made themselves masters of Canterbury, Maidstone and Rochester; they seized country gentlemen and their families and held them as hostages; they stopped pilgrims on the way to Canterbury[41] and made them go down on their knees and swear, "to be faithful to King Richard and his commons," never to agree to any tax except the familiar fifteenths, and "never to accept a king named John." These demands doubtless referred to the unpopular poll taxes and the much hated John of Gaunt, Duke of Lancaster, uncle of the young king, whom they suspected of planning to dethrone him.[42]

The rebels on either side of the Thames below London were at

[40] Froissart, *Chronicles* (Thomas Johnes Translation, London, 1845), chap. ccclxxxi.

[41] These might almost have been Chaucer's Canterbury pilgrims, for it was only five years later that he began putting their tales into their immortal form.

[42] Walsingham, *Historia,* I, 455; Henry Knighton, *Chronicon,* II, 131.

the same time communicating with one another by boat and agreeing on common action. As usual, leaders appeared among the rioters, Thomas Barker and Jack Straw in Essex, and in other parts of the country, Geoffrey Lister, a dyer, in Norfolk, Robert Cave, a baker, Abel Kerr, and, most influential of all, Walter or Wat Tyler in Kent. As if by common consent the various bands flocked toward London hoping ingenuously for the help and leadership of the young king. By Wednesday, June 12, the Kentishmen were gathered at Blackheath, the Essex men were massed outside of Aldgate in the east of London. The next day the people of the Hertfordshire villages and of St. Albans rose, took possession of the town, beleaguered the abbey and, leaving a guard, hurried on in a great crowd toward London. There were thus three hordes converging on the capital. From Blackheath the Kentishmen made an attempt to communicate with the king, who was at the Tower, surrounded by his ministers and courtiers. He was rowed down the river but did not land, the rioters thronging the shores, as a chronicle tells us, "shouting like thirty thousand devils." No conversation being possible, the king and his party returned to the Tower while the rioters pressed on to Southwark.[43]

By the connivance of one of the city aldermen the drawbridge had been let down and before Thursday was over the mob had swarmed across it into the city and had been joined by the rebels from the east and the north. They found abundant support from the lower classes of the capital. The "Peasants' Insurrection" is wrongly so called; it included artisans and city proletarians as well. The combined rioters burned the Savoy palace of John of Gaunt, the Temple, then, as now, the abode of lawyers, and the building of the Knights Hospitallers at Clerkenwell. They dragged the unpopular Flemings from the Vintry and from the churches where they had taken refuge, murdered several of them and chased the German merchants to their fortified Steelyard. They were not after plunder, for when one man stole a silver cup from the Savoy palace his companions threw him and his loot together back into the fire. But they had no such compunction about the wine cellars of rich citizens. Many drank themselves insensible. Old scores were

[43] Knighton, *Chronicon,* II, 131-134.

settled by the murder or beating of citizens now powerless in the hands of former servants or apprentices.

The night of Thursday was a night of terror for the city and of apprehension for the government. As the young king and his councillors in the Tower and his mother in the little Palace of the Wardrobe nearby looked out over the smouldering fires in the city and on the distant horizon; as they heard the drunken shouts of the mob, they may well have dreaded the next day. But it opened calmly enough. An appointment seems to have been made for an interview with the king at Mile End, or it may simply have been a chance meeting between him and a body of the rioters, but here they put their demands before him. The king gave the ready promise of those who do not intend to keep their word, asked the rebels to appoint some of their number to stay and receive the written grants, and bade the rest return to their homes. Many of them, especially the Essex men, seem to have done so, while clerks in the chancery were set to work to draw up charters of emancipation and pardon.[44]

In the meantime another body of rioters were taking into their own hands the punishment of the "traitors"—that is, the ministers—which the rebels had demanded at Mile End. They found the Tower unguarded, made their way in, seized the lord chancellor, Archbishop Sudbury; the lord treasurer, Robert Hales, and some lesser ministers who had not accompanied the king, took them out to Tower Hill, put them through the semblance of a trial, then beheaded them and carried their heads through the streets on poles. Friday night was a repetition of the night before, though there was no more burning. On Saturday morning some of the rebels, perhaps dissatisfied with the grants of the day before, or tempted to go further by their bloody triumph at the Tower, met the king again, this time at Smithfield, and made much more extensive demands.

What more was in the minds of the leaders we can only guess from the confessions put into their mouths by those who chronicled their later downfall—which is poor testimony. They confessed according to these, to having planned to drive out all the clergy,

[44] Thomas Walsingham, *Historia Anglicana,* I, 417.

except perhaps the mendicants; to put to death all the nobles and gentry and to seize their lands; to kill all judges, lawyers and ministers of government—a charge made probable enough by their actions—then to put the king himself to death and to set up in each county a ruler chosen from their own number.

Which, if any, of these were among their projects, the power to carry them out passed away with the sequel of the Smithfield conference. Their downfall was as rapid as had been their rise. The story familiar from the history books is taken from Froissart, who must have been there or heard of it from an eye-witness. It is clear enough and picturesque enough, though other chroniclers contradict him in some respects, and indeed contradict one another.[45] But there is no reason to doubt the main facts of the accepted narrative. The king on horseback with some courtiers, the mayor of London and other city officials rode into the open square of Smithfield, where the market now stands, while a body of the rebels under their leader Wat Tyler, riding a "little horse," pressed in from the opposite side. The rebel leader, now for the first time in the presence of the king and doubtless drunk with success and perhaps with wine, rode forward and grasped him cordially by the hand; he also called for beer to quench his thirst and in a manner unseemly in the royal presence drank and rinsed out his mouth. He is also said to have tossed a dagger from one hand to the other as if in defiance. Two or three of those around the king, resenting this familiarity, or seeking a quarrel, or resuming a previous altercation, dashed forward, dragged Tyler from his horse and stabbed him to death.

The mob did not at first, apparently, see what was going on, for a cry arose that the king was knighting their leader. When they realized that he had been assassinated, they began to draw their bows against the king and his party. Richard is said to have then ridden forward, offered himself as their leader and bade them follow him. One may doubt whether a boy of fourteen, even if endowed with the precocity and duplicity of Richard, could have so easily made his peace with a mob long out of hand. But what-

[45] *Chronicon Angliae,* by a monk of St. Albans (Rolls Series), 209; George Kriehn, "Studies in the Sources of the Social Revolt in 1381," *American Historical Review,* VII (1902), 274-85.

ever the cause, the morale of the rebels was lost. London was soon abandoned. That night proclamations were issued ordering all vagrants to return to their homes; the city gates were closed; those magistrates who had favored the rebels were arrested and later brought to trial.

In the meantime the insurrection had spread through much of the south, east and midlands of England, and even to the north and west.[46] In addition to St. Albans, rioters seized the monasteries of St. Edmunds at Bury and St. Mary's at York. Ten counties with their principal towns were for a few days in the hands of the riotous populace. Some seventy-five named places—cities, towns, villages, abbeys, castles—appear as scenes of disorders on the rolls of the courts or in other records. They were pillaged, burned or their authorities overawed while the rebels worked their will. Chief Justice Cavendish, Prior John of St. Edmunds, John of Lakenheath, Reginald of Eccles, Edmund of Walsingham and other justices of the peace were killed at one or other of their manor houses, or, as in the case of Cavendish, while trying to escape across country. The monks of St. Albans were forced to allow certain houses objectionable to the townsmen to be torn down. The stone handmills which the abbot had seized from his tenants and used to pave his parlor were taken up and restored to those who claimed them.

Above all, the rioters burned and destroyed charters and court rolls wherever they could find them, in manor house, abbey or church. These were the records of their services, rents and disabilities; if the records were destroyed the burdens might be thrown off. The lawyers who administered the estates, kept the records and enforced the requirements of law or custom fared hardly better than the documents themselves. As one chronicle says, "They punished by beheading each and all who were acquainted with the laws of the country. . . . They were eager to give old records to the flames and lest any should for the future make new ones they put all such as were able to do so to death. It was dangerous to be recognized as a clerk and such as were found with an inkhorn by

[46] A particularly good account of the rebellion in one region is Edgar Powell, *The Rising in East Anglia* (Cambridge, 1896).

their side seldom escaped their hands. . . . The memory of ancient things having been lost the lords would not in the future be able to vindicate any kind of right against them."[47]

The reaction in England was as rapid as in most other countries. The nobles, knights and gentry of the countryside, including some militant prelates, put down the local disorders and inflicted punishment with scant attention to the formalities of trial and conviction. The bishop of Norwich, absent from his diocese, when he heard of the tumults there gathered a group of his servants and hastened homeward. When he met a body of the rebels he put on helmet and armor and with his followers attacked and scattered them. Two who had been captured he ordered hung from a nearby tree, but, mindful of his priestly office, first heard their confessions and held their heads from striking the ground as they were dragged to execution.[48]

The disintegration of the rebellion at London discouraged the rioters elsewhere. The king promptly issued a series of proclamations revoking all promises and ordering all men to return to their homes and to perform their usual services. Special sessions of the courts were held in the disturbed districts; the annotations "hung" or "beheaded" that occur so frequently on the margins of the court rolls indicate the steps taken in the stamping out of the embers. When Parliament met in the autumn an act of indemnity was passed for those who had acted illegally in putting down the rising, along with some other statutes favorable to the landlords. To the king's proposal that an act for the abolition of serfdom should be passed in place of his withdrawn charters of general manumission, "they all cried out with one voice, No! No!" While the courts were slowly punishing offenders throughout the country, a general pardon—with some 300 exceptions, tailors and weavers and brewers, several clergymen, a "soothsayer" and others—was announced in Parliament. Before the close of the year the revolt of 1381 and its immediate consequences were a thing of the past.[49]

[47] Walsingham, *Historia,* I, 455; II, 9. (Rolls Series.)

[48] George Macaulay Trevelyan, *England in the Age of Wycliffe* (London, 1909), 245-6, Chapter vi of this work is a vivid account of the whole insurrection.

[49] Stubbs, *Constitutional History of England* (fourth edition, Oxford, 1896), II, 481-5; *Rotuli Parliamentorum,* III, 100-13; 5th Richard II, *Statutes,* I, chaps. vi, vii, ix; 6 Rich. II, *Statutes,* I, chaps. iii, xxix; *Statutes of the Realm,* II, 20-1.

Returning to the two interviews between king and rebels at Mile End and Smithfield, it is not their picturesqueness or their tragedy that gives them their special interest, but the fact that the rebels presented a list of demands formulated by themselves. They were the *cahiers* of a Fourth Estate. They give us our principal clue to the public desires of typical members of the lowest level of organized society. It is to be remembered that the Commons in Parliament, the Third Estate in France and similar groups in other assemblies represented at this time an aristocracy, not the mass of the people. It is only on this and a few other occasions that we can hear the common people making their own demands. They want no more serfdom; in 1381 serfdom was an antiquated system, an occasion for burdensome fines and disabilities, no longer an integral and natural part of manorial agriculture. They want no more compulsory service to employers under the Statutes of Laborers. They want to be freed from the payment of toll in local markets and to be charged no more than fourpence an acre for rent of land—perhaps a dollar an acre in modern terms—a low rent. The use of all woods should be common, and hunting and fishing should be thrown open to everyone.

There are few political claims. They want pardon for their rebellion and the release of all prisoners then in jail. They ask for the execution of fifteen "traitors," to be named by the petitioners, doubtless the ministers then in office whom they held responsible for the unpopular taxes, the lack of success in the war and the general inability or unwillingness of the government to make the lot of the common people a happier one. They want the king in future to be guided in his actions by the Commons, in their sense of the word. There are even fewer religious demands, though the two made at Smithfield—that the possessions of the church should be confiscated, and that there should be only one bishop for all England—were doubtless echoes of the Lollardy that must have been widespread among the people while Wyclif's ministry was still being exercised from Lutterworth.[50]

These were relatively clear-cut though hopeless aspirations; there were others that can perhaps be inferred from the actions or words

[50] George Kriehn, "Studies in the Sources of the Social Revolt in 1381", loc. cit.

of the rebels on other occasions or that were attributed to them by their enemies, but they were vague and doubtful. This, like all other popular revolts, represented an ebullition of social discontent rather than a definite program of popular reform. Like all the movements we have discussed it was largely a movement of release of the spirit as well as the body—a wild, angry revolt of the class at the bottom of society against suffering, injustice and monotony. These insurrections were quite different from revolutionary movements which have a relatively definite program. Revolt, insurrection, must be clearly distinguished from revolution. It is not merely the difference between failure and success. There is a more fundamental distinction. Revolt has usually arisen from despair and has almost always failed; revolutions have occurred when conditions were improving or at least when there was a trend which men of perception could recognize and guide toward the ends they desired. Revolutions have been successful, sooner or later, because they have been steps in social development; mere revolts have been hopeless struggles against fate.

Many conditions of the time doubtless served as incentives to this English rising; the new poll taxes, the bad progress of the French war, the too slow decay of serfdom, the influence of radical agitators, religious ferment. It must be remembered that in 1381 large parts of the English Bible were scattered through the country, and that much of Wyclif's teaching was subversive. But the movement of revolt was a general European, not merely an English, phenomenon; there must have been deeper and more universal causes. So we are brought back to the quest for an answer to the problem of the prevalence of popular revolts in the fourteenth century.

One answer is to be found in the unsettled nature of the period. As has been observed, a narrative of the fourteenth and fifteenth centuries is not a narrative alone of advance, but also of decline; not only were new institutions arising, but old institutions were decaying. The agricultural transformation on the manor, the breaking up of the old demesne, payments in money instead of in personal service, the substitution of competition for immemorial custom, purchase from the towns for rural needs instead of supplying them by local production, the growth of liberty, must have worked a change in the position and ideas of the peasantry none the less real because it cannot be measured by statistical means. Class divisions in the towns, the growth of the craft gilds, the segregating effect of capitalism, the pervasive influence of foreign trade, the participation of townsmen in national government, the action and reaction of royal intrusion and withdrawal, made the towns the native home of restlessness and class conflict. Feudalism was disintegrating; the church, as will be described in a later chapter, was in this century in a condition of conflict and decadence, while religion itself was a matter of deep concern. Some of the heresies of the period came especially close to the common people.

All periods are periods of change, periods of transition, if the observer looks into them closely enough, but there seems to have been something in the age of Wyclif and Hus, of the Vision of Piers Plowman, of the sermons of John Ball and his ilk, of the doctrines of social equality and of the indefensibility of private property, spreading so widely in such obscure channels, that was especially destructive of such settledness as there had been in the middle ages proper. Instability in institutions and thought was one of the main characteristics of the fourteenth century.

Secondly, the mass of the people had no organ of expression. There existed newly attained representation of the middle classes in parliaments and other national bodies—estates, cortes, diets. The desires and interests of nobles, churchmen, landowners, merchants, lawyers, citizens could be expressed in these assemblies. But in what forum could the peasant, the workingman, speak? He had no representation anywhere, in any general or local assembly. An English parliament which had recently passed the statutes of laborers, the game laws, the sumptuary laws; the prelates and lords temporal, knights, citizens and burgesses who had answered the king's proposal to emancipate the serfs with the cry "this consent we will never give, were we to die in one day,"[51] was obviously an upper and a middle class body. The people who demanded at Smithfield the abolition of serfdom, the repeal of all laws which

[51] *Rotuli Parliamentorum,* III, 100.

gave compulsory rights of service to employers or which prevented the rise of wages, which wanted a restriction of rent to a third the prevailing rate, and common rights to hunting and fishing in all woods and streams, was an entirely different class, an employed not an employing or a privileged class. The first was represented at Westminster, the second could only express itself by insurrection.

The same thing was true throughout Europe. The common man was unrepresented, therefore he rebelled. Lacking means of asking for even partial reform through the existing assemblies, the lower classes made a series of pathetic attempts to reach their vague ends by brutal, uncorrelated and futile means. Here and there some chance occasion or casual influence destroyed the already unstable equilibrium; the usual order of life was deserted, the people struck out at whatever was nearest that at all represented the objects of their dissatisfaction. They gained confidence by numbers and won success by the suddenness of their onset. A leader arose gifted with natural eloquence or with abilities suited to the immediate requirements—almost nameless, half-mythical, emerging momentarily from obscurity—some butcher or weaver or poor priest, only to fall a victim to the vacillation of his own party, or to the success of the organized powers of the time. The rising was put down, the embers were stamped out, only to flare up again in a few years, or in a different place.

Insurrections of the people continued to occur in the fifteenth and in later centuries, but in the main they took on a different character. They must be looked upon in the light of the circumstances characteristic of those periods. The special type of class rising we have been dealing with was a phenomenon of the later thirteenth, the fourteenth and the early fifteenth centuries.

Chapter Five

THE HUNDRED YEARS WAR

AN INQUIRER imbued with the scientific spirit, seeking ultimate causes and fundamental influences, may find them in the economic history of the time, but the outline picture of this period, as of so many others, must be drawn against a background of almost constant war. The later decades of the thirteenth and the earlier decades of the fourteenth century were filled with the half-feudal, half-national contests by which the rising French monarchy was striving to assert its supremacy over Flanders in the north and Gascony in the south. The English kings were at the same time trying to conquer Ireland, Wales and Scotland. Wars between Castile and Aragon and between both kingdoms and the Moors of Granada were almost constant. The Swiss cantons by successive wars with their Austrian overlords were fighting their way to freedom. Italy was several times invaded and was repeatedly torn by internal wars. In Germany there were wars of succession in the princely states and wars for the imperial crown. In the north one Scandinavian kingdom fought for supremacy over the others, to bring about or to break away from a union, or to block the advance of the Hanseatic League. The warlike activities of the Teutonic Order furnished a field for endless military adventure in Prussia, Poland and Lithuania; the bitter Hussite wars devastated Germany; the waves of Turkish invasion were breaking upon the eastern frontiers of Europe. But the most famous of all these wars was the series of English invasions of France which extended from 1338 to 1452, and which has come to be known as the Hundred Years war.

I. THE CAUSES OF THE WAR

An old French poem, *The Vows of the Heron,* attributed the outbreak of the Hundred Years war to the malign influence of a certain Count Robert of Artois. "He began the war and the terrible strife" is the theme of the poem.[1] At a court dinner at Windsor, after a hawking expedition in which Count Robert's falcon had captured a heron, "the most cowardly of birds, because it is afraid of its own shadow," the count had the heron roasted, placed on a platter and offered by a young lady to the English king and his nobles, charging them with cowardice because they were afraid to claim Edward's rightful inheritance of the crown of France and appealing to them to vow on the heron to enter France in the king's quarrel. In answer to this appeal the king declared his intention of claiming his crown and each knight vowed to do some deed of gallantry for his king and his ladylove. Robert, a disinherited claimant to the county of Artois, was an exile from France, where he had, so it was charged, murdered some of his relatives, forged documents, and, what was worse, used sorcery in seeking the death of the king. He threads in and out of the history, romance and poetry of the time and certainly exercised a fascination over the young King Edward III. He finally lost his life at Crécy, fighting on the English side, but it is unlikely that he had much to do with precipitating the war between England and France.

The causes of the Hundred Years war were more deep-seated than any personal ambitions, and, although it may be contended that no war was ever absolutely unavoidable, it would have required more wisdom and self-control than Edward III or Philip of Valois possessed to resist the progress of so nearly manifest a destiny. The war was a natural outcome of the conditions of the time. The unstable feudal equilibrium between the French and English kings, the difficult position of Scotland, sailors' disputes, the struggle for the wool market, the influence of foreign adventurers, the latent ambition of Edward III to gain the French crown, and the rising spirit of nationality all combined to bring about a more serious and prolonged conflict than any which had previously troubled the relations between England and France. The wars of Edward I and Edward II with France, so recently as 1294-1303 and 1324-27, were in the main feudal contests fought

[1] *Political Poems and Songs Relating to English History,* edited by Thomas Wright (Rolls Series), I, 1-25.

with feudal levies. The time was not then ripe, as it was a decade later, for the beginning of the long series of English national invasions of France.

The feudal relations of the two sovereigns who faced each other across the Channel were especially disturbing. In his own country the English king was a proud and independent ruler, heir to the ancient national sovereignty, to the lordship over his own vassals and to that "divinity which doth hedge a king." On his accession all men bowed before him and took their oaths of allegiance to him. In France, on the other hand, though nominally lord of a great congeries of territories—duke or count or lord—of Normandy, Anjou, Poitou, Guienne and many other provinces that had come to him by inheritance or marriage, he was for all of them vassal of another man, ruler only by sufferance, so to speak. For these dominions across the Channel he had to go on his knees and swear homage and fealty to the King of France as his feudal lord.

On the other hand, even this limited control of French territory by the English king was against the whole centralizing tendency of the French monarchy. Step by step the royal line of France, Philip Augustus, St. Louis, Philip the Bold, Philip the Fair, had transformed their feudal headship over duchies, counties, viscounties and lordships into something approaching actual sovereignty. This development was still continuing, but in the provinces held by a lord who was also a king the process met a hundred obstacles. The greatness of a vassal king was necessarily a contradiction of the spirit of strong monarchy. The kings of England clung to every feudal and financial claim; the kings of France strove to carry their policy of unification into the English-controlled south as they had into the other parts of France. Friction was engendered especially on occasions of the paying of homage. Over and over again there was dispute, and the antagonism became ever more embittered. In 1324 Edward II, summoned to France to swear allegiance to Charles IV, refused to come in person and sent his brother in his stead. The difficulty was thus postponed for a time, but in 1328 came the unavoidable crisis. A new king of France demanded the homage of Edward III, the young king of England who had never yet, although almost two years on the English throne, acknowledged his vassalage for his French lordships. Delay after delay was met by repeated messages of reminder until in May 1329 Edward, a boy of sixteen, crossed to the Continent and at a great ceremony in the cathedral of Amiens swore his fealty.

In the midst of the ceremony a difficulty presented itself. Was it simple or liege homage that was being performed? Was Edward merely agreeing to be faithful to the French king, or was he promising to fight for him against all his enemies? Was it enough that he should kneel as he was, in his armor, or must he with belt loosened, helmet and sword laid aside, place his hands between those of his lord as he swore? The lawyers of the two kings consulted, and it was only after the ceremony had been tentatively completed and after some months that the English king acknowledged that this, which was destined to be the last of such ceremonies, was full homage.[2]

More than in any earlier case this ceremony was hollow. The reason was that Edward had hidden in his bosom a strong belief that he should himself rightfully be the King of France. In the minds of all concerned, in fact, must have been the question of this possible hereditary claim. The question extended back fully ten years. The house of Hugh Capet had been fortunate for more than 300 years in having had a male heir ready for the throne as each successive occupant left it. But in 1316 the direct descent in the male line was broken. Louis X died leaving only daughters. The French peers unhesitatingly gave the crown to the late king's brother, not to his daughter. They had no mind to bring in the foreign husband of a daughter of the royal house to rule over them. The same thing happened on Philip's death in 1322. He left only a daughter and therefore his next brother, Charles, became king. When Charles in turn died, in 1328, also without a son, there was abundant precedent for excluding women from the throne. So neither a daughter of the late king, nor his sister Isabella, who was married to Edward II of England, nor yet this sister's son, Edward III of England, was accepted. Instead the crown was given to Philip of Valois, cousin of the late three kings. It was to this representative of a collateral line, Philip VI, his distant relative, that Edward in 1329 took his oath of fealty, obviously not without

[2] D. Hughes, *The Early Years of Edward III* (London, 1915).

secret reservations. "They were friends according to their outer countenance," says the chronicler. Isabella indeed had made claim for the throne for her young son when he became King of England. But the French barons were even more opposed to an English king than to a Continental ruler and paid no attention to the demand.

Later, when there was more opportunity for argument and less occasion for action, this decision of the French feudal court was generalized. An old law of the Salian Franks prohibiting the bequest of land to a woman was claimed to include the crown, and the so-called Salic Law declared that the crown of France should never descend to a woman—a famous rule still more widely extended later. All this was, for the time being, buried beneath the oath of allegiance, but none the less it was in Edward's mind, a fixed idea to be brought up later if needed.[3]

Scotland was one of the sources of contention between the two monarchs. The French king never acknowledged the English overlordship of Scotland. In the disputes concerning the succession to the throne of that troubled land the claimant who was refused the support of the English king could always count on the favor of the French. While Balliols were on the throne the Bruces were protected in France. French adventurers were always in the Scotch armies; money was loaned by the French king, or on his credit, to Scotch pretenders, and French ships carried over Scottish exiles when they were ready to return and try again for independence.

The Hundred Years war was not merely a feudal nor primarily a dynastic war. It was the first of modern national wars, a conflict in which the people as well as the monarchs were interested. Antagonism between neighbors is traditional, easy to awaken and difficult to appease. Hostility between the French and English kings had been spreading to the peoples. Between the rising trading and fishing towns on the south coast of England—Dover, Sandwich, Rye, Hastings, Portsmouth, Plymouth and others—and the line of towns on the north coast of France—Morlaix, St. Malo, Cherbourg, Harfleur, Dieppe, Boulogne and Calais—there had grown up a border warfare not unlike the conflict on the English-

[3] Rymer, *Foedera* II, ii, 765, 797, 805, 813.

Scotch border, or the raids of Christians and Moors on the frontier between Castile and Granada.

Knighton's chronicle of a series of incidents which took place during a period of strained relations between the English and French kings will give a first-hand impression of these conflicts. In 1293 two sailors from an English vessel lying in a Norman port went ashore to get fresh water. They fell into controversy with a group of Norman sailors; words led to blows, knives were drawn, one of the English sailors was killed and the other escaped with difficulty to his ship, pursued by twenty of the Frenchmen. The English ship got safely to sea, reported the incident in home ports and sought help in obtaining revenge. In the meantime the Norman vessels had followed in pursuit, and a few days afterward came up with six English ships. There was a fight, it went against the English, the French captured two of their ships, killed some of the men, threw others overboard, and hung the rest to their yardarms, "making no difference between a dog and an Englishman," as the chronicler complains. Stirred by this outrage, an English fleet was collected. Not finding any French vessels at sea, it sailed into Swyn harbor, captured and carried off six French ships, killed many in the fight and drowned others. There were reprisals and counter-reprisals. Arrangements were finally made through messages exchanged by English and French towns, and a day was set to fight it out. The English got some Irish and Hollanders to join them, while the Normans enlisted the support of other Frenchmen and Genoese. On April 4, a day of snow and hail, an all-day battle took place, and, as the English chronicler puts it, "Omnipotent God gave us the victory." After killing "many thousands," and drowning "an infinite number" in their sinking ships, the English fleet brought back many vessels loaded with booty. As this was in a time of nominal peace between the two countries the French king naturally protested and demanded repayment for losses. The English king retorted that the French were the aggressors, but agreed to confer; the dispute, however, dragged on till it was lost in the war which eventually followed.[4]

Accounts of similar incidents are spread over the pages of the

[4] Knighton, *Chronicle* (Rolls Series), I, 334-7.

contemporary chronicles. A French ship puts into Hythe unexpectedly and the crew, finding the population at their mercy, kill forty men and burn several boats in the harbor. Some French galleys run into Portsmouth, burn most of the town and sail away burdened with spoil. An English admiral during a dispute between the two kings goes on a raid down the Channel, captures 120 French ships and carries them into English harbors. The sailors of Yarmouth burn Cherbourg, gut the abbey of the Canons and carry one of the monks back with them to England for ransom.[5]

Similar atrocities and border incidents disturbed life in southern France, though barbarism was seldom so unbridled on land as at sea and was often transfigured by romance and legend. In addition there were rivalries in the wine trade of Bordeaux and the wool staple in Flanders. Nor must the ambitious, precocious personality of the young English king—a monarch at fourteen, a husband at fifteen, a commander in the field at sixteen, a father at seventeen—be lost sight of as a factor in the outbreak of the war.

II. THE EARLY ALLIANCES OF THE WAR

Edward in all probability contemplated, from the very time of his oath of allegiance, an invasion of France to settle these old disputes and to garner glory. In 1337 he was at last ready. To pit England, a small country, against France, which was much larger, more populous and more wealthy, he had to have allies. In April of 1337 he sent a deputation consisting of a bishop and two noblemen, with a train of clerks and servants, to Valenciennes, the residence of his father-in-law, Count William of Hainault. Within the next few months these envoys proceeded to weave a network of alliances between Edward and the princes, nobles and gentry of the Netherlands and the lower Rhine. There are few better means of obtaining an impression of the incoherency of political relations in the early modern period than to follow these negotiations in detail. Ranging from dukes and counts who agreed to serve with a thousand men-at-arms down to mere noblemen with a handful of followers, under agreements varying all the way from veritable treaties to mere personal promises to fight, a system of alliances

[5] Ibid., 350-2.

was built up to form a continuous eastern front stretching from the North Sea almost to Switzerland. The dukes and great counts of Brabant, Hainault, Lorraine, Holland, Gueldres and Juliers, the count palatine of the Rhine, the duke of Bavaria, an Adolf count of Monte with 100 men-at-arms, a John Quatremas with ten men-at-arms, a Robert of Terburg with thirty lances, Cray de Hofstad with four followers, Sir Henry de Graischef and Sir Arnold de Baghaim, each for himself, and a scattering of others agreed to serve the English king and did homage and fealty to his representatives, the greater ones reserving their allegiance to the Emperor.[6]

England was already entering upon that system of providing funds for impecunious but warlike Continental groups that has played so large a part in all her subsequent foreign policy. These agreements were small subsidy treaties. It was then, as it has always been, an expensive system. A regular tariff was established, fifteen gold florins a month for each man-at-arms, in addition to money needed for equipment. The subsidies went to civilians as well as to nobles and knights, and were often hard to distinguish from bribery. A canon of Cambrai, a secretary of the count of Hainault, a chamberlain of the archbishop of Cologne, all received payments as "counsellors of the king."[7] Successive sums of money were placed in the hands of the king's representatives, Parliament was induced to grant the king the value of half the year's export of wool, and a plan was agreed upon with the merchants to export this half at monopoly prices by holding back the other half. The loans Edward was forced to solicit from English, Italian, Flemish and German money-lenders have already been described. These loans laid the foundations for Edward's bankruptcy a decade later.

In July 1338 Edward himself went to the Continent, landing at Antwerp, where he confirmed all the engagements his representatives had entered into. A month later, accompanied by the queen and his little daughter Joan, now two years old, he set out on a journey up the Rhine to meet the Emperor, who had joined the

[6] E. Déprez, *Les Préliminaires de la Guerre de Cents Ans* (Paris, 1902); and the admirable study of H. S. Lucas, *The Low Countries and the Hundred Years War, 1326-1347* (Ann Arbor, 1929); J. de Sturler, "Les Relations Politiques de l'Angleterre et du Brabant, 1272-1326," *Revue Belge de Philologie et d'Histoire,* XI (1932), 627-50.

[7] Rymer, *Foedera,* II, ii, 966-8.

alliance in July on the understanding that he should supply 2,000 men at Edward's expense, and who had appointed Edward Vicar-general of the empire west of the Rhine. With striking exactitude the king followed the same route a modern tourist would take, stopping at Cologne to visit the famous shrines there and contributing a sum equivalent to about $5,000 to advance the erection of the cathedral. At Bonn he dined with the archbishop, made the rest of the journey by boat, visited the usual sights, paid the regular fees and gave tips, all of which happens to be recorded in a contemporary list of his expenses.[8]

Ultimately he reached Coblentz, where a conference with the Emperor was held amidst much festivity and in the intervals of the sittings of the Reichstag, which had been called at the same time. Edward's title as Vicar of the Emperor was confirmed, a closer treaty negotiated and an agreement made for the marriage of the little princess with the Emperor's son. The two sovereigns then parted, Edward returning to Antwerp, the Emperor to Munich, taking the little girl with him to be brought up, as it was expected, by her future parents-in-law.

So the line of the eastern frontier was closed, except for the all-important section of Flanders. Before describing its entry, it may be observed that the negotiations which Edward had been carrying on at the same time with the kings of Castile and Naples, with the count of Geneva and other princes to the south and west had been unsuccessful. The leanings of those powers were rather toward France than England.

One of the first steps in the recently arisen dispute between England and France had been the laying of an embargo on the export of wool and foodstuffs from England to France, including Flanders. Then the manufacturing towns of Flanders were as completely dependent on English wool as was Lancashire 500 years later on American cotton. When a year, even eighteen months, passed without the usual supply of raw materials and food the Flemish towns were reduced to desperation. The representatives of the English king were constantly urging them to enter into al-

[8] W. Stechele, "England und der Niederrhein bei Beginn der Regierung König Edwards III," *Westdeutsche Zeitschrift*, XXVII (1908), 91-151, 441-73.

liance with him. Their loyalty to their suzerain, the King of France, and to their count, Louis, who was largely under French influence, was finally stretched to the breaking-point, and in December 1337 a rising took place in Ghent under the lead of a rich but rather democratic merchant, Jacob van Artevelde. His policy was to offer Edward the neutrality of Flanders in the approaching war, in return for the removal of the embargo on English wool. The rising spread rapidly from Ghent to Bruges and Ypres and finally to all the towns of Flanders. Edward had for the time to content himself with Flemish neutrality. The count and the French king agreed to it rather than contemplate the complete defection of the Flemings. So the first short campaign of the war, in the autumn of 1339, was fought in eastern France by Edward with a small English army and a body of plundering allies from the Netherlands but without the military cooperation of the Flemings.[9]

But neutrality as a permanent policy was impossible. Artevelde drew closer and closer to Edward and in January 1340, at a great ceremony in the market-place at Ghent, treaties were signed by which the Flemings accepted the claims of Edward, who on this occasion assumed the title of King of France, so that the inhabitants of Flanders might avoid the charge of treason to their lord. It is said that the first official use of Edward's new arms, the lilies of France quartered with the leopards of England, was on a cloak made for this occasion by a tailor of Ghent. The King agreed to place the English staple of wool at Bruges for fifteen years, to keep a navy on the sea to protect trade between England and the Netherlands and to give a subsidy of £140,000 to the three leading cities of Flanders. As a matter of fact he did not carry out any of these stipulations, nor for that matter did the Flemings take any appreciable part in the war.[10]

Philip made no such extensive plans for defense as Edward was making for attack. He relied on the greater power, wealth and extent of his country, or was at a loss to find allies, so he watched and waited instead of actively preparing against invasion. As of

[9] Lucas, *The Low Countries and the Hundred Years War,* 188, 190, 200, 203, 257-279. On the economic side there is much of interest in the volume edited by G. Unwin, *Finance and Trade under Edward III* (Manchester, 1918).

[10] Lucas, op. cit., 339, 351, 358, 365, 385-424.

old, the French depended on Scotland to make an attack on the north when England was engaged on the Continent. There were also some negotiations for the help of a Genoese fleet and force of crossbowmen, and certain efforts were made to block the policy of England in Flanders and Spain. But in the large the attitude of the King of France, so far as external alliances were concerned, was a passive one. It is true that France was already showing that power of attraction that has always been one of her sources of apparent strength and real weakness. More than one prince, a wanderer or a fugitive from his own dominions, was at Philip's court. There were, for example, John, the old king of Bohemia, of whom it was said that "Nothing happens without God and King John," and his son Charles of Luxemburg, later the emperor Charles IV; there were James, king of Majorca and Jerusalem, Louis of Nevers, the Count of Flanders, and other princes of lesser degree. But these princes, with their gallant knight errantry and their precipitancy in battle, were to prove a burden rather than a help in the war.

As a matter of fact both sovereigns anticipated, like later antagonists in the same region, a prompt and definitive arbitrament of their dispute; that 100 years should pass by before a decision was reached was one of the ironies of fate. Edward had engaged his allies only for a few months; he expected to throw them against the king in one short and overwhelming campaign. The Emperor announced that he would go in person into France with the English king because he believed there would be a *magnum campestre bellum*, a great fight in the open field. From the confused accounts of the chroniclers it would seem that efforts were made in the early days of the war to bring the armies together for a decisive battle at some appointed place or even to have the sovereigns meet individually to settle their dispute in single combat. The course of events was absolutely the opposite. There was a year of delay before Edward actually assembled his host. Most of the carefully built structure of alliances of 1337 and 1338 fell like a house of cards. Many of his friends, including the Emperor, changed their allegiance or their policy; they either did not appear or they withdrew early in the autumn of 1339.[11] The invasion of France from the

[11] Henry Knighton, *Chronicle* (Rolls Series), II. 10; Lucas, op. cit., 330-1.

Netherlands in the autumn of 1339 and a long siege of Tournai in 1340 entailed no fighting on a large scale. Nor was any battle of importance, except that of Sluys, fought for almost a decade.

III. THE RAVAGING OF FRANCE

These early and inglorious campaigns, however, foreshadowed what was to be one of the most marked and deplorable characteristics of the war. It was to be a war of devastation. As the invaders marched through the country, villages and crops were burned, orchards cut down, farm animals seized and the people harried. On the very day of Edward's entry into France he "put to flame the whole vicinity of Cambrai and for the whole succeeding week did not cease from burning everywhere those parts." On the march he sent his troops ahead "devastating on all sides a space from twelve to fourteen leagues a day." In a campaign purely futile, so far as the objects of the war were concerned, more than 1,000 villages were destroyed.[12] At the very beginning of the war the French seamen, already hostile, landed on the southeastern coast of England and ravaged and burned as far inland as they dared go. Without the facilities for destruction of modern warfare, the ax and the torch supplied many of its deficiencies.

Mingled with devastation and inseparable from it was pillage. Some of the ravaging of the country was pure destruction; its only object, apart from the venting of anger or revenge, was the desire to sting or shock the enemy into open fight or into a willingness to come to terms. But there was much opportunity to secure plunder. There was evidently nothing to prevent either officers or common soldiers from taking whatever of value or attraction they could find in the invaded country. As a result the English troops were usually loaded with plunder on their way back from a foray. Much booty was taken back to England and this in turn built up a body of supporters of the war as a source of predatory wealth.

The chroniclers tell of a multitude of conflicts between small groups of fighting men, but these were little more than fleeting scenes against the background of pillage and destruction. Battles were almost chance interludes. There was little chivalry in the

[12] Knighton, *Chronicle,* II, 10; Lucas, op. cit., 330.

whole war. It was largely a matter of money. A king, nobles, knights and citizens were captured and held for ransom. The keenest disputes among knights and common soldiers alike were over their conflicting claims to the ransom money for those they had jointly captured. Cruelty was omnipresent. After the capture of the city of Limoges, the Black Prince, ill in his litter, lay and watched the burning of the cathedral and the town, while the townsmen were put to the sword by his orders. A few conspicuous cases of knightly generosity have given a fictitious glamour to a period from which generosity was almost completely absent. A mantle of romance and gallantry has been thrown over betrayal, cruelty and infinite destructiveness.

Through conscious policy, through habits of destruction or through love of plunder, great stretches through Artois, Brittany, Normandy and Gascony, were successively reduced to desolation. When an English army landed in Normandy in 1355, expecting to find allies and an opposing army, they did not find either. So they turned the campaign into a long-drawn-out foray in the neighboring provinces. In 1373 John of Gaunt marched southward from Calais through Artois, Picardy and Burgundy, then through Auvergne and central France and all the way to Bordeaux, devastating the country as he went. *Incendit et vastavit,* "they burned and wasted," is the ever-recurring formula of the chroniclers when giving the history of a campaign. The French themselves devastated the border provinces that had taken the English side and the rich southern regions which had remained faithful to their English feudal lords.[13]

Walled towns were immune from capture, at least during the early period of the war, because of the lack of adequate artillery, and because time could seldom be taken to starve them into submission. But undefended churches and monasteries, villages and the countryside were never spared. The piety of the time was no more

[13] Knighton, *Chronicle,* II, 478-79; J. Froissart, *Chronicle.* Including the material he borrowed from Jean le Bel, Froissart gives an account of the Hundred Years War in great detail from its beginning to 1405. His narrative can be most satisfactorily consulted in the modern translation by Thomas Johnes (two volumes, London, 1803-10 and later editions), or in the 16th Century translation by Lord Berners (reprinted, London, 1901-03), or in the original, edited by Kervyn de Lettenhove (twenty-five volumes, Brussels, 1863-77); or in the edition edited for the Société de l'Histoire de France by Siméon Luce (seven volumes, Paris, 1869-78).

adequate than its chivalry. The detailed narratives, either in the chronicles of the time or in the classic modern work of Deniflé, stagger the imagination by their unbroken records of devastation.[14] Modern warfare is certainly barbarous enough, but at least it does not call for purposeless destruction, indiscriminate violation of women, strangling of guards, cutting the throats of stragglers and stabbing helpless prisoners after a battle.

In times of truce and above all after the signature in 1360 of the treaty of Brétigny, which proved to be only a 9-year armistice that was not very scrupulously observed, there appeared the "free companies." These were bandits, organized from the English, French or mercenary troops who were discharged to save money whenever a momentary peace was made and who were left without occupation, frequently without the means of reaching home. Largely denationalized, habituated to pillage and anticipating re-engagement later, the soldiers formed themselves into bands large enough for self-protection, led by captains aggressive enough to obtain for them occupation and strong enough or popular enough to win obedience. The names of the leaders of these bands were at that time as familiar as those of nobles or other famous soldiers; they dominated whole sections of the country, levied tribute on towns, villages and churches, seized women for their wives or mistresses, clergymen for their accountants and correspondents, children for servants, goods for their needs or desires. Attempts to scatter them by diplomacy or force failed. Even when the leaders took service for their men outside France, as du Guesclin did in Spain and Hawkwood in Italy, they eventually returned. The free companies remained a problem and an affliction until a more orderly condition of society deprived them of any reason for existence.

Devastation fell on the coasts as well as the interior; there were few sea-fights, but much ravaging of the coasts and islands on both sides of the Channel. It is true that the first considerable incident of the war was a great naval battle, the sea fight off Sluys, in June 1340. The army which had invaded the northeastern districts of France in the futile 5-month campaign of the autumn of 1339 was

[14] H. Deniflé, *La Désolation des Églises, Monastères et Hopitaux de France pendant la Guerre de Cent Ans* (Paris, 1897-99).

made up largely of Edward's Netherlands allies, but these were now scattered and he had gathered at home an expeditionary force which sailed from Orwell June 22, 1340, in 200 or more vessels. The fleet appeared the next morning before Sluys. That town, the port of Bruges, named from the sluices or locks by which the river Swyn enters the sea, was the easiest place of entry into the Netherlands. In the bay of Sluys, in modern times largely silted up, Philip had ordered the assembling of all the ships available in the Norman harbors, to which he had added some hired Spanish ships and Genoese carracks. There were perhaps 200 in all, somewhat fewer than the English, under the command of three famous seamen, Quiérat, Béhuchet and the Genoese admiral Barbavera. It was said, probably with the usual exaggeration, that there were 35,000 men aboard. Originally gathered for a sudden descent on England, the fleet was now massed to prevent the landing of the English army of invasion. The scene was reminiscent of more than one historic gathering of ships in the same waters. The earlier expeditions were intended for the invasion of England. Now the English were reversing the process, and it remained to be seen whether they could force a landing on the Continent. For many hours it was doubtful. The English fleet, the king himself aboard, pressed in vain on the long line of French vessels lashed together across the harbor. Then the English, feigning retreat, made for the open sea; the French broke their line and followed. The English turned and their archers, in one of the earliest triumphs of the long-bow, drove the Frenchmen from their decks by a rapid and steady flight of arrows. Soon the antagonists were grappled ship by ship in a hand-to-hand contest. The French vessels were one after another forced to take flight or else were boarded and captured. The soldiers and sailors were killed and thrown overboard or, by the fierce custom of the day, hung from the yards. The victory was complete; unopposed the king with his army landed in Flanders the next day.

But there were few engagements of so decisive a character. In 1342 the English fleet relieved Hennebont in Brittany which was held by their allies; in 1346 they fought a battle off Cortoy which completed the blockade of Calais. Until near the end of the war the fleet managed to keep the Channel open while expedition after expedition was sent into France. It was more difficult for the English to keep in touch with southern France. One obstacle was the prevalence of southwest winds, which made it hard to weather the Breton capes. In those seas they also had to meet Spanish allies of the French. In 1350 off Winchelsea, they destroyed a Spanish merchant fleet on its way from Bruges to Spain. On the other hand in 1372 an English fleet burdened with men, horses and equipment for a campaign in the south was attacked, defeated and its commander captured by a combined French and Spanish fleet.[15]

Apart from these engagements in the Channel the harrying of the coasts was as common as the ravaging of the country. Even before the outbreak of the war there was a recrudescence of French attacks on the south coast of England. In 1337 they harassed the Channel Islands; in September and October 1338, while Edward was still engaged in knitting up his Netherlands alliances, French privateers sacked and partly burned Portsmouth and Southampton, and the next spring ships from Normandy and hired ships from Genoa attacked Dover and Folkestone, burned Hastings and ravaged the coasts of the western counties. When Edward landed in Normandy for the campaign that ended in Crécy, he took time before marching inland to devastate the shores around La Hogue, to sack the town of Barfleur and to burn French fishing boats in the harbors. In 1360, while the English army was carrying desolation up to the very walls of Paris, a French fleet made a descent on Winchester, burned the town and rivalled the brutalities that made the English land campaign of the same year notorious. The incident that marked the resumption of hostilities after the Peace of Brétigny, in 1369, was a French attack on the Isle of Wight and another burning of Portsmouth. In 1370 Rouen was used as a base for two successive French naval expeditions led by a fugitive Welsh prince to ravage the coast of Wales. The old hostility between the two sides of the Channel was given abundant opportunity for gratification during the long war. Yet whatever the injuries inflicted on the coast population, it was inland France that

[15] Walsingham, *Historia Anglicana,* I, 274-5 (Rolls Series).

suffered the worst ravages. It was only resilience—that patient clinging to the soil—the persistent energy of reconstruction so characteristic of the French people, that repaired the repeated ravages of the war and, notwithstanding their sufferings and losses, kept a numerous population alive for ultimate recuperation and for better days.

IV. THE EARLY COURSE OF THE WAR

The Hundred Years war may fairly be divided into three periods: the initial phase from its outbreak to the treaty of Calais in 1360; the long period of desultory fighting from the resumption of the war in 1369 to the invasion of Henry V in 1415, and the gain and loss of mastery by the English in the remaining thirty-seven years of the long struggle.

The two ineffective early campaigns in northeastern France had been brought to a close with a truce that was prolonged till 1345. In the meantime, however, Edward had interfered against the king in the civil war in Brittany. A contested claim to that duchy gave him an opportunity to take sides and receive the support and the fealty and homage of two successive dukes. The Breton harbors furnished convenient access to the country and the plunder of its peasantry under the name of protection gave support to a certain number of English troops and local partisans. There were countless small engagements; Brittany was long a battleground of English and French, on which soldiers got experience. Strong places were lost and recaptured, but no appreciable influence was exerted on the outcome of the war. In 1345 the sphere of operations was extended by the landing of an English army at Bordeaux and the invasion of Gascony under the Earl of Derby.

In 1346 Edward himself landed in Normandy, which had not before been touched by the war. In the course of a pillaging tour in the direction of Flanders he was headed off by the French king with an army much larger than his own. Edward was forced to take up a defensive position near the little town of Crécy. The battle, the delight of contemporary chroniclers and the pride of patriotic Englishmen, described so often and so brilliantly, can claim only a few lines in this short chapter, the object of which is rather to portray the character and point out the significance of the war than to narrate its events.[16] The choice of position and the arrangement of troops by the English king showed generalship and experience; the French king, if he planned the battle at all, was overborne by the hasty and inconsiderate bravery of the nobility and knighthood that made up the larger part of his army.

Place and time were also favorable to the English. The rising slope which the French had to storm, the sudden downpour of rain which wet the bowstrings of the Genoese crossbowmen, the level western sun on the backs of the English and in the eyes of the enemy, the weariness of the French footmen after a day's tramping, combined with the steadiness of the English and the precipitateness of the French to make the victory an overwhelming one for Edward. It was in this fighting that the Prince of Wales, the Black Prince as he came to be called, first won his reputation and seized from the helmet of the defeated king of Bohemia the three feathers that have since been the accompaniment of his title.

It was here also that the great value of the English longbow was first clearly demonstrated. Developed, apparently, in the wars of Edward I in Wales and Scotland, it rivalled in directness of aim, in range and accuracy the arbalest or crossbow, the characteristic weapon of the most famous Continental footmen; in other respects it surpassed it. The longbow was aimed from the eye with the arm drawn above the shoulder, not below, as shown for instance in the Bayeux tapestry of 300 years earlier. This gave it power and ease of aim. In rapidity of use it was far and away the best missile-throwing weapon of its day. The flight of arrows from the English bowmen fell "like snow" upon the French at Crécy, according to Froissart's somewhat inapplicable if picturesque simile. With a quiver of arrows at his side or several thrown on the ground before him, an archer could with a single movement pick up an arrow, fit it to the cord, draw it to its head, discharge it and reach or bend for another.

Compare with this simple procedure the complicated operation of the crossbow. This had to be held to the ground by means of a

[16] Monographic studies are those of J. Wrottesley, *Crécy and Calais* (London, 1898), and of J. Vicard, "La Campagne de juillet-août, 1346 et la Bataille de Crécy," *Le Moyen Age,* XXVII (1926), 1-84.

stirrup while the short thick bow was bent by turning a ratchet till the cord fitted into the cross slot. The bolt was then put in place and the weapon lifted to the shoulder for discharge. As to the relative accuracy of the two weapons there was a long controversy. The claims for both are equally incredible, and as a matter of fact the uses to which they were put in battle required but little accuracy of aim. Discharged in a shower upon an approaching body of cavalry or pikemen, the English arrows never failed to slow up the charge of horsemen or to throw an attacking body into confusion, especially when, as at Crécy, the enemy had to advance uphill. Then came the opportunity to attack; the knights swept down upon the disordered mass of their opponents or dismounted and fought at an advantage over those whose horses had been pierced by arrows and had fallen under them. At other times the bowmen, advancing in groups along with cavalry or pikemen or spearmen, by their constant discharge of arrows fatally weakened some point in the enemy's line preparatory to a charge. These tactics were employed in many smaller engagements and aboard ship in the sea-fight off Sluys.[17]

Whatever the elements of good fortune for the English and ill fortune for the French, there was much hard fighting at Crécy before the French army was dispersed, leaving great numbers of nobility and common men dead or captive. Philip fled, though only with reluctance. The news of the battle spread far and wide through Europe; the defeat of the proud French chivalry seemed incredible, and the English gained great prestige. Edward turned directly westward to undertake the siege of Calais, which continued through the subsequent winter and until the capture of the city in the spring of 1347. This was perhaps the most important incident of the war. The French inhabitants were expelled and an English population introduced. Calais remained a firm foothold of England on the continent, a military outpost, the seat of the Continental staple of English wool and the location of a mint where foreign money was recoined into English. It was a source of national pride and its loss 200 years later helped break the heart of

[17] See especially C. Oman, *The Art of War in the Middle Ages* (Oxford, 1885).

Mary Tudor and brought bitter humiliation to the proud spirit of Elizabeth.[18]

Over and over again the south was ravaged by plundering expeditions carried on at one time by the Duke of Lancaster, at another by the Black Prince, from Bordeaux, the principal city of the English possessions in the south.[19] In 1356, as the prince was returning from one of these predatory journeys, John, now King of France, threw himself in the way and forced the English to fight a battle near Portiers. It was a repetition of Crécy. The English, on the defensive, had a relatively superior position among vineyards and protected by hedges. The French with their vastly superior numbers could not resist the temptation to attack, but were hampered in their advance by the narrow passages between the hedges, by the deep mud of the freshly plowed fields and by the steady rain of arrows from the English longbows. They soon fell into confusion, and the English victory became a slaughter. The most serious consequence for the French, worse even than the capture of the king and a number of the highest nobility, was the demoralization, which was so complete that large numbers of nobles fled, thereby throwing discredit on their whole class. This discredit reacted, as we shall see, on the wavering political conditions at the time. The English, on the other hand, enriched themselves by the ransoms of these high-born captives.

Four more years of alternate truce and ravaging and a futile treaty negotiated by the imprisoned king in London but rejected at home, were necessary before exhaustion obliged the English to offer a treaty intended to conclude the war. The French accepted what was really a dictated peace. Although the English king agreed to yield his claim to the title of King of France, all the southwestern provinces, the old group of English fiefs, with some additions, were to be separated from France and handed over to the English king without fealty or homage. These terms implied the creation of a new state in Europe, a principality dependent on the English crown. In addition, a war indemnity of 3,000,000 crowns,

[18] Wrottesley, *Crécy and Calais,* 1-52, 53-57, with representations of the banners and numerous notes, reproduces two contemporary accounts. See also J. Vicard, "Le Siège de Calais," *Le Moyen Age,* XXX (1929), 129-89.

[19] See J. Moisant, *Le Prince Noir en Aquitaine* (Paris, 1894); R. P. D. Pattison, *The Black Prince* (London, 1910).

equal perhaps to $30,000,000 in modern value, was imposed upon the French and the king, two of his sons and a number of French nobles were to remain in England as hostages until it was paid.[20] This treaty, signed at Brétigny and confirmed in the autumn of 1360 at Calais, though drawn up and ratified with all formalities, proved to be but a temporary cessation of the war. The dismemberment of France was unenforceable and the war indemnity was probably beyond the power of the impoverished country to pay. In 1369 the war was resumed. A long period of alternating warfare and peace followed, the former largely unfavorable to the English, the latter scarcely profitable to the French because of the continuance of disorder and internal conflict. In 1396 a truce of twenty-eight years, equivalent to a peace of compromise, was signed, and guaranteed by the marriage of the young English king to the daughter of the King of France. It was the revolution in England in 1399 that robbed this second attempt at settlement of the war of its validity.

V. LATER STAGES OF THE WAR

Whatever may have been the inevitableness of the war in its early stages, the invasion of France by Henry V in 1415, the conquest of Normandy and the campaign that led to the battle of Agincourt in 1415 were a deliberate war of conquest, and the Treaty of Troyes of 1420 that brought the war nominally to an end for a third time was again a peace dictated by the conqueror.[21] The refusal of the dauphin and his party to accept this peace, by which he was disinherited, made the treaty ineffective and there was again an alternation of campaigns and truces. Truces played a large part in the whole war. At least temporary cessations of warfare were necessitated by the exhaustion of both combatants. By the later years of the war the devastation of the French country-side was so great that the English armies had to take over horseshoes, nails and hay for their horses. The old days when the war largely paid for itself,

[20] E. Cosneau, *Les Grands Traités de la Guerre de Cent Ans* (Paris, 1889), 30-68; E. Perroy, "Charles V et le Traité de Brétigny," *Le Moyen Age,* XXIX (1928), 255-81.

[21] On this phase see especially J. H. Wylie and W. F. Waugh, *The Reign of Henry V* (three volumes, Cambridge, 1919-1929); and Richard A. Newhall, *The English Conquest of Normandy, 1416-1424* (New Haven, 1924).

when plunder and ransom money went far to repay expenses and to ensure popularity, had passed away and each campaign necessitated a hard struggle in Parliament to obtain appropriations for equipment and equally serious sacrifices on the part of France to prepare for defense. Yet the truces, however frequent, were badly kept. Provincial struggles, the activity of the free companies, guerilla warfare, all made the nominal peace agreements almost nugatory. Nevertheless they were breathing-spells. Neither England nor France could have endured continuous warfare for three successive generations. Of the whole 112 years from the first English expedition sent across the Channel to conquer France to the last futile invasion of Gascony, some sixty-eight years were at least nominally years of peace, only forty-four were years of war.

As the war dragged on many changes revealed themselves. None was more marked in its effects than the increased use of gunpowder. The early years of the war still belonged to the period of the pike and the lance, the arbalest and the longbow, the mounted and armored knight, using spear and long sword and battle-ax. In the later days cannon and musket were asserting their dominance in modern warfare, and the use of gunpowder for undermining and battering down the walls of cities was giving an entirely new character to attack and defense. It was doubtless due largely to this development of the use of gunpowder that the concluding phase of the war was predominantly one of sieges. When Henry V renewed the war in 1415 and brought an army into Normandy, he did not enter immediately upon a pillaging campaign as Edward III had done when he landed near the same spot. Instead, Henry trained his cannon, the "Messenger" the "King's Daughter," the "London" and others, named according to the fanciful practice of the time, on the walls of Harfleur, the nearest French city. Within a month he had captured it.[22]

It is true that a few weeks later Henry was forced to fight the battle of Agincourt. It was an almost pathetic massacre of a French host which, though much superior in numbers, was so crowded, so deep in mud, so wearied by a long march and a night in the rain,

[22] Newhall, op. cit., has a particularly illuminating discussion of the change in strategy in the later phases of the war.

so ill-fed, and so inflamed with a futile bravery that left no place for caution or discipline, that it was hewn down by an English army of only about a quarter its size. The smaller numbers of the English enabled them to move freely to the attack and so to slaughter the immobile French as if they were cattle.

The battle of Agincourt, like the charge of the light brigade, was glorious, but it was not war; at least it was not characteristic of the war as it was fought by Henry V and his successors. Such pitched battles as took place were fought under the walls of beleaguered towns. A sortie from inside the walls or an effort to relieve the city from outside occasionally precipitated a battle, but marching armies seldom met. In 1416, 1417 and 1418 Henry plodded systematically across Normandy, reducing one city after another, Caen, Bayeux, Lisieux, Alençon, Falaise, Cherbourg, and finally Rouen itself, a city as large as London.

Rouen, notwithstanding the artillery brought to bear upon its walls, required a 6-month siege and great expenditure of life and money by the besiegers, to say nothing of the appalling suffering of those inside the town. The cannon of the time were seldom adequate to make an immediate breach in well built town walls, and starvation of the inhabitants by as close an investment as possible had to be resorted to as an auxiliary weapon. At the siege of Rouen the governor soon found it necessary, if the soldiers and citizens were to be fed, to expel all refugees and the poor who had no food of their own. So some 12,000 miserable souls were driven out of the gates. They were refused passage through the besieging English lines and reentry by the French garrison. So they lay cold and starving through November and December of 1418, till on the last day of the year the city succumbed to combined assault and hunger and the surviving refugees shared with the citizens in the food brought in by the captors.

Rouen was well treated after its fall, but there was seldom a surrender which did not have among its conditions the execution of some of the defenders. Henry V hanged sixteen prisoners before the gates of Montereau as a warning to the governor of the castle of the results of hopeless resistance. On the surrender of Meaux he hanged the French governor from an elm outside the city gate in retaliation for his execution of prisoners; he put to death as traitors some Scotch volunteers because their king was in the French camp, and also a trumpeter who had disrespectfully directed his blasts from the walls toward him. The same thing happened at Mélun, where two monks, a number of the garrison and some Scottish men-at-arms were hanged. A city which held out till it had to yield unconditionally was at the mercy of its captor, to be given up to plunder or ransomed according to his will. Its population was subjected to pillage, slaughter and rape if the common soldiers demanded it, or was reduced to poverty if the anger or the policy of the commander preferred to impose a crushing war indemnity upon it.

One of the developments of the long war was the production of a group of trained and veteran commanders. Members of the royal or great ducal families; nobles and commoners became soldiers of experience, some of them of great military capacity. Such were Bertrand du Guesclin and Olivier de Clisson, Sir John Chandos and Robert Knolles. These men, as responsible governors of provinces or cities, often kept order and imposed a rough military justice. But under them were the leaders of auxiliary forces—men of a different type, bastard sons of kings or dukes, self-made men who had risen from the ranks, captains of companies or guardians of castles—largely uncontrolled in their operations, who were often hard, cruel and mercenary, even toward their own people. These were called in the parlance of the time *écorcheurs*, "skinners," because they despoiled their victims, even those whom they were set to protect. Roderigo de Villandrando, Antoine de Chabannes, the Bastard of Bourbon, the Bastard d'Armagnac, La Hire, scores of others, however regular their appointment, differed little from the leaders of the free companies of the early part of the war. They and their bands of soldiers were often left without pay, due to a truce or to demoralization of the government or the death or incapacity of their superiors. They had little recourse but pillage; it is small wonder, then, that they became mere brigands, living on the land, under one banner or another or under no banner, and making the people their victims. There were few sections of France, from the valley of the Loire to the highlands of Auvergne, from Normandy to Languedoc, which did not at one time or another suffer from the companies of the *écorcheurs*. Estates of provinces met and granted money to the leaders of the bands, but the plunderers returned. The estates of Burgundy met fifteen times in ten years and appropriated 80,000 livres to the bands of soldiers in their district.[23]

There was much emigration of the common people from the most troubled districts. Population declined. Some statistics remain; the 221 parishes of the diocese of Rouen had in the thirteenth century a population of 14,992, in the fifteenth of 5,976. In 1435 Toulouse had lost just one half its inhabitants; another southern city which formerly had a population of 10,000 had but 400. After the capture and sack of Limoges only five persons were living among the ruins of the old and populous city. These figures may be doubtful, as are all early statistics, and some regions were more fortunate than others. But the contemporary statement that in the winter of 1438 wolves wandered through the half-depopulated suburbs of Paris, attacking women and children and penetrating at times into the old city itself, is well substantiated. There were few spots in France untouched by the war, during one or another of its periods.

VI. THE ADVANCE OF NATIONALISM

During the latter part of the war there were repeated manifestations of the increasing influence of that intangible but powerful force which in its higher forms we call patriotism, in its lower a more or less narrow nationalism. The English in their endeavor to conquer France were not only attacking a larger and more populous country, but were struggling against a current of increasing strength, the French sentiment of national separateness and unity. Neither the French nor the English, probably, were aware of the growth, perhaps not of the existence of this force, but it was nevertheless a potent one. There are many evidences of it. One is the successive defection of England's French allies.[24] The early foreign alliances proved to be of no value. Except for the assistance given France by the Castilian navy and a certain amount of diversion

[23] A. Tuetey, *Les Écorcheurs sous Charles VII* (two volumes, Montbéliard, 1874).

[24] Cf. especially the interesting essay of G. Grosjean, *Le Sentiment National dans la Guerre de Cent Ans* (Paris, 1927).

from the side of Scotland, the war was fought between the French king and his native supporters on the one side and the English king and those French princes who took his side on the other. These French adherents of the English king ultimately left him, drawn away by the attraction of their own nationality. Four of them—Brittany, Normandy, Aquitaine, Burgundy, their princes or the influential classes of their people—were at one time or another effective supporters of the English king. One after another they were lost to his cause. If the steps by which these defections took place should be traced it will be seen that in each case an assertion of nationalism was the fundamental cause.

VII. JOAN OF ARC

But the real surge of national feeling must be sought not so much among rulers and among the great, as among the middle and even the lower classes, the permanent reservoir of primitive emotions. It was the peasant girl, Joan of Arc, who represented most fully and awakened most effectively the passion of patriotism in fifteenth century France. The story is a familiar one.[25] On the 6th of March, 1429, a young girl presented herself at the court of the dauphin in Chinon, declaring that she was sent by the King of Heaven to free Orleans, long under siege by the English, to take the dauphin to be crowned as his fathers had been at Rheims and to drive the English out of France. The court of the dauphin was an inhospitable place for the reception of such a message. It was a gathering of defeatist nobles and demoralized soldiery around a *fainéant* prince. Charles had been called King of France by his adherents since the death of his father in 1422, but had done little to make that title a reality.[26] "King of Bourges" he was called in derision by the English party. He seemed satisfied to loiter away his time in that city or in passing from one of his chateaux to another in the Loire country which almost alone remained in his obedience. He was supported by a phantom government while the English captured one province after another and

[25] The literature on Joan of Arc is far too voluminous to be analyzed here but will be treated in the Bibliography.

[26] See Gaston Dodu, "Le Roi de Bourges," *Revue Historique*, CLIX (1928), 38-78.

finally besieged Orleans, the only remaining military barrier of independent France.

After some opposition Joan was allowed to deliver her message to the dauphin in person. She may even then have awakened in him some credence. Sent to the kitchen, her simple and unquestioning faith in her mission soon found acceptance among the servants, and spread higher and higher till it captured the imagination of some of the younger nobles and men of war—La Hire, Dunois, the duc d'Alençon and others. She was sent to Poitiers to be examined by the bishop for any indication of sorcery, and on her return was able to rouse the dauphin to some degree of activity. He ordered the preparation of a body of troops and its despatch under some old officers to the relief of Orleans. Joan, to her great delight, was allowed to go along, provided with a horse, a man's armor and a banner on which she had her motto inscribed, "Jhesus Maria." She did not know how to read or write, but in accordance with her belief in her mission she dictated letters to the English regent and other leaders commanding them in the name of the King of Heaven to abandon the cities they had captured, to leave the government of the country to its true rulers, and to withdraw with their troops and followers from France.

Arrived before Orleans she was able, with a little party, to enter the city from the river side, for the place had never been completely invested. Among the garrison and the inhabitants of the city she revived the spirit of confidence which led to a series of successful sorties by the French, the capture of several of the English bastions, and after three days to the abandonment by the English of their 7-month siege. The "Maid of Orleans" Joan of Arc has been called ever since.[27]

Two or three unwonted victories for the French in the open field followed. Joan then returned to Chinon and urged the reluctant dauphin to make the journey to Rheims to be crowned. The opposition of many of the nobles, jealous of her leadership or incredulous of success, and Charles' own indolence and indecision held him back, but the will of Joan and the activity of the forward

[27] See H. Barande, *Orléans et Jeanne d'Arc; Étude Critique et Stratégique du Siège d'Orléans* (Paris, 1910).

party ultimately gained the ascendency. On June 29, 1429, little more than three months after the Maid's appearance at court, Charles, accompanied by an army of 12,000 men, set out over the 250 miles of the Orleanais and Champagne to the old royal coronation city. En route one city after another, Troyes, Sens, Chalons, opened their gates, while the English-Burgundian garrisons withdrew. Other towns far to the north, Compiègne, Laon, sent offers to receive them, and on the 17th of July the dauphin was formally crowned as Charles VII, King of France, in the cathedral at Rheims.

Once they were again in the Loire country king and court sank back into apathy. Joan was given permission, but no support, for an advance on Paris. She suffered the bitterness of her first defeat and received a slight wound in an unsuccessful attempt upon the walls, and thereupon returned to the south to be cured and to pass a restless winter of inaction. Compiègne, so often captured and recaptured, was now being held by the French against the assaults of a Burgundian force, and in March Joan with a small body of troops slipped away from the court, gained entrance to Compiègne and joined the garrison in a sortie against the besiegers. By some mischance she failed to get back with the other troops when the gates were shut on their return, was seized in the mêlée by a Burgundian soldier, and came eventually as a prisoner into the hands of the Duke of Burgundy. There were a dozen possibilities by which the King of France could have obtained her release; ransom—all prisoners were objects of repurchase in those days; a threat of retaliation upon English and Burgundian prisoners; a resumption of negotiations for peace with Joan as a pawn. All these methods were available, but Charles made no move and Joan was soon betrayed, for a price, to the English, carried to Rouen and thrown into prison.

The report of the English regent that "a disciple and leme of the fende called the Pucelle used fals enchantements and sorcerie" measured the English fear of her influence and established the English tradition that lasted to the time of Shakespeare. It was to the English party a necessity of war that she should be removed and her prestige destroyed. This was the work of the ecclesiastical court which was appointed for her trial at Rouen under the presidency of the Bishop of Beauvais. For more than ten weeks in forty sessions of this court—sometimes there were two a day, sitting three hours at a time—this ignorant girl was questioned, scolded, threatened, led into what were intended to be verbal or logical traps. Of no other trial of the fifteenth century have we a report approaching this in detail and accuracy. The record gives the questions put to her and her replies to them. They are remarkably direct and full, not infrequently touched with the native shrewdness of the French peasant, occasionally resentful of repetition or of the incredulity of her hearers.[28] There emerges from the record the story of a sensitive child, raised in simple piety, for whom the saints were as real as the people she saw around her, and who saw St. Catherine, St. Michael and other saints just as they were represented by their images in the parish church. As she grew to adolescence the stories she heard of the ravages of the English in her country became part of her general conception of warfare of the powers of evil.

What set her apart from other young girls—she grieved over it in her testimony—was the intense conviction of her personal mission—the voices of the saints told her she must herself go to the aid of the dauphin. He had been appointed by God to rule France and it was her duty to see that he was placed upon the throne. It was this impulsion that brought her reluctantly and after overcoming a long series of obstacles to Chinon, to Orleans, to Rheims, to Rouen. The expulsion of the English, the rescue of France from her enemies, was also part of her mission and of her strength. It was her pure and vivid patriotism that gave her power. She embodied the growing conception of a single, united France, free under her king from foreign occupation or interference. It was this mission that made her an important factor in the political history of the time.

The trial at Rouen could end in but one way. She was in the hands of those who could not afford not to destroy her. A moment of weakness on Joan's part gave them the opportunity. Wearied, frightened by threats of torture and tempted by hopes of release, abandoned, as she thought, by her "voices," she broke down, declared herself an impostor, confessed that her voices had been

[28] The trial may be conveniently followed in P. Champion, *Procès de Condemnation de Jeanne d'Arc; texte, traduction et notes* (two volumes, Paris, 1920-1921).

feigned and threw herself on the mercy of the court. Sentenced to perpetual imprisonment, returned to a cell and subjected to neglect and insult, she regained her courage, withdrew her confession and sought peace in the reassertion of her guiding voices and the reality of her mission. This was her end. She was summoned again before her judges, declared a relapsed heretic and a sorceress, and on the 30th of May, 1431, she was burned at the stake in the market-place in Rouen.

The exclamation of the English soldier, "God forgive us; we have burned a saint," was formally justified 375 years later when St. Joan was canonized in a great ceremony at Rome. Only ten years after her execution, however, the belated recognition by Charles VII of the greatness of her services, the rising patriotism of France and the breach between England and Burgundy opened the way for a review of her sentence. A new court was appointed, this time at Paris and in the hands of the French king; the testimony was reviewed, the conclusion of the earlier court reversed and the Maid declared innocent.

There may seem to be no sufficient excuse for giving so much space to the life of this peasant girl in a brief chapter on the Hundred Years war. But so seldom has the historian such abundant and trustworthy material for his narrative, especially for a narrative of devotion to a high and unselfish cause; so few are the spotless characters in history that he may be excused for dwelling on the personality of Joan of Arc for its own sake. But, as has been more than once intimated, her career has a deeper and wider significance. It is one of the earliest and best indications of what is more and more impressed upon the student in the study of this period. It is in this time that we find imbedded the roots of one of the most powerful of the forces, whether good or bad, that were to influence all modern history, the sense of nationality, the response of peoples to the appeal of patriotism, the united support by the whole people of a centralized government.

VIII. THE CLOSE OF THE WAR

The twenty years of the war that ensued after the brief career of Joan of Arc cannot easily be reduced to simplicity or unity. A gathering of the representatives of the English, the French, the Burgundians and some outside powers at Arras in 1435 failed to bring the war to a close. Successive efforts and long negotiations for peace took place from time to time, but the English delegates were unwilling that their king should surrender the title of king of France, and Charles was now strong enough to refuse peace without that promise. Some 10,000 English soldiers were scattered as garrisons through those parts of France still under English control, but they could seldom be reinforced and were not strong enough for any advance. France was sufficiently well-armed and sufficiently unified to make such expeditions as England was likely to make against her almost sure to fail. Nor was the spirit of England or her rulers still warlike. Economic and moral forces were working in other directions. England's commerce was being taken over by Englishmen in the place of foreigners. The leaders of public opinion and the controllers of policy to England were less warlike, more interested in this growing commerce. There were even stirrings of an intellectual opposition to war and an interest in the new learning. The war continued, then, because no means presented themselves of bringing it to an end. An occasional capture and sack of a town or a minor success or defeat in an open battle, a few reinforcements or a languid campaign simply served to keep the war alive. In 1449 the French definitely took the field to expel the invaders. The cities of Normandy were captured one after another till the English retained nothing in the north except Calais. In the south, in the same year, many places were taken by the French. Bayonne became French and Bordeaux was captured, though soon again recaptured. In 1453 a desperate battle was fought when the English troops from Bordeaux tried to relieve what was almost their last foothold, the town of Castillon, from an attacking French army well provided with artillery. The French were victorious and the English commander, the Earl of Shrewsbury, an old and able soldier, was killed in the engagement. Castillon and soon afterward Bordeaux itself fell; no further expeditions were sent, and without any treaty or settlement beyond the withdrawal of the English troops, the war came to an end.

The Hundred Years war was in more than a material sense a

war of destruction. The transfer of allegiances, the breakdown of loyalties, the changes in military science went far to destroy feudalism as a form of political organization. The haunting medieval conception of a united Europe, a single Christendom, did not survive the bitter antagonism of the early modern wars, of which this was the most extended. The belief of the English king and people that they could conquer France or annex some part of the European continent was disproved by experience. The English never afterwards did more than try to retain, or, when lost, to regain in Calais a foothold in France. Their adventurous spirit when it later reasserted itself took the form of renewed efforts to complete the subjugation of Ireland, to send out trading voyages, to make conquests and settlements in America and the Far East, but never again did they enter upon a war of conquest on the Continent.

On the other hand the Hundred Years war introduced much that was new; the use of gunpowder, already adverted to; new devices and increased amounts of taxation; the strengthening of representative bodies as a result of the constant demand for funds for the war or for defense against invasion; greater English familiarity with the Continent. The spirit of nationality, hardly perceptible at the beginning of this period, took form, as has been observed, gained strength and became of great influence by the time of its close. This change has already been noted in connection with the economic history of the period. It will play its part in the political and religious history still to be narrated, but in none has it appeared or will it appear more clearly than in the incidents of the Hundred Years war.

Chapter Six

THE DECLINE OF THE CHURCH: THE WEAKENING OF THE PAPACY

THE medieval church was a body of men and women set apart by ordination or vows from the rest of the community. When King John in the first article of the Great Charter promised that "the English church shall be free and shall hold its rights entire and its liberties uninjured," he went on to explain that this freedom consisted in its members being undisturbed in electing to its offices. The English church, that is to say, was a certain body of men who were promised by the king the privilege of keeping their organization free from royal interference. So it was elsewhere. Some thousands, perhaps some hundreds of thousands, of men and women in the various countries of Europe, of different degrees of ordination and under various rules, holding ecclesiastical offices and performing ecclesiastical duties of the most diverse description—bishops and canons, priests and deacons, chaplains, vicars, curates, monks, friars and nuns, notaries and university students—were separated from the rest of the world by their membership in a definite and recognized organization, the church.[1]

This membership not only separated them from laymen but bound them together. The church had for many centuries been highly institutionalized and, like all institutions, devoted much of its attention, perhaps the greater part of its attention, to keeping its organization intact, to the preservation of its immunities, the increase of its power, the extension of its functions and the maintenance of the uniformity of its doctrine. Its members, therefore, were much occupied with adopting rules and exercising discipline within their own body, attending meetings of various groups of

[1] There are, of course, other definitions of the church, more mystical or more modern; but it is important for purposes of historical discussion to have clearly in mind the contemporary conception of the medieval church as a definite group of persons.

churchmen, settling internal disputes, holding elections or making appointments, and gaining for themselves or others promotion within the church.

Quite as absorbing as the problem of preserving its character as an institution was the church's devotion to securing the income and administering the endowments that supported its members and enabled it to carry out its objects. A very considerable part of the land in the various countries of Europe was in the possession of the church, whose income and expenditure were both very large. Many of its members received fees, salaries or payments of various kinds. All this income, from the tithes of the parish priest to the feudal dues of the bishops, the rents of the monasteries and the taxation, annates and judicial fees of the popes,[2] had to be administered and frequently had to be extorted from unwilling debtors. The administration of its funds required so much attention from churchmen that it troubled deeply the thought and conscience of many of the best men in the church. The collection and expenditure of income was the subject of much criticism both inside and outside the organization. The church of course had religious duties and fulfilled religious functions, but these were on the whole a minor part of its activity. An analysis of ecclesiastical correspondence and official records, as the student finds them in the thirteenth, fourteenth and fifteenth centuries, shows far the greatest part of the time and attention of churchmen devoted to matters of finance and organization.

It is with the loss of power of this organized church that we have to deal. It is a study in the history of an institution, not of religion. In the middle of the thirteenth century this mighty structure, although beaten upon by many storms, still stood practically unshaken. Its dominion over the minds of men, its means of obtaining obedience, its recognition by the state, were all so great that it seemed all-powerful in its wide sphere. But the events of the 200 years with which we are engaged wrought a profound change. Its foundations were sapped, its fabric was weakened, it was subjected to new and adverse forces both from within and from with-

[2] W. E. Lunt, "The Financial System of the Medieval Papacy," *Quarterly Journal of Economics,* XXIII (1909), 251-95.

out. By the middle of the fifteenth century it was an organization relatively impotent, awaiting the dismemberment and spoliation of the Reformation and the rejuvenation by the Counter-reformation that came a generation later.

I. THE CONFLICT BETWEEN POPE BONIFACE VIII AND THE KINGS OF FRANCE AND ENGLAND, 1294-1303

Notwithstanding the extension of the church through all middle and western Europe, as an institution it was highly centralized. All its members, secular and regular, looked to the pope, the bishop of Rome, the successor of Peter, the vicar of Christ on earth, as their head. The loss of power and prestige by the pope, and the weakening of the authority of the church itself were processes which, though by no means identical, were closely connected. The change in the pope's position became evident first. The old struggle for preëminence between emperor and pope was already largely past. Frederick II, the last emperor to enter into a serious contest for supremacy, died in the year in which our period opens, 1250. Even though successive emperors, Henry VII, Lewis of Bavaria, Charles IV, still went to Rome to be crowned, they did so rather to strengthen their power and prestige as rulers in Germany and in Italy than either to acknowledge or to defy the popes as European over-lords in either the temporal or spiritual fields.[3]

But as the thirteenth century progressed and the fourteenth opened, a challenge was issued to the pope which he could not fail to recognize as a more serious danger to his authority than the antiquated and at best tenuous claims of the emperor. This was the rising power of the national monarchies, backed by the support of the newly enfranchised middle classes. The centralized power of the king that was fast destroying the independence of the nobles was not likely to spare the wealth or respect the privileges of the clergy if it found them a serious obstacle to its policy or saw an opportunity to use their resources for royal needs or ambitions.

An attack was made upon the immunities of the church at al-

[3] A number of well-chosen extracts and translations from works on the subjects dealt with in this chapter are given in J. F. Scott, Albert Hyma and Arthur H. Noyes, *Readings in Medieval History* (New York, 1933), 512-54.

most exactly the same time by the kings of England and France, politically speaking, the two most advanced countries of Europe. They were both strong kings, Edward I and Philip the Fair. Nor was it an unassertive opponent with whom they had to deal. Benedetto Gaetano, who ascended the papal throne as Boniface VIII in 1294, was a vigorous Italian priest. He had occupied many official positions in the church and held the highest views of the papal powers. The conflict was precipitated in each country by an attempt of the king to tax the property of the church.[4] In the "Model Parliament" of 1295 it was only with reluctance that the English clergy made the grant demanded of them for the Scotch war, and in a parliament at Bury the next year they refused to make a payment unless the pope were asked for and gave his consent. Earlier grants to the crown had been made by the clergy, it is true, but only for semi-religious objects, to finance a crusade or to reimburse the king for losses suffered through the exile of the Jews. This new demand was for general purposes.

The same claim was made in France. In 1294 Philip the Fair obtained from the French clergy the payment of a tithe for the prosecution of his war against the English, and in 1296 he sought the renewal of the tax. Some of the clergy protested and appealed to the pope to support them in a refusal. Boniface gave his support by issuing the bull *clericis laicos*, which declared it unlawful, under pain of excommunication, for lay governments to tax church property and forbade clergymen to pay such impositions without papal consent. This bull was published in France in the midsummer of 1296, in England in January 1297. Both sovereigns took up the gauntlet. Edward immediately demanded from the clergy a tax of a fifth of the income from their temporal property. When at their convocation in 1297 they failed to grant it, he ordered the judges to refuse all protection to clergymen, and instructed the sheriffs to

[4] The classical work on this controversy is Pierre Dupuy, *Histoire du Différend entre le Pape Boniface VIII et Philippe le Bel, Roi de France*, with many documents (Paris, 1655). It is strongly royalist. Almost the whole of vol. XVIII of H. K. Mann, *Lives of the Popes in the Middle Ages* (London, 1906-1932) is devoted to Boniface VIII. A judicious account of this dispute, still valid, notwithstanding its age, is to be found in E. Boutaric, *La France sous Philippe le Bel* (Paris, 1851), 88-118. Jean Rivière in *Le Problème de l'Église et de l'État au Temps de Philippe le Bel* (Louvain, 1926), devotes himself exclusively to the doctrinal side, giving a good discussion of the arguments of both parties and of contemporary controversial writing.

seize and hold the church lands. Philip forbade the export of money from France, thus cutting off from the papacy much of its regular revenue. Both countries had the same problem. Edward succeeded in solving it, as will appear, by firm but somewhat indirect methods. The King of France entered into a direct contest.

A rain of bulls fell from Rome. *Ausculta fili,* "Listen, my son," addressed directly to Philip, enumerated his ill-doings and repeated the familiar claims of the papacy. *Super Petri solio* threatened the king with excommunication and released his subjects from their allegiance. *Salvator mundi* withdrew all previous papal grants and favors from the king. *Ante promotionem* ordered all French prelates to come to Rome to attend a council for the preservation of the liberties of the church.[5] A war of pamphlets broke out. The flood of writing to which every crisis in the church and many in political and economic life and in the philosophic world now gave rise was a premonition, or perhaps an early stage, of the Renaissance.[6]

At the jubilee of 1300 the pope, in the midst of brilliant ceremonies and before the 200,000 pilgrims who are said to have visited the Eternal City in that year, reaffirmed his supremacy in Christendom and exalted his demands upon kings. But all these high-sounding words echoed against a firm wall of national resistance. The English king demanded and received from the clergy as individuals, without papal sanction, payments of heavier taxes than those they had by papal command refused as a body. In France the clergy, assembled in convocation by order of the king, acknowledged that in time of national danger they must contribute to the national expenses and the pope himself found it wise to make this concession.

The contest, however, still went on. Charges of tyranny, betrayal,

[5] The custom of referring to papal letters and decrees by the first two or three words of their Latin text is a familiar one. Translations of *clericis laicos* and some other bulls are to be found in R. G. D. Laffan, *Select Documents of European History, 800-1492* (New York, 1930), 114-416; J. H. Robinson, *Readings in European History* (Boston, 1904), 488-90, and elsewhere.

[6] Rivière, op. cit., and R. W. and A. J. Carlyle, *A History of Medieval Political Theory in the West*, V (London, 1928), chaps. ix, x, go over the polemical material in some detail. See also W. I. Brandt, "Pierre Dubois, Medieval or Modern?" *American Historical Review*, XXXV (1929-1930), 507-21, and C. H. McIlwain, *The Growth of Political Thought in the West from the Greeks to the End of the Middle Ages* (New York, 1922), 236 ff.

perjury and even of heresy were made to and fro. "Mother church which was wont of old to rule her children is now reduced to bondage, nay, trampled under foot," complains one ecclesiastic. New claims were advanced on both sides. In 1302 Philip called the Estates General and obtained from them a unanimous vote of support in his dispute with the pope. In April 1303 the pope issued a final bull declaring that, unless by the 8th of the succeeding September Philip should withdraw his opposition, amend his ways and yield to discipline, he would be excommunicated and all France laid under an interdict. There was little probability that such a threat would be carried out, but it precipitated the end.

In the contest the pope had been pressed further and further into a position of ineffective scolding and now he was subjected to actual violence. The way was prepared by a declaration by the king of the illegality of the election of Boniface to the papacy and an appeal to a general council of the church to provide for the election of a new pope. This move was intended not only to depose and humiliate Boniface, but to invalidate all the bulls which he had directed against the king. The prosecution of the pope was directed by William of Nogaret, a learned lawyer, a trusted minister of the king, but a man of violent spirit. Before an assembly at the Louvre in June 1303 he brought formal charges against Boniface not only of illegitimacy of election, but of simony, immorality, violence, irreligion and heresy, and obtained authority from that court to seize the pope in order to bring him before the proposed council.[7]

Boniface was then with his cardinals at the little town of Anagni, his native place, seeking refuge from the heat of Rome on the slopes of the Apennines. On the 7th of September, the day before that set for laying the interdict on France, Nogaret appeared at the gates of Anagni accompanied by a few hundred soldiers, drawn partly from the pope's enemies at Rome, partly from a neighboring rival town. The captain of Anagni had been bribed to admit the conspirators and within a few hours the houses of the cardinals had been sacked, the papal treasury looted and Boniface himself seized, rudely treated and made a prisoner. He was eighty-six

[7] R. Holtzmann, *Wilhelm von Nogaret* (Freiburg, 1898); R. Scholz, "Zur Beurtheilung Bonifaz VIII und seines Charakters," *Historische Vierteljahrschrift*, IX (1906), 476-515.

years old, vigorous, dignified and a noteworthy representative of his high office. But although his captors found it impossible to carry him to France, as they had probably intended, and the populace both of Anagni and Rome rose and forced his release, his return to Rome left him nothing but humiliation and depression. On October 11, 1303, he died, leaving the usual charges of poison and tales of a deserted and despairing death-bed with surrounding portents.[8] The papacy and the kingship had come to grips, each embodied in a vigorous champion, and the latter had won. Never again were such high claims made by or for a pope and never afterward was there any doubt that such a struggle against an independent king would be futile. Indeed the conflict of Philip with Clement V concerning the Templars which followed a few years later led to a similar humiliation of the pope who, notwithstanding his resistance, was forced to bend to the will of the king.[9]

II. THE AVIGNON RESIDENCE OF THE POPES, 1305-1378

Rising financial claims of the papacy and the increasing resistance to them on the part of the temporal rulers were both connected with the pope's adoption of Avignon as a place of residence. The "Babylonian captivity," as churchmen called it, lasted from 1305 to 1378. Clement V, who became pope in 1305, was a native of Aquitaine, a Frenchman, even though a subject of the king of England. He was at the time of his election Bishop of Lyons, where he received the notice of his elevation and where he was consecrated. He never found opportunity to take up his residence in Rome or even to visit the city with which the fortunes of the popes had been for so many centuries connected. Nor did his six successors through seventy years. This absence from Rome was not at first, or scarcely indeed at any time, a deliberate policy. John XXII, who was elected in 1313, planned to return to Rome, as did Benedict XII on his election in 1334, but each successive pope was

[8] There is still much difference of opinion as to whether Boniface was physically maltreated. P. Fedele: "Per la Storia dell' attentato di Anagni," *Bolletino dell' Istituto Storico Italiano,* XLI (1921) believes that he was; Walther Holtzmann: "Zum Attentat von Anagni," *Festschrift für Albert Brachmann,* Weimar, 1931, 492-503, holds the opposite view.

[9] Henry C. Lea, *History of the Inquisition in the Middle Ages* (three volumes, New York, 1888), III, 238-329; on the much-vexed question of the Templars see now E. J. Martin, *The Trial of the Templars* (London, 1928).

a French prelate and the college of cardinals remained predominantly French. Rome was a distant, decayed and turbulent city, the policy of the kings of France favored the retention of the popes within their sphere of influence and a papal capital was soon built up at Avignon, more free from disorder and far more comfortable than Rome itself.[10] Clement V, anticipating an early establishment in Rome, while he lived at Avignon, occupied with his court only a few rooms in the buildings of the Dominicans. John XXII, however, was before his election Bishop of Avignon, and as pope continued to occupy and to extend the episcopal buildings. Benedict XII bought for the bishop a new dwelling, and he and his successor, Clement VI, rebuilt the old episcopal residence into the great palace of the popes as it continued to be occupied by the next three pontiffs and much as it remains to the present time. The city of Avignon itself became a papal possession when the heiress of Provence granted it for a money consideration to Clement VI in 1348.[11]

Here the vast organization of the central government of the church was concentrated. It was evidently the moral force, not the numbers, the material wealth or the activity of the church that was suffering a decline. At no time was its missionary and its diplomatic activity, its increase in centralized power and in money income more rapid than in the period during which the papal court was situated at Avignon. It was a ceremonious and brilliant court, the most distinguished in Europe. A vast number of chamberlains, officials of all kinds, councillors, chaplains, domestic servants, diplomatic representatives, visitors and messengers thronged the palace, claimed the attention and struggled for the favors that flowed from the pope. He was, moreover, frequently surrounded by members of his family, by personal friends and dependents who had served him from the time before his election to his high office. His court was a personal as well as an official establishment.

[10] Moreover, in the preceding half century the pope had seldom spent much time in Rome. G. Mollat, *Les Papes d'Avignon, 1305-1378* (fifth edition, Paris, 1924), xi-xiv. This small work gives an excellent general account of the papacy during this period. Elisabeth Kraack, *Rom oder Avignon?* (Marburg, 1929) makes a thorough scholarly analysis of the causes and beginnings of the Avignon captivity.

[11] See L. H. Labande, *Le Palais des Papes et les Monuments d'Avignon au XIVe Siècle* (Marseilles, 1925) and R. Brun, *Avignon au Temps des Papes* (Paris, 1928).

An extensive financial, judicial and administrative machine carried on the work of the great corporation, the church. The papal chancery prepared and sent out thousands of letters in the name of the pope or of established branches of his government; suits on appeal reached Avignon from all the lower courts of the church throughout Christendom; appointments were made within all the national churches; directions were given to missionaries, inquisitors, legates and special commissioners; heresies were reported and discussed and measures taken for their extirpation.

In addition to the papal court were the establishments of the cardinals. Between twenty and thirty of these great princes of the church spent most of their time at Avignon, each having a palace or dwelling of his own, each surrounded with a group of officials, servitors and often relatives and friends, and each sharing in the work of central administration of the church as well as looking after his own ecclesiastical and personal property and attending to such duties as were assigned by the pope.

In all this life and activity there was little that was new or peculiar to Avignon. It was simply a heightened and intensified development of what had existed in Rome from the thirteenth, even from the twelfth century. It was a period of secular interests and luxurious living. It was not a life conducive to piety nor to spiritual elevation, nor in many cases even to a decent morality.[12] It was "the sinful city of Avignon," referred to in a resolution of the English Parliament already quoted. It was the life of Avignon that Petrarch lashes in his letters, calling it Babylon. The poet's life was practically coterminous with the period of the captivity and much of it was spent at Avignon. His descriptions are doubtless exaggerated—they are the words of a satirist—but there is much sober testimony to justify them. "Here reign the successors of the poor fishermen of Galilee: they have strangely forgotten their origin." "Babylon, the home of all vices and all misery. . . . I know by experience that there is no piety, no charity, no faith, no reverence, no fear of God, nothing holy, nothing just, nothing sacred." "All you have ever heard or read of perfidy, of deceptions,

[12] E. Müntz, "L'Argent et le Luxe à la Cour Pontificale d'Avignon," *Revue des Questions Historiques*, LXVI (1899), 5-44, 378-406.

of hardness, of pride, of shamelessness and unrestrained debauch; in a word all examples of impiety and evil manners which the world has to show you, you can find collected here." "One loses here all good things, first liberty, then successively repose, happiness, hope, faith, charity."[13]

Whether corrupt or only worldly, the papal court at Avignon was expensive. All those devices which had been invented in the preceding century for increasing the income of the central government of the church—papal levies on the income of benefices, on national churches in any way under papal control, annates, tenths, procurations and a score of other forms of payment—were extended, diversified, made regular and imposed upon local church officers and bodies by successive papal orders. A system of papal collectors was established throughout Europe and payments were required from holders of local benefices, from bishops and canons, abbots and priors, archdeacons and chaplains, holders of judicial offices in the churches and of positions created by papal grant in universities and charitable institutions.[14] These impositions bore especially upon the monastic orders, so much more closely dependent upon the pope than were the secular clergy. All these dues, besides the taxes demanded and the gifts requested from time to time, were collected as described in an earlier chapter by papal officials in the far ends of Europe. Payments were made in kind or in local money, and transmitted through the services of the Italian bankers to the papal court at Avignon.[15]

This papal harvest was gleaned largely from new fields of profit. The old claim of the papacy to fill vacancies in local churches when the incumbents died at the papal court or on their way to or from it, was in this period extended on one plea or another to a practice of nominating to almost all positions where there was anything unusual in the form of appointment or in the relations of the appointee to the pope. The claim was carried further by grants of papal "reservations" and "provisions," that is to say, prior

[13] *Epistolae sine Titulo,* 5, 14, 17, 18.

[14] See C. Samaran and G. Mollat, *La Fiscalité Pontificale en France au XIVe Siècle* (Paris, 1905). There were twenty-three collectors scattered through the thirteen archbishoprics of France alone.

[15] See, e.g., J. P. Kirsch, *Die päpstlichen Kollektorien in Deutschland während des 14ten Jahrhunderts* (Paderborn, 1894).

rights to election or appointment to certain church positions to become operative immediately after the death of the existing incumbent. These might apply to any country and might be at the expense of any patron or his appointees. Men traveled to Rome or Avignon from all countries hoping to obtain such "provisions." The pope, like other generous but straitened masters, was glad of the opportunity to reward his servants at the expense of endowments often in distant countries and intended for very different uses.[16]

III. ANTI-PAPAL LEGISLATION

It was not likely that in a time of growing national self-assertion these somewhat sordid encroachments of the general church upon the local churches would fail to arouse opposition, however overmastering the financial or political needs of the papacy. Long before the height of the Avignon period, in a convocation of the French clergy at Paris in 1283, in a German church assembly at Würzburg in 1287, at the Spanish cortes of Zamora in 1301, and at the parliament of Carlisle in England in 1307, remonstrances were made in varying forms against the papal grants of provisions, the diversion of monastic funds from their proper uses, the appointment of foreigners to native benefices, the harsh exaction of first-fruits, and the newly devised papal levies and the undue extension of ecclesiastical jurisdiction.

But it was not till the middle of the fourteenth century, when the intrusion of the papacy in the field of appointments had gone much farther, when the loss of wealth by its transfer abroad had become serious to national treasuries and when the court of Avignon had lost much of the prestige that belonged to Rome, that the full force of national opposition showed itself. The prominence of England in this opposition was doubtless due to her entrance in 1338 into the war with France. When a French pope was wearing the tiara, living in a city on the very borders of France, surrounded by French cardinals and presumably largely under the control of the French king, it seemed intolerable that he should make appoint-

[16] The financial system of the Avignonese popes is well described in A. C. Flick, *Decline of the Mediaeval Church* (two volumes, London, 1930), I, chaps. iv and v. On provisions see G. Mollat, *La Collation des Bénéfices Ecclésiastiques sous les Papes d'Avignon* (Paris, 1921); A. Clergiac, *La Curie et les Bénéfices Consistoriaux* (Paris, 1911).

ments to English church positions, part of the income of which was intended for his treasury.[17]

A provision by which such an appointment was made, as has been explained, was a document given to a cleric by the pope, stating that the pope had reserved to himself the appointment of a successor to the present incumbent of a certain benefice and naming the holder of the provision as that appointee. The death of the incumbent was the signal for the production of the pope's provision, and the installation of the appointee would naturally follow. Such provisions were usually for deanships or canonries at a cathedral, sometimes for a judicial position or for a large parish, sometimes even for a bishopric or abbey. In the former cases it deprived some patron, lay or ecclesiastical, of the right of appointment, in the latter it infringed upon the cathedral chapter's right of election. Sometimes the pope simply gave to the applicant a mandate to a certain bishop requiring the latter to give to the person named the next available appointment, leaving it to the bishop to find him a place.

The practise increased with the pressure for funds at the papal court. The English records are filled with such documents. In the diocese of Salisbury in 1326, the dean, precentor, treasurer, two archdeacons and twenty-three holders of prebends had been nominated by the pope, and there were eight known holders of provisions awaiting vacancies. Pope Clement VI, who ruled from 1342 to 1352, during the early years of the Hundred Years war, was especially lavish in such grants. With ill-judged levity some one in 1349 drove an ass into the presence of the pope and cardinals at Avignon with a petition hanging around his neck asking that he also be given a bishopric.[18]

In England opposition began in earnest in 1343. In the parliament of that year a strong remonstrance was drawn up by the nobles and commons and put in the hands of one of the judges,

[17] After the English victory at Poitiers a distich was circulated:

> "Now the Pope has become French and Jesus has become English,
> You have seen which is greater, the Pope or Jesus."

[18] W. W. Capes, *The English Church in the Fourteenth and Fifteenth Centuries* (London, 1900), 85-7; see further A. Deeley, "Papal Provisions and Royal Rights of Patronage in the early XIVth century," *English Historical Review*, XLIII (1928), 4[illegible]-527.

Sir John Shoreditch, to be taken to Avignon and presented to the pope and cardinals in person. He was received with scant courtesy. When the pope challenged his complaints he said "Holy Father, you gave the deanery of York to Cardinal Talleyrand of Périgord whom we all consider a deadly enemy of our king and of his realm." After some further altercation Shoreditch left the papal city suddenly, apparently in fear of his life. In the same year the king issued an ordinance prohibiting English clerics from seeking such provisions.

Complaints were made in almost every parliament. In 1346 the Commons urged that benefices granted to foreigners should be taken into the king's hands and the possessions of foreign priories confiscated. In 1351 they charged that cases in the king's courts were appealed to the higher church courts outside of England and decided in favor of the pope's appointees. In 1376 in "a bill against the pope and the cardinals" they complained bitterly that the papal collector was living like a prince in London, with an army of clerks engaged in sending great sums of money out of England to a court consisting of cardinals almost to a man Frenchmen and enemies of England, yet drawing their incomes in many cases from English benefices. They charged alien priests, monks and nuns with taking treasure abroad and betraying secrets to England's enemies.

They made high claim to the independence of England. The action of the pope they declared was "to the open disherison of the same crown and destruction of the regalty of our lord the king . . . the crown of England hath been so free at all times that it hath no earthly sovereign . . . nor should it be submitted to the pope, and the laws and statutes of the realm by him defeated and avoided at his will. . . . Wherefore all the liege Commons of the same realm will stand with our said lord the king and his said crown and regalty in all points to live and die." The lords temporal adopted the same expressions, and, with some reservations, the lords spiritual agreed.

The result of these complaints and petitions to the king was the passage of half a score of laws known as the Statutes of Provisors and Praemunire, the earliest in 1351, the latest in 1393. Their object was to make all papal appointments in England invalid and to limit to its narrowest bounds the exercise of papal jurisdiction and administrative action in England.[19]

Other questions of the limits of papal rights came up. The old payment of a certain sum in acknowledgement of the feudal dependence of England and Ireland on the pope, dating from John's time, being in arrears, was claimed in 1365, but positively refused by a joint vote of the three estates in Parliament. In 1374 when the pope demanded a subsidy on feudal grounds for a war with the Florentines, an assembly of lords temporal and spiritual at London unanimously refused the demand.

The pope, on the other hand, threatened excommunication and from time to time sent messengers and scolding letters to England. As far as he was able he disregarded this hostile legislation. In 1374 a conference was called at Bruges to smooth out friction, but nothing was accomplished, although the conference was memorable for bringing John Wyclif, sent as a representative of the king, on the scene for the first time. The dispute was renewed with much bitterness under Pope Martin V between 1415 and 1420, but parliament refused to repeal the Statutes of Provisors, as he requested.[20]

The heat of these disputes, the popular hostility to churchmen in various countries and the dissensions presently to be described might lead the reader to expect a great breach in the fabric of the church, such as occurred later. But the strong restraining influence of custom and the many countervailing tendencies of the time must be constantly borne in mind. In England one of the influences favoring continued unity was the policy of the king. The assertion of nationalism at this time was largely parliamentary and popular. The king shared in it far enough to enact the nationalistic legislation demanded by Parliament, and Edward III, Richard II and their Lancastrian successors used it for their military ends. Per-

[19] The principal statutes, in addition to the king's proclamations of 1343 and 1349, are 35 Edward I; 25 Edward III, Stat. 4; 25 Edward III, Stat. 5, c. 22; 27 Edward III, c. 1; 38 Edward III, Stat. 2; 3 Richard II, c. 3; 7 Richard II, c. 12; 12 Richard II, c. 15; and 16 Richard II, c. 5. The expressions quoted in the text are from the last of these statutes.

[20] Capes, *The English Church in the Fourteenth and Fifteenth Centuries,* 85-100, 169-75.

haps they were themselves affected by patriotic sentiment. On the other hand they steadily weakened the force of the laws against papal appointments by seeking the help of the pope in placing their own nominees in ecclesiastical office. Nothwithstanding the law, English bishops and many other churchmen owed their position to the connivance of the king with the pope in breaking it. Clement V in the first years of his reign made twenty provisions in England and John XXII in his first three years gave 351. In addition to the cases already mentioned the volumes of "Papal Relations" with England are loaded with applications for such favors, their grant and the payments made for them. This tide continued to flow between England and Avignon, and then Rome, till it was cut off by the Reformation. The shocking traffic carried on by Wolsey was simply the culmination of a custom that dated back to the fourteenth century.[21]

It was the same with other countries; more reservations and expectancies were given in France than in any other country. For the Empire we have scattered statistics, such as the twenty-six papal provisions granted in the archbishoprics of Cologne and Trier by Clement VI in his first year and the forty-one given in three churches of Strassburg between 1324 and 1330. Thousands of such papal appointments must have been made in the various national churches during this period of extension of financial claims. In the Vatican Library there are still twenty-two huge manuscript volumes containing petitions and letters concerning appointments.[22]

Legislation to limit or prevent this papal intrusion is therefore to be found in other countries than England. The whole spirit of the determinations at the meeting of the German electors at Rense in July 1338 and at the diet at Frankfort in August of the same year was one of self assertion of the German church as well as of the state and insistence on the retention of all its privileges. There was legislation in both France and Spain to forbid papal appointments in those countries. The pragmatic sanctions of Bourges and Mainz which completed this series of nationalistic efforts, adopted in 1438 and 1439, were only the culmination of a long struggle.

[21] *Great Tudors,* edited by Katherine Garvin, (London, 1934), 73-80.
[22] A. C. Flick, *The Decline of the Medieval Church,* I, 120.

IV. THE GREAT SCHISM, 1378-1415

In the meantime the popes had returned to Rome. Notwithstanding the dignified ease and the secular grandeur of their captivity, they had continued to look upon their establishment abroad as temporary. The poverty, the turbulence, the crudity of Rome contrasted harshly, it is true, with the peace, good order, comfort and luxury of Avignon, but after all it was Rome, the episcopal seat of Peter himself, the inheritor of the tradition of the ancient and the medieval empire. Dante had deprecated their original departure from Italy and Petrarch with his last breath pleaded for their return. Certain saintly women, St. Brigitta of Sweden, who visited Rome in the Jubilee year of 1350, and St. Catherine of Siena, who visited Avignon in 1376, pleaded with the pope to abandon France and return to Italy. Repeated delegations of citizens and clergy from Rome came to urge his return.[23]

There were also more material reasons. United opposition to the pope's temporal rule in Italy, a distant echo of that nationalism so prevalent in Europe at the time, was showing itself. The "good state" of Rienzi was a Roman rather than a papal conception. In 1375, under the lead of the Republic of Florence and of Bernabo Visconti of Milan a league of eighty or more cities, including Genoa, Pisa, Bologna, Perugia and Ferrara, the last three in the States of the Church, was formed to oppose the activity of the French "barbarians" sent by the pope to administer his territories and collect his Italian revenues. Although this rebellion was put down, it required 10,000 Breton "free companions" from France under the militant cardinal, Robert of Geneva, and a series of excommunications, interdicts and plunderings to accomplish it. It might well be that if the pope were himself in Italy disorder would be restrained, and prosperity restored to the old city of emperors and popes. The poverty and ruin of Rome were a scandal to Christendom. Lacking the papal court and the concourse of officials, diplomats, visitors and pilgrims, the ancient city had become a second-rate Italian town, the roofs of many of its churches fallen in,

[23] E. von Seckendorff, *Die Kirchenpolitische Tätigkeit der Heiligen Katherina von Siena unter Papst Gregor XI* (Berlin, 1917).

sheep pasturing on the grass that grew around the altars of St. Peter and the Lateran.[24]

Nor was Avignon itself so secure as in the past. The banditti that threatened its walls, the discharged soldiers of the truces of the Hundred Years war, have already been referred to as a constant danger. Between 1360 and 1370 the companies swayed to and fro between France and Spain and at any time they might again overawe Avignon as they had in 1361 and again under Duguesclin in 1365.

The first attempt at a return to the old capital was made by Urban V in 1367.[25] A man of piety, holding high views of the duties and powers of his office, he recognized the strength of the Roman appeal and overrode the opposition of the French cardinals who surrounded him. He took ship at Marseilles accompanied by a fleet of sixty vessels provided by Italian cities, partly for protection and partly as a matter of honor, and in October he established himself in the Vatican. Mass was celebrated by a pope at the high altar of St. Peter for the first time in more than sixty years. But the confusions and difficulties in Italy were too great and the appeals of the French cardinals too strong for Urban's determination, and in 1370 he returned to Avignon. His death immediately afterward was considered by the Italians a punishment for his desertion.

A second attempt was hardly more fortunate. The successor of Urban, Gregory XI, scion of a noble French family, a scholar and a man long engaged in the diplomatic and administrative work of the church, was impressed with the need of transferring the papal capital to Rome. When he was elected at Avignon in 1370 he announced his intention of returning to Italy and in 1374 he wrote to the Emperor asking for his protection on the journey. In October 1376, with even more éclat than Urban, he sailed with a great entourage from Marseilles to Corneto and then made his way to Rome. The whole expedition cost something like $300,000 in modern value.

This was nominally the end of the papal absence from Rome;

[24] Ludwig Pastor, *Geschichte der Päpste*, (second edition, Freiburg, 1891), I, 59-65.

[25] The return to Rome has been studied by J. P. Kirsch, *Die Rückkehr der Päpste Urban V und Gregor XI von Avignon nach Rom* (Paderborn, 1898), and by L. Mirot, *La Politique Pontificale et le Retour du Saint-Siège à Rome en 1376* (Paris, 1899).

practically it was the beginning of a period of still greater confusion. A troubled year followed, and a proposed return to Avignon was precluded only by Gregory's death in March, 1378. When the conclave of cardinals met in the Vatican in April the clamor of the populace outside demanding the choice of an Italian pope, and the rift inside between Italian, Provençal and French cardinals, with their various interests, ambitions and rivalries, led to a hasty and ill-considered choice. The new pope was a Neapolitan, the Archbishop of Bari, not well known to the cardinals but considered a compromise candidate. He took the name of Urban VI. He was a man of sixty, learned in the canon law and ready to enforce obedience to it, rough in his manners and determined to utilize the absolute powers traditionally belonging to him as the earthly representative of Christ. Disputes immediately broke out between him and the cardinals. He reproved their way of life openly in consistory, cut off some of their sources of income and threatened to create a large number of new Italian cardinals. The cardinals soon repented of their choice and planned a change of masters.[26]

Slipping away from Rome, one by one, they gathered at Fondi just across the border in the kingdom of Naples, announced that the election of Urban was void because of the intrusion and threats of force of the Roman mob, called on him to resign and, when he refused, issued a manifesto declaring the papal throne vacant. They proceeded to elect as pope one of their own number, Robert, Cardinal of Geneva, a Frenchman, young, highborn, already known as a soldier-priest. He took the name of Clement VII. After a short and ineffective campaign for the capture of Rome, which would have given him at least ecclesiastical control of Italy, he returned with the cardinals to Avignon, where the old papal offices were reëstablished. He was acknowledged with enthusiasm by his relative the King of France and soon afterward by the sovereigns and countries in alliance with France—Aragon, Castile, Navarre, Sardinia, Sicily, Scotland and some parts of Germany. Clement VII was thus able to hold in his obedience and to rule from Avignon,

[26] M. Creighton, *A History of the Papacy during the Period of the Reformation* (Boston, 1882), 48-50, 55-64. The first volume of this work, notwithstanding the title, covers the period of these paragraphs, 1378-1418.

so far as the power of the church was concerned, the greater and richer part of Europe.[27]

But Rome also was the seat of a papacy. Urban refused to accept his deposition, created twenty-nine new cardinals, mostly Italians, and announced the deposition and excommunication of those who claimed to have deposed him. He was supported by the remaining states of Europe, England, Flanders, the northern kingdoms and most of Germany. Thus arose the Great Schism, the official split in the church, which endured for fifty years, threatened to subordinate the head of the church to his prelates and as a matter of fact went far to complete the subjection of the church as a whole to the control of the lay rulers of Europe.

On the death of Urban in 1389 his new-made cardinals, relying on their appointment by a regularly chosen pope, proceeded to elect a successor, Boniface IX, and carried on the line by electing successively Innocent VII and Gregory XII.

The same thing happened at Avignon. Clement died five years later and the cardinals who had elected him chose as his successor a Spaniard, Pedro de Lima, who became Benedict XIII. Thus the two lines, one at Rome the other at Avignon, were established, like two rival dynasties, the representative of each line claiming to be the legitimate ruler of the whole church.[28]

At the beginning of the schism each claimant tried to make good his position by military force, either directly by troops hired at his own expense and under his own control, or by using the arms of some princely adherent. "Crusades" were declared from time to time in the interest of either line. These warlike efforts were futile. Spiritual weapons were as ineffective as temporal. Each pope directed against his rival formal, verbose and abusive bulls of deposition and condemnation. Boniface at Rome excommunicated the pope at Avignon and was in turn excommunicated by him, and this occurred again on the death of Boniface and the election of his successor. The arguments of scholars were as divided and as inept as in the struggle between Boniface and Philip the

[27] Louis Salembier, *Le Grand Schisme d'Occident* (fifth edition, Paris, 1921), presents a viewpoint favorable to the Roman popes, while Noël Valois, *La France et le Grand Schisme d'Occident* (four volumes, Paris, 1896-1902), gives the Avignonese side. Valois' book is now the outstanding treatment of the whole subject.

[28] Creighton, *The Papacy during the Reformation*, I, Book i. "The Great Schism."

Fair or in the controversy concerning the Spiritual Franciscans. Books, essays, sermons and resolutions of offense and defense issued from the universities and from the studies of learned men, more voluminous and scarcely less vituperative than those emanating from the two papal chanceries. The rival popes and their adherents were, however, in the main dependent for their support on the decisions of temporal rulers, and these were made entirely on the lines of temporal policy. The church, though with much expostulation, traveled the road marked out for it by the state. The clergy in each country, and through them the laity, had relations only with the pope whose title was approved by the government; the Clementine group were the countries under the influence of France, the Urbanists were the rest of Europe.

In the meantime the division of Christendom, or at least of the western church, into two hostile and mutually abusive factions was a scandal, and the church itself was fast losing the respect of the laity. The fundamental strength of the church as a claimant to authority over the religious life of the people lay in its unity, as a single organization supposed to have been established by Christ and his apostles. But no such unity and therefore no such authority now existed. "No man can serve two masters." Moreover, many of the abuses of the church were intensified by the double headship. Two papal courts, two colleges of cardinals, two groups of ecclesiastical judges and two sets of officers of papal administration were a heavy load for the people of Europe to support, when even one, whether at Rome or Avignon, had in earlier times required financial pressure approaching extortion. The warlike expeditions directed by each pope against the other were supported by heavy taxes or by the dubious practice of selling indulgences. It was by no means a matter of chance that the rapid spread of the Lollard heresy in England and its inception in Bohemia fell in the midst of the great schism. The crusade of the Bishop of Norwich in Flanders in 1383 in support of Pope Urban, and the intervention of the pope in his own interest in the civil war in Naples, with their accompanying pressure for funds, were occasions for concern to many pious souls, as the sale of indulgences had always been.

Finally, the old traditions of lavish expenditure still prevailed, especially at Avignon, where Clement VII and his successor held a princely court that required the use of every possible source of income, even the most questionable. The court of Rome if less brilliant was not less greedy of money, equally generous in the grant of reversions and provisions and even more reckless in the issue of indulgences. An English cleric after long service at the pope's court declared "At Rome everything is bought and sold, so that benefices are given not for desert but to the highest bidder; whence every man who had wealth . . . kept his money in the merchant's bank to further his advancement. . . . As therefore under the old dispensation, when the priests were corrupted with venality, miracles ceased, so I fear it will come to pass, under the new dispensation; and methinks the danger standeth daily knocking at the very doors of the church."[29]

At Avignon it was certainly no better; "The virtues of our ancestors are quite neglected, boundless avarice and blind ambition have invaded the heart of churchmen. 'Freely give for freely ye have received' is now most vilely perverted. 'Freely I have not received, nor will I freely give, for I bought my bishopric for a great price and must indemnify myself for my unprofitable outlay.' "[30] Even orthodox churchmen were revolted at a pope pronouncing excommunication when he was himself under excommunication; carrying on war and political intrigue; living a life of irregular morals in a corrupt, self-indulgent court, and at the same time claiming to speak authoritatively in the name of Christ. Men inclined to heresy went further in opposition. It was during the first decade of the schism, while Urban was ruling at Rome and Clement at Avignon that Wyclif wrote those essays in which he denied the divine authority and the practical value for religion of the whole papal and hierarchical system of the church.

Heretics might look with a certain equanimity on a split in the church which exposed its corruption and weakened its authority; but all others, layman and ecclesiastic, scholar and political ruler, even the rival popes themselves, deplored the schism as a source

[29] Adam of Usk, *Chronicon,* (second edition, London, 1904), 196. The chronicler was a Welsh ecclesiastical lawyer writing about 1415.

[30] H. von der Hardt, *Magnum Oecumenicum Constantiense Concilium* (Frankfurt, 1700), I, 104, quoting Nicholas of Clémanges and Dietrich Vries, contemporary churchmen.

of much evil. The church was too closely interwoven with the political, economic and religious life of the time, too strong in its privileges and duties as a national body, and too important as the only international organization in existence, to show evidences of dismemberment and decay without creating general dismay. Efforts to heal the breach were therefore constantly made.[31] At first the respective popes tried to bring about unity, each by deposing his opponent, or by the prohibition of the election of a successor to his rival on that rival's death. Claims to legitimacy and the opposition of the two colleges of cardinals prevented the success of this plan. Then negotiations were undertaken by each in the hope of inducing his rival to resign, but again without result, although each offered to give his rival, if he should abdicate, high power and position and great influence at the papal court.

The schism had already endured thirty years when the fourth pope in the Roman series, Gregory XII, succeeded so far as to obtain an engagement from the second Avignon pope, Benedict XIII, to come to a personal conference, with the expectation that they might both abdicate and leave the way open for the election of a single successor. But although they came as near as Savona and Lucca, only fifty miles apart, small difficulties intervened and the meeting never took place.

It was obvious that the cardinals could, if they would, solve the problem. Each group agreed more than once, before they entered into conclave, that the one elected pope should make every effort, even to the extent of abdication, to bring about unity in the papacy. Once elected, however, ambition or the tradition of the office or, it may be, a sense of duty or responsibility induced a Gregory or an Innocent or a Benedict to enter upon the office and to continue to assert his right of occupancy of it even at the cost of a continuance of the schism.

V. THE PERIOD OF COUNCILS, 1409-1449

The solution finally came from the general acceptance, at least for a generation, of an old and frequently asserted and as frequently

[31] G. J. Jordan, *The Inner History of the Great Schism* (London, 1930), studies the various methods advanced and used to overcome the crisis and reëstablish unity in the church.

controverted claim of the superiority of an assembled council of the whole church over the elected head. It was an age of assemblages. Parliaments in England, meetings of the estates, general and local, in France and Spain, and of Diets and Landtagen in Germany became a regular procedure. Provincial, diocesan and other synods of the church were frequently convoked. Councils of the monastic orders were held regularly. The kings of France and England and the Emperor called frequent councils of princes and higher clergy, in addition to the meetings of the estates. There were gatherings of lawyers, of merchants, of the Commons without the Lords. Leagues of cities, like the Hanse of Germany and the *hermandades* of Spain, were held together by frequent representative gatherings. It would have been strange if the great schism had not given occasion for an assembly of the church to consider the situation.

The way was prepared by France. Weary of the schism, offended by the election of a Spanish pope at Avignon, and guided by liberal leaders of the University of Paris, a council of all the higher clergy of France met in 1395 and urged the newly elected pope to resign. Nothing having been accomplished, three years later the King of France called an assembly of eleven French archbishops and sixty bishops, who proceeded to withdraw their allegiance and the financial support of the French church from the pope at Avignon, Benedict XIII. This action was alternately supported and opposed by the crown, but the French church proceeded to organize itself on national lines and in partial independence from papal rule. This reorganization, known as "Gallicanism," was completed at a council of the French church in 1407. Somewhat similar action was taken at about the same time in Bohemia and Hungary. The church was in danger of breaking up; at any rate the lines of division among the nations were being drawn much deeper. Benedict issued a bull of excommunication against the French bishops, but this was burned. He then left Avignon for Perpignan on the Spanish border, while the church in France remained largely independent.

In 1408 the majority of the cardinals of both groups, abandoning the respective popes, met and issued a call for a general council of the church to meet the next year at Pisa, under the protection of the Republic of Florence. The summons was widely welcomed. Reformers dissatisfied with the worldly life of churchmen and with the manifold abuses in the church, evils which had proved too strong for the power of individual popes, bishops and heads of orders, had long since appealed for a council. It was hoped that it would bring about "the reform of the church in head and members," an expression first used as early as 1330 by William Durand, Bishop of Mende, in his book *General Councils and the Reformation of the Church.*

An organic union with the Greek church, at that time threatened by the advancing Turks, might also be obtained by securing their appearance at a general council. Men of learning charged with heresy had appealed to a general council against papal and local ecclesiastical judgments. Above all it was only through a council, apparently, that the great schism could be healed. As a means to this end it had been urged at one time or another by almost all powers concerned, even by the rival popes themselves, though they might afterward have recoiled from its implications. Treatises were written and circulated which almost uniformly advocated the assembly of a council. In some of these writings the supremacy of the pope was rudely assailed. It was argued that the cardinals as well as the popes were responsible for the welfare of the church and that if the pope failed to call a council when needed the cardinals might do so.

This theory, when developed, became the familiar parliamentary doctrine applied to the church.[32] Obedience might be withdrawn from a wicked and recalcitrant pope; the pope, since he had been elected by the cardinals, might be deposed by them; the pope's power existed only in so far as he represented the universal church; he might therefore err like other men, and might, like other men, be judged. This view, defended then and later by certain theologians and church lawyers, especially by doctors of the University of Paris, conceived of the church not as an essentially absolute monarchy, but rather as a continuing body whose interests must be conserved no matter what the cost to its head. The responsibility for its preser-

[32] One of the best analyses of this conciliar theory is that of J. N. Figgis, *Studies in Political Thought from Gerson to Grotius, 1414-1625* (second edition, Cambridge, 1916), but see also the very penetrating study of Johannes Haller, *Papsttum und Kirchenreform* (Berlin, 1903), and McIlwain, *Growth of Political Thought,* 346ff.

vation lay, in default of a united or sufficiently wise papacy, with the cardinals, the princes of the church. This reserve of power in the hands of the church itself, with the authority of a general council in the background, was the "conciliar theory." It would have made the church an oligarchy. It was not out of line with the prevalent tendency toward limited monarchy, though it failed of universal acceptance then and was not destined to be the ultimate ideal of the church.

There had been no council since that of Vienne in 1312, where the dissolution of the Templars had been so inadequately achieved. The summons to Pisa in 1409 was to begin a new series which characterized the next quarter of a century, the "conciliar period," as it is called in church history. Contemporaneous with the assembly at Pisa small rival councils were called at Perpignan in Spain by Benedict and in Venetia by Gregory. The council at Pisa was followed by the great world council at Constance, which dragged on from November 1414 to April 1418. Reunions of it took place at Pavia and Siena in 1423 and 1424, and the series of councils was continued by a meeting at Basel which began in opposition to the pope in 1431 and ended in rebellion against him in 1443. A council of the rebellious party then met at Lausanne while the obedient elements met successively at Ferrara, Florence and Rome. The movement did not die out until 1449. The colorful record of these councils we must, in the interests of space, deny ourselves here.[33] No royal court nor feudal assemblies, no meeting, diplomatic, academic or civil, or ecclesiastical gathering within the boundaries of one nation could compete with these international councils in interest, in attendance, in splendor, in intrigue and in dramatic action.

The procession which made its way into the cathedral at Pisa for the opening of the council in 1409 included some twenty-two cardinals and fourteen archbishops; sixty-nine bishops, priors, grandmasters and generals of monastic and crusading orders; more than a hundred representatives of absent prelates; ambassadors of the Emperor, kings and princes; delegates from all the learned institutions of Europe, and a great number of individuals distinguished in

[33] The great standard treatment of the councils is C. J. von Hefele, *Conciliengeschichte,* best used in the enlarged French translation of H. Leclerq, *Histoire des Conciles* (eight volumes, Paris, 1907-1921).

learning, in the law and in diplomacy. It was said that the council drew more than 9,000 strangers to Pisa.

The two popes, both of whom had protested against the assembly, were summoned by their personal names to come before the council. When they failed to appear, they were declared deposed because of their contumacy. The cardinals present proceeded to elect one of their own number, who took the name of Alexander V. But neither Benedict nor Gregory accepted the act of deposition, and both obtained enough temporal support to continue nominal courts, Benedict's at Perpignan and later at Peniscola in Spain, Gregory's in a distant part of the old States of the Church. The pope elected by the Pisan cardinals established himself at Rome.

Even a council therefore had failed to heal the schism. On the death of Alexander the next year the cardinals at Pisa, still unable to obtain the resignation of Benedict or Gregory, proceeded to elect another pope, John XXIII, a man unfortunately of low morals and mediocre abilities, capable only of guaranteeing military protection to the council. Few of its other objects were attained, though various abuses in the church were discussed. Nor were any reforms accomplished by the council which Pope John, in accordance with the arrangements made at Pisa, though against his own desires, called at Rome in 1412.

VI. THE COUNCIL OF CONSTANCE TO THE ELECTION OF MARTIN V, 1414-1417

The most promising attempt at solving the church problem through a council was initiated, as were so many of the ecclesiastical movements of the time, by a temporal ruler, the Emperor Sigismund, who exercised pressure upon Pope John to convoke a meeting somewhere outside of Italy. This greatest of all the councils of the period met at Constance in November 1414.[34] It was given distinction by the attendance of both the pope and the emperor. The two or three thousand participants, cardinals and other prelates, noblemen, representatives of governments, religious orders and universities and distinguished individuals, surrounded, it was said, by a

[34] J. H. Wylie, *The Council of Constance to the Death of John Hus* (London, 1900); A. Main, *The Emperor Sigismund* (Oxford, 1903).

hundred thousand of their followers—clerks, merchants, minstrels, soldiers, prostitutes and beggars—swamped the little German city and the surrounding country. They set themselves at once to the threefold task for which the council was called. The leaders hoped to attain church unity, to define and stamp out heresy and, the best of them, to reform the church itself. With the first of these objects all lay and most church elements were in accord; the schism had accentuated national conflicts, increased the expenses of governments and people, debased the coin of religion. With respect to the second point, so persistent was the dread of heresy, so great the dominion of the church over the minds of men, that lay delegates might be expected to adopt and carry out whatever conclusions the ecclesiastics might reach. As for the third, the reform of the church "in head and members," it was universally accepted as desirable, but the great difficulty was to keep up to their task those whose interests and established position in the world would necessarily suffer from reform.

At Constance the pope was in the hands of stronger powers, clerical and lay, than his own; and these powers had determined upon the deposition of all three claimants in order to place a single pope on the throne. With John they had a comparatively easy task. He was perhaps the worst of all the popes. His character and recorded actions made him defenseless. Under the theory already accepted at Pisa, he was, in May 1415, deposed from the papacy by decree of the council on grounds of heresy, schism and wickedness as pope and priest and man. Confronted with his record of personal vices and crime, and faced with the judgment of the council agreed to by the cardinals, John accepted his sentence, announced his surrender of the papacy, promised never to resume its powers, gave up his seal and drew off his fisherman's ring. He was kept a prisoner in a nearby castle for some years, then bought his release, returned to Italy, settled at Florence and was appointed by his successor bishop and cardinal. He died before entering upon his new office.

Gregory XII, the Roman pope, when called upon by the council to abdicate, found himself abandoned by his last princely protector and his few cardinals. He therefore waived his claims to the papacy, was given the title of cardinal-bishop, first in rank after the pope, and soon died, at the age of ninety. Benedict XIII, pope in the old Avignon line, was at his refuge in Spain. Though abandoned by his protector, the King of Aragon, and urged by the emperor in person and by a deputation from the council, he still refused to abdicate. Thereupon, in April 1417, the council, already in its third year, deposed Benedict as a schismatic, a heretic and a disturber of the peace. As a matter of fact he lived to be ninety-four, still claiming to be pope. In 1424 he urged his two remaining cardinals with his dying breath to choose a successor. A phantom pope was actually chosen but soon abdicated and became bishop of a Spanish diocese.

Notwithstanding Benedict's obstinate refusal and shadowy claims, the papal chair was counted as vacant from the day of his deposition by the council, and the bells of Constance were rung in recognition of the freedom of the church from its divided allegiance and the opportunity to choose a single head for Christendom. After much intrigue this was accomplished; the cardinals and a group of other members of the council met in conclave in the old merchants' hall at Constance and elected a Roman cardinal as pope. He took the name of Martin V, was borne to the cathedral, placed on the high altar and acknowledged and congratulated by the crowds who passed by him for hours. The great schism was over.

VII. MYSTICISM AND HERESY

The papacy was never the same after the Avignon period and the great schism. Almost three generations of exile from its natural centre at Rome, the pronounced French influence and character of the papacy during that period, the increasing insistence on its financial prerogatives, all this had diminished the devotion and affection formerly felt toward the head of the church. The schism with its conflicts and jealousies left the organization weakened. And yet these were but episodes in the history of the church. The capital could be reestablished at Rome; the schism, as has just been seen, could be healed. A more serious threat claimed the attention of the council at Constance. This was the spread of heresy, which was a danger not only to the organization of the church but to its internal unity and coherence. Heresy had been on the increase during the period of the captivity and the schism, favored doubtless by the widespread criticism of church morals and intensified by the intellectual activity of the age, but it had been a serious problem for a long time. It is necessary therefore to go back to the beginning of our period and trace its growth.

There was little sympathy with heresy which was recognized and acknowledged as such. At a time when the church was identified with Christianity, heresy, that is to say, any belief officially condemned by the church, was in the minds of orthodox Christians treason to God, betrayal of the common faith, the worst of crimes, setting the heretic apart from all other men, depriving him of all rights and making him, like other traitors, an object of contempt as well as condemnation. But in the thirteenth and fourteenth centuries there were great numbers of men whose beliefs differed, whose doubts were not set at rest and whose religious longings were not satisfied with what the official church provided. What was heresy and what was truth was not clear.[35]

There was mysticism, always closely allied to heresy. Widely scattered on the continent were the writings and the prophecies of the half-mythical Abbot Joachim of Flora. He seems to have been in real life a worldly young nobleman of Calabria, who on a visit to the Holy Land about 1175 was converted, saw visions, was inspired, so he claimed, with prophetic powers, and was commissioned by God to speak and write concerning things to come and to interpret the scriptures. He was miraculously provided with the necessary scholarly equipment by drinking deeply of a river of oil in a vision. He returned to Italy, was ordained priest and took the vows of the Cistercian Order. Unwillingly made abbot of the monastery of Curazzo, he fled from his charge in order to devote himself to still more rigorous self-discipline and to obtain freedom to preach and to write. He wrote *The Harp with Ten Strings, The Unfolding of Revelation, The Harmony of the New and the Old Testament.* His sayings and writings and the legends that grew up about him became a great mass of popular tradition. What Merlin was in the field of romance Abbot Joachim became in the field of religion.

[35] Henry C. Lea, *The Inquisition in the Middle Ages* (three volumes, New York, 1888), I, 236-7. See also the Catholic view in E. Vacandard, *The Inquisition* (New York, 1908), and the good semi-popular account of A. S. Turberville, *Medieval Heresy and the Inquisition* (London, 1920). A. L. Maycock, *The Inquisition from Its Establishment to the Great Schism* (London, 1926), is a suggestive defense of the institution.

He could explain all the mysterious meanings of the Bible and foretell the future. His books were added to in the thirteenth century by a series of works popularly attributed to him, *The Prophecies of Cyril, Commentaries on Jeremiah, Prophecies of the Popes, The Seven Ages of the Church*, and others.[36]

No brief analysis can give even the gist of the often incoherent sayings and writings of Abbot Joachim. They interpret every episode of the Old Testament in terms of the New and of both in the terms of later history. Each Biblical character or event represents some person or occurrence or condition in the present, or prefigures some state of man or of the church in the future. There are three periods of the world: the period of the Law or of the Father, the period of the Gospel or of the Son, the period of the Holy Spirit. The second, in which we are living, is marred by avarice, lustfulness and irreligion in the church and unhappiness among the people, but it is approaching its end. That should come in 1260, forty-two generations from the birth of Christ; for did not Judith remain in widowhood three years and a half, which is forty-two months, which is 1260 days, and each day is a year? Then the present church, that which is founded in Peter, will be purified, the present hierarchy will disappear, a new order of monks, truly spiritual men, will guide mankind, and the human race will enjoy its long Sunday rest.[37]

In symbolic drawings, in oral, in written and indeed long afterward in printed form, the dreams, the fantastic analogies, the predictions, the allegories of Abbot Joachim furnished much of the food of the marvelous on which it seems the souls of mankind must largely feed. At the very beginning of our period, in 1255, they were given new currency by their reappearance as a single work under the name *The Everlasting Gospel*, with an explanatory introduction by an unknown hand. It is said that laymen and even women bought copies of the new work from booksellers on the pavement of Notre Dame at Paris, and we know that it was passed

[36] A classic study of Joachim is J. J. Döllinger, *Prophecy and the Prophetic Spirit in the Christian Era* (translated by A. Plummer, London, 1873), chap. vii. See also Henry Bett, *Joachim of Flora* (London, 1931). Emmanuel Aegarter, *Joachim de Flore, l'Évangile Eternel* (two volumes, Paris, 1928) is little more than romancing.

[37] *Expositio magni prophete Abbatis Joachim apocalipsim . . . cui adjecta sunt ejusdem Psalterim decem Cordarun* (Venice, 1527).

from hand to hand among the people in the south of France. Its ideas and sayings spread and burgeoned in the favorable soil of the thirteenth and fourteenth centuries far beyond their influence at the time of their origin. With its bitter condemnation of existing religion, its free criticism of the church, its prophecies of a new era soon to begin, in which ecclesiastical observances would be superfluous and men would live in a continual ecstasy, the lore of Joachim, while it excited the fancy, must have obscured the teaching and lessened the authority of the church in the minds of hundreds of thousands.

Much of this mystic lore was too vague to be subjected to doctrinal tests and too widely disseminated to be brought under authority. But Joachim's essay on the Trinity was condemned as heretical in 1213, eleven years after his death, and a council at Arles in 1260 condemned his writings and those who accepted them. Nevertheless Dante reverenced Joachim and placed him in Paradise, and his influence is clearly recognizable in the work of Roger Bacon. His vague cult spread widely, especially in Languedoc, where the Albigensian doctrines had presumably been crushed by the crusade against them and the few smoldering embers of that heresy were supposed to be put out by the bull *ad extirpandam* of 1252, but where the people were still unsettled in belief.[38]

Much more conformable to the thought of the time was that wave of mysticism which between 1300 and 1400 spread from the valley of the Rhine to the Netherlands and showed itself always on the borderland between acceptance of the practical religious ministrations of the church and an effort to obtain a more personal, intimate and direct union with divinity. Master Eckhart and his two disciples Tauler and Suso, all Dominicans, spent their lives of study, preaching and writing at Cologne, Erfurt and Strassburg, with periods of study, refuge and educational work at Paris, and in Switzerland and Bohemia. It was perhaps from their teaching that John Ruysbroeck in Brussels received the ideas that found expression in his mystical and devotional works, the *Adornment of the Spiritual Marriage*, the *Kingdom of the Lovers of God*, the *Sparkling Stone* and others. The practical piety that accompanied this

[38] Lea, *The Inquisition in the Middle Ages*, III, 10-20.

search for God, the constant use of the Bible as a source of knowledge, the distaste for what seemed to them the empty or misused ceremonies of the church, led them to the formation of group after group of adherents of a contemplative life. The "Friends of God," the "Brethren of the Common Life," the students of the "new devotion," followers of Gerard Groote, founder of the school at Deventer, gave to the later fourteenth and earlier fifteenth centuries, on one side an independent educational movement at Windesheim, Zwolle and elsewhere in the Netherlands, on the other the dreamy piety of the *Imitation of Christ.* Both alike were lacking in ecclesiastical regularity and many of the ideas emanating from them were subsequently condemned as heretical.

But what was heresy? It was by no means certain. Independent thinkers claimed that what the pope or bishop or their opponent in controversy called heresy was really the true doctrine of the church. In the unending theological disputes of the time the charge of heresy was brought so freely that it became little more than a term of abuse and was disregarded unless pronounced with formality and followed up with force. A leading independent thinker was the English scholar William of Ockham. He was a master of arts and doctor of divinity of Oxford and Paris, entered the order of St. Francis and became so famous as a reasoner that his students at Oxford called him "the invincible doctor." At the University of Paris, in the ready academic internationalism of the age, his career and his ideas became inextricably bound up with those of Marsiglio, an Italian, and John of Jandun, a French scholar, so that seldom is one spoken of without the others. They were all drawn into the current controversy on "evangelic poverty."

This dispute between two factions of the Franciscans spread widely and bade fair to split not only the order but the church itself. It was the teaching of the "Spiritual Franciscans" or the "Fraticelli," as in their exuberant modesty they called themselves, that as Christ and the apostles lived entirely without property they had left this as an example to be followed by the church.[39] Such an example the church had certainly not followed, since its organization and

[39] There is an immense literature on this subject, for some guidance in which the reader is referred to the Bibliography in this volume.

work had from an early period been founded mainly on endowments and obligatory payments. To deprive the church of its endowments was to destroy the organized church altogether. Naturally this teaching received prompt and unhesitating condemnation from the pope. In the course of the controversy the charge of heresy was bandied back and forth, and in 1327 the pope imprisoned at Avignon on the charge of heresy Ockham, Michael of Cesena, at that time General of the order, and some other Franciscans.

Lewis, duke of Bavaria, was at this time engaged in a struggle with the pope for recognition as emperor, and had gone to Italy to strengthen his claims through the secular arm. Although his dispute was on quite other grounds than evangelical poverty, he was not disinclined to utilize the intellectual support of those already in conflict with the pope. He therefore offered a refuge to the Franciscan captives at Avignon.[40] On May 25, 1327 they escaped by boat, were rowed down the Rhone to its mouth and taken in a galley to Pisa, where they came under the emperor's protection. The next year they went with him to Munich and from the Franciscan convent there Ockham poured out during the next twenty years a succession of works discussing philosophical and political themes, including bitter personal attacks on the opinions and the lives of two successive Avignonese popes, John XXII and Benedict XII. He was excommunicated on June 6, 1328. The next year the pope declared the whole Franciscan doctrine of the necessity of complete poverty a heresy. In his essay, *Errors of the Pope,* on the other hand, Ockham charged John XXII with seventy errors and seven heresies. He declared "Jesus came among men not to gain dignities and powers but to submit to contempt and injury, to be crowned not with a diadem of precious stones but with a crown of thorns. His reign was not temporal but celestial and spiritual; all doctrine opposed to this is heretical and blasphemous. The manifest heresy of John XXII deprives him of all power and separates him from the universal church."[41]

The most significant of Ockham's writing, however, was not his

[40] R. Möller, *Ludwig der Bayer und die Kurie im Kampf um das Reich* (Berlin, 1914).

[41] A. Renaudet, in L. Halphen et Ph. Sagnac, *Peuples et Civilisations,* VII, *La Fin du Moyen Age* (Paris, 1931), 101.

personal attacks on the pope, nor even his advocacy of evangelical poverty, but his vehement opposition to the claims of the church to act in the temporal sphere. The same doctrine was urged with still greater force and popular appeal by Ockham's friend, Marsiglio of Padua.[42] A student since his youth of the Roman law, and citizen of a community governed on its principles, Marsiglio was imbued with Roman imperial principles even before he entered the scholastic atmosphere of the University of Paris. Here he was lecturer, became rector in the year 1313, and had come, as already stated, in contact with the keen mind of William of Ockham. As a result of these influences Marsiglio wrote his great work *Defensor Pacis*, "The Defender of Peace." This was a bold assertion, in the first place, of the supremacy of the state over the church, and, secondly, of the equality of all members of the church, indeed of all Christians, before God. In Marsiglio's demonstration of these points, the special claims of the pope were practically all argued away, and the authority of the priesthood was much diminished. Judgment and absolution are no more significant when they come from the pope than if they came from any other priest, and in neither case are they of any validity unless they represent the judgment of God. The pope may, like any other man, be mistaken or misled or influenced by hatred or favor.

John of Jandun joined in these views and assisted in the publication of the *Defensor Pacis*.[43] The book and its teachings, like the question of poverty, became the center of heated controversy. The pope declared all the writings of Marsiglio and John heretical and themselves heretics. In 1326 they both left Paris and joined Ockham and the other Spiritual Franciscans in their refuge at Munich, all receiving from Lewis of Bavaria protection for the remainder of their lives, John of Jandun till 1328, Marsiglio until 1343, and

[42] An admirable brief analysis of the work of Ockham and Marsiglio and of this whole conflict is in R. L. Poole, *Illustrations of the History of Mediaeval Thought* (London, 1884), chap. ix, 264-81. Ockham's *De Imperatorum et Pontificum Potestate*, and his *Epistola ad Fratres Minores* have recently been edited by C. K. Brampton (Oxford, 1927, 1929). On Marsiglio consult E. Emerton, *The "Defensor Pacis" of Marsiglio of Padua* (Cambridge, 1920), and C. W. Previté-Orton, *The Defensor Pacis of Marsilius of Padua* (Cambridge, 1928).

[43] M. J. Tooley, "The Authorship of the Defensor Pacis," *Royal Historical Society Transactions*, IX (1926), 85-106.

William of Ockham, apparently, till 1349.[44] The book of Marsiglio continued to be read, notwithstanding its condemnation. In 1376 a French translation appeared at Paris, so that it obtained still wider circulation.

The arguments which emanated from these men were addressed to scholars. They were dependent for their reception, in so far as they exercised an influence, on the learning, the keenness of mind and the habit of discussion of the intellectual classes of the time. The whole question whether their authors were heretics or not was a matter of debate. Such works were sometimes declared heretical by one pope only to have his judgment reversed by his successor, or indeed, in some cases, under pressure, by himself. In the meantime they were widely held to be orthodox even among learned churchmen. The church was not absolutely homogeneous or settled beyond question in its beliefs.

The church might not have been seriously weakened by a certain amount of such learned internal dissent if there were no heresy among the mass of the people. But such there was. If there has ever been an "age of faith," an age when the official teachings of the church satisfied men's minds and spirits and obtained universal acceptance, or when the authority of the church in matters of belief was acknowledged by all, it was not the period now under consideration. It is impossible to describe here, difficult even to enumerate all the heresies that troubled the thirteenth and fourteenth and early fifteenth centuries. The Inquisition was established in Italy, France, Burgundy and Spain from the middle of the thirteenth century forward, with the task of rooting out these divergences of belief. But scarcely had it made headway against heterodoxy in one form and lighted the fires which were intended to purify the church, when a new heresy showed itself or an old one was revived. The old heresy of the Albigenses or Cathari, with its anti-sacerdotalism and its dualistic conception of God, crushed out in the open country, lived on in the remote valleys of the Pyrenees, the Alps, the Apennines and the Abruzzi, and even in the obscure purlieus of some of the Italian cities. Indeed, it worked its way

[44] J. Sullivan, "Marsiglio of Padua and William of Ockham," *American Historical Review*, II (1896-1897), 409-26, 593-610; C. K. Brampton, "Marsiglio of Padua, Life," *English Historical Review*, XXXVII (1923), 1-19.

back through Istria, Dalmatia, Croatia and Servia toward eastern Europe, from which its half-oriental doctrines had originally made their way along the old trade routes from east to west.[45]

The Waldenses, who were like the Cathari, except that they were mostly poor men, were still scattered through the southeast of France and extended their influence southward into Italy and northward along the Rhine and into Bavaria, Moravia and Bohemia.[46] The Beghards or Brethren of the Free Spirit, the Beguines, the Brethren of the Cross, the Guglielmites, the Flagellants, the Dolcinists, the Sagerellists, the Luciferans, the continental Lollards of whom unfortunately we know so little,—devotees or dreamers or seekers who so easily passed the border which separates individual piety from heresy,—went their ways of deviation from the narrow paths of orthodoxy until they were forced by bishops or inquisitors to conform or to become martyrs to their faith.[47]

How many heretics there were, what proportion of the population was in silent or active opposition to the doctrines and ordinances of the church, it is impossible to tell. When a contemporary chronicler declares that "You would hardly meet two men upon the highroad of whom one would not be a Lollard"; or we read of fifty-four being burned in Paris, or note the hostility to clergymen shown by so many peasant insurgents, or hear the charge of heresy so freely made, one gets the impression that religious disaffection was ubiquitous, disrespect to the church or even hostility to it well-nigh universal. But further study gives a different impression. Careful consideration brings the conviction that, except in certain places and at certain times, the number of non-conformists was slight in comparison with the number of those obedient to the teachings and the authority of the church. At the Jubilee of 1300, of the 200,000 pilgrims who visited Rome and kissed the hands of Pope Boniface VIII, in all probability not only churchmen but far the greater number of laymen hated heresy and despised heretics.

[45] Of the extensive literature see especially T. de Cauzons, *Les Albigeois et l'Inquisition* (second edition, Paris, 1908); E. G. A. Holmes, *The Albigensian or Catharist Heresy* (London, 1925); H. J. Warner, *The Albigensian Heresy* (two volumes, London, 1922-1928).

[46] T. de Cauzons, *Les Vaudois et l'Inquisition* (third edition, Paris, 1908); H. Haupt, "Deutsch-böhmische Waldenser um 1340," *Zeitschrift für Kirchengeschichte*, XIV (1894), 1 et seq.

[47] Lea, *The Inquisition in the Middle Ages*, III, 30-175.

There is little doubt that a great body of the population, as far as they were interested at all, accepted naturally and dutifully, often unthinkingly, the existence and authority of the organized church, obeyed its requirements and used its ministrations.

As for outward submission, that was practically imperative. The church had sufficient material power to coerce all but the most highly placed of laymen. But there was, even among the masses of the people, an attitude of obedience and in some a heart-felt attachment to the church. It would be a falsification of history if, in tracing the decline of the church and making the necessary reference to its abuses, we failed to remind the reader of the protection, the support and the consolation it gave to vast numbers of people. Yet on the whole in these centuries the structure of the church could be kept intact and even formal obedience preserved only by constant disciplinary action and frequent prosecutions by local officials and by the officers of the Inquisition who were scattered through most countries of Europe.

As the period progressed, criticism became more and more outspoken, the church itself less and less satisfying to the intellectual and spiritual needs of the people, its own standards lower. It is not only to the critical historian but to the apologist for the church that this seems a low period in her history. Devotion seldom sprang up of itself within her boundaries and when it did it met a chilling reception from her governors. The greater freedom and vigor of thought that accompanied life in the cities, the increase of wealth and the extension of international intercourse in this period found no echo of liberalism in the church and were forced to take refuge either in secularism or in heresy.

1. THE RICH MERCHANT, GIOVANNI ARNOLFINI, OF LUCCA.
A portrait attributed to Jan van Eyck, c 1435

2. THE FLORENTINE MERCHANT, PIETRO MELLINI.
A bust by Benedetto da Maiano

3. SKETCH OF THE PIAZZA, DOGE'S PALACE, AND GRAND CANAL, VENICE.
From a manuscript in the Bodleian Library

4. THE HOUSE OF THE MERCHANT, MARINO CONTARINI, ON THE GRAND CANAL IN VENICE, CONSTRUCTED 1421-1434

5. LOADING A SHIP.
From a manuscript in the Germanisches Museum, dated 1441

6. SHIPS OF THE HANSE.
A fresco in the Mariakirche at Lübeck (Fifteenth century)

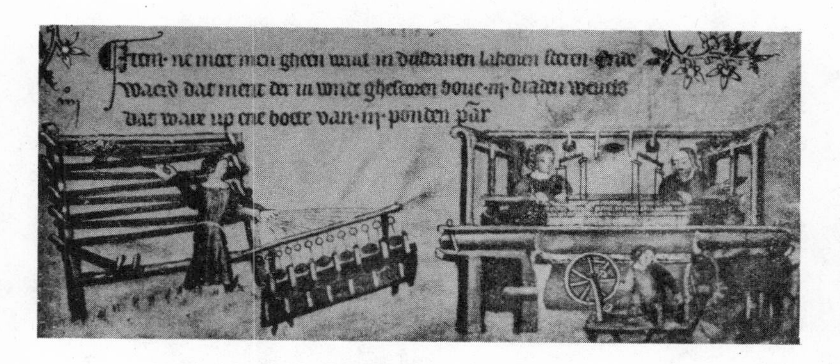

7. FLEMISH WEAVERS AT WORK.
From a fourteenth century manuscript at Ypres

8. THE CITY HALL AT BRUGES, CONSTRUCTED ABOUT 1400

9. THE HOUSE OF JACQUES COEUR AT BOURGES.
One of the finest extant houses of the Middle Ages

10. A SHIP OF JACQUES COEUR, PICTURED ON GLASS, ABOUT 1400.
From the Bourges Museum

11. SAINT ELOI OF LIMOGES, PATRON SAINT OF THE GOLDSMITHS
A fifteenth century painting by Petrus Christi, 1449

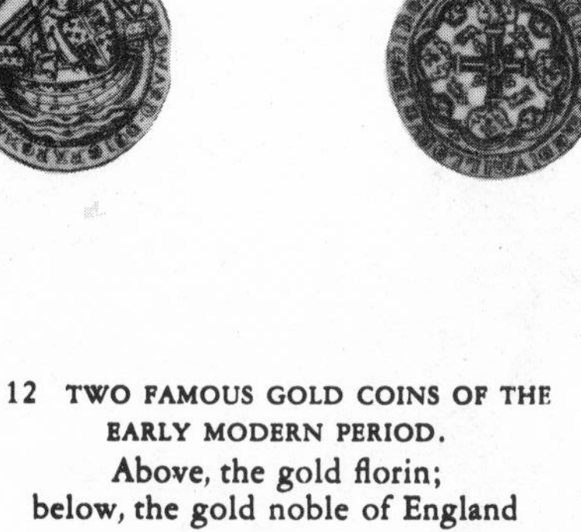

12 TWO FAMOUS GOLD COINS OF THE EARLY MODERN PERIOD.
Above, the gold florin;
below, the gold noble of England

13. A MONEY-CHANGER OF THE FIFTEENTH CENTURY.
From a manuscript in the Bodleian Library

14. POPE BONIFACE VIII, OPPONENT OF PHILIP IV.
A bust by Arnolfo di Cambio, c. 1300

15. THE ASSAULT ON THE POPE AT ANAGNI.
A miniature from the Villani manuscript in the Chigi Library

16. KING ALFONSO THE WISE OF CASTILE.
From a manuscript of the *Cantigas del Rey Don Alfonso el Sabio*, in the Escorial Library

17. THE THREE ESTATES.
From the *Arbre des Batailles*, a manuscript of about 1450 in the Bibliotheque de l'Arsenal

18. THE THREE ESTATES OFFERING THE KING OF FRANCE AN AIDE.
A miniature from the *Grandes Chroniques*

19. CHARLES OF NAVARRE PREACHING TO THE POPULACE OF PARIS DURING STEPHEN MARCEL'S RISING.
A miniature from the *Grandes Chroniques*

20. A PARLIAMENT OF EDWARD I.
From a medieval drawing in the Society of Antiquaries

21. THE GREAT PESTILENCE AT TOURNAI, 1349.
From a miniature in a manuscript in the
Brussels Library

22. COLA DI RIENZI.
A relief in the Palazzo Barberini, generally supposed to be the only contemporary likeness of the great tribune

23. THE MILITIA OF GHENT.
From a fresco, now destroyed, in the Chapel of St. John and Paul. This picture gives an excellent idea of the cross-bow

24. A MEETING OF THE FOLLOWERS OF JOHN BALL AND WAT TYLER.
A miniature in the British Museum

25. EDWARD, THE BLACK PRINCE, WITH ENGLISH AND FRENCH ARMS.
From his tomb at Canterbury

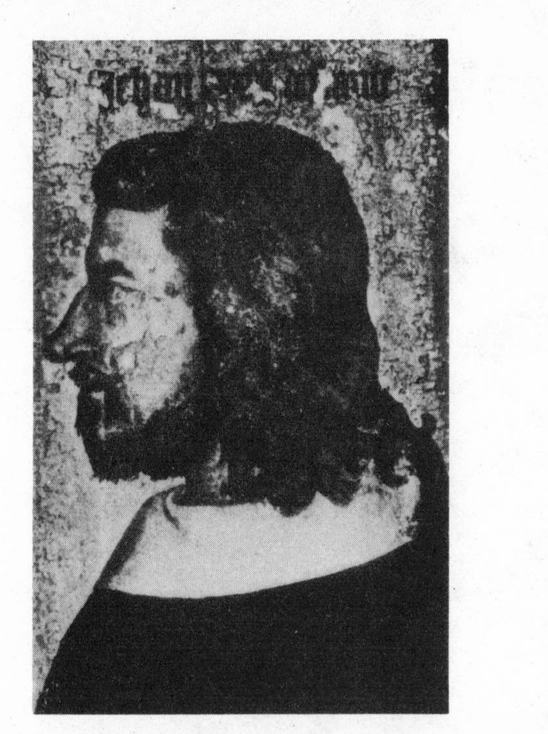

26. JOHN II, KING OF FRANCE, CAPTURED AT THE BATTLE OF POITIERS

27. KING CHARLES VII OF FRANCE, THE DAUPHIN OF JOAN OF ARC'S TIME.
Painted about 1450 by Jean Fouquet

28. AN EPISODE OF THE HUNDRED YEARS' WAR. THE RETURN OF KING JOHN TO LONDON.

A miniature from the *Chronique de Règnes de Jean II et de Charles V*

29. A CAVALRY BATTLE, AS REPRESENTED IN THE FRESCOES BY SPINELLO ARETINO (C. 1390) IN THE CAMPO SANTO AT PISA

30. HENRY V. KING OF ENGLAND, REGENT OF FRANCE.
National Portrait Gallery, London

31. JOAN OF ARC ARRIVING AT THE CHATEAU OF CHINON IN 1429.
From a tapestry of German origin, supposed to be contemporary

32. THE GREAT FORTRESS-PALACE OF THE POPES AT AVIGNON

33. THE EMPEROR SIGISMUND.

A portrait study by an unknown Austrian artist, probably done from life between 1435 and 1438. This painting, in the Vienna Museum, has been recently identified

34. THE POPE ENTERING CONSTANCE FOR THE GREAT COUNCIL.
From the illustration in the Aulendorf manuscript of Richental's *Chronicle* (1419)

35. JOHN HUS BEING BURNED AT THE STAKE.
From the illustration in the Aulendorf manuscript of Richental's *Chronicle* (1419)

36. POPE MARTIN V, ELECTED AT THE COUNCIL OF CONSTANCE.
A tombstone done by Donatello

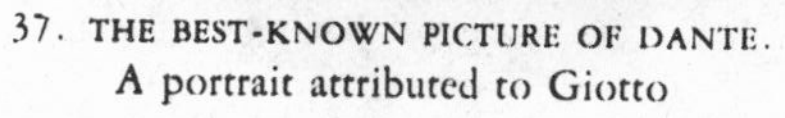

37. THE BEST-KNOWN PICTURE OF DANTE.
A portrait attributed to Giotto

38. GIOVANNI BOCACCIO.
A painting by Andrea del' Castagana, now in Florence

39. GUARINO OF VERONA, HUMANIST AND TEACHER AT FLORENCE AND FERRARA.
A medal designed by Matteo da Pasti

40. PETRARCH, A PEN-AND-INK SKETCH BY LOMBARDO DELLA TOLA, IN THE BIBLIOTHÈQUE NATIONALE

41. GEOFFREY CHAUCER.
From a manuscript in the British Museum, written 1412

42. THE FIRST MODERN EQUESTRIAN STATUE.
Gattamelata, done in bronze by Donatello, now at Padua

43. COSIMO DE' MEDICI.
A marble tablet by Verrocchio or one of his pupils

44. KUBLAI KHAN.
From a Chinese engraving

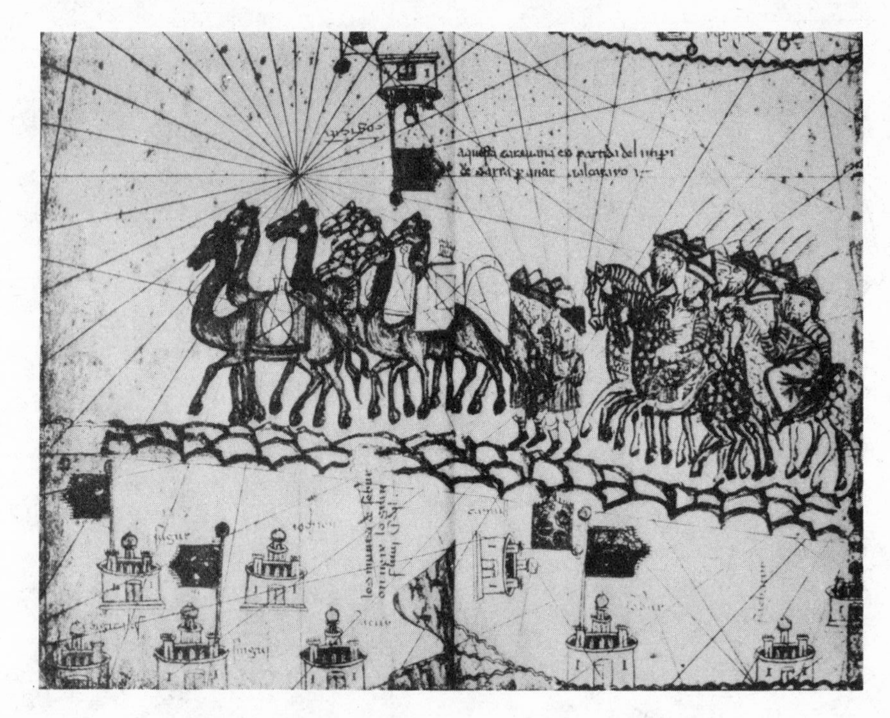

45. THE POLO BROTHERS SETTING OUT WITH THEIR CARAVAN.
A picture from the famous Catalan Atlas (1374) in the Bibliothèque Nationale

46. THE MARIENBURG, CASTLE AND HEADQUARTERS OF THE TEUTONIC KNIGHTS

47. RUSSIANS AT WAR.
From a fourteenth century manuscript in the Novgorod Museum

48. THE FIRST OF THE GREAT PORTRAIT MEDALS OF THE RENAISSANCE.
John Paleologus, done by Pisanello at Ferrara, 1437, during the Emperor's visit to the Council to secure help against the Turks

49. JOHN CANTACUZENE PRESIDING OVER A COUNCIL.
A miniature from a manuscript in the Bibliothèque Nationale, and one of the few works of Byzantine painting on non-ecclesiastical subjects

50. MOHAMMED II, THE CONQUEROR.
A portrait painted from life by Gentile Bellini

Chapter Seven

THE SPREAD OF HERESY

I. JOHN WYCLIF

ENGLAND through the middle ages had preserved a singular immunity from heresy. She seems to have heard little of the "Everlasting Gospel"; the Catharism of the south hardly reached her; the quarrels between the orthodox and the heretical Franciscans awakened at the time only distant echoes there; she produced almost no indigenous heretics, and was largely unaware of the tides of heresy that flowed across the Continent. She was only a late comer into the conflicts in matters of belief and ecclesiastical organization that were rending the church in other parts of Europe. It is true that the Englishman William of Ockham was declared a heretic in 1327 and exercised a deep disruptive influence on the succeeding generation, but his influence at the time affected only the Continent. It was only later and indirectly that it reached England.

All this was true till late in the fourteenth century. Then, in the same half-century that saw the ravages of the Black Death, the principal gains and losses of the Hundred Years War, the storm of the Peasants' Rebellion, the Statutes of Provisors and Praemunire and the beginnings of English popular literature in the vernacular, in short in a half-century of restless activity, a religious revival, the most marked characteristic of which was its interpenetration with heresy, swept through England.

Large movements in history usually spring from a variety of causes, and this was probably true of English Lollardy. But so far as surviving records indicate it took its rise directly from the teachings of one man, John Wyclif.[1] The events of his life centered about the University of Oxford; he took his degree in divinity and began lec-

[1] The best study of the life and work of Wyclif is Gotthard Lechler, *John Wyclif and His English Precursors,* translated by Peter Lorimer (two volumes, London, 1878); but see also G. M. Trevelyan, *England in the Age of Wycliffe* (fourth edition, London, 1909), and H. B. Workman, *John Wyclif* (two volumes, Oxford, 1926).

turing there about 1360, and until 1378, six years before the end of his life, was seldom long away from those academic surroundings. He preached occasionally in London churches and elsewhere and became rector of Lutterworth in Leicestershire in 1374, but must, until shortly before his death in 1384, have been frequently an absentee from his parish in order to lecture at the university.

Wyclif was first of all a scholar, a learned man, a bold and independent thinker, a subtle disputant. He was described by contemporaries as "peerless in logic, philosophy, divinity, morality and speculation," "the most eminent doctor of theology of those days," "in philosophy second to none, in scholastic learning incomparable." He was "the flower of Oxford scholarship," and even those graduates of Oxford who disapproved of his doctrines were proud of him as "a great clerk." He was familiar with the Fathers, with Aristotelian and scholastic philosophy and, to an unusual extent, with the Bible. Like Ockham and Marsiglio, he was early drawn into the discussion of the temporal claims of the papacy. At the request of the king he wrote and spoke in opposition to papal provisions and was sent as envoy to a conference with papal representatives at Bruges in 1374. He also wrote for the use of Parliament an argument against the feudal payment claimed from England by the pope. He was a busy teacher, preacher and writer in both Latin and English.

It was in this academic and public activity, warmed with an eager spirit of religious controversy and desire for reform, that he developed those ideas and teachings that made him the greatest intellectual and religious force of his time in England, carried his influence across intervening lands to a distant corner of Europe, and made his name famous in his own time and since.[2]

The development of the heretical ideas of Wyclif was doubtless progressive, and the exact stages of their growth in his mind cannot be traced. His disregard of the authoritative teaching of the church and reliance on the Bible as the adequate source of faith and of moral teaching certainly dated from an early period. His constant references to the Scriptures led his students at the university to

[2] W. W. Capes, *The English Church in the Fourteenth and Fifteenth Centuries* (London, 1900), chap. vi, an excellent chapter, as indeed is this whole work, though but slightly sympathetic with the Lollard movement.

call him "the evangelical doctor." One of his works alone contains 700 Biblical quotations. Many of his sermons and tracts are little more than extracts from the Scriptures with a running commentary. His Vulgate was apparently always by him and his memory was stored with Biblical expressions and incidents. He had little of the Joachimite ingenuity in discovering hidden meanings; the Bible was to him merely a source of doctrinal and moral teaching. At first he urged that it be interpreted in accordance either with the teaching of the Fathers or the guidance of learned men, but later he expressed his full confidence that the Holy Spirit would enlighten even ignorant men in discovering its meaning, if they were in earnest. Neither the tradition of the church nor the authority of pope or council, he held, was of any weight in matters of religion when compared with the words of the Bible. This was perhaps his most fundamental divergence from the conceptions of the official church.

Equally destructive of the accepted organization of the church was his vehement assertion of the evil effects of its endowment. It has already been pointed out that no single criticism of the church in the thirteenth and fourteenth centuries was more general than the belief that its possessions were its curse. From Walter von der Vogelweide to Dante, from Ottokar of Harnack to John Hus, in chronicles, in the teachings of the Cathari and in the writings of learned scholars of France and Italy, there was the reiterated complaint of the ill service Constantine did to the church in making his donation of land to Pope Sylvester.[3] The story of a voice from heaven warning of its results appeared again and again:

> "Whene Constantyn of his cortesye holy kirke dowede
> With londes and leedes, lordshepes and rentes,
> An angel men hurde on high at Rome crye
> 'Dos ecclesie, this day hath ydronken venyme
> And tho that have Petre's power aren poysened alle.'"[4]

One might suppose the writer of *Piers Plowman* was merely translating the chronicler of the early fourteenth century, John Parrhisiis,

[3] Gerhard Laehr, *Die Konstantinische Schenkung in der Abendländischen Literatur des Mittelalters bis Mitte des 14ten Jahrhunderts* (Berlin, 1925).
[4] *Vision of Piers Plowman,* C text, passus XVIII, ii, 250-7.

Quod in donatione illa audita est vox angelorum dicentium in aere, hodie in ecclesia venenum effusum est. But the story was widespread and appears in many forms.

It was not merely the apocryphal donation of Constantine and the endowment of the papacy that the reformers of the fourteenth century, Wyclif most vigorously of all, had in mind. Like the Spiritual Franciscans half a century before, the English scholar wrote and spoke against the possession by the clergy, either secular or regular, of lands, property or legal income. Christ and his apostles had lived as poor men and "it belongeth not to Christ's vicar nor to priests of holy church to have rents here on earth." Over and over again in his speaking and writing he comes back to the evil results, the simony, the covetousness, the diversion from their spiritual duties, of a clergy who lived from endowments and tithes, payments and fees, instead of depending on the free offerings of the people. Since the mendicant orders had acquired houses, lucrative appointments and other possessions their "stinking orders" were equally to be condemned. "These irreligious that have possessions, they have commonly red and fat cheeks and great bellies." Wyclif gave only too many proofs of being a master of the coarse, unrestrained vituperation which was the common speech of controversy at the time. The prelates are "horned fiends to be damned in hell." They "made God's law unsavoury . . . with stinking words and law." On the other hand his opponents called him "Mahomet" and "the devil's instrument," "the heretic's idol," and transformed his name into "Wickedlife." The pope charged him with "vomiting forth from the recesses of his body false and heretical propositions."

It is but a short step from denying to the church temporal property to denying to it temporal office. Wyclif asserted boldly that churchmen had no right to interfere in matters of government. Temporal rule belonged alone to the civil powers. It was their right and duty to prevent the clergy, whether pope, bishops or priests, from passing beyond their strictly spiritual sphere. Prelates who were also great officers of government; ecclesiastical judges who fined and imprisoned laymen for religious offenses; the pope, who claimed to depose kings and to be himself a sovereign and who made wars for temporal ends, all were alike unchristian and should have their temporal powers and possessions wrested from them by kings and governors.

The whole theory of an organized church system gradually disintegrated under Wyclif's critical thinking. He denied the existence under Christ's authority of any difference of rank in the church. Ordination, confirmation, consecration of churches, could be as well performed by any plain priest as by a bishop. Indeed any good man might act as a priest. The whole body of ceremony and symbolism, confession, penance and absolution, pilgrimages to the shrines of saints, the use of holy water, the veneration of relics, prayers for the intercession of the saints and of the Blessed Virgin, the claim of the clergy to excommunicate, all this should be abolished, for "Jesus Christ and his apostles useden them not." He gave a Protestant, indeed a Calvinist, definition of the church. It was made up not of the clergy alone but of all Christians, at least of all who were destined to be saved.

His early respect for the pope as a possible reformer of discipline in the church did not survive the great schism and the hatreds and conflicts that accompanied it. In a series of pamphlets he attacked the principal papal claims. The pope's power to excommunicate he denied, as had the scholastic heretics of the Continent, unless Christ himself had condemned the sinner; he questioned the primacy of Peter, and ridiculed the claims of such a wicked man as Urban VI to infallibility. He declared the claim of the pope to grant indulgences or to dispense the accumulated merits of the saints a "fond blasphemie." His teaching concerning transubstantiation was obscure and later declared by the pope to be heretical.[5]

Years of such teaching in such conspicuous surroundings could hardly pass unnoticed and unrebuked. Yet the actual efforts to silence Wyclif in his own lifetime were curiously slight, tardy and ineffective. His academic superiors were indisposed to interfere with his teaching. Only twice was he required to answer personally for his questionable views; both times by reluctant ecclesiastical authorities and both times without serious results for himself. In February 1377 Archbishop Sudbury summoned him to appear before convoca-

[5] R. L. Poole, *Wycliffe and Movements for Reform* (London, 1889), a small but excellent work; Creighton, *The Papacy during the Reformation*, I, 108-10.

tion at St. Paul's in London. There was much disorder and no action was taken. The pope then intervened. Opponents at the university or listeners to some of his outside sermons had sent to Rome a series of theses which he was said to have advocated. These were officially declared by the pope to be either heretical or erroneous and, using them as a basis, the pope, in May 1377, addressed a series of bulls to the Archbishop of Canterbury, the Bishop of London, the king and the university. The chancellor and masters were appealed to "in consideration of the favors and privileges conceded to your University of Oxford by the apostolic see," and "as warriors and champions of the orthodox faith, without which there is no salvation of souls." They were charged with allowing "tares to spring up amidst the pure wheat in the fields of your glorious university." They were required on apostolic authority to put an immediate end to all discussions of the doctrines of Wyclif, to arrest him and send him under guard to the Archbishop of Canterbury and the Bishop of London and to silence and remove all other supporters of doctrines condemned by the church.[6]

Perhaps resenting this outside interference, perhaps preoccupied with the death of the old king and the coronation of the new and with the renewal of the French war, those appealed to took no action for many months. Early in 1378, however, Wyclif was summoned by the archbishop to Lambeth Palace. Again there was a disorderly intrusion of Londoners and the clergy present simply recommended that the accused clergyman cease supporting in public or at the university the articles recently condemned by the pope. He accepted the admonition, withdrew from public preaching and largely from the university, retired to his parish of Lutterworth and spent the remaining six years of his life in varied writing, the most considerable part of which was the composition of some of those massive Latin works which have lately been published by the Wyclif Society. He died in 1384.[7]

[6] H. Gee and W. J. Hardy, *Documents Illustrative of English Church History* (London, 1896), 105-8; *Translations and Reprints* (University of Pennsylvania), Vol. II, no. 5, sect. iii; John Lewis, *Life of Wycliffe* (London, 1720; new ed., Oxford, 1820), valuable because of its appendix of documents.

[7] An interesting essay, laying stress on Wyclif's public career, is in Reinhold Pauli, *Pictures of Old England* (London. 1861), Essay viii.

II. THE SPREAD OF LOLLARDY IN ENGLAND

In the meantime his teachings seem to have taken firm hold at Oxford. In 1382, four years after his retirement, the chancellor, Robert Rigge, appointed as preacher of the English sermon on Ascension Day Dr. Nicholas Hereford, well known for his Wyclifite views. As preacher of the Latin sermon on Corpus Christi Day he appointed Philip Reppingdon, who had lately taken his doctor's degree and in his first lecture had declared that in moral matters he intended to defend the teaching of Wyclif, and that in regard to the sacrament of the altar he would "place a finger before his lips till God should further enlighten the hearts of the clergy." In his Corpus Christi Day sermon he declared Wyclif's opinion of the sacrament to be true, and the chancellor congratulated him on his views. In the same year, a student named William James, in the presence of all the masters in Arts, declared the Eucharist as the church celebrated it to be mere idolatry, the chancellor interposing mildly only to remark "speaking philosophically"! John Aston was one of those Oxford masters who not only lectured there but preached what was certainly heresy throughout the country. Oxford long continued to remember with reverence her great teacher and to discuss and even accept, so far as overmastering authority permitted, his characteristic doctrines.[8]

Lollardy, as this body of opinion came gradually to be called, was far from being merely a university interest; it penetrated all society. It existed in high places. Queen Anne, coming from half-heretical Bohemia, with her copy of the gospels in Latin, German, Bohemian and English, must have been at least a well-wisher. The Duke of Lancaster supported Wyclif, at least in his early life. Henry Percy, Earl of Northumberland and lord marshal of England, was charged with being a "fautor" of the Lollards; John Montague, Earl of Salisbury, who had married the daughter of a Londoner, is described as "a friend of Lollards, a derider of images, a scoffer at sacraments." When he came into the possession of the manor of Shevley he removed all the images of saints placed in the chapel

[8] *Fasciculi Zizaniorum* (Rolls Series), 304, 306, 307; Henry Knighton, *Chronicon* (Rolls Series), II, 176.

by his predecessors and laid them away in obscurity, except that he allowed a certain figure of St. Catherine to be placed in the kitchen, as a special favor to the servants, who were much attached to it. Even at the point of death at the hands of the mob at Cirencester long afterward he refused confession and absolution.

The knights and gentry seem to have been especially responsive to the new doctrines. Wyclif praises them as a class for their willingness to read the Bible in English, and they are blamed by the clergy for giving protection to Lollard preachers. Certain knights were given the sobriquet of *milites capuciati*, "hatted knights," because they refused to remove their hats when the host was carried through the streets. At least three members of King Richard's council, Sir Lewis Clifford, who had fought with the Duke of Lancaster in Spain, France and Africa; Sir Richard Stury, an old councillor of Edward III and fellow ambassador with Chaucer in Italy, and Sir John Clanvowe, were known as Lollards. It was somewhat later, in 1400, that Sir Thomas Cheyney was removed from his position of Speaker of the House of Commons because he was a Lollard, though he occupied many other less conspicuous positions.

In 1395 Clifford and Sir Thomas Latimer were responsible for introducing into the House of Commons, and probably for tacking up on the doors of St. Paul's and Westminster Abbey, the "twelve conclusions" of their group. These went over the whole ground of Lollard opposition to the existing organization, property-holding and doctrines of the church: Her endowments ought to be taken away, monastic vows and vows of chastity by the secular clergy are injurious, the miracle of transubstantiation is idolatry, the blessing of holy water and other objects is mere jugglery, prayers for the dead are ineffective, churchmen ought not to hold worldly office. They call upon parliament to introduce reforms in these matters.[9]

No attention was paid to this appeal, due apparently to the opposition of the king, but over and over again attacks upon the church came up in the Commons. In 1404 and again in 1406 there were proposals to confiscate the lands and other temporal possessions of the church, which can hardly have arisen from any other source than the Lollard proclivities of the knights and gentry who were rep-

[9] J. H. Wylie, *England under Henry the Fourth* (London, 1884-98), I, 51-3, 174-86, 410, etc.

resented there. In 1410 it was rumored that the knights of the shire in Parliament were planning to propose a general act of confiscation of the lands and goods of the clergy, and it was claimed that this would provide sufficient endowment to maintain fifteen earls, 1500 knights, 6200 esquires, 100 almshouses and still leave £20,000 for the king's treasury. The king's rebuke checked this extreme proposal, and the Commons asked only for some mitigation of the existing statutes against heretics and for confiscation of half the revenue of absentee churchmen and papally appointed holders of benefices. Even this petition received no attention. It was the last of the parliamentary threats against the church. The special Lollardy of the knighthood of England seems to have run out, except in the most famous case of all, that of Sir John Oldcastle, which may be left till the still wider extension of heresy through England, especially among the lesser clergy and the townsmen, is noted.[10]

Wyclif himself, notwithstanding his scholastic training and habits, was more interested in spreading a simple and devout religion than in academic controversy. In addition to his own preaching he encouraged traveling preachers, who became known as his "poor priests," to go through the country. An orthodox opponent has described them, "on foot, clothed in long garments of russet, all of one cut, sowing their errors among the people and preaching them publicly in their sermons." Many of the reformer's homilies and expository tracts, largely duplicating one another, filled with texts from the Bible and their explanation and application, were evidently intended for use among the common people.[11] He blamed the beneficed clergy for their neglect of preaching and wrote a special treatise on "The Pastoral Office." The prevalence of preaching in this period has already been mentioned. The number of wandering preachers, exhorting the people and often teaching unauthorized doctrine, was a source of constant trouble to the bishops. Sermons were evidently a gratification to the mental restlessness of the age.[12]

[10] W. Stubbs, *Constitutional History of England,* III, 47, 64, etc.

[11] G. Lechler, *Wyclif,* I, 283-323; H. L. Cannon, "The Poor Priests," *American Historical Association, Annual Report,* 1889, I, 449-82.

[12] See G. R. Owst, *Preaching in Mediaeval England* (Cambridge, 1926); A. Lecoy de la Marche; *La Chaire française au Moyen Age, specialement au XIIIe Siècle* (second edition, Paris, 1886); F. R. Albert, *Geschichte der Predigt in Deutschland bis Luther* (3 parts, Gütersloh, 1892-1896).

Large parts, eventually the whole of the Bible, translated from the Latin Vulgate into easy vernacular English, were spread abroad at this time. It was a natural step. English was rapidly making its way forward as the single national language. In 1362 it was required by act of parliament that pleadings in the courts of law should be in English and in 1363 for the first time the lord chancellor used English for his speech opening parliament. *Piers Plowman,* the mystical writings of Richard Hampole and the poetry of Hoccleve were all written in English, and Chaucer had already begun the *Canterbury Tales* while Wyclif was at Oxford. Moreover it was an age of translations, including translations of the Bible. Parts were extant in French from early in the fourteenth century, and a new translation of the whole Bible from Latin into French was being made between 1398 and 1407 at the expense of the Duke of Orleans; there were translations in Catalan and Castilian before 1300, though the Catalan translation was suppressed as early as 1266 by decree of the King of Aragon, and the Castilian version which had been made on the order of Alfonso the Wise in 1269 was driven out of use by the church authorities. There is, however, a copy still in the Escorial. In 1422 Don Luiz Gonzales, Master of the Order of Calatrava, engaged a learned Jew to translate the Old Testament anew into Castilian, on the ground that the old Spanish was now antiquated and obscure. This work was finished in 1430. There were also German and Bohemian versions.[13] Wyclif says, "The worthy realm of France, notwithstanding all lettings, hath translated the Bible and the Gospels, with all other true sentences of doctors, out of Latin into French. Why should not English men do so?"

Just who made these translations into English, the part taken by Wyclif, and the origin of other contemporary translations have long been matters of erudite discussion; but certain it is that they became common by 1400. One hundred and seventy manuscripts of various portions of the Bible in English, all dating from the fourteenth century, have survived official destruction and the casual ravages of time. Some of these are finely written and handsomely bound, books that might have befitted nobles or those knights of

[13] Marcelino Menendez Pelayo, *Heterodoxos Espanoles* (three volumes, Madrid, 1880-81.) I, 435; II, 704; H. C. Lea, *Chapters from the Religious History of Spain* (Philadelphia, 1890), 17-9; F. Falk, *Die Bibel am Ausgange des Mittelalters* (Cologne, 1905).

whom Wyclif says that they "have wille to rede in Englische the gospel of Cristis lyf." Others are small and rough, such as might well have belonged to poor men. Queen Anne had a copy of the four gospels in English which she submitted to Archbishop Arundel, who assured her that they were correctly translated. Another handsomely illuminated copy was in 1397 in the possession of the Duke of Gloucester, and still another is among the books once belonging to "Good Duke Humphrey."[14]

There was no heresy in the Wyclifite translation of the Bible, but from that vast repository of story and teaching, from its record of personal experience and its prophecy of future reward and punishment, from its poetry and spiritual appeal, the unguided reader or the reader guided only by such inspiration as his own needs, desires and aspirations provided, was sure to draw doctrines different from those the official church prescribed. The Bible has never been put into the hands of common men without awakening not only devotion but much divergence of opinion and often bizarre individual interpretation. For good or ill, after about 1380, the Bible was in the hands of the people and so it remained for more than a generation, notwithstanding the disapproval and the efforts of the bishops and the more conservative clergy. "This Master Wyclif translated from the Latin into the tongue of the Angles (not of the angels) the gospel which Christ intrusted to the clergy and learned men of the church in order that they might gently minister it to the laity and to the weak, according to the exigencies of the times and the need and mental hunger of each one. Thus to the laity and even to such women as can read this was made more open than formerly it had been, even to such of the clergy as were well educated and of great understanding. Thus the evangelical pearls have been scattered abroad and trampled by the swine."[15]

The result desired by Wyclif and dreaded by most churchmen followed. Over and over again when heretics were prosecuted it was part of the charge that they were found to have copies of the Eng-

[14] Wylie, op. cit., II, 34; J. H. Penniman, *A Book about the English Bible* (New York, 1920), 336-43; Capes, *English Church in the Fourteenth and Fifteenth Centuries*, 124-31; Margaret Deanesley, *The Lollard Bible and other Medieval Biblical Versions* (Cambridge, 1920); F. A. Gasquet, *The Old English Bible and Other Essays* (London, 1897), expresses opinions on the translations different from the prevailing ones.

[15] Henry Knighton, *Chronicon*, II, 151-2 (Rolls Series).

lish Bible in their possession. Long afterward the denouncers of a certain Richard Hunne, who was burnt for heresy, said of him "There lay his English Bible open and some other works of his, that every man might see the places noted with his own hand." Ralph Mungyn, who was in trouble in 1428 for criticizing the pope for indulging in unchristian warfare, was found to have had the gospels of Wyclif in his possession for twelve years. A parish priest in Sussex, who was suspected of heresy and brought up for trial before the bishop, confessed that he had the gospels in English and some other books of Wyclif. A group of heretics were known as "Bible men." There emerged many of those deviations from traditional doctrine that naturally follow a literal interpretation. One man insisted that the seventh day, not the first, must be kept as the sabbath, another that pork must not be eaten, another that it is wicked to take oaths, another that imprisonment for debt is forbidden in the Bible. Some were so literal as to object to capital punishment and to war. Reading the Bible in the vernacular did not necessarily produce heresy, but it did stimulate independent thought and thus superseded one of the main functions of the church, the guidance of the religious life of the laity.

Notwithstanding the number of men of good family who were Lollards, the great mass of religious dissent in England was among the lower clergy and the common people. The leavening effect of the Scriptures in their own language, the preaching and teaching of Wyclif himself and of the "poor priests" and the receptive mood of the nation carried Lollardy far afield. The Lollard meets us at every turn. In a chapel just outside the town gates of Leicester crowds gathered to listen to the preaching of a heretical priest named Swynderby. When he was forbidden by the bishop to preach in any church or chapel in the diocese he chose as his pulpit a pile of millstones set up for sale by the roadside and declared his intention of preaching there, "so long as he had the goodwill of the people."

Some were fanatical or eccentric, some impious. A certain Wiltshire knight, Sir Lawrence St. Martin, when handed the consecrated wafer rose from his knees, took it home with him, broke it into three pieces and ate one with oysters, one with onions and one with wine, to show that it was no different from ordinary bread. Another split up an image of St. Catherine for firewood to boil his cabbage. A woman in London set up a private altar in her house, dressed her daughter as a priest and travestied the mass. In Salisbury some of the lower clergy ordained colleagues to the priesthood. On the other hand a knight, Sir Cornelius Clowne, long a disbeliever in transubstantiation, was converted by seeing the word "Jesus" in bloody outline on the whiteness of the communion wafer as the priest dropped it into the cup.[16]

So a knight, a priest or chaplain here and there, a poor mechanic, a weaver, a tailor, a woman, is named in the contemporary records as instance, as illustration or as culprit in a trial. We hear of crowds coming, after persecution had begun, to kiss the ground where those they considered martyrs were burned and to carry off their ashes as relics. So the Lollard appears as a familiar character in the poetry and prose of the time; such as Chaucer's parson who objects to the host's profanity and is jestingly called a Lollard, or the "Master Lollard" of the Townley Plays.

III. THE SUPPRESSION OF ENGLISH LOLLARDY

The best measure of the extent and seriousness of the Lollard rebellion against the official church is the time and effort required by church and state to put it down. It took thirty years to reduce Lollardy to unimportance and a full half-century to drive it into complete obscurity. This struggle, although full of dramatic incident, need not be told in detail here. This chapter is engaged with the failures, not with the successes, of the medieval church, or perhaps, more fairly, with the ruinous cost of such successes as she won. The crushing out of Lollardy was one of these successes, but the price of it was increased dependence of the church on the civil government, the substitution, in many cases, of cold conformity for warm piety, of a submissive but stagnant Oxford for one full of life and independent thought.

In extirpating heresy the church received indispensable support from three successive kings, Richard II, Henry IV and Henry V, and from the majority in Parliament. Royal ordinances and parlia-

[16] Knighton, *Chronicon,* II, 163-4; Thomas Walsingham, *Historia Anglicana,* I, 450-1; II, 253.

mentary statutes succeeded one another in 1382, 1395, 1401, 1406, 1414. The great Lollard statute of 1401 "for the burning of heretics," introduced and pushed through Parliament by the clergy, required sheriffs and other local officers to receive heretics after their conviction in a church court "and them before the people in a high place cause to be burnt, that such punishment may strike fear into the minds of others."[17]

Thus the theory that churchmen should possess control over the faith and religious practices of the people, and that the civil government should support them in their powers, even to the infliction of the death penalty, was introduced into English law and remained a weapon in the hands of the church authorities for a century and a half. Henry IV's approval of this statute, the connivance of Prince Henry with the burning of Sawtrey, and, after he became king, with the prosecution for heresy of his old friend and companion in arms Sir John Oldcastle, are only the most striking indications of the aggressive orthodoxy of the crown.

The actual suppression of Lollardy was, however, the work of the organized church. The Peasants' Rebellion of 1381 had helped to stem the tide of heresy by building up a dike of reaction. Religious and social disaffection were closely intertwined and a conservative fear of further violence showed itself in varied action against any deviation from accustomed ways in either church or state. The death in the insurrection of Archbishop Sudbury, a man of the people and perhaps not himself unsympathetic with the ideas of Wyclif, brought into the archbishop's chair Courtenay and after him Arundel, both members of noble families and both determined upholders of authority. Vigorous action was brought to bear by the archbishop, the provincial and diocesan councils, and the bishops of London, Hereford and Salisbury upon all who were disobedient to authority. Statements of orthodox doctrine and rules for securing conformity were drawn up in 1382, 1396, 1407, and 1409 in successive meetings of the clergy and these were enforced by the church courts. After the statutes against heretics were passed, the church-

[17] *Rotuli Parliamentorum,* III, 122, 132; 5 Richard II; 2 Henry IV, c. 15; *Statutes of the Realm,* II, 23, 26, 125-8.

men had the assistance of sheriffs and other officers. Oxford was with much difficulty and after long conflict reduced to submission.[18]

It is a curious fact that the first generation of the Lollards in almost all cases recanted. There was no Inquisition in England, nor was torture a part of English court procedure, civil or ecclesiastical, but so strong was the tradition of authority, so complete the control of the organized church over all forms of religious and intellectual life, so overwhelming the sense of powerlessness of the unsupported individual standing alone before the representatives of universal ecclesiastical authority, that, when brought before such a forum, offenders almost uniformly succumbed, signed recantations of their former beliefs and performed such penance as was imposed upon them. It was not till years had passed and heresy had become more familiar in England that men became more firm and furnished new contingents to "the noble army of the martyrs."[19]

When once courage was gained and when once the fires provided for by the statute of 1401 were lighted the list of those who endured to the end began to lengthen. There was Badby, the tailor of Evesham; White, the relapsed heretic, and the two priests of Norwich (Norwich was always a restless city); "A ribald tiler . . . who despised the seven sacraments" and Richard Wych, a clergyman, who like several other clerics was burnt on Tower Hill. So some fifty or more came to their end at the stake or, when treason was combined with heresy, as in the case of Sir John Oldcastle, on the gallows. Many even yet recanted. The church wanted above all things obedience, acknowledgment of its authority, and therefore was willing to make large offers of mercy. After a certain heretic had been burned to death at the stake in Norwich, 120 Lollards in the diocese recanted on being offered mild penance. Men and women, stripped to their shirts, carrying fagots or candles as penance for holding heretical beliefs, were a common sight before St. Paul's or in the market-places of Leicester or Bristol.[20]

Gradually the long struggle of the church was successful; the purging of the university was achieved, the books of Wyclif were

[18] Capes, *The English Church in the Fourteenth and Fifteenth Centuries,* 141-4, 149, 151, 157, 169, chap. ix.

[19] E. P. Cheyney, "The Recantations of the Early Lollards," *American Historical Review,* IV (1909), 423-38.

[20] Capes, op. cit., 145-9; Wylie, *England under Henry IV,* III, 423-49.

burned in the market-place of Oxford, the silencing of wandering preachers was accomplished; the crushing of Lollardy as a political danger was completed with the execution of Oldcastle in 1417. The tide of heresy ebbed to a low level. Viewing the long procession of these rebellious spirits as they appear in the contemporary chronicles, as they pass through the pages of Foxe or as their trials and beliefs are more critically discussed in the pages of modern writers, one is struck with the hunger of a multitude of souls for something which the church was not giving them. Amid all the contentiousness of fanaticism, all the crude and ignorant interpretation of the Scriptures, all the impatience of the heavy hand of authority, there was a longing for spiritual satisfaction. The period was one of restlessness, of criticism, of insurgency against fixed conditions. Just as the serfs wanted freedom, just as the man of the middle class grasped at the share in the government of town or nation that guaranteed protection to his interests and gave scope to his enterprise, just as the soldier and the traveler sought adventure, so the pious soul wanted to seek out its own salvation. For this desire the church had little sympathy or guidance. Obedience to its authority, acceptance of its teaching, satisfaction with its sacraments, material support of its members, such were its offerings and its claims.

The Lollard rebellion against these ideals gradually died out or became obscured and by the middle of the fifteenth century, the end of our period, it was quite insignificant. If there was dissent, it was silent. If "Wyclif's Wicket," "The Lanterne of Light," "The Booke of the New Law," or the Scriptures in English were read, they were read in secret. The church had her way; heresy all but disappeared from among clergy and people alike. But the victory of the church was a pyrrhic victory. As already remarked, the religious zeal which might have inspired it with new life was lost to it, and there remained only a lethargic willingness on the part of the church and the people to accept whatever form of religion their rulers presented to them. The political support on which the church had relied for success against the Lollards had in due time to be paid for in the coin of ecclesiastical submission to royal supremacy. It was two and a half centuries afterward that Milton declared, "Had it not bin the obstinat perverseness of our prelats against the divine and admirable spirit of Wicklef, to suppresse him as a schismatic and innovator . . . the glory of reforming all our neighbors had bin compleatly ours."[21]

IV. THE RELIGIOUS AWAKENING OF BOHEMIA

English Lollardy did not die with its submergence in England; it reappeared in Bohemia. That country offered at the time a peculiarly receptive soil. It was, in the first place, experiencing a vigorous awakening of national feeling. A Slavic nation extending like a great wedge into the Teutonic centre of Europe, it had long submitted to the pervasive influence of the more aggressive, more commercial and more cultured Germans who made their way in as ecclesiastics, colonists, merchants and officials, controlling state, church, learning and economic life.

From the middle of the fourteenth century the tide turned. Charles IV, king and emperor, who ruled in Bohemia from 1333 in 1378, notwithstanding his German name and origin, was a son and grandson of Bohemian kings and encouraged Bohemian nationality in every practicable way. He planned to make Prague a great European capital and to a large extent he succeeded. The Bohemian nobles were encouraged to follow local customs and respect national tradition. The Czech language was given, like other vernacular tongues of the period, more extended recognition and usage. Collections of laws and customs were issued in the native language, and works of literature and science appeared in national dress. It was the golden age of Bohemia. In 1344 the bishopric of Prague was separated from the province of Mainz and became an independent archdiocese, over which a succession of vigorous metropolitans held sway. In 1348 a university was established on the model of Paris, Oxford and Bologna; it not only became a centre of the national movement but rivalled the older institutions in numbers, learning and attraction to foreign students.[22]

Accompanying this national revival was a movement for ecclesiastical and moral reform. The churches received the doubtful ad-

[21] *Areopagitica*, pub. Nov. 1644, *Works of John Milton* (London, 1867), IV, 436.

[22] Count F. H. von Lützow, *Bohemia, an Historical Sketch* (first edition, 1896; Everyman Library, London, 1909), a popular work by a learned historian; Gerald G. Walsh, *The Emperor Charles IV* (New York, 1924), chap. iii.

vantage of numerous grants of land and bequests from the crown and nobles. Ecclesiastics of local birth, though often of foreign training, were placed at the head of the local churches, and new sets of rules of a reformatory nature were issued. This religious revival was spread by popular preaching. In the generation overlapping that of Wyclif, just as he and his followers preached evangelical sermons at Oxford, in London and throughout England, so a succession of famous Bohemian preachers—Conrad of Waldhausen, Milicz of Kremsier, Albert Ranconis, Thomas of Stitny, Mathias of Janov, John of Stekno, John Hus and others—preached in the churches of Prague and other Bohemian towns and in country parishes. Just as the English preachers used Latin or English according to the character of their congregations, so the Bohemian preachers spoke in Latin, in German or in Czech, as their audiences required. Some of their sermons were collected and published as models and material for young preachers, much as were Wyclif's tracts and homilies.[23]

This movement was independent of the established church. At Prague two men of means, a merchant named Kreuz and a knight, John of Mühlheim, in 1391 erected and endowed Bethlehem Chapel, a place for public preaching independent of the cathedral or of any parish church. The endowment provided for a chaplain, who should always be a secular clergyman and should preach to the people in the Czech language on all Sundays and holydays. It was a product of the national movement and of popular piety.[24]

In all this there was no heresy. The popular preachers were or at least intended to be entirely orthodox, and in the few cases when the soundness of their teaching was questioned, they, like the early English Lollards, yielded to authority. Indeed, the repression of heresy was stated to be one of the special objects of the new statutes issued by the archbishop and was urged in the instructions to

[23] See V. Novotný, "Les Origines du Mouvement Hussite en Bohême," *Revue d'Histoire des Religions* (1929); V. Kybal, "Étude sur les Origines du Mouvement Hussite en Bohême; Mathias de Janov," *Revue Historique,* CIII (1910), 1-31.

[24] Franz Palacký, *Geschichte von Böhmen* (Prague, 1845), Band III, Abth. i. 160-230. Palacký's classic history is strongly colored by his fervent nationalism. As an antidote one might consult the correspondingly anti-Czech accounts of A. Bachmann, *Geschichte Böhmens* (two volumes, Gotha, 1899-1905), written as a reply to Palacký, and the more readable but even more hostile narrative of Berthold Bretholz, *Geschichte Böhmens* (two volumes, Reichenberg, 1921-1922).

young clergymen. The heresy they had in mind was doubtless the teaching of the Waldenses which, as it was rooted out in France, had spread eastward and was now prevalent in Bohemia, Moravia and Poland.

Nevertheless the revivalists were strict moralists and did not hesitate to blame the lives of the clergy as well as of the laity, even of those in high places. They were, besides, devoted to the Bible and treated it constantly as the principal if not the only source of religious teaching. "From youth up I have loved the Bible and called it my friend and bride, the very mother of fair affection, of knowledge, of fear and blessed hope," writes Mathias of Janov. He wrote, somewhere between 1380 and 1382, *Rules of the New and Old Testament,* which declared as positively as Wyclif ever did that the Bible alone is the standard of faith. Familiar reformed doctrines propounded by Mathias—that salvation is by faith alone; that it is belief in Christ, not baptism or confirmation, that makes the Christian; that ceremonies, pilgrimages, the veneration of relics and images only serve to turn the mind away from more spiritual worship—these can have been overlooked by the church authorities only because they appear solely in his Latin writings and no conspicuous effort was made by him to spread them among the people. Thomas of Stitny, however, wrote in the language of the people tracts repeating criticism of churchmen, appealing for more spiritual religion based on a study of the Scriptures, and speaking with scant respect of ceremonies and of the intervention of the priest.

The Bible, or at least the Gospels and the Psalter, were already known among the people. Before the fourteenth century was over they had the whole Bible in their own language. There was an antiquated Czech version dating from quite early times, but a more modern translation was known to English scholars about 1388; the copy of the Gospels in Bohemian, German and Latin possessed by Queen Anne about the same date has already been referred to. The popularity of the Bible in the vernacular is shown by the existence of some thirty-three manuscripts of the whole Bible in Czech, and twenty-two additional manuscripts of the New Testament, all dating from a period before the invention of printing.

What would have been the course of development of this popular revival, already verging on heresy, if it had remained a purely native movement, cannot now be known, for it was soon subjected to a powerful impulse coming from abroad. This was the influence of English Lollardy. There were several bonds that bound the two countries together at this time. In 1381 Anne of Bohemia, daughter of Charles IV and sister of Wenzel and Sigismund, successive kings of Bohemia, came to England as the wife of Richard II and lived there till 1394. Bohemians came in her train, and embassies passed to and fro between the two countries. Henry of Lancaster visited Prague in 1392 and later Sigismund visited England.

The common interchange of students among the universities of Europe brought occasional English students to the new university of Prague and Bohemians to the old intellectual centre of Oxford. The latter was made a regular practice by a foundation established by Adalbert Ranconis, a graduate of Prague and probably himself a former student at Oxford, long a lecturer at the university and dean of the cathedral at Prague. In 1388 he made a will providing for the support of a certain number of Bohemian students devoting themselves to the liberal arts or theology at Paris or Oxford—a group of traveling fellowships. An echo of the prevailing nationalism exists in the provision of the will that the holders must be Czechs on both father's and mother's side and that the administrators of the fund must also be Czechs living in Prague and from there remitting the money to students at Paris or Oxford.[25]

Recipients of this fund may well have been the principal transmitters of the writings of Wyclif to Bohemia. There were in the last decade of the fourteenth century, perhaps in the time of Wyclif himself, Bohemian students in England who became familiar with his teachings and writings. Jerome was a student at Oxford in 1399 who, impressed by Wyclif's learning and repute, copied at least two of his treatises and brought them back with him to Prague in 1401 or 1402. There are still at Prague manuscripts of works of Wyclif, with the names of their copyists, made in the little English village of Braybrooke in the year 1407. The national and religious revival in Bohemia and the prevailing tendency to criticize the church encouraged the immediate spread of these writings. It was said that

[25] The will is printed in *Oesterreichische Mittheilungen,* XVII, 210-3.

ninety separate works of Wyclif were available there in many copies. A few years later they were so well known and so widely disseminated that 200 manuscripts were collected and burned. Notwithstanding this and much other destruction numerous copies have survived to our own time.[26]

V. JOHN HUS

Many of the students and theologians at Prague acknowledged that their previous beliefs and judgments had been changed by the writings of the English master lately introduced, but of transcendent importance was the influence exercised by these writings on the scholar, writer and preacher John Hus or Husinec.[27] Born in a remote part of Bohemia of humble parentage and raised amid hardships, he was attracted to the clerical life, as he himself admitted, by its greater ease; but he soon became, like Wyclif, a devoted university scholar. He worked his way through the University of Prague, graduated Master of Arts in 1396, began lecturing in 1398, and rose to be dean of the faculty of philosophy in 1401 and rector in 1403. He was also a canon of the cathedral and became confessor to the queen. But it was as a preacher that he exerted his greatest influence. Ordained a priest in 1400 he gained early popularity and was appointed chaplain of Bethlehem Chapel in 1402. The writings of Wyclif, at first those of a philosophical, then those of a theological and still later those of a purely devotional nature, attracted him as soon as he came into contact with them. He began to quote from them, to praise and recommend them to his hearers, to argue from them and to use them as the basis of his religious teachings. He himself says of Wyclif in a letter to a critic, "I am drawn to him by his writings, by which he seeks to bring back all men to the law of Christ, and especially so the clergy, to the end that they may dis-

[26] Wylie, *England under Henry IV*, III, 450-5; G. von Lechler, *Wyclif*, II, 322-41; see also O. Odložilík, "Wycliff's Influence on Central Europe," *Slavonic Review*, VII (1929), 634-62.

[27] The great standard biographies of Hus are available only in Czech. They are discussed at length by Joseph Šusta, "Histoire de la Tchécoslovaquie," *Revue Historique*, CL (1925), 67 ff., and CLXXII (1933), 88 ff. Franz Strunz, *Johannes Huss, sein Leben und seine Werke* (Munich, 1927), is a brief compilation, with extracts from Hus' writings and sermons. Jan Herben, *Hus and His Followers* (London, 1926), is a competent popular sketch.

miss the splendor and glory of the world and with the apostles live after the life of Christ."[28]

Hus, like his English master, lived in two separate but by no means completely disconnected spheres, that of university lecturer and controversialist and that of popular religious agitator. In both fields he obtained many adherents, but, considering the source from which so many of his ideas were derived, he quite naturally aroused much opposition among conservative clergymen. In May 1403 two of his fellow canons of the cathedral handed in to the university a series of forty-five points of Wyclif's teaching, which, as they pointed out, had already been declared heretical, and demanded that all lecturers in the university should be forbidden to teach or preach them. This was agreed to by a slight majority of the masters and thus began a deep rift in the university, among the cathedral and city clergy and among the populace. Hussite or Wyclifite doctrines soon spread through all classes and became in Prague and in much of Bohemia the prevailing belief of the community.

When the university, led chiefly by the German element, took grounds against the new doctrine, local patriotism was brought to bear. A split occurred, the Germans and most of the other foreigners left Prague, and the reform party came uppermost. The university became the patriotic centre of the nation, the great upholder of the new doctrines and thereby a patron of heresy.[29]

At the cathedral Hus was for some years regularly appointed to preach the semi-annual Latin sermon to the assembled clergy, but as he diverged more widely from accepted doctrine and became more outspoken in his criticism of the clergy, the archbishop and several of the canons turned against him. In 1409 they appealed to the pope for further powers to contend against heresy. The necessary bull soon came. In accordance with its provisions the archbishop issued an order that all persons having copies of Wyclif's writings containing any of the forty-five condemned articles should

[28] See the remarkable series of parallels in J. Loserth, *Huss und Wyclif* (new and augmented edition, Munich, 1925). Loserth was the great exponent of the theory of Wyclif's influence, which is minimized by Novotný and some, though by no means, all recent Czech writers. See, in addition to Šusta's review articles, K. Krofta, "L'Aspect National et Social du Mouvement Hussite," *Le Monde Slave,* V (1928), 321-51.

[29] Creighton, *The Papacy during the Reformation,* I, Book II, chaps. iii-v, gives step by step the sequence of these events. Appendices nos. 11, 13 and 16 are of special value.

surrender them, and that all preaching in any place except the cathedral and the parish churches should cease. More than 200 manuscripts, as has been said, were turned in and in July 1410 there was a holocaust of Wyclif's books in the courtyard of the archbishop's palace. While the cathedral bells were tolled and the cathedral clergy sang Te Deum, as if for a victory, the university, now purely Czech and largely Hussite, protested against the destruction. Hus and some others of the clergy appealed from the archbishop to the newly elected pope, John XXIII, and Hus continued to preach, notwithstanding the archbishop's order, to thousands in Bethlehem Chapel. The pope, instead of accepting his appeal, ordered his appearance for trial at Rome. Hus refused to go and a few days later the archbishop proclaimed his excommunication and that of all others who had disobeyed the orders of the church to bring in heretical books and cease unlicensed preaching.

Riots and tumult spread through the city. In a sermon Hus defied the church authorities and appealed to the people. "I know not whether the pope who has just died, the one who has issued orders to burn the books of Master John Wyclif where many good things are to be found, is in heaven or in hell, but I have appealed against him. Will you support me?" His hearers in the church shouted their assent. Hus urged them to stand firm and not to fear excommunication; "let us gird ourselves, and stand for the law of God after the example of the old covenant."

So through three years more, from 1410 to 1412, Prague and much of Bohemia were torn by religious conflict. King Wenzel at one time appealed to the pope and the archbishop to allow freedom of preaching and to release Hus from his excommunication, at another ordered the rebellious clergy to obey their superiors in the church. An interdict was laid upon the city, the cathedral treasures were taken to the castle for safe-keeping, and an attack was made on Bethlehem Chapel by a group of townsmen injured by the interdict. On the other hand the indulgences being sold to pay for Pope John's crusade against the King of Naples, protector of his rival, aroused anew the opposition which the sale of indulgences has never failed to produce, stirred Hus to bitter attacks on the head of the church, and gave occasion for riots in which students, led by Jerome, drove the pope's messengers out of the city, piled the pardons on a cart, carried them through the streets and then burned them in the market-place. In July 1412 three young men were tried and beheaded in the city ditch for sharing in these riots and shouting in a church that the indulgences were lies and the pope a liar. But the crowd hailed them as martyrs.

There is a threat of rebellion in all heresy where the state and the church are closely united, as had been seen in the case of the Albigensians in France and even in the plots of Sir John Oldcastle in England. In Bohemia force was in evidence both above and below from the very beginnings of the Hussite movement, which was now fast entering upon a phase of more material struggle than could be confined to university lecture halls, pulpits, church courts or even occasional riots in the streets. The pope's emissaries appealed to the populace of Prague to raze Bethlehem Chapel as a mere nest of heretics, while Hus talked of unsheathing the sword, and his congregations threatened bloodshed if they were interfered with.

King Wenzel himself was troubled at the fast spreading waves of turbulence and appealed to Hus to suspend his preaching in the city. As Wyclif at the request of convocation had left Oxford to avoid conflict thirty years before, so Hus left Prague about Christmas, 1412, and took up his residence at the castle of a friendly nobleman some distance in the country. Here and in other retreats, busily writing books, pamphlets, letters of appeal to his people at Bethlehem Chapel and to the university, and occasionally preaching in the villages, he remained while his doctrines were taking deeper and deeper root through the country until in 1414 he was summoned to appear at the council of Constance.

VI. HUS BEFORE THE COUNCIL OF CONSTANCE

The gathering of the council and its work in settlement of the schism has been already described. It entered early upon its second task, the definition and, as it hoped, the extirpation of heresy. Its efforts centered upon the teachings of Wyclif and Hus. All earlier disputes concerning heresy were forgotten in the recency and extent of these and their danger to the authority of the church. A definitive decision had to be reached.[30]

Soon after the opening of the council two successive commissions were appointed to consider extracts from the writings of Wyclif placed before them. These were the forty-five articles that had been recently presented by the conservative party at Prague, and some 200 sent by the party now in control of the University of Oxford. They were promptly condemned as heretical by both commissions and then by the whole council. All the writings of Wyclif were ordered to be destroyed wherever found; his body was to be dug up and cast out from consecrated ground. Manuscripts of Wyclif had already been burned at Oxford, Prague and Rome and there was some further destruction as a result of the orders of the council; but there were enough left to serve as material for devotion and contention at the time, and for reproduction and study by modern scholars.[31] The sentence of desecration of his bodily remains was carried out twelve years later by the bishop of his diocese. There is no indication that these bitter attacks on his writings and on his remains served to diminish his influence or his reputation; so great has been the power of constituted authority over material things, so little over ideas.

Hus had welcomed the emperor's suggestion that he go to Constance, anticipating an opportunity to show that his teachings had Biblical support and trusting in his skill as a controversialist to defend his views before a body less prejudiced against him than the cathedral clergy of Prague. Before his departure from Bohemia, however, he procured from the archbishop and the Inquisition testimony to his orthodoxy concerning transubstantiation, and also a safe-conduct from Emperor Sigismund.

When he arrived at Constance on November 3, 1414, great numbers of people received him affectionately, because of his reputation for piety. The pope, too, showed him respect, in consideration of the favor he enjoyed with the emperor. For a few weeks his

[30] C. J. von Hefele, *Histoire des Conciles* (French translation by H. Leclerq, Paris, 1907-1921), VII, Pt. 2, 223-7.

[31] See T. Arnold, *Select English Works of Wyclif* (three volumes, Oxford, 1869-1871); F. D. Matthews, *English Works of Wyclif hitherto unprinted* (Early English Text Society, London, 1880); *Wyclif's Latin Works* (Wyclif Society, London, 1883-1913), thirty-two volumes.

lodgings were a centre of popular religious discussion. This was distasteful to the pope and cardinals, whom his Bohemian opponents were busily stirring up against him. Late in November, therefore, he was formally accused of heresy, arrested and placed in confinement in a convent on a little island in the lake, where he was treated with much rigor and interrogated on his religious views according to the usual inquisitorial process. At the same time a commission of the council examined witnesses and drew up a more definite statement of the heretical views charged against him.[32]

His friends and, after his arrival, the emperor protested against his imprisonment, but the pope supported the well established rule of the church, that a person charged with heresy lost all civil rights until the charges were disproved. Sigismund, perhaps overpersuaded by the authorities of the church, perhaps fearful of the dissolution of the council before its work was accomplished, perhaps yielding to his own hatred of heresy and vexation at the stiffness of Hus under examination, to his eternal discredit ceased to assert the validity of his safe-conduct and acquiesced in all later proceedings against Hus.

Before these were taken, however, the reformer was kept in prison for seven months, much of the time chained to a post, poorly fed, and under the charge of alien and disrespectful guards. Eventually, on the demand of his friends, he was allowed to appear before the general council. On his first appearance, June 5, 1415, the confusion and interruptions were so great that the sitting had to be suspended. For the next two days there was open discussion. He acknowledged his admiration for Wyclif, though disagreeing with him on transubstantiation. His desire to discuss theological and legal questions was refused on the ground that there were definite charges against him which he must first recant or be held guilty of heresy. He angered the emperor and the clergy alike by throwing doubt on the right of those in mortal sin to rule either in state or in church, and introduced the unfamiliar conception of the church, held by Marsiglio of Padua and Wyclif, who regarded the church not as the body of ordained clergy, but as all those, whether clergy or laity, who were predestined to salvation. Such opinions could

[32] Creighton, *The Papacy during the Reformation*, I, 331-55.

not be condoned by those holding authority, political or ecclesiastical. Beliefs were rather recklessly charged against Hus that he declared he did not hold, and he tried hotly to argue that those which he did hold were not heretical.

But the crucial question was not arguable. Was he or was he not willing to submit himself to the judgment of the church speaking through the council, the pope, the cardinals and other ecclesiastical judges? He still asserted his right to accept or not accept their judgment and was therefore, according to the theory of the church, necessarily condemned. No doubt was expressed of his personal piety or his gifts of teaching and public preaching; no one questioned whether he was a man of deep learning and devout life; whether he was a beloved and helpful teacher of students at the university and a powerful influence for a good life among the people of Bohemia; whether he was a good shepherd of sheep wandering far afield.

These questions were not raised at Constance. No doubt Hus was provocative, defiant and obstinate; no doubt his judges were overbearing and contentious. He had all the pride of the theological controversialist; they represented ecclesiastical authority, the most arrogant of all forms of power. The only question was of obedience to the church, as represented by the clergy there present. When Hus refused this there was no alternative to condemnation. Strong pressure was brought to obtain his recantation; it had been received from others a hundred times in the past two generations. Various forms of abjuration were placed before him, but each of them offended either his reason or his conscience. After four weeks passed in negotiation, he was brought before the whole council assembled in the cathedral of Constance, formally declared guilty of heresy, deposed from the priesthood, divested of the robes and symbols of his standing as a clergyman, and a paper fool's cap painted with devils put on his head. He was handed over to the secular power for punishment, with the usual specious avoidance by the church of responsibility for the infliction of the death penalty approved at that time by both canon and secular law. He was then led to the meadow outside the city walls where the monument to his martyrdom now stands, and burned at the stake. He died with serenity. His ashes were gathered by his executers and thrown into the Rhine. There should be no relics of the martyrdom.

Jerome, his follower and friend, the old Oxford and Prague student, the fiery missionary to Poland and Bohemia, a year later revoked the recantation he had at first made, declared that Hus was no heretic but a witness for the truth who had died a martyr. He was himself burned on the same spot.[33] Poggio Bracciolini, an Italian ecclesiastic attending the council, a devotee of the rising study of antiquity, wrote, characteristically, to a friend in Italy that Hus and Jerome endured death "with as much firmness as any ancient philosopher."[34]

It was not the stoicism of the philosopher nor even the patience with which a good man can accept a harsh and unjust punishment that made the victory of the Council of Constance over Hus and Jerome a barren one. It was rather that they were representatives of a large and growing number of persons determined not to accept the authority of the Roman church. They were a symbol of the increasing inability of that organization to retain its unity and to exercise such unquestioned dominion as it had once, but no longer, possessed.

We must follow the progress of that decline somewhat further, in two of its forms, the Hussite wars and the effort to reform the church from within through a succession of general councils. To neither of these need much space be given; the former was mainly a political and military struggle, the latter a chronicle of ineptitude and failure.

VII. THE HUSSITE WARS

The news of the harsh treatment and execution of Hus roused Prague and all Bohemia not only to anger but to arms. The execution of a Czech by a distant and alien body set fire to all the smoldering embers of nationality; the insistence of the council on rigorous orthodoxy as against any individual or national variation from the doctrines it laid down strengthened the Bohemian love of religious controversy and warmth of religious emotion. Above all, one of

[33] Hefele, *Histoire des Conciles,* VII, Pt. 2, 40-8, 215-83, 298-331, 396.
[34] Ortvin Gratius, *Fasciculus Rerum* (London, 1690), I, 170-174.

the most deeply loved and widely admired of national leaders in all history had been betrayed by his native sovereign and burned by foreign ecclesiastics. As a result, in September 1415, at a series of meetings in Prague 452 nobles and knights affixed their seals to a protest against the condemnation and execution of Hus, and more than half of them entered into a solemn covenant to uphold for the next six years their national religion and to resist any external attack upon it.[35]

It was long, however, before any agreement could be reached as to what this religion was, how it differed from that insisted upon by the pope and the council, and which of the various groups in Bohemia should be able to impose its views upon the others. After some five years of controversy, as a compromise, there were formulated and widely accepted "The Four Articles of Prague," providing for freedom of preaching, the giving of both bread and wine to the laity in the communion, the exclusion of the clergy from civil office and the possession of property, and the punishment of both clergy and laity for moral offenses. In the meantime there had been bitter dissensions throughout the country; supporters of the pope and council opposed Hussites, and the Hussites themselves split into two great divisions: Utraquists, the moderate party, and Taborites, the extremists. There were widespread riots; churches and convents were attacked and burned; priests, monks and laymen were killed in the conflict; images and relics were destroyed. King Wenzel wavered between Catholics and Hussites. At one time a papal legate was received and had three men burned at the stake for expressing views then almost universally held in the country; at another a wild crowd in Prague, seeking the release of some Hussite leaders, stormed the city-hall and threw the city councillors out of the windows to their death.

When, in 1419, Wenzel died, his brother Sigismund, now King of Bohemia as well as emperor, came to Prague with the intention of restoring his kingdom to orthodoxy and order. But the city gates were shut against the betrayer of Hus; on November 1, 1420, he was, with his German troops, defeated by a body of his rebellious

[35] An account of these events is the main subject of Count Lützow's *Bohemia* (Everyman Library, London, 1896), pp. 109-61; see also his *The Hussite Wars* (New York, 1914); E. Denis, *Huss et les Guerres Hussites* (Paris, 1930).

subjects, mostly peasants, under the walls of the city. He was forced to flee and it was not till 1436, sixteen years later, that he entered his capital.

There intervened the "Hussite wars," which troubled and devastated much of eastern and central Europe for almost twenty years.[36] They were at once civil and foreign wars, like the Hundred Years war in France, with the latter part of which they were contemporary. They were also religious wars. Sigismund was early declared deposed by a section of his subjects, but war broke out repeatedly between orthodox parties formed in his support and favoring a return to the church, and nationalist parties favoring a more or less independent religious policy. The more extreme and warlike party, the Taborites, developed leaders of resourcefulness, native genius and continued energy. John Ziska, and after him Procop the Great, are regularly listed among the world's great generals. The armies they built up were fired with a fierce national and religious enthusiasm.[37] At first they were almost purely Bohemian, but, as in most long war periods, they gradually drew in a large mercenary and alien element, and ultimately became an ever-victorious veteran professional army against which few opponents could stand. The old, half-barbarian eastern practice of using their baggage wagons arranged in a circle or square as bulwarks was combined with the new use of field-cannon and handguns which defended these ramparts until a wearied and demoralized attacking army, repulsed, became stubble before the flame of their sorties. The slaughter of the defeated armies, frequently but half-hearted in the contest, was terrible.

Sometimes, as during the civil wars between 1422 and 1426, the opponents were fellow-countrymen, but the campaigns were usually fought against invading bodies of so-called "crusaders." Five successive "crusades" were declared by the pope against the heretic nation. These armies were usually made up of German feudal or

[36] These confused conflicts can be best traced in Palacký, *Geschichte von Böhmen,* III, i, 407-21; ii, Book vii.

[37] It is worth noting that a recent biography of Ziska by Joseph Pekař, *Žižka a jeho Doba* (three volumes, Prague, 1927-1930), tends to overturn the idealized conception of Palacký. Pekař regards the whole Hussite wars as a national disaster for the Czechs and regards Ziska as a fanatic who prevented a reasonable compromise with the Emperor (see J. Šusta in the *Revue Historique,* CLXXII (1933), 88 ff.).

mercenary troops and led by German princes. Twice an English bishop-soldier, Cardinal Beaufort, brother of Edward IV, acted as one of the leaders against the Hussites, but twice the troops he helped to collect either dissolved before the Taborites or were diverted to meet more immediate needs in France.

In the years that followed 1420 and, after a period of civil war in 1426 and 1427, successful defensive campaigns were fought, in which all invaders were driven out and all Bohemia was brought under the control of the native army and its leaders. Then in 1428 there was a change. The Hussites themselves became invaders, at first of Moravia, Silesia and Hungary, to the east, then of Germany to the west. In destructive raids they reduced the regions through which they passed to despair and no power seemed able to withstand them. In 1429 and 1430 they penetrated to the very heart of Germany and sent plundering bands far to the north into Saxony and to the west almost to within sight of the Rhine. Germany was evidently powerless against these invaders. The last attempt at a counter-attack was made in 1431 when a crusading force under Cardinal Cesarini and Frederick of Hohenzollern entered Bohemia. On August 14, near the city of Taus, they were met by Procop and the Hussite army, singing its battle hymn, "All ye warriors of God," and driven back in helpless confusion and with great slaughter.

These events were the occasion for a series of successive stormy meetings of the German Reichstag from 1422 to 1434, in which attempts were made to introduce financial, military and constitutional reforms in Germany. Proposals were made in 1422 at Nürnberg and in 1427 at Frankfurt to organize an imperial standing army supported by a permanent tax, as was done in France in 1430, with the hope that it would withstand the Hussites; the invading Bohemians playing the same part in Germany as the invading English did in France. But the forces of decentralization were too strong; the armies of Germany remained the same ill-organized and poorly paid bodies that had formerly fled from the Hussites. In 1429 a papal legate met them on their retreat at the frontier and in his anger tore the imperial standard down and trampled it under foot but he was powerless to change the course of events. The proposed army reforms remained a dead letter.

VIII. THE END OF THE COUNCILS

The narrative of the Hussite wars now leads back to, as it had emerged from, a council of the church, for the Council of Basel, which met in July 1431, as provided for at the Council of Constance, came to the conclusion that negotiation with the heretic army and nation was absolutely necessary, if peace in Europe and good order in the church were to be attained. Even the pope, Eugenius IV, who in 1431 succeeded Martin V, feared the extension given to Hussite doctrines by the military successes of the Bohemians. News of the beliefs of the Hussites had spread with the news of the wars to the far confines of Europe, and the hope expressed at Constance that all discussions on matters of doctrine would be silenced was evidently vain. In many cities, especially in Germany, burgher governments were following the example of Prague, so far at least as to drive out domineering church officials.

The pope, the cardinals and the doctors of the church were therefore ready to make concessions. Sigismund had long been anxious to obtain his restoration, and the more moderate Hussites, including Procop, whose influence was great, desired peace for their country, so long a prey to warfare. When therefore in 1432 an invitation was sent from Basel to the Bohemians to send representatives to the council, it was for the purpose of reaching a compromise. The Four Articles of Prague were accepted as a basis of negotiation by both sides and guarantees of personal safety and free opportunity to argue their beliefs before the council were provided. Eight Bohemian clergymen and seven nobles representing the various Hussite factions appeared at Basel in January 1433; they were received, not as culprits before their judges, as Hus and Jerome had been at Constance, but with courtesy and at least outward willingness to hear the defense of their doctrines.[38]

While these discussions were in progress the internal troubles of Bohemia came to a crisis. A league for peace on any reasonable terms with the church and with the deposed king was formed

[38] Hefele, *Histoire des Conciles*, VII, Pt. 2, 715-21, 755-89.

among the nobles and the more conservative clergy and citizens of Prague. At the same time the elements favoring democracy and the social equality that, as has been observed, ran through all the popular movements of the time, gathered strength for resistance. Military leaders on both sides were old officers of Ziska and Procop, and both bodies had the strength and the weakness of long existing warfare. But the moderates were the more numerous and at the siege of Pilsen in 1433 and at a battle near Lipa in 1434, the remains of the old Taborite army were destroyed and Procop himself killed.[39] A triangular negotiation between the Bohemian leaders, the king and the council resulted in the "Compacts of Prague," signed in July 1436. So far as Sigismund was concerned, he agreed, as far as he was able, to protect Bohemians from external intrusion on their ecclesiastical semi-independence; archbishops and bishops of the Bohemian church should be elected by the Bohemian clergy; no foreigner should grant benefices in Bohemia or its dependent state, Moravia; nor should any natives of those countries be cited before a foreign tribunal. He received the oaths of fealty of the Bohemian nobles and at last entered Prague in state, August 1436.

The religious concessions of the council were less extensive, though in their implications hardly less important. The old demand of the Hussites that the laity should receive both bread and wine in the communion was conceded to all Bohemians and Moravians who should ask for it; preaching was to be free to all duly authorized, and the punishment of mortal sins was to be inflicted on all, clergy as well as laity. The right of holding property by the church was acknowledged and protected, but its administration was to be "according to the teaching of the Apostles and the Fathers," whatever that may have meant. It is evident that these vague terms saved the authority of the church so far as to make the council willing to agree to them, but yielded enough to the moderate Hussites to satisfy them and to strengthen them for the contest in which they trampled out the resistance of the more radical party.

The "compacts" seemed few and unimportant, and bore small proportion to the large liberties more radical reformers had claimed. But from the point of view of the power, authority and unity of

[39] F. Palacký, *Geschichte von Böhmen,* III, iii, 163-9.

the church they were of the greatest significance. They were wrested not only from the pope but from the general church. They authorized divergent practices among Christians as against the uniformity so constantly insisted on before by the church. They were not merely a denial to church authorities of excessive claims to rights of appointment and taxation, as were the Gallican liberties of France and the anti-papal legislation of England, but self-chosen and positive rights, forced from a reluctant hierarchy. Above all they were the poor but genuine remains of a great popular revival of piety, morality and independent thinking in Bohemia and far-off England. The council at Basel, with which the compacts of 1436 were signed, was the first assembly of importance that had met in obedience to the bull *frequens*, providing for regular meetings of a council every five years, decreed by the Council of Constance in 1417. It is true that in accordance with that requirement a council met in 1423 at Pavia, which for political reasons was immediately removed to Siena, but it was scantily attended and after a few months of irregular sessions was dissolved without having accomplished much. The council at Basel lasted from 1431 with varying activity and with many interruptions till 1449. There were long contests between the council and the pope as to their respective powers and much appeal to and interference by temporal rulers.[40]

Ultimately dissension between the council and Eugenius IV became so great that in 1437 he announced its transfer to Ferrara, later to Florence and in 1443 to Rome. A minority of the bishops and other attendants at Basel obeyed these summons and made up a small but obedient assembly. The majority of the attendants at the council at Basel, on the other hand, declared again that a general council of the church was superior in authority to the pope, refused to obey his summons, and continued to sit at Basel. In 1438 they claimed to suspend Eugenius from the exercise of his papal functions, and a year later declared that his insistence on his superiority to a general council was heresy, excommunicated him and finally announced his deposition. They proceeded to elect a new pope, Felix V, who succeeded in obtaining the acknowledg-

[40] See Noël Valois, *Le Pape et le Concile, 1418-1450; La Crise religieuse du XVe Siècle* (two volumes, Paris, 1909), for a detailed narrative of the Councils of Pavia-Siena and Basel; also P. Lazarus, *Das Basler Konzil* (Berlin, 1912).

ment of some of the smaller, but of none of the more important countries of Europe, which continued to recognize Eugenius as pope.

This condition, in which there were for a short time rival councils and rival popes, bade fair to become another schism, but in 1447 Eugenius died. The cardinals in the council at Rome elected a new pope Nicholas V. In 1449 the Basel council, having in the meantime moved to Lausanne, secured the abdication of Felix and by agreement chose as pope the same Nicholas V. There was therefore now but one pope; the rival council soon disappeared. On April 25, 1449, the Council of Basel-Lausanne finally dissolved itself; the council Basel-Ferrara-Florence-Rome, weary of its long controversies, disintegrated and dissolved.

At Basel in 1435, at Constantinople in 1437 and at Ferrara and Florence in 1438 and 1439 the principal object of interest was a series of attempts to unite the Greek Orthodox with the Roman Catholic church. This old division of Christendom seemed to demand reunion now that the Mohammedan Turks were pressing on the lands of the Greeks beyond their powers of resistance. In 1438, after long negotiations, a great embassy from the east, including the Greek Emperor, the Patriarch of Constantinople, twenty-two bishops of the eastern church and a great number of priests and laymen, arrived at Ferrara in a fleet hired by the pope and council from Venice. A vague formula of union was drawn up and accepted by both parties, but when it was announced in the east it was almost universally repudiated, and the division of Christendom remained much as it was before. As our period closes there was again but one pope, Nicholas V, who was ruling with such moral authority as remained to his office and such political power as he could secure or preserve in the midst of the rising autocratic monarchies. No further council was called for more than a century. The "conciliar period" was over.[41]

The general reformation "in head and members" which had been so constantly in the minds of the better men in the councils as one of the principal objects for which they were called, and which might have turned back the decline of the medieval church, had

[41] Valois, *Le Pape et le Concile,* I, 95-339; II, 344-51.

made so little progress and had been so reluctantly entered upon by the popes and the great body of the clergy that it left universally recognized abuses practically untouched. At Constance, at Siena, at Basel, measures had been adopted which promised improvement in discipline and morals, but they were passed halfheartedly and never enforced. Reform from within any organization, government or party has traditionally been difficult, and the history of the church during this period was a notable demonstration of this principle. So great are the vested interests in any institution, so complicated the involvements, so incapable its members and beneficiaries of approaching its problems in a critical spirit, that usually only outside and often only hostile influences can improve it. So the medieval church failed to reform itself peacefully in the fifteenth century. To resist force, if that should be exerted for its reformation, it had far less strength in 1450 than it had possessed two hundred years before.

Chapter Eight

LANGUAGE, LITERATURE AND ART

NEITHER the church nor the political world, nor even economic conditions, changed so much during this period as did literary and artistic practices and standards. The roots of modern languages and literature and of all forms of later art and intellectual interest lie deep in the soil of the middle ages, but their first flourishing and promise of fruitage was in these early centuries of modern times. The middle ages, however rich in things of the mind, were relatively stationary ages. The period with which we are dealing was, on the other hand, a period of great change. This change laid the literary and artistic basis of the modern world.

The languages of Europe were taking on approximately their permanent form. All written production, except for certain professional purposes and among the learned few, came to be in the recognized vernacular of each country. Men began to write in the language in which they spoke when they spoke most carefully, and the written language characteristic of this period became the standard for all later times. These centuries gave birth to an abundant and varied literature in each of the European languages.

The subjects and the fashions of literature and learning went through a somewhat similar change. As we have seen, there was during this period no cessation of scholastic interest or mystical thought, but the culture of Greece and Rome, the antithesis of scholasticism and mysticism, obtained a higher esteem; its literary survivals were more sought after and their contents more carefully studied and more widely disseminated. Contemporary with these changes in language, literature and learning and in some ways parallel with them, were the beginnings of a new and rapid development in art. Lastly, an elusive but real alteration in the mental attitude of the more thoughtful classes, not unconnected with the renewed study of the classics, but broader and more critical, became one of the characteristics of all later intellectual life.

I. THE PREVALENCE OF LATIN AND FRENCH

At the opening of this period Latin was still entrenched as the written language in the universities, the church, law, government, diplomacy and records. It was as natural to write in Latin as it was to speak in one's mother tongue. But Latin was not the only language preferred to the common language of the people. French too was almost an international language. Martino da Canale, an Italian scholar, about 1260, translated a Latin chronicle of Venice into French rather than Italian, "because the French language is current throughout the world and is more delightful to read and to hear than any other." Brunetto Latini, Dante's teacher, about 1265, gave two reasons why he, an Italian, was writing his *Trésor* in French; one reason was that he was then living in France; the other that the French language was "the most delectable and most familiar to all people." Dante himself spoke of it as being "an easier and pleasanter vulgar tongue" than any other of the romance languages. In the early fifteenth century French was spoken of by Christine de Pisane as "the best known language in the whole world."[1] The book of Ser Marco Polo appeared first in dialectical French and its earliest translation was into a more familiar form of the same language.

We hear of minstrels at Bologna "singing of Roland and Oliver," presumably in French, and the frequency of Italian baptismal names taken from the *chansons de geste* testifies to the popularity in Italy of the principal subjects of French literature. Through Savoy and Piedmont merchants, minstrels and pilgrims, on the way to Rome, using a language far superior to the native patois of those districts and meeting as yet no acknowledged form of Italian, spread the use of French far down into Italy. At the other end of the peninsula, for at least a half century during the domination of the Angevin rulers, French was the official, mercantile and literary language of Naples.

[1] *De Vulgari eloquentia,* Book I, chap. x; F. E. Brunot, *Histoire de la langue française* (Paris, 1905-), I, 358-60.

Carried on the waves of conquest to England, Naples and Flanders, taken by Crusaders to the east, spoken by merchants at inland fairs and along the western coasts of Europe, and spread with the repute of French chivalry among the knightly class in all countries, the innate merits of French, the interest of its literature and the variety of its verse-forms made the use of it habitual throughout much of Europe. The early deposit of a deep stratum of French words and forms in the language of Germany and the transformation of many Gallic legends into Teutonic folklore are proofs of the early prevalence of the French language and of the familiarity with French epic poetry in the regions along the Rhine. Royal marriages, political alliances and constant trading intercourse carried it far to the east of that border region. We are told that the great lords of Germany had French teachers for their children, and that the ability to speak French was used even by German poets as a test of courtly training. Wolfram von Eschenbach in his *Parsifal* makes the chief of the pagans speak French. The *Assises* of Jerusalem and of Antioch were in French, and in the official documents of the Armenian neighbors of the Crusaders, French was used as a second language.[2]

II. THE RISE OF MODERN ENGLISH

The rise of the respective native languages to national recognition and to literary and official use therefore involved, in many cases, the deposition from their dominant position not only of Latin but of French. This was especially true of England, where the Norman and the Angevin conquests, the successive waves of French-speaking adventurers and the prevalent literary fashion had seemed to make it as likely that French as that English would ultimately predominate. But the use of English had never been abandoned by the mass of the people, and it was always understood and even spoken by many of those who more habitually used French. Gilbert Foliot, made Bishop of London in 1164, though of Norman descent, preached fluently in English as well as in French and Latin. The same was true of Abbot Samson

[2] Adenet le Roi, *Bête aux Grans Pies,* 148-50, quoted in Brunot, op. cit., I, 359; Dulaurier, *Documents arméniens, Recueil des histoires des Croisades,* preface.

of Bury St. Edmunds about 1200, "but in the dialect of Norfolk, where he was born and bred," and half a century later of Bishop Grosseteste.[3] Stewards and bailiffs of manors, merchants frequenting towns and fairs, monks and the lower clergy, children in mixed families, however aristocratic, must have absorbed English from contiguity or from the requirements of their position. It is not hard to pick up the essentials of another language by ear and by frequent contact; bilingualism is a familiar phenomenon. Even the stream of native literature, though it had narrowed, had never dried up.

From the middle of the thirteenth century, however, the use of both written and conversational English rapidly increased. It is evident that for many purposes it was becoming necessary. Although the Provisions of Oxford, wrested from the King in 1258, were drawn up in Latin and French, when copies were sent to the shire courts to be read before the rural knights and freeholders, the letter accompanying them was in English.[4] Evidences of the increasing familiarity with English of the king, ministers and upper classes, and of willingness to give it recognition, became more and more numerous. When in 1257 Richard, Earl of Cornwall, was elected emperor, one of the claims for his choice was his familiarity with English, which, in the view of the chronicler, "is similar in sound to German."[5] In 1295 Edward I appealed to the patriotism of his subjects by charging the King of France with "threatening to destroy the English language from the face of the earth." When a representative of the king urged the Parliament of 1337 to approve his invasion of France, he spoke in English "to the end that he might be better understood by all."[6]

Certain privileges which the king had granted to London in the same decade were explained in English to the city council in the guildhall by one of the aldermen, although he had himself written a legal treatise, *Le Miroir de Justices,* in French. In 1362, on

[3] Walter Map, *De nugis curialium,* I, xii; Jocelin de Brakelonde, *Chronicle,* translated by E. Clarke (London, 1899), 32; R. S. Stevenson, *Robert Grosseteste* (London, 1903), 62.

[4] A. J. Ellis, *Transactions of the Philological Society,* 1868, 1-135; W. W. Skeat, *ibid.,* 1880-87, appendix vi; M. B. Ogle, *Royal Letters to Oxford* (Oxford, 1892), gives a facsimile.

[5] Matthew Paris, *Chronica Majora,* III, 289 (Rolls Series).

[6] Froissart, *Chronicles* (edit. by Kervyn de Lettenhove), II, 326.

the petition of the city of London, a statute was passed requiring all pleadings and judgments in all courts in England to be in the English tongue, since French "is much unknown in the said realm."[7] In the same year and almost regularly thereafter Parliament was opened by the chancellor in an English speech. The parliamentary deposition of Richard II in 1399 and his renunciation were read in English as well as in Latin, "so that all might understand"; and Henry IV made his claim to the throne in English.[8]

By the middle of the fourteenth century it is evident that English was the native language of all classes. Students at the universities and novices in the monasteries would break the rules by using English, when by the statutes they ought to have spoken Latin in their more formal converse and French in their leisure hours. Text-books in English for the study of French give the best testimony to the fact that young people of the upper and middle classes used English as their mother tongue, and soon after the middle of the century boys in the grammar schools construed their Latin by means of English, not of French.[9]

Even catastrophe played its part in the change to English. When the Black Death left monasteries and vicarages empty, they were filled largely from below, from the classes that spoke English not French, and often read sadly little Latin. The rise of the middle classes to prosperity and political recognition, the rise of the lower classes to freedom, meant the rise of the English-speaking classes.

But all this, or most of it, had to do with the spoken language. The progress of the written word was slower. French had come into use in records along with Latin early in the thirteenth century and had eventually in the fourteenth come to predominate over it. There was therefore a triple contest between Latin, French and English. As a matter of fact, in records, the two former long survived. The statute that required the use of English in the courts was itself in French and provided that judgments should be enrolled in Latin. The statute book is a French record with occa-

[7] 36 Edward III. Stat. 1 c. 15; *Statutes of the Realm,* I, 375; A. C. Baugh, *History of the English Language* (New York, 1935), 169, 182.

[8] J. H. Wylie, *History of England under Henry IV,* I, 7-16.

[9] Ralph Higden, *Polychronicon,* translated by John of Trevisa in 1385.

sional lapses into Latin until well beyond the end of this period. The Rolls of Parliament and the records of the king's council are a curious jumble of French, Latin and English entries, with the last tending to preponderate by 1450. But the professional lore of the clerks doubtless induced them to keep the records in their own jargon—for legal French was little else—long after it was understood by no one else.[10]

In less official circles English made its way earlier into documentary use, though even here slowly. In the early fifteenth century private letters, wills, town and gild ordinances appeared occasionally in English. The brewers of London, in ordering a translation of their early statutes, said in 1422, "Our mother tongue—that is the English tongue—hath in modern days begun to be honorably enlarged and adorned . . . and many of our craft of brewers have knowledge of writing and reading the said English tongue, but other languages, that is Latin and French, before these times used, they do not in any wise understand."[11]

The national language had by this time been "enlarged and adorned" by a noble national literature. The fourteenth century was indeed one of its greatest periods. In the early part of that century the stream of native writing in English and of translation from the Latin and French into English ran fuller and fuller; in its later decades Wyclif and his companions were disseminating their vigorous English sermons, tracts and translations among the common people; the mysticism, the satire and the picturesqueness of the *Vision of Piers Plowman* were making it one of the most admired and most frequently reproduced of English poems; before the century closed Chaucer was writing the *Canterbury Tales* in spirited English verse, the model for which, however, he found in a country far away from England. By the middle of the fifteenth century the change was complete. England had a vernacular in use in every phase of her national life and literature

[10] See F. W. Maitland, "The Anglo-French Law Language" (*The Cambridge History of English Literature*), I, chap. xx.

[11] W. Herbert, *Twelve Great Livery Companies of London* (two volumes, London, 1836-7), I, 106; see, in addition to the *Statutes of the Realm* and the *Rolls of Parliament*, such town records as H. T. Riley, *Memorials of London and London Life, 1276-1417* (London, 1868); Mary Bateson, *Records of the Borough of Leicester* (London, 1901-1904), volumes I and II; and *The Paston Letters*, in many editions.

whose richness, flexibility and vigor have proved sufficient for all demands ever made upon it.

The use of Latin declined even more rapidly than that of French. It continued to be the language of national chroniclers longer than in most countries, though the advance of city-life is reflected in a number of chronicles written by city men and largely occupied with city affairs, occasionally in French, but mostly in English. Ralph Higden's popular general chronicle was also translated into English by John of Trevisa in the fourteenth century and the rhymed English chronicle of Robert of Brunne was written in 1338, as he says,

> "For tho that in this land wonn
> That the Latyn no Frankys conn."[12]

III. THE USE OF SPANISH IN RECORDS AND LITERATURE

The parallelism already mentioned between the early constitutional development of England and Spain extended to the languages which record the early steps of that development. Just as there were unexpectedly early instances of representation of the middle classes in the cortes, so there are many official documents in the common speech of Castile scattered among those in the more customary Latin. The Treaty of Cabrera of 1206 between Leon and Castile was drawn up entirely in the common language.

But the general change in written usage from Latin to the language of the people occurred during the reign of Alfonso X, "the Wise" (1252-1284), and was largely due to his personal influence. Soon after his accession he ordered that all public documents formerly issued in Latin should in future be drawn up and published in the popular language. Thus the Castilian chancery used the vernacular in advance of all other countries of Europe. Latin was reserved for foreign correspondence, and even then Castilian was regularly used in letters to the King of Portugal and occasionally in communications to the rulers of England and Aragon.[13] The first translation of the old Visigothic code from Latin into Castilian,

[12] C. Gross, *Sources and Literature of English History* (second edition, London, 1915), Section 48; H. Root, *The Poetry of Chaucer* (second edition, London, 1922), etc.

[13] E. S. Procter, *The Castilian Chancery during the Reign of Alfonso X*, in *Oxford Essays in Mediaeval History*, presented to H. E. Salter (Oxford, 1934), 105-6.

begun in the reign of his father, was completed in Alfonso's time. His *Mirror of Rights* and *Code Royal* were issued in Castilian in the earliest years of his reign, and his great digest of the laws, *Los Siete Partidas* ("the Seven Divisions"), one of the greatest of all codes, worthy to stand alongside those of Justinian and Napoleon, was also drawn up in Castilian and completed in 1265.

Popular chronicles and popular literature reflected the same royal influence. The *Gran Conquista de Ultramar*, a history of the Crusades brought down to the middle of Alfonso's reign, the *General Chronicle of Spain*, the *Chronicle of the Cid*, a prose parallel to the popular ballads that had grown up about that popular hero, and the translation of the Bible, previously referred to, all bore the impress of Alfonso's authority and in some cases of his hand.

Even at this early date Spain experienced one of the greatest periods of her native literature. Fourteenth-century Spain resounded with ballads in the vernacular. Hundreds, indeed thousands of poems, mostly by nameless authors, told and retold the stories of Alexander, Charlemagne and the Twelve Peers, and repeated the incidents of the long conflict with the Moors. The influence of the Arabic language and literature is clearly recognizable. Moorish incidents are intermingled with Christian. "Woe is me, Alhama" is the refrain of both a Castilian and a Moorish song. Nor is it hard to recognize in the bold and defiant tone of Castilian poetry in the fourteenth century the same spirit that we have seen braving the king in the cortes and carrying on feudal warfare against him in the field.

The fifteenth century did not produce in Castile so original and interesting a body of literature as the fourteenth. Nevertheless the mass of allegories and sonnets that marked that century—136 poets are named in one *Cancionero*—and the first Spanish drama, written in 1414, as well as the large body of chronicle literature and of legislative record, did much to make secure by the middle of that century the position of Castilian as the official and literary language of Spain.

IV. FRENCH OF PARIS

The emergence of French as the language of official usage, of chronicles and of a generally understood literature, while it belongs to the same period as the rise of the vernaculars of England and Spain, had marked characteristics of its own. It was a question not only of the use in writing of a language before only spoken, but of the choice of the language of one particular region in preference to all others. As late as the middle of the thirteenth century each neighborhood had its own well-marked dialect. Roger Bacon, traveling in France in 1260, remarked that the speech of the Normans, the Picards and the Burgundians was so different that what was said quite properly in the language of one shocked the inhabitants of another.[14] The great distinction was of course that between the north and the south, the *langue d'oil* and the *langue d'oc*. Even in Languedoc, Provençal and Limousin or Catalan must be distinguished. In the north there were the Picard, Burgundian and Norman, to which Bacon refers, the Walloon, the dialect of Lorraine, the dialects of Franche Comté, of Champagne, of Anjou and, above all, that of the old duchy of France, of which Paris was the capital. These dialects were not merely patois. Some of them had their literary as well as their spoken forms of the old *romance* common to the whole country. The troubadours had made Provençal famous before Simon de Montfort, in his barbarous crusades in the first half of the thirteenth century, had trampled out both the heresies of the Albigenses and the whole civilization of the south. Both epic and lyric poetry, the romances of the Round Table and translations from the Latin, were familiar in the east and northeast; there were poems in the language of Artois and poetry in the Anglo-Norman dialect that existed on both sides of the Channel.[15]

But it was the language of Paris and its immediate vicinity that was destined to become, indeed already at the opening of this period was well on its way to becoming, classical French. The dialect of that region had been raised to preëminence since the eleventh century by the presence there of the king and the court. Government documents were, of course, traditionally drawn up in Latin; the chancery was a direct descendant of the Roman imperial administration and to this day its language is permeated not only with Latin

[14] His word is *horrescit*. *Opus Majus*, III, 14. See for a detailed and scientific study of the origin and growth of the French language Ferdinand E. Brunot, *Histoire de la langue française des origines à 1900* (Paris, 1905-); this subject is discussed in vol. I, 15, 304-30, etc.

[15] Gaston Paris, *Littérature française au moyen âge* (fifth edition, Paris, 1914), introduction, pp. 6, 7.

forms but with Roman conceptions. The earliest unquestioned instance of French being used for such purposes dates from 1254, when an acknowledgment of vassalage from the Duke of Brittany, still lying duly sealed in the Archives, was drawn up in the French of Paris. Scarcely later, in 1259, a treaty with the King of England, likewise in French of that form, was signed and still reposes in the English Record Office. Its use became more and more frequent, until, in the fourteenth century, it equalled and before the end of that century predominated over Latin as the language of documentary use. As the central government grew in activity, power and prestige, as the treasury and the chancery became more highly organized and poured forth a constantly increasing stream of royal letters and ordinances, the pressure exercised through its written instruments became overwhelmingly great and its extension throughout the kingdom inevitable. It was soon used for all official purposes in all parts of France, even in the south and in Navarre and Naples, when French dynasties ruled there. By the middle of the fifteenth century only the records of the church, the voluminous correspondence with the popes, and an occasional exceptional treaty or ordinance were drawn up in Latin.[16]

This official use only reflected the practice among the upper classes. The court was a social and a literary quite as much as it was a political centre. Paris, the principal residence of the king and his relatives, the gathering-place of nobles and officials, the source of patronage for authors, the location of the most famous university of Europe—Paris had incomparable social and literary advantages. The language of the court, that is to say the language of Paris, dignified by official use, polished by literary expression and spread by social influence, came to be recognized as French in a universal sense. Jean de Meun, in his translation of Boethius about 1300, apologized for the crudity of his work on the ground that he was not born at Paris but spoke the language his mother taught him when she nursed him at Meun. The trouvère Adenet le Roi of Brabant declared that Queen Berte, daughter of the King of Hungary, spoke such good French that one would believe she was born at Saint Denis. When a deaf and dumb man, cured of

[16] A. Giry, *Manuel de Diplomatique* (Paris, 1894), 464-72.

his infirmity by touching the remains of Saint Louis, began to speak, it was not in his native dialect of Burgundy, but in the correct French of Paris.[17]

France is remarkable for the early date, the varied interest and the wide dissemination of its chronicles in the native language. Not only the long narratives in verse of the twelfth century, such as the *Brut* and the *Rou*; not only the three famous names in historical prose, Villehardouin, Joinville and Froissart, each of which illustrates a century, from the thirteenth to the fifteenth; not only the *Grands Chroniques*, which give a semi-official contemporary record from 1274 well through the fifteenth century, but a long series of minor writers whose subject was the events of their own time gave vogue and familiarity to their national language. The great mass of early French literature, the *chansons de geste*, the "songs of exploits," the romances, the *fabliaux*, the lyric poetry, the miracle and mystery plays, the chronicles and above all the *Roman de la Rose*, the most popular poem of its age, were by 1450 familiar everywhere in France and many of them in England, Italy, the Netherlands and Germany.

V. DANTE AND THE ITALIAN VERNACULAR

The rapid development, the beauty, the widespread influence of the Italian language, its achievements in literature and its accompaniments in art, all tend to obscure its relatively late appearance as a recognized vernacular. Its adoption was no earlier, indeed it was rather later, than the languages of England, Spain and France. On the threshold of modern times, in this as in so many other aspects of life, stands the massive figure of Dante. In his essay *De Vulgari Eloquentia* ("Concerning the Common Speech"), written in Latin about 1305, he surveyed the various dialects of Italy and denied to all of them, even to Tuscan, the honor of being that "illustrious Italian vulgar tongue" in which the highest poetry should be composed by the worthiest writers.[18] Unfortunately he left his work and his argument incomplete, but already in the early part

[17] Brunot, op. cit., I, 229-30.

[18] *De Vulgari Eloquentia*, translated by A. G. F. Howell (London, 1890), XIX, 22-43, 47.

of the thirteenth century a whole school of poets, the "Sicilians," as they are called from their connection with the court of Frederick, King of Naples and Sicily, had written in a mixed but flexible Italian dialect. Dante himself spoke in the *Convito* of the Italian "precious mother tongue," and condemned those who, to seem learned, used Provençal or some other foreign speech.

In his sonnets and *canzoni* Dante had already written graceful poetry, and in the *Vita Nuova* ("The New Life") good clear prose, in a language which, although possibly, as he claims, composite or selective, was in the main the language of Tuscany. Other poets, his friend Guido Cavalcanti, his early teacher, Brunetto Latini, Guido Guinicelli of Bologna, Guittone of Arezzo, Jacopone of Todi, Cino of Pistoia, were all using Tuscan and were busy polishing and purifying it into the *dolce stil nuovo*, the "sweet new fashion" which soon came to be what all knew and admired as Italian. The impress which Dante placed on this new language by his poetry was perhaps his greatest achievement.[19]

Except for this and for his influence in placing a high valuation upon poetry, and apart from the inescapable challenge of his greatness, there is little reason to consider Dante a forerunner of modern times. In his ideas of religion, of the church, of the empire, of philosophy, he belongs rather with the age that was passing away than with that which was growing up about him. When Henry VII came to Italy in 1310, Dante received him with eager letters of appeal for a restoration of imperial powers, and in the midst of a world of local princely despots he wrote his Latin essay on monarchy of the old world type. He was a man of medieval learning; he knew such of the classics as were commonly known in his time, he was familiar with the great scholastic writers, and some things he had learned from Arabic scholars, but in the philosophic conflicts of his own time, the groundwork of the future, he took little interest. He was harsh in his criticisms of the church, but was not a heretic. Yet in his influence he stands, by common

[19] See the early chapters of Francesco de Sanctis, *History of Italian Literature* (New York, 1931), a work which, although almost a century old, has had so strange a history and is so much a book of ideas that it has been frequently reëdited and translated, even in recent times.

consent, as the first great figure in the new intellectual life of Italy.[20]

The events of his own life are familiar. Born in Florence in 1265 of an old aristocratic but not wealthy family and exiled in 1302 at the age of thirty-one as the result of a political feud, he wandered from one of the petty courts of the rising princely families of Italy to another, studied for a time at Bologna and perhaps at Paris, read, meditated, wrote. It is largely to this lonely career of a great spirit thrown back on itself, embittered by exile, haunted by poetic visions, that we owe the greatness and the distinction of his work. His character was sombre and remote, and his career was a tragedy. There is a certain loftiness in every expression that has come down to us from his lips or his pen. From the first line of the sonnet he wrote when he was eighteen years of age and had just been overwhelmed by the kind salutation of Beatrice Portinari, to the last lines of the *Paradiso*, written at Ravenna during the closing years of his life and sent after his death to his early patron, Can Grande de la Scala, there is the same note of distinction, of elevation, of independent and original force.

His contemporary and neighbor, the chronicler Giovanni Villani, says of him: "This man was a great scholar in almost every branch of learning, albeit he was a layman; he was a great poet and philosopher and a perfect rhetorician alike in prose and verse, a very noble orator in public speaking, supreme in rhyme, with the most polished and beautiful style which has ever been used in our language. . . . He wrote the *Comedy*, wherein in polished verse, and with great and subtle questions, moral, natural, astrological, philosophical and theological, with new and beautiful illustrations, comparisons and poetry he dealt and treated in one hundred chapters or songs of the existence and condition of Hell, Purgatory and Paradise, as loftily as it were possible to treat of them. . . . This Dante, because of his knowledge, was somewhat haughty and reserved and disdainful, and after the fashion of a philosopher, care-

[20] Among recent books on Dante the following are outstanding: Paget Toynbee, *Dante Alighieri, His Life and Works* (fourth edition, London, 1910); C. H. Grandgent, *Dante* (New York, 1916); C. A. Dinsmore, *Life of Dante Alighieri* (Boston, 1919); K. Federn, *Dante und seine Zeit* (third edition, Stuttgart, 1921); K. Vossler, *Medieval Culture; an Introduction to Dante and His Time* (London, 1929).

less of graces and not easy in his converse with laymen; but because of the lofty virtues and knowledge and worth of so great a citizen it seems fitting to confer lasting memory upon him in this our chronicle, although indeed his noble works left to us in writing are the true testimony to him."[21]

All his other work has been thrown into relative unimportance by the grandiose mass of the *Divine Comedy*, with its sublime subject, its complicated structure, its alternatively lovely and lurid images, its constant reference to living or recently living personalities—twenty-two of them his own fellow Florentines—and its unending procession of strange thoughts, flexible verse and surprising rhymes. All his work, Italian and Latin alike, received prompt recognition from his fellow-countrymen. We hear of blacksmiths and donkey-drivers chanting his verses as they went about their work, and reciting them so badly that the author belabored them for the injuries they inflicted upon his poetry.

More than 500 manuscripts of the *Divina Commedia* still exist, and four commentaries on his works appeared within a few years of his death, one by his own son Jacopo. Scores of studies of parts or of the whole of his work were written before the invention of printing in 1450. Except for a short visit to Venice, he spent the last years of his life as a guest of the Da Polenta family at Ravenna and died there in his fifty-seventh year, September 14, 1321. Yet he always remained a Florentine and would gladly have returned there if his opponents, who had procured his exile and still remained in power, had permitted it. He says of himself, "Since it was the pleasure of the citizens of the fairest and most renowned daughter of Rome, Florence, to cast me out from her sweet bosom, wherein I was born and brought up to the crowning point of my life, and wherein I long with all my heart, with their good leave, to repose my weary spirit and to end the days allotted to me, wandering through almost every region to which our language reaches, I have gone about as it were a stranger and a beggar."[22]

The particular satisfaction of a recall to his native city was denied to Dante, but fifty years after his death, seventy since his exile,

[21] Giovanni Villani, *Selections from the Florentine Chronicles*, translated by Ross E. Selfe (Westminster, 1896), Book IX, p. 136.
[22] *Convito*. I, 3, 11, 15-40.

when his fame had long become a pride to his native city and his works had been copied and recopied, a group of citizens of Florence petitioned the signory to appoint a man "well trained in the book of Dante" to lecture on that book to all wishing to hear it. The lecturer was to hold his position for a year, to lecture on all days except holidays and to receive 100 gold florins. One Giovanni Boccaccio, then living at Certaldo, just outside Florence, who had known and imitated Dante's work for fifty years, had made with his own hand a complete copy of the *Divine Comedy* as a present for his friend Petrarch and had written the first life of the great poet, was appointed to the position and gave his first lecture in the church of St. Stephen on October 23, 1373. Dante had in a certain sense returned to Florence.

VI. BOCCACCIO AND THE DECAMERON

Boccaccio took his lectures seriously, reading and commenting on the *Comedia*, stanza by stanza, in popular language but with a great display of literary, scientific and philosophical learning. But he was already an old man, in poor health, and after a few months he suspended his lectures. He died two years later, in December 1375.

It was part of the inconsistency of the age that the great epic of the Christian world, with its sense of sin and of divine punishment, should have been reverently commented on by the portrayer of a world devoid of all religious sense, which knew nothing of guilt or penitence or divine retribution. For Boccaccio, for all his many-sidedness, was above all the compiler of the *Decameron*. He was by birth a Florentine, though, like so many of his fellow-citizens, long a wanderer.[23] His father was a partner of the Bardi and was living in Paris when Giovanni was born, in 1313, of a nameless, presumably a French, mother. The boy was sent home to learn the reading, writing and bookkeeping necessary for his business career, and was then sent to Naples to get further training among the Florentine merchants there.

He was an uninterested apprentice and business man and soon

[23] See G. Volpi, *Il Trecento* (Milan, 1898), and E. Rodocanachi, *Boccace: Poète, Conteur, Moraliste, Homme Politique* (Paris, 1908). The best single book on Boccaccio is Henri Hauvette, *Boccace, Étude biographique et littéraire* (Paris, 1914).

turned his attention, first to law, then to literature. At Naples, at the rich, brilliant and enlightened court of King Robert, he studied at the university, learned much of life and pursued his amour with Maria d'Acquiro, his "Fiametta," who filled the place in his poetic inspiration occupied for others by a Beatrice, a Laura, a Stella, a "Dark Lady of the Sonnets," or one of the other lady-loves of troubadours and poets of all time.[24] It was to an Italy of poetry, literature and art, that Boccaccio turned from business. It was characteristic of the Florentine spirit that, as an apprentice, he read Ovid's *Metamorphoses* and himself wrote Latin verses, and it was typical of Neapolitan life that he made friends with scholars interested in the classics and with courtiers reading French verse.

When the Bardi failed, in 1346, he returned to Florence. There and in various other towns of Italy as well as at Avignon he sought a livelihood, knowledge and adventure. In middle life he settled down at Florence, became prosperous, was elected a member of the governing council of the city, and divided the rest of his life between public appointments and literary interests. He carried a gift of money from the society of the Or San Michele of Florence to Dante's daughter, who was a nun at Ravenna, and he entered into a life-long friendship and correspondence with Petrarch. He was lifted high in the estimation of his time by his Italian poems, collected in his *Ninfale, Visione* and *Fiametta*, as Dante had collected his in the *Vita Nuova*; by his scores of letters in polished Latin, exchanged with literary men; and by his compilations of classical, medieval and mythological lore, a form of writing especially popular in a society not creative but hungry and thirsty for information and always fond of a story.

The Decameron, written soon after he had returned to Florence, between 1350 and 1354, was one of these compilations, but it was a compilation so skilfully constructed, so spirited, so witty, so interesting, so excellent in style, so many-sided a reflection of its time, that it has remained, notwithstanding official condemnation and unofficial disapproval, one of the most widely read of the world's classics. Its setting was felicitous. The sombre details of the Black

[24] An excellent picture of the Neapolitan court is given in W. Goetz, *König Robert von Neapel; seine Persönlichkeit und sein Verhältniss zum Humanismus* (Tübingen, 1910).

Death as, during eight months in 1348, it reduced the civilized life of Florence to barbarism, are lightly and swiftly sketched. Contrasted with the horror of the city are the simple ease and luxury of the villas about Fiesole, where the four young women and three young men of the party had taken refuge from the epidemic. Their device of telling stories to while away the time, the detachment with which each of the tales is set out as a separate piece of literary art, and the clear-cut outlines of the stories reproduced from a dozen ages and countries are all so masterly as to defy criticism.

It would be hard to conceive of a more complete contrast than that between the *Decameron* and the *Divine Comedy*. The stories of Boccaccio are purely pagan; the book includes no element of Christianity except the barest of formalities—the story-tellers fast on Fridays. It plays on all the strings of human nature except those that Dante commends. It has few or no examples of self-sacrifice, of spiritual religion or exalted patriotism. It is no wonder that the church early placed it on the *Index expurgatorius* and retained it there until in recent times its literary repute rescued it from that condemnation.

On the other hand it deals with men and women such as, unfortunately, many of them really were and are. Within its sphere, and that rather a wide one, it was a true transcript of life. Its salacity has no doubt commended it to many readers of the grosser sort who have small capacity to recognize its literary charm. Boccaccio himself in later life regretted its licentiousness, as Chaucer regretted the looseness of the Canterbury Tales; but prurience alone would not have given Boccaccio's work so long and varied a life. It is its literary skill, its accurate reflection of certain aspects of its time, its satire on life in all times, its appeal to the sense of humor of its readers, that have justified the scores of editions and translations in which it has appeared.

VII. PETRARCH AND KNOWLEDGE OF THE CLASSICS

The literary tone of Italian society and especially the classical interests of that society were, more largely than is usual, the result of the life and popularity of one man, Francesco Petrarca (1304-1375). The old conception of the Renaissance as a sudden rediscovery of antiquity and a resulting spring forward of the human spirit into greater light and freedom, every modern scholar must deprecate. The background of the middle ages was much less dark, the advance of knowledge much more gradual, the superiority of the new over the old much more subject to reservation than such writers as Burckhardt, Symonds and Geiger assumed.[25] Nevertheless "there were giants in those days," and Petrarch, measured by his influence on his time, was one of the world's great creative spirits. Like Dante he was an exile from Florence, though for most of his life a voluntary one. He was born at the neighboring town of Arezzo in 1304, when Dante was in his fortieth year. When a boy of eight, his father at Pisa pointed out to him and perhaps introduced him to his great predecessor, already famous. It was the only time their lives crossed. Dante soon left Pisa for Verona and Ravenna, and his death came nine years later. In the same year Petrarch was taken by his parents to Avignon, the residence city of the popes, which had become a gathering-place for Italian exiles, bankers, ecclesiastics and literary men.[26]

Here and in its vicinity, at school at Carpentras and at the University of Montpellier, Petrarch spent his boyhood and youth. He was fortunate in his friendships. Evidently attractive personally, of cheerful disposition and alert mind, he made friends at school and college with boys who subsequently became men of influence. At the papal court he was befriended by Giacomo Colonna, afterward Bishop of Lombez, by Giacomo's brother, Cardinal Giovanni Colonna, and by his father, Stefano, a Roman noble. At an early age Petrarch, like most scholars, took lower orders in the church. The Colonni were all interested in poetry, art and travel, and it was no doubt the early indications of the genius of Petrarch that attracted

[25] Of the many discussions of this problem see especially W. Goetz, "Mittelalter und Renaissance," *Historische Zeitschrift,* XCVIII (1907), 30-54; K. Brandi, *Das Werden der Renaissance* (Göttingen, 1908); A. Philippi, *Der Begriff der Renaissance* (Leipzig, 1912).

[26] The basic study of Petrarch is still Gustav Körting, *Petrarcas Leben und Werke* (Leipzig, 1878). The best recent study is P. de Nolhac, *Pétrarque et l'humanisme* (second edition, two volumes, Paris, 1907), partially translated under the title *Petrarch and the Ancient World* (Boston, 1908). J. H. Robinson and H. W. Rolfe, *Petrarch, the First Modern Scholar and Man of Letters* (new edition, New York, 1914), contains many selections with commentary. Edward H. R. Tatham, *Francesco Petrarca, the First Modern Man of Letters* (two volumes, New York, 1925-1926), is a good semi-popular biography.

them to him. It was probably through their influence and that of other learned and well-to-do friends that Petrarch lived a life of relative ease and of freedom from that poverty that had embittered the austere spirit of Dante. He was given several ecclesiastical livings, from which he drew the income but which he seldom visited. His religious life was largely formal. Like Dante he criticized the wicked lives of many churchmen. His denunciations of the papal court at Avignon were, as we have seen, among the bitterest diatribes ever written, but he had nothing to say against the church as an institution. He had apparently little interest in matters of theology. Curiosity to see the world, love of adventure, or the opportunity for patronage carried him from city to city in Italy and abroad, as it did so many of his fellow-countrymen. A list of his journeys and sojournings in Italy, France, Flanders, Germany and Switzerland would be a long one; they covered most of his life of seventy years. But it was restlessness, not poverty, that made him a wanderer. He soon became famous for his learning and literary productiveness and had for hosts and correspondents, kings, princes, popes, cardinals, bishops, noblemen and scholars.

The most famous of his literary triumphs came early in life. Some scheming by his friends, perhaps a suggestion of his own, brought to him at the age of thirty-five the grant of the laurel crown, which Dante was too proud to accept so long as he was a banished man. One day in the year 1340 brought him offers of the crown from the University of Paris and from the Senate of Rome. At a loss which offer to accept, or desirous of making the ceremony as conspicuous as possible, Petrarch wrote to King Robert of Sicily, then the great patron of all poets, asking his advice, and followed this up by a visit in person. After an interview and a formal display of his classical learning, Robert gave him his hearty recommendation for the Roman offer. On Easter Day, 1341, the ceremony took place. The presiding officer of the Senate, himself temporarily wearing the laurel crown, was seated on a raised chair on the Capitoline hill, surrounded by twelve boys dressed in scarlet and six in green, carrying flowers, all sons of aristocratic Roman families. Amid the sounding of drums and fifes the president summoned Petrarch to appear. The poet, wearing a long robe, came forward and cried three times "Long live the Roman people, long live the Senate of Rome, God preserve them in liberty." Then he knelt and the president took the laurel wreath from his own head and put it on that of the poet, saying, "The crown is the reward of merit." The poet-scholar then rose, recited a Latin ode in honor of the ancient Romans, and delivered an oration complimentary to their descendants. Accompanied by the Roman crowd, always ready to applaud a spectacle, he proceeded to St. Peter's and deposited the wreath before the high altar. Bombastic as all this may seem, it was the spirit of the Renaissance and of Italy. The same homage to antiquity was paid ten years later by the same Senate and populace when they acclaimed Cola di Rienzi tribune of a restored Roman Republic.[27]

However much the life of Petrarch was marked by such ceremonies, however much spent in courts and cities, filled with pleasurable companionship and warmed by adulation, he would have declared, probably sincerely, that he took greater delight in quite rural, homely things. His little farmhouse at Vaucluse, his two servants, his dog, his garden—above all his garden—the simple life, the remoteness from the world—Vaucluse was only fifteen miles from Avignon, but separated from it by a wooded ridge—his walks there, his meditations, his books, have become as familiar to lovers of literature as the associations of any one spot on the earth's surface. Here, from his thirty-fourth to his forty-eighth year, he spent most of his time, going out into the larger world, making journeys and visits, as has been told, but always coming back to Vaucluse. Here he spent his time studying, musing, perfecting his taste, writing, altering, rewriting till he was satisfied, becoming constantly more infatuated with the writings of the ancients and pouring out a series of graceful sonnets in Italian and a flood of letters to his friends in classic Latin. The last ten years of his life, from 1364 to 1374, from his sixtieth to his seventieth year, he lived for the most part in a small house he had built for himself among the Euganean Hills, at Arqua, about ten miles from Padua.

His interest in the classics was his earliest, his latest and his most constant passion. In one of his letters he says, "From my earliest

[27] See M. E. Cosenza, *Francesco Petrarca and the Revolution of Cola di Rienzo* (Chicago, 1913).

childhood I brooded over the books of Cicero, either from natural sympathy or because of the encouragement of my father, who was a great worshipper of that author." He rejoiced, he says, to hear his father read the orations in sonorous Latin even before the boy could understand what they meant. He had good classical teachers. Convenevole, his master at Carpentras; Giovanni of Florence, a papal official and an old friend at Avignon; Raimondo Soranzio, a lawyer and book collector at Avignon; Dionisio da Borgo San Sepolcro, professor of divinity at the University of Paris; Marco Barbato, chancellor of King Robert of Naples; Boccaccio, and many others whom we know principally through his letters concerning their common interests, were all classical scholars.

He gradually built up for himself a respectable library of manuscripts of the ancient writers. When he was a law student at Bologna, he began his collection with Vergil and a Cicero's *Rhetoric*. Soon he added a volume containing not only Vergil but Servius Statius and the *Odes* of Horace, a volume on which his own annotations may still be seen. While still young and poor he made copies of many manuscripts loaned him by others. On his journey to the north he bought manuscripts in Paris from the dealers who, then as now, had their tiny shops along the Quais, and he had at least a glimpse of those in the new library of the Sorbonne. Sometimes he kept his companions waiting while he copied with his own hand manuscripts shown to him. It was the same on his first visit to Rome. By the time he retired to Vaucluse he had not only Cicero, Vergil and Horace, his first loves, but Seneca, Boethius, Livy, Florus, Sallust, Suetonius, Macrobius, Ovid, Juvenal and Lucian.

Even in his retirement he continued to borrow and copy manuscripts. His friends made him presents; some even that he could not read, for he had a Plato and a Homer in the original Greek which he could look on only with reverence, not with understanding. A large part of this literature reappears in an infinite amount of quotation and reference in his various writings. In the forty-five books of his Latin letters, his twelve philosophical and moral works, the three groups of Latin poems, and his epic poem *Africa*, there are few extended passages which do not contain quotations from the classics or comment drawn from classical examples or classical opinion. It was through this body of ancient literature, read and reread, that he gained that familiarity with their contents and that reflection of their style which runs like a constant stream through all his writings. Even more than an Italian poet, Petrarch was a classical scholar. At the very last he was engaged on a life of Caesar, and the half-finished page still lying in the Bibliothèque Nationale at Paris, over which he was bending when he died, is an excerpt from one of the letters of Cicero to Atticus.[28]

It was through his contagious enthusiasm for the classics that he exercised his greatest influence on his age. His poems in Italian were, no doubt, with their beauty and grace, endless variety and perfection of form, the main source of his fame in his own time and of much of its permanency. But it was his Latin writings, above all his hundreds of letters to correspondents, cast into graceful literary form, concerning themselves with such a great variety of human affairs, reflecting and extending the new interest in the classics, that have made him in the judgment of later times the pioneer of a new intellectual world.

VIII. HUMANISM

This enthusiastic addiction to the study of the writers of Greek and Roman antiquity, which has come to be known as humanism, was not, however, at least in Petrarch's case, a philosophy of life. He was too much of a poet, too much a man of his own time, too much of a Christian, to enter readily into the spirit of an age which had a simpler, more direct and less inhibited attitude toward the world. His approach to ancient literature and ancient thought was a romantic one, that of the explorer rather than of the colonizer. He venerated the classical authors rather than understood them. He represented nevertheless one of the most characteristic interests of Italy in his day, one destined to spread widely, one which was indeed already spreading widely there and beginning to extend to all Europe. Boccaccio himself turned, during his later life, from poetry and the telling of tales to the composition of Latin works of erudition and to his long correspondence with Petrarch, much of it on classical subjects. The influence of Latin models even on his

[28] Pierre de Nolhac, *Pétrarque et l'humanisme,* chap. i, *Pétrarque Bibliophile.*

Italian prose style is evident. He tells the tales in the *Decameron* and elsewhere in a much less simple, less direct style than does his contemporary Sacchetti or, in her letters, Saint Catherine of Siena.

Florence was as prominent in classical studies as in literature. Humanism was much advanced by three successive chancellors of the Signory, Collucio Salutati, who held that office from 1375 to his death in 1406; Leonardo Bruni, his pupil, who served from 1427 to 1444, and Poggio Bracciolini, who was chancellor in 1453. These men, enthusiastic students of the ancients and adventurers in literary style, clothed their official letters, negotiations and records in elegant diction wherever Latin could be used, and introduced expressions of grandeur and patriotism drawn from the classics into the vernacular when Italian was requisite. They also used their position as secretary to collect ancient manuscripts.[29]

Not only at Florence but at Rome there were classical scholars in official positions. Poggio, who was like Bruni a disciple of Salutati and owed to him a secretary's position with the pope which took him to Constance, to France, to England and back to Rome, was one of the most devoted and most successful hunters of old manuscripts for half a century before he was called back to Florence. At Constance, in Paris, in London, he ransacked dusty libraries and found long forgotten works of Statius, Lucretius and Quintilian, as well as twelve of the comedies of Plautus.[30]

Everywhere in cathedral and monastic libraries and in obscure repositories, enthusiastic search was being made. Previously forgotten or unknown works of classical writers were discovered and acquired, often with difficulty and at great price. The Florentine Niccoli spent his whole fortune in buying books and finding lost manuscripts of Cicero, Lucretius, Pliny and others. Guarino of Verona brought back with him from a visit to the east in 1408 some fifty Greek manuscripts. Aurispa, a learned book-collector from Sicily, obtained from various quarters and brought back to Venice in 1423 more than 200 manuscripts. Filelfo, who was in 1420 sent to Constantinople as secretary of the Venetian legation, obtained and brought home with him copies of the works of some forty

[29] See especially K. Brandi, *Die Renaissance in Florenz* (fourth edition, Leipzig, 1913), and F. T. Perrens, *La Civilisation Florentine du 13ième au 16ième siècle* (Paris, 1893).

[30] See E. Walser, *Poggius Florentinus: Leben und Werke* (Leipzig, 1914).

Greek authors. Cardinal Bessarion spent 30,000 gold florins in buying about 600 manuscripts of early writers and bequeathed them to St. Mark's in Venice.[31]

Many manuscripts were copied for those who wished to acquire them; there were whole companies of copyists in the larger and more literary cities. One great merchant prince just at the close of our period engaged forty-five copyists, who in somewhat less than two years copied 200 volumes. Frederick of Montefeltro of Urbino (1444-1482) kept thirty to forty copyists at work in various places and spent altogether some 30,000 florins for his library, later sold to the Vatican. There are but few of the classical or early Christian writings which we now possess that were not already in one or other of the collections in Italy by 1450.[32]

Long before that date Italian scholars had learned to go back of Latin thought and expression to the Greek that underlay so much of it, and to read the great mass of Greek literature in its original form. A Latin translation of Homer covered with annotations in Petrarch's own hand still lies in the Library at Paris; this was as near as the first great humanist got to the original Greek. But in the next half-century Greek scholars taught in Italy, Italians went to Constantinople to study, and translations from Greek into Latin were numerous.[33]

From 1297 onwards humanism made its way into the universities. Under the head of rhetoric, the language, the literature and matters dealt with in the ancient literature were alike lectured upon. It was not till seventy years after the death of Petrarch that, with the publication by Laurentio Valla in 1444 of his *Elegancies of the Latin Language*, the romanticism which its founders had impressed on humanism was cured and the classics became a subject of critical and scientific study.[34] But by this time humanism had secured for

[31] See L. Mohler, *Kardinal Bessarion als Theologe, Humanist und Staatsmann* (two volumes, Paderborn, 1923-1927).

[32] See R. Sabbadini, *Le Scoperte dei Codici Latini e Greci ne' secoli XIV e XV* (Florence, 1905), and the materials in T. Klette, *Beiträge zur Geschichte und Literatur der Italienischen Gelehrtenrenaissance* (three volumes, Greifswald, 1888-1890).

[33] Cf. Louise R. Loomis, "The Greek Renaissance in Italy," *American Historical Review,* XIII (1908), 246-58; see the section "Byzantium and the Italian Renaissance" in A. A. Vasiliev, *History of the Byzantine Empire* (Madison, 1929), 433-44.

[34] W. Schwahn, *Lorenzo Valla: ein Beitrag zur Geschichte des Humanismus* (Berlin, 1896).

itself a safe, indeed a dominant, position as a widespread and influential intellectual movement, one which was still advancing in recognition, which was already drawing the eyes and would soon draw to Italy the steps of foreigners from all other countries of Europe.

Humanism was not the only intellectual interest of the time in Italy; indeed it had to face opposition. A dark side of the picture was already being noted by some. The movement implied a reversion to pre-Christian ideals, and there were many who objected to Greek and Roman mythology and the traditions of ancient heroes superseding the lives of the saints and the traditions of western countries. To many churchmen epicureanism or even stoicism seemed a poor exchange for the lessons of the cross. Humanism, besides, preferred Latin and even Greek to the vernacular and thus endangered the lately won glory of the national language. It lent itself readily to the support of autocracy so that the most famous humanists were often flatterers of the new tyrants.[35]

Yet it had no serious rival. The church was secular and corrupt, its bureaucracy steeped in classicism; the pope, Nicholas V, elected just at the close of this period, in 1447, was himself a trained humanist. At Florence Cosimo de Medici combined the old prestige of banking, commerce and political leadership with enthusiastic patronage of the new learning. Moreover humanism did not stand alone; it was accompanied by a vigorous corresponding movement in all fields of art; it was linked with all other phases of the Renaissance.

IX. NEW MOVEMENTS IN ART

Notwithstanding the supremacy of the fifteenth century in all fields of art, the hand of originality already lay visibly upon much of the work of the fourteenth. Giotto, as Vasari, his sixteenth-century biographer, says, "succeeded in resuscitating art and restoring her to a path that may be called the true one." The endless patient research of later critics, the invaluable advantage of a longer perspective and a broader knowledge have found in each of a number of fourteenth-century artists in other countries as well as Italy in-

[35] E. Walser, "Christentum und Antike in der Auffassung der Italienischen Frührenaissance," *Archiv für Kulturgeschichte,* XI (1913), 273-88.

dications of originality and have ascribed to them their respective forms of influence. Nevertheless, Giotto stands, much as Dante stands, at the entrance of the path to modern artistic development.

Indeed there was much that bound Giotto and Dante together. They were probably born but a year apart and for fifty-five years they were contemporaries.[36] Giotto was born in Florence itself, like Dante, or in a village in the valley of the Mugello, but a few miles away. They were, according to the contemporary chronicler, "intimate friends." They met at Padua soon after the poet's banishment, when the painter was engaged on one of his first tasks outside of Florence. They were in Avignon at the same time and quite possibly together in Paris. Dante in the later days of his life induced his friend to visit Ravenna and paint for the Da Polenta family. It is to Giotto that we owe the only contemporary portrait of Dante, that on the wall of the Bargello, and in return he is described in the *Comedy* as the most famous painter of his time. The contemporary story that the painter's scenes in his "Apocalypse" at Naples are due to the suggestions of the poet is not without probability.

The wide spread of the repute and influence of Giotto and Dante in their respective spheres is no less striking. One of the most impressive characteristics of the new intellectual and artistic life was its dissemination through Italy. Florence did not lose her prominence, but the names of Siena, Rome, Padua, Ravenna, Milan, Naples, Rimini, Assisi, Arezzo, Avignon, the successive fields of Giotto's work, are only suggestive of the extension of fourteenth-century artistic production, not only in painting but in sculpture and architecture.[37] The artists of the time, it must be remembered, were artisans, the more successful of them masters with workshops, others journeymen and apprentices. Those whose names have been preserved and whose productions are studied as proofs or products of the Renaissance are only a tithe, or perhaps a hundredth of the

[36] C. Bayet, *Giotto* (Paris, 1907), 5; see further M. G. Zimmermann, *Giotto und die Kunst Italiens im Mittelalter* (Leipzig, 1899).

[37] Besides the great histories, like A. Michel, *Histoire de l'Art* (Paris, 1905-), and A. Venturi, *Storia dell'Arte Italiana* (Milan, 1904-), see A. Philippi, *Die Kunst der Renaissance in Italien* (two volumes, Leipzig, 1905); J. A. Crowe and G. B. Cavalcasalle, *A New History of Painting in Italy* (three volumes, New York, 1908-1909); F. J. Mather, Jr., *A History of Italian Painting* (New York, 1923); G. Scott, *The Architecture of Humanism* (second edition, London, 1924); W. J. Anderson, *The Architecture of the Renaissance in Italy* (fifth edition, London, 1927).

more or less gifted and trained painters, sculptors and architects who were available for the artistic adornment of a rich and cultured Italy.[38]

The other great requirement of art, patronage, sprang from the same industrial and financial source we have seen productive of so many other forms of progress in that age. The fact that the Italians were an industrial people and that the main interests of the cities were manufactures, commerce and finance did not prevent the existence of a passion for art. The Bardi, the Peruzzi, the Spinelli, the Baroncelli and other banking families in Florence, the Tolomei in Siena, commissioned painters to decorate chapels for them in the principal churches, and many individual merchants, like Pandolfo Petrucci at Siena, ordered the execution of those triptychs and other paintings in which sacred scenes are made the occasion for painting admirable portraits of the donors. Similarly Felix Brancacci of Florence in his will left money to construct and decorate in the church of the Carmine, that chapel which has ever since given testimony to the skill of Masolina and the genius of Masaccio.

Even the despised earnings of usury might be turned to artistic uses, as in the case of Reginaldo Scrovegno, whom Dante saw in a rain of fire in the *Inferno*, but whose son Enrico engaged Giovanni Pisano to build the little church of St. Mary of the Sands in Padua and Giotto to fill it with some of the earliest and greatest products of his genius.

The governments of the cities were equally ready to spend the income from trade on public buildings and the beautification of the city churches. The long records of the *Campo Santo* at Pisa show continuous expenditure by the city government in fees to painters from many different regions for more than a century. The cathedral and the *Palazzo Pubblico* at Siena, alike the work of the city commune through a century and a half of construction, were both adorned in the early fourteenth century with paintings which established in Duccio, Simone, Pietro and Ambrozzio Lorenzetti and others a new and characteristic school of art and introduced new subjects more germane to the life of the city than the sacred sub-

[38] See lists from the city records in Crowe and Cavalcasalle, op. cit., I, 131, 145, 156, 267, 277, 329, 369, 418, and in Vasari, notwithstanding his restriction to "the most eminent" painters. See also L. Hautecoeur, *Les Primitifs Italiens* (Paris, 1931).

jects of tradition. The walls of the palace of the Podestà in Florence were early covered with allegorical paintings of which there remain to us almost alone a group of portraits, among them that of Dante, itself invaluable.

Scarcely less liberal in their patronage of art were the authorities of the church. The pope, prelates and monastic orders built or rebuilt churches and convents, filled them with carved pulpits, altar-pieces, screens and shrines, and engaged painters to cover the walls with pictures. The church of St. Francis at Assisi by its engagements and rewards served as a training school for at least two generations of painters and is now the principal shrine for the study of early Tuscan art. The workshops attached to public and church buildings were training places for architects, sculptors and painters; so that those who had worked at one place carried its ideals and practices far and wide and helped to spread the influence of that particular school of art. Even beyond the bounds of Italy there was originality in the fourteenth century. In Flanders, in Burgundy, in war-torn France itself there were evidences of spontaneity in painting and sculpture, if not in architecture.[39]

In the fifteenth century the patronage of princes and kings came to count for more than that of great merchants or wealthy churchmen. Several of the rising princes of Italy, rude despots though they sometimes were, were surrounded by scholars and popular artists and yielded to these artistic influences till they themselves became patrons of all kinds of creative art. Yet no rich man or even sovereign ever did so much for art as Cosimo de Medici (1389-1464).[40] He made possible much of that artistic production that his remote modern successors in the line of men of wealth now painfully and with still greater expenditure collect. He was, at the opening of the fifteenth century, head of one of those banking families that had risen on the declining fortunes of the Bardi, Peruzzi and their contemporaries. The peculiar organization of the Florentine government made it possible for an able, astute and wealthy citizen

[39] Cf. L. Dimier and L. Réau, *Histoire de la Peinture Française* (Paris, 1925), volume I.

[40] See W. H. O. Smeaton, *The Medici and the Italian Renaissance* (New York, 1901); K. Dorothea Ewart, *Cosimo de'Medici* (New York, 1899); and Cecily Booth, *Cosimo I* (Cambridge, 1921).

to exercise without show an influence equal to the princely power being seized elsewhere by violence and in Florence itself at a later time only assured by the possession of a title. The wealth of Cosimo was very great, his influence in the period from his return from banishment in 1434 to his death in 1464 almost unbounded. Much of his wealth and influence was utilized for the encouragement of art, literature and learning.

Cosimo was a great builder. Churches and convents were constructed, furnished, decorated and endowed at his expense, and chapels were built and beautified in the older churches. He built for himself the Riccardi palace in the Via Larga to take the place of the old family dwelling in the market place, in addition to his four summer residences outside the city. He collected and had copied, as mentioned before, great numbers of manuscripts. As a banker and leading citizen Cosimo made the fortunes of whole families, and as a patron of art and literature formed personal friendships with painters, architects and men of learning and secured for them office and support. All this expenditure, so far as it was an expenditure of money, was supported by the wide banking operations of the Medici family, which had by this time branches in Paris, London and Bruges and included under its name the fortunes and investments of several other families.

But the services of Cosimo indicate the opening of a new era in the world of art and literature. The promise of the early part of the fourteenth century, except perhaps in the field of humanism, was not immediately fulfilled. Either support or genius was lacking, and there was a slowing up of artistic and literary production. The lessons of that period were available, its standards were accepted, but it was not till well into the fifteenth century and under the encouragement of princely patrons like Cosimo de Medici that art and literature resumed the progress that led to the triumphs of a new age.

Chapter Nine

THE REVELATION OF THE EAST

THE Italians were as manifestly the forerunners of modern geographical discovery as of modern commerce and banking and of the modern fashions in learning, literature and art. Their avidity for maritime enterprise was remarkable. No shores of the Mediterranean or of its connected waters were unfamiliar to them, and both the Genoese and the Venetians early took courage to sail through and beyond the Straits of Gibraltar. It was Genoese navigators who first of modern Europeans saw the islands of the western ocean, the Madeiras, the Canaries, the Azores, one by one rise before their eyes from the sea. Though the voyage of the Genoese Launcelot Malocello in 1270 to the Canaries, the "Fortunate Isles" of ancient tradition, is but poorly authenticated, it is certainly true that within the next few years his fellow-countrymen had made more than one voyage thither. Petrarch, who was born in 1304, refers casually to such voyages "in the time of my parents," and before the end of the fourteenth century they had become a commonplace.

As these island groups came to be treated as stepping-stones to bolder discoveries to the southward and westward, they passed into the hands of Portugal and Spain, but the Italians were still the instruments of which the sovereigns of those countries made use. In 1317 King Diniz, creator of the modern Portuguese monarchy, appointed Emmanuel Pezagno of Genoa lord high admiral of Portugal. Pezagno brought with him twenty trained Genoese seamen to act as captains and pilots and passed his office down to his son and grandson. It was in the same year with this appointment, that the Venetian fleet made the first of its regular voyages to Flanders and England.

In 1341, when three ships were sent from Lisbon by Alfonso IV, equipped for a systematic exploration and possible occupation of the Canaries, the crews were still largely Genoese. The captain of one of the ships was a Nicoloso de Recco of Genoa, and a narrative of the expedition has come down to us, written by a certain Florentine merchant long resident in Seville, who accompanied it. Petrarch was present at Avignon in 1344 when Pope Clement VI was induced to disregard the Portuguese claims and make to a Spanish prince a grant of the Canaries to be held as a papal fief. Before 1350 the Canaries, the Madeiras and even the distant Azores were all brought within the circle of familiar European knowledge.[1] Notwithstanding this knowledge, so few and so tentative were the steps taken in westward exploration during this period that its further progress may well be left for treatment in a later volume. The Far East, however, with all its wonders and romance, was opened to the knowledge of Europeans well within the thirteenth, fourteenth and early fifteenth centuries. That knowledge and the mental expansion to which it gave rise were a part of the intellectual equipment of even the earliest modern times.

Two inducements dominated travel and exploration in the east—religion and trade. The two incentives can hardly be separated, and they were both permeated with the spirit of personal adventure, the desire for knowledge of the world. "In order to know the real truth concerning the various regions of the world take this book and read it," is the appeal of a thirteenth century narrative.[2] It is to be remembered that both trade and Christianity were old in the east. Certain perennial streams of commerce had from time immemorial flowed to and fro in Asia, through eastern Europe and around the shores of the Mediterranean and the Euxine. Much of the commercial enterprise that led to further geographical knowledge consisted in attempts to tap these profitable trade routes at their source or at least at some earlier point in their course; the creation of entirely new lines and materials of import and export belongs to a later period.

In the same way Christianity in various early forms, the Nestorian, the Jacobite, the "St. Thomas," the Armenian and even the Greek Orthodox, were known in the nearer and even in the more

[1] The basic account of African exploration in this period is C. de La Roncière's, *La Découverte de l'Afrique au Moyen Âge* (three volumes, Cairo, 1925-1927).

[2] G. Pauthier, *Marco Polo* (Paris, 1865).

distant parts of Asia. Much of the vigor of the Roman church in sending out those missions which did so much for geographical knowledge was induced by the hope of superseding these sects by the Catholic organization. The historian cannot but observe that some of the most eager Christian missionary service in all ages has been devoted, not so much to carrying the name of Christ where it was unknown before, as to substituting what the missionaries have considered a more pure or more authoritative form of Christianity for that already known there. This period was no exception and idolaters, Moslems, Buddhists and heretical Christians were alike the objects of efforts at conversion.

I. THE EAST AS A REALM OF TRADING ADVENTURE

The best known of these early glimpses of the east, "The Book of Ser Marco Polo," was, however, more a narrative of adventure and a report of observations than either a missionary or a trading record. Marco Polo represented much that we have observed to be typical of his time and of his nation—the exuberant energy and precedence of the Italians in so many fields, the extension of trade, the habit of traveling, the spread of information from country to country. The story of the Polos is a familiar one, but will bear retelling.[3]

In the middle years of the thirteenth century, just at the beginning of the period covered by this volume, three brothers of this typical Venetian family were engaged in trade—Maffeo and Nicolo between Venice and Constantinople, and Marco (the older) in Soldaia, a port on the north coast of the Black Sea, within Tartar territory but occupied for the most part by a numerous and enterprising population of Italians. In the year 1260 Maffeo and Nicolo Polo visited their brother in Soldaia and, possibly on his advice, proceeded further eastward to the capital of the Khan of the Kipchak Tartars at Serai to dispose of some valuable jewels. They were successful in their trading and remained at his court or in the vicinity for a year or more. Cut off from return by the outbreak of wars and invited to

[3] Numerous editions are available. The fullest and best is the great work of Sir Henry Yule, *The Book of Ser Marco Polo, the Venetian* (third edition, revised by Henri Cordier, London, 1903). See also H. Cordier, *Ser Marco Polo: Notes and Addenda to Sir Henry Yule's Edition* (New York, 1920); one of the most convenient editions is *The Travels of Marco Polo, the Venetian* (Everyman Edition, London, 1908), given some distinction by an Introduction by John Masefield.

go on to the court of the Great Khan himself, then established in China, they traveled eastward in the company of one of his great officials till they arrived at Cambaluc, the modern Peking. They were received at court, and their replies to the inquiries of the Tartar lord aroused his curiosity concerning the customs, learning and religion of the west. He ordered the travelers to return to their home and ask the pope to send out a hundred learned missionaries, who might perhaps confute the priests and magicians of other religions established at his tolerant court. He wanted also some oil from the lamp that was kept burning at the Holy Sepulchre in Jerusalem. The Italians were given the services of a Tartar guide and were provided with letters to the pope and with a general warrant from the Great Khan which secured them protection and support through the whole breadth of his domains.

They made their way homeward only to find the papacy vacant by the death of Clement IV, and they met, therefore, almost insuperable difficulties in carrying out their mission. However, Nicolo Polo found at Venice that while he and his brother had been on their long journey his son Marco, whom he had left a child with his mother, had grown to be a young man of fifteen, and when the brothers returned to China with such fulfilment of the Khan's request as was possible they decided to take the young man with them. Marco was born in 1254; he was therefore almost an exact contemporary of Dante, Giotto and Marsiglio of Padua. It is Marco around whom the story gathers; it was he who played the leading part in the drama of their adventures, and it is his narrative of their explorations and observations that has given fame to their journey. The older Polos serve merely to introduce the younger man and they soon fade from the picture.

Their return to the east was begun in the year 1271, the year after the voyage of Malocello through the Straits of Gibraltar. It was characteristic that at the same time a Genoese should be voyaging westward and a Venetian eastward, both in search of distant lands. Going by sea from Venice to Acre, then on to Layas, the best-known Syrian termination of Asiatic trade routes, they began their land journey; at first southward and eastward through Mesopotamia and Iraq to Ormuz; then northward through Persia and eastward along ancient caravan routes, through the mountain regions of Badakshan, to the Pamir, "the roof of the world," then from stage to stage through old trading cities, Bokhara, Samarkand, Kashgar, Yarkand, Khotan; then across Gobi, one of the most arid and most interesting deserts of the world, the place of deposit of some of the earth's most revealing fossils, possibly the cradle of the human race.

After further travel the Venetians arrived again at the court of the Great Mogul. It was the center of the eastern world. Kublai, the third successor of Genghis Khan, still half-barbarian notwithstanding the long residence of the dynasty among the highly cultured Chinese, was now sixty years old and ruled over a wider extent of territory and a greater number of subjects than any monarch of his time, perhaps than any ruler of all time. Marco's description of his palace in Shangtu, near the capital, its eight miles square of enclosed ground, its barracks for his guard of 12,000 men, its storehouses for military equipment and for the Khan's wardrobe, its dwellings with their scores of rooms, the great hall set on its high marble terrace, where fourteen times a year a great festival for his thousands of nobles was celebrated, its series of apartments for his four wives, his numerous concubines and his sons, each of whom had his own court, his train of 5,000 elephants with their harness of silver and precious stones; the buildings ornamented with colored tile, paintings and sculpture, the groves and artificial lakes and gardens—all these as Marco describes them were the witchery that filled the half-drugged senses of Coleridge when he dreamed

> "In Xanadu did Kublai Khan
> A mighty pleasure dome decree
> Where Alph the sacred river ran
> Through caverns measureless to man
> Down to a sunless sea." . . .

The adjoining city, six miles square, with its shops, its handsome dwellings, its guard-houses, its curfew, its thousands of public women and their superintendents, its twelve wide-extending suburbs, its multitudes of inhabitants "greater than the mind can comprehend," the thousand carts and packhorses loaded with raw silk that made their entry into its market daily, and other merchandise and supplies in proportion are all described with an exuberance which afterward gave Marco the sobriquet of *Il Milione*, "the man who talks in millions." But after all he was a traveler, an Italian and a man of the thirteenth, one of the most wonder-loving of centuries; on the whole his statements have with a few exceptions been fully corroborated by later travelers.

The observations he made on his way to the east and on his return are of the greatest interest. His route and his reports have been made the object of minute, learned and vivacious study and description, and are still the basis of much of our early geographical knowledge, as they were the attraction of his narrative for his contemporaries. But we must restrict ourselves to what was most significant, the revelation he gave to the western world of China, a country of numbers, wealth and civilization far superior to its own.

The young Italian attracted the favorable notice of the Great Khan, was taken into his service and so remained for seventeen years. His opportunities for seeing the eastern world were unsurpassed. He made his way on one mission or another through all parts of Cathay, or northern, and Mangi, or southern, China, using the effective system of post-horses and boats ready for government service. The roads were kept constantly in order, paved and raised above the surrounding soil so that they might drain easily; thousands of stone bridges spanned the rivers, and the Grand Canal, through which 200,000 merchant vessels passed each year, was a main artery of traffic north and south. It was shortly before his arrival that the Grand Canal had been brought to completion by joining its links in one continuous channel of more than 500 miles, forming then, as it does still, an actively used waterway through the heart of the country from Hangchow in the south to Tientsin in the north. Marco named and described sixteen Chinese provinces and forty-seven cities, though he explained that he had not mentioned those which lay to one side or other of the route of his journeyings. He estimated that those he had named were not one-twentieth of those that existed and that there were 1,200 cities and walled towns in southern China alone, an estimate not very different from modern figures.

Over one of these towns, Yangchow, a manufacturing and trading center of over a million inhabitants with twenty-five lesser towns under its jurisdiction, Marco served as governor for three years. A week's journey from Yangchow was Hangchow or Quinsai, the "Celestial City," the ancient capital of southern China, which Marco visited frequently. This city is of special interest, not only because of the detailed and enthusiastic description of it given by the traveler, but because of the impression this description of it seems to have made on the mind of Columbus, who believed that he was in its vicinity when he reached the West Indies 200 years later.[4]

Marco declared that "it surpasses in grandeur, wealth and beauty every other city in the world" and claimed to have made notes at the time of its extent and customs. There were in it, he said, 12,000 bridges, doubtless a great exaggeration, though Hangchow is still a city of a multitude of bridges spanning the watercourses connected with the Yangtse river, the Grand Canal and the lake. Some of these bridges are high enough to allow vessels with masts to pass under them, which was not true at that time of any bridge in Europe. There were ten principal market-places, each more than 300 yards square, surrounded by buildings which were dwelling houses above and shops below, and each crowded three days in the week with 50,000 to 60,000 people buying and selling supplies, especially the abundant fish from the lake, vegetables and fowl from the surrounding country, and fruit and wine of the neighborhood. There were also great stone warehouses along the canal, built to accommodate the merchandise coming from India and elsewhere. As an instance of the extent of foreign commerce Marco said, he "learned from a customhouse official that the city imported of pepper alone daily forty-three loads, each load of 243 pounds," equalling some six tons. He described also the city police, the fire towers and stone buildings to which household goods could be taken in case of fire. There were great buildings on two islands in the lake outside the town, erected by the citizens in common, provided with furniture, tableware and table linen, where as many as a hundred wedding feasts or other sumptuous entertainments could be given at one time, all accommodated in separate pavilions or rooms.

[4] C. R. Beazley, *The Dawn of Modern Geography* (three volumes, Oxford, 1897-1906), III, 117-23; Yule, *Book of Ser Marco Polo,* 193, 212.

The people of Hangchow, as of the south generally, were more luxury-loving than the inhabitants of the more abstemious north. Many of them had retired from business or were masters of some of the 12,000 workshops of the city, "each workshop furnishing employment to ten, fifteen, twenty or sometimes as many as forty workmen," and did not themselves labor. Dressed, like their wives, in silk and wearing many jewels, they lived in fine houses in which they collected paintings and carvings. They were handsome in person and courtly in manners. They spent the evenings and much other time driving in hired carriages or being poled up and down the lake with their wives or mistresses in barges holding ten to twenty persons, decked over above and fitted below with gilded cabins in which they might dine while they looked out of the windows at the scenes of beauty along the shore, or at the city with its handsome houses, temples, convents and gardens, and with its great trees growing down to the water's edge. To the Venetian traveler the plain gondolas of his native city passing up and down its Grand Canal must have seemed simple and rude indeed compared with all this rich abandonment to pleasure and display of wealth.

The seaports of Kangui and Zayton, the modern Canton and Amoy, were far to the south of Quinsai and were reached by traveling through a country crowded with so many towns that to the stranger they seemed like one continuous city. This region produced much sugar, ginger, camphor, silk, cotton, salt, saffron and porcelain. The great number of ships lying in these ports, larger than any known in Europe, with crews of 200 to 300 men and loaded with such goods as spices, sandalwood and jewels, paid to the Great Khan, as Marco himself saw from an inspection of the customhouse accounts, 16,800,000 ducats, perhaps $200,000,000, a year.

This port of Zayton, second only to Alexandria as the greatest trading port of the world, according to Marco, to which, as he says, a hundred times more pepper came than reached Christendom through Alexandria, was destined to attract the long-continued attention of western navigators, missionaries, merchants and monarchs. In 1308, only sixteen years after Marco Polo's visit, there was a Roman Catholic bishopric and a settlement of Christian merchants at Zayton. "I am in front of Zayton and Quinsay," Columbus wrote in his journal of November 1, 1492, as he threaded his way among the West Indies.

There are, in Marco's story, distant echoes of Zipangu, or Japan, which, according to his information, was 1,500 miles from the mainland. It was civilized and rich; its sovereign had a palace of which the roof was covered with plates of gold, as the roofs of the Venetian churches were covered with lead, but Marco had not himself been there and few merchants from China visited it; its traditional exclusiveness was already a characteristic. Even this glimpse of a golden island was, however, a lode-star for western navigators. In the margin of Columbus' copy of Marco Polo is a mark pointing to the passage about Zipangu, and in John Cabot's petition for permission to send out an expedition of discovery from England to the westward he expresses the hope of reaching "the island of Cipango."

Marco was much interested in the vast number of islands in the sea to the eastward. He meant apparently all the great archipelago to the southward also, including the Philippines and even the Moluccas, for he stated that he had learned from mariners and fishermen that there were 7,448 of these islands, that they produced sandalwood, spices and drugs and that of all the trees that grew upon them there was none that did not emit a fragrant smell. He called attention to the fact, again starred by Columbus, that the China Sea is not a separate body of water, but "a part of the ocean."

Either some journey made by Marco or his interest in his Tartar employers, led him to describe the lands of their native steppes and other regions far to the north of his own travels. Fifty days' journey to the north of Lake Baikal you reached the northern ocean, he reported. This was so far to the north that "the pole star seems to be behind you, and to have in part a southerly bearing," an astronomical statement that Marco would never have repeated if he had actually gone that far north. But the sparse population, the reindeer, the falcons, the winter's cold—so bitter that men could not live at the farthest north—are all unmistakable characteristics of Siberia. If these early travelers had only made more careful inquiries and taught Europe the vastness of the distance to which the northeast of Asia stretches, it might have saved later men from their heart-breaking search for a "northeast passage," based as it was on the belief that, the north capes of Scandinavia once passed, the coast of Asia turned rapidly toward the south and made the approach to China easy; one of the most tragic mistaken guesses in all geographical history.

More directly a result of observation was the knowledge of India which Marco obtained and passed on to the world. This was partly a result of a journey Marco made on the business of the Khan, partly of his experiences and inquiries on the way home to Venice. This return journey began in 1292, seventeen years after the Polos arrived at Peking. Permission to leave was obtained only with difficulty. The Polos were anxious to return to Venice and were moreover fearful that the high favor they enjoyed under Kublai might not be retained under a successor. The Khan was now seventy-eight years of age, and did, as a matter of fact, die two years later. But the old Khan liked them and valued their services and gave them leave to depart only when it was necessary to have well-informed guides to accompany a princess he was sending by sea to Persia to become wife of a distant relative.

It was in this three years' voyage that Marco was able to add to his previous knowledge and to transmit information of the regions along the eastern and southern shores of Asia and the eastern coast of Africa. His accounts were, of necessity, concerned especially with islands—Java, Sumatra, Candore, Singapore, the Nicobars and Andamans, Ceylon, Socotra, Madagascar and even Zanzibar. Of the provinces on the mainland of India and in the interior of Java and Sumatra, however, he gave some description, probably from hearsay; Abyssinia attracted his interested attention from the Christian belief of its ruler, but Marco did not recognize him as the "Prester John" of tradition, with whom he was later identified by the Portuguese. Notwithstanding the familiarity he obtained with Zanzibar and Madagascar, he heard nothing of a way around the southern coast of Africa. Merchants from all countries came to Madagascar, he said, for ivory, sandalwood, ambergris and other products; those from the Malabar coast of India reached it in twenty to twenty-five days: but "there is no resort of ships to the numerous islands further south, this and the island of Zanzibar alone being frequented."

The fact that there was open sea to the south and that Venetian navigators might sail in that direction and back home through the Mediterranean was all unknown to him, as it remained for almost an even 200 years afterward.

He gave some description of the regions around the mouth of the Red Sea, Arabia and Somaliland, and described anew the trading route through that sea, Cairo and Alexandria, although this had been long familiar to all Europe. With a hasty return to a description of the eastern parts of Russia, of which he had seen something and heard much, but which he had omitted from the earlier part of his narrative, Marco brought his book to an end. As a matter of fact he had returned with his father and his uncle, by an almost complete sea-route, along the shores of southern China, Annam, Burma and India, to Persia, where they left their charge, the Tartar bride, in tears at separating from them, and so to the Black Sea, thence to Constantinople, and so through the Mediterranean to Venice, which they reached in 1295.

The circumstances under which Marco's narrative was drawn up are of interest: The year after his return, as a wealthy citizen of the republic he was in command of one of the galleys at the fatal battle of Curzola of 1296, when the Venetian fleet was destroyed by the Genoese and he, with 7,000 other Venetians was captured, thrown into a Genoese prison and, notwithstanding attempts at ransom, kept there for three years. Perhaps to while away the time, he recounted his adventures to his fellow-prisoner Rusticiano of Pisa, who apparently wrote them from Marco's dictation. He called it his "Book of Various Experiences" and it is fairly named. It was, as has been observed, made up largely of descriptions of the natural features of the countries through which he had passed and of their productions, of the cities and their inhabitants, their trade, their religion, their customs, their appearance, and of China, in which he had lived a third of a lifetime. Indeed, so detailed and varied were his statements that there have been skeptical students who have considered the book to be really an encyclopedia of medieval knowledge of the Orient, and the voyages of the Polos to be a mere literary device to give interest to the compilation. But no serious scholar has supported this view, and certainly no casual reader will get that impression. There is too much that is individual and characteristic, too steady a stream of adventure running through it, too much of it was new to the western world to allow it to be considered a thirteenth-century handbook of general knowledge.

The story as put down in dialectical French by Rusticiano in the prison at Genoa was soon translated into better French, then into Italian, into Latin, and ultimately into all other civilized languages. Some of the early forms were revised by the traveler himself, for Marco lived for thirty years after his return, dying in 1324, three years after Dante, when Petrarch was a young man of twenty. Copies of his book were widely disseminated. In 1301, only nine years after it was dictated, Marco Polo himself gave a copy of the narrative, "the fourth copy which had been made," to a French nobleman, Thiébault de Çépoy, then on a mission to the Republic from Charles of Valois. Marino Faliero, who was Doge of Venice in 1354, possessed a copy of the book said to have been made by the traveler himself, besides a ring given to Marco by the Great Khan. The maker of a map of 1375 was evidently familiar with Marco's narrative, for on it appear not only the new discoveries in the west, but an excellent representation of all those regions described by him and far the best outline that had ever yet been made of the whole continent of Asia. The Florentine chronicler Giovanni Villani (1280-1348) advised all who wanted to know about the Tartars to read "the book of Messer Marco Polo of Venice."

There is an interesting translation, made perhaps a century later, from Latin into Irish for Florence MacCarthy and his wife, Katharine Fitzgerald, embedded among romances and lives of saints in the manuscript known as the *Book of Lismore.* As early as 1426 the Signory of Venice, evidently proud of their fellow-citizen, gave to a visiting prince of Portugal a copy of Marco's book accompanied with a map, unfortunately now lost, which may possibly have had some influence on the series of Portuguese explorations then just begun. There are now in existence altogether eighty-five manuscripts of the book made before the invention of printing in 1450. Since that time there have been numberless printed editions. One student lists seventy-three, in twelve languages, including the Latin translation with annotations in the handwriting of Columbus now in the library of Seville.[5]

But it was in its first impact upon the western world that the narrative of Marco must have exerted its greatest influence. It suddenly doubled the size and increased manifold the variety of the known world. The panorama of races, cities, ships, new animals, unknown religions and strange social customs, spread before the eyes of the people of western Europe, must have stretched the medieval mind to something of modern requirements. The vast, rich, populous, civilized and tolerant east must have been an attraction and a lesson as well as a source of wonder to the men of the thirteenth and fourteenth centuries.

The travels of the Polos had been initiated by the desire for trade. However much the love of adventure, desire for knowledge and the interest of service under the Great Khan may have provided incentives for Marco's wanderings and observations, the trading interest was never absent. The merchant and his wares were the constant objects of his mention. The people of Kashgar "subsist by commerce and manufactures, particularly works of cotton. . . . Abundance of cotton is produced here, as well as flax and hemp. Merchants from this country travel to all parts of the world." He described Ormuz, "whose port is frequented by traders from all parts of India, who bring spices and drugs, precious stones, pearls, gold tissues, elephants' teeth and various other articles of trade." "Yezd is a considerable city on the confines of Persia where there is much traffic. A species of cloth of silk and gold manufactured there is known by the appellation of Yezdi and is carried from thence by the merchants to all parts of the world." In the city of Chin-Kian-Fu in China the remarkable fact that there were there three churches of Nestorian Christians was not allowed to obscure the statement that the inhabitants "gain their living by trade and manufacture and are wealthy. They weave tissues of silver and gold." The people of Tibet were of minor interest because "they are not a commercial but an agricultural people." Japan received scant mention apart from its wealth in gold and pearls and the idolatry and independence of its

[5] Beazley, op. cit., III, 20, 545-54.

people, because "few merchants visit the country, nor is it frequented by much shipping from other parts."

II. THE EAST AS A SPHERE OF MISSIONARY ENTERPRISE

With the Polos, however, purely trading and exploring journeys to the eastward came, at least for the time, to an end. Somewhat later when they were resumed and we hear vague reports of Europeans making their way backward along the old Asiatic trading routes, the travelers did not see fit to leave us any record of their journeys. On the other hand there were other incentives that took travelers into the same regions and helped to familiarize Europe with Asia. Missionary zeal was offered an opportunity at the very beginning of this period which the church was not likely to disregard. This opportunity was the conquest of the whole of northern and central and much of western Asia by the Mongols or Tartars.[6]

In one of those curious sudden dispersions of a formerly stationary race so characteristic of the history of Asia, the Mongols, under their leader Genghis Khan and his immediate descendants, in the first half of the thirteenth century swept across that continent eastward, southward and westward. The southward and eastward invasions gave them the China of Kublai Khan and the Persia and Turkestan of his dependent chieftains. To the west their conquering hordes spread across the plains of Russia and far into Poland, Moravia, Silesia, Hungary and Bulgaria before the original impetus was lost. About the beginning of our period, after the battle of Wahlstatt in 1244, the tide turned. But for the time being the whole continental stretch from the eastern borders of Europe to the sea of China and Japan, and from the Arabian deserts, the Hindu Kush and the Himalaya mountains indefinitely northwards, was under one ruler. A letter of protection from the Great Khan or an official guard provided by him, such as the Polos received from Kublai, guaranteed comparative security and opportunity for safe travel in the whole of this vast territory. Moreover, from a religious point of view the Mongols were a tolerant power; they might pos-

[6] An account of this conquest in brief form with the latest bibliography is given in L. Halphen and Ph. Sagnac, *Peuples et Civilisations* (Paris, 1931), VII, 176-88.

sibly be receptive to a superior religion, such as Christianity—or, as afterwards proved to be the case, to Mohammedanism. Under Genghis' descendants the great empire fell into four divisions: first, the Far East under the Great Khan himself, who had established his capital at Peking; second, the Chagatai of Central Asia and Turkestan; third, Persia and its surrounding regions, whose ruler was known as the Il-Khan, and fourth, the Mongols of Kipchak, or the Golden Horde, with its capital at Serai on the Volga, who were the rulers of greater Russia. But even then all the Tartar dominions were still open to the passage of traders and there was no opposition to religious propaganda.

These conquering and godless Mongols, the native races they had subjected to their rule, the teeming millions of China and Central Asia, all seemed open to the missionary efforts of the church. There was besides always the hope of uniting the scattered sects of early Christianity, and perhaps the Orthodox Eastern Church itself, under the Roman headship. Missionaries were available in the cohorts of Franciscan and Dominican friars, detached from local responsibilities and pledged to the service of the church. The increasing wealth of Europe could easily provide for the necessary expense, the Crusades as an outlet for religious fervor had run their course, and interest in them, except for a few knightly and pious souls like St. Louis, had died out.[7]

It would seem that conditions were unusually favorable for an insistent effort of the Roman church to subject to its special doctrine, ritual and organization all these potential converts. A century of missionary effort followed. From 1245 to 1340 a series of expeditions were sent, at first only to those lands beyond the Black and Caspian Seas most recently overrun and most accessible, but later to Persia and the lands of the Il-Khan, to Almalik and Karakorum, and finally to India and to China, to the court of the Great Khan himself.[8]

There was even some diplomatic intercourse between Europe and

[7] The change wrought by the opening up of Asia by the Mongols is thoughtfully discussed in Eileen Power, "The Opening of the Land Routes to Cathay," in A. P. Newton, *Travel and Travellers of the Middle Ages* (London, 1926), chap vii.

[8] There is now an exhaustive study of the relations of the Papacy to the Tartars and of the narratives of papal emissaries and missionaries, in Giovanni Soranzo, *Il Papato, l'Europa Cristiana e i Tartari* (Milan, 1930).

the Near and the Farther East. Three times during the later years of the thirteenth century messengers came with letters from the Il-Khan to the kings of England and France and to the emperor, proposing joint military action against the Mohammedans, who were now pressing upon him. In 1307 a Tartar embassy appeared before Edward II at Northampton for the same purpose. With the pope also there were exchanges of letters, mostly concerning the plans of the church. Missionaries and messengers passed repeatedly between Peking and other Tartar capitals and Rome and Avignon.

A long list of names, most of them, though by no means all, Franciscans, and mostly Italians, give testimony to the extent and devotion of this movement. John of Monte Corvino, Gerard and William of Prato, Anthony of Parma, Andrew and Peter of Florence, Matthew of Arezzo, Arnold of Cologne, Peter of Castello, Nicholas of Apulia, Thomas of Tolentino, Andrew of Assisi, John of Cora, Gregory of Hungary, Ricold of Monte Croce, Oderic of Pordenone and scores of others appear as participants in these eastern journeys, singly or in groups with others, named or nameless. Three Dominicans were sent out as preachers by Boniface VIII in 1296, three Franciscans died of disease immediately after entering India in 1308. In the year 1338 an embassy from the Great Khan arrived at Avignon, asking for the re-opening of good relations and expressing an interest in the horses as well as the religion of the west. In return a group of thirty-two missionaries under the Italian John of Marignolli, provided with letters and gifts, made their way from France to Italy, thence through Constantinople across the Black Sea and, by a route now becoming familiar, to the courts of the Kipchak and Chagatai Khans, and finally, after three years of travel, reached Peking, where they remained for three years engaged in religious work. John returned by sea and has left an admirable account of his experiences.[9]

Bishoprics and even archbishoprics were by this time established from Armenia to China, in India and Turkestan, even where clergy and laity were few or wanting; organization often preceded conversion. There was an archbishopric of Cambaluc and a bishopric

[9] Beazley, *Dawn of Modern Geography,* III, 184-5, 288-309; P. Schlager, *Mongolenfahrten der Franziskaner* (Trier, 1911); P. L. Lemmens, *Geschichte der Franziskaner Missionen* (Münster, 1929).

of Zayton; in 1306 there were three churches in the former and at least two in the latter; in 1340 Marignolli was able to perform service in the cathedral at Peking.[10]

At one time, around the middle years of the fourteenth century, as many as forty Franciscan houses were scattered through northern and eastern Turkestan, Persia, Central Asia, China and Tartary. Nor were converts wanting. There were continuous hopes and occasional rumors of one or other of the Tartar Khans accepting baptism. Religion was, as has been said, held lightly by them; they were tolerant of all creeds, and might readily, it was believed, make their decision in favor of Christianity. Many common people were baptized—at one time in one year, it was claimed, 5000 in China. John of Monte Corvino, the founder of the church in India and China, who was in Peking the year after the Polos and may have passed them on their return, bought 150 boys between seven and eleven years of age, baptized them and taught them enough Latin to chant the Roman service, to the great delight of the Khan, now an old man of eighty, as he listened to them from his palace.

Although this extensive missionary enterprise went to pieces before the end of the fourteenth century, it led nevertheless to an immense amount of writing of narratives, reports and letters descriptive of the east. Two of the earliest accounts, those of John de Plano Carpini, the Italian, and William de Rubruquis, the Fleming, are among the best of all narratives of travel, though their journeys did not take them far beyond the Black Sea.[11] *The Book of Marvels* in which the French Dominican, Jordanus of Severac, described his travels in India and Abyssinia, is an early report of more distant regions. In the *Directions for Crossing the Sea*, composed in 1330 by another Frenchman, on the other hand, the "sea" is the Mediterranean and the "crossing" the journey from France to the Levant; incidentally he described his travels in Asia Minor, Syria, Persia and Russia. The letters written in 1338 by Pascal of Vittoria from Almalik, in what is now southern Siberia, are contemporary with the accounts of the lands along and beyond the Baltic, introduced

[10] A. C. Moule, *Christians in China Before the Year 1553* (London, 1930).

[11] C. R. Beazley, *Texts and Versions of John de Plano Carpini and William de Rubruquis* (Hakluyt Society, extra series, London, 1903), vii-xx; Henri Cordier, *Les Merveilles d'Asie de Jourdain Catalan de Severac* (Paris, 1925).

by John Marignolli into his *Annals of Bohemia,* written at the request of the Emperor Charles IV.

A Franciscan monk, Oderic of Pordenone, one of the best of narrators, set out eastward about fifty years later than the Polos, "to win gain of souls," followed almost exactly their route, spent three years in Peking, and has left a *Description of Eastern Regions,* dictated to a friend in Padua, which rivals Marco's book in interest and minuteness and corroborates it in a hundred instances. We have the same account of the size and luxury of Quinsai and additional de scriptions of Canton, "three times as large as Venice," Zaiton "twice as large as Bologna," of Nanking, Yangchow and the whole line of cities along the Grand Canal. Oderic's narrative was almost as popular apparently as Polo's, as some seventy-five fourteenth and fifteenth century copies of it still exist. Notwithstanding his religious motives for travel he was a good observer, a lover of adventure, a man of wide and varied interests. Among his observations it is of interest to note that in Zaiton, the Amoy of modern China, the Christian monks who had a convent there, had established a *fondaco,* with a bathhouse, for the use of European merchants trading there, probably Genoese, who came by land or by land and water, since almost 200 years were yet to elapse before the all-water route around the Cape of Good Hope was known.[12]

In Oderic's story as in Polo's and running vaguely through many other narratives of travel is the elusive person and country of "Prester John," that is "Presbyter" or "Priest" John, a half mythical ruler of a wonderful land, a Christian, a great potentate. Oderic visited what he thought was his land, about fifty days' journey westward of Peking, but was disappointed; his capital city of Chosan, which must have been somewhere on the upper waters of the Hoang-ho River, although head of a group of cities, was no larger than the Italian city of Vicenza; and the king-priest had no great distinction except that he always received a daughter of the Great Khan as his wife. Polo considered that he found Prester John's country south of the Gobi desert. Its ruler was a "King George" or "Wang Khan," sixth in descent from the original Prester John. Others reported that

[12] Oderic of Pordenone's narrative is translated in Yule, *Cathay and the Way Thither* (second edition, revised by Henri Cordier, three volumes, London, 1913-1915), 1-162.

his country was on the shores of Lake Baikal, or elsewhere. The whole story is tenuous, much mixed up with Gog and Magog, partly an explanation of the existence of tribes early converted to Nestorian Christianity, partly an effort to find a material location for the country described in a forged letter from "Prester John" to the Pope, which had been current in various forms in Europe since the twelfth century. The story played its part in all early exploration; it changed its location from Asia to Africa and was later identified, no doubt correctly, with Abyssinia or Ethiopia and its Christian king.[13]

III. COMPILATIONS OF EASTERN TRAVELS

The popular interest in distant lands in the fourteenth century is indicated by the appearance of compilations of travels. The *Pratica della Mercatura* or "Merchant's Handbook," written by Francesco Balducci Pegolotti of Florence is said by a modern scholar to be "perfectly unreadable by the general public of any age, medieval or modern," yet "of supreme value to traders of the fourteenth century; to all students of medieval life, medieval travel and medieval traffic beyond price." This judgment seems justified by the fact that but one manuscript of it is known, and it has so far been printed in but one edition and never translated, yet it is constantly referred to as a standard work. It was written in Italian by a clerk in the banking house of the Bardi, serving successively in Antwerp, London, Cyprus and Cilicia, from 1315 to 1335. It gives, in addition to much purely mercantile lore, a full description of all known trade routes between Europe and the Far East.[14]

The same indication of a growing familiarity with the geography, peoples and productions of eastern lands is shown in the *Secrets of the Faithful Crusaders* of Marino Sanuto, the Venetian, written

[13] Beazley, *The Dawn of Modern Geography,* III, 88-90, 284-5; E. Denison Ross, "Prester John and the Empire of Ethiopia," in A. P. Newton, *Travel and Travellers of the Middle Ages* (London, 1926), chap. ix. A translation of the forged letter is given in this essay. The whole question is critically reviewed by Richard Hening, "Das Christentum im mittelalterlichen Asien und sein Einfluss auf die Sage vom Priester Johannes," *Historische Vierteljahrschrift,* XXIX (1934), 234-52.

[14] Beazley, op. cit., III, 324. Extracts from it are scattered through Yule, *Cathay and the Way Thither,* III, 137-73. A new edition is being prepared for publication by the Mediaeval Academy of America.

in Latin. His book, first presented to the pope in 1307 and extended by additional chapters in later years, was an argument for a new type of Crusade, directed primarily against the Moslems of Egypt and the Syrian coast, impoverishing them by laying an embargo against all Christian trade with them.[15] Of great interest in itself for its ingenious and statesmanlike plans and proposal of "economic sanctions," the excuse for the mention of this work here is its wide sweep of geographical knowledge, its discussion of Asiatic ports and trading cities with the same detail and in the same connection in which it proposed a combination of various Mediterranean, Hanseatic and Slavic towns. It is evident that to Sanuto and his readers the greater part of Asia had come within the circle of common knowledge. The twenty-two copies of his book still surviving in manuscript testify to the number of its contemporary readers.[16]

Vastly better known than any writers who utilized common geographic knowledge for other ends was one who professed to describe his travels for their own interest. This was "Sir John Mandeville." Long supposed to be a real person telling a real story, he is now known to have been, under that name and in that guise at least, a pretender, a wholesale plagiarist. The author who used the name and who claimed to be an Englishman, descendant of that once famous family, and himself a traveler in the lands he described, was in reality a French physician of Liège, Jean de Bourgogne. So far as influence is concerned, what his book lacked in veracity it made up in popularity. It was written in French about 1360, half a century later than the book of Marco Polo, and was translated immediately into English, Latin, Italian and other languages. It attained an astounding celebrity. Two hundred and twenty-five manuscripts of the fourteenth and fifteenth centuries are known to exist; it was early printed in many editions and was long accepted as a true account of travel and observation. Although in its personal narrative it is mendacious and in its descriptions inferior to many of the authentic accounts from which it was plagiarized, the fact that such a compilation was possible discloses the

[15] J. Bongars, *Gesta Dei per Francos* (Hanau, 1611), II, 1-288.
[16] C. R. Beazley, op. cit., III, 311-9, 549.

amount of material already available; its popularity indicates the general interest in new knowledge of the world, and in turn it must, with all its deficiencies, have done much to spread that knowledge abroad.[17]

Two fifteenth-century travelers, Clavijo, the Spaniard, who wrote an account of his adventures while on a mission from Henry III, King of Castile, to Tamerlane in 1403-6, and Johann Schiltberger, a German soldier, captured at the battle of Nicopolis and living among the Tartars from 1396 to 1427, who dictated his *Reisebuch* after his return to his home near Munich, have left admirable records of eastern lands, but they visited no places not already known and already described by western travelers. The same is true of the vast amount of "pilgrim literature," the sixty or eighty narratives of western pilgrims who in the wake of the Crusades visited the holy places of Palestine between 1250 and 1450. These were more generally Germans, French, English, Russians or Poles than were the churchmen who had tried to establish Roman Christianity in the Far East. There were also merchants who in the early fifteenth century wrote longer or shorter accounts of their journeys and observations, but no one of them compares in value with their predecessors of the three or four preceding generations, and as a matter of fact the unveiling of the East had already been accomplished in the fourteenth century.

These varied writings and the oral reports of so many travelers must have made knowledge of China and India, Thibet and Turkestan, the lands of the Near East, Persia, Mesopotamia, Arabia, the adjacent parts of Asia Minor, the lands south of the Caucasus and around the Black and Caspian Seas, the northern and western parts of Russia, all the shores of the Baltic and even much of Siberia and Mongolia, familiar to all but the most ignorant and those living in the most secluded parts of the western world. The scene of Chaucer's "Knights' Tale," written between 1380 and 1400, is at Serai, the capital of the Tartars on the Volga, and the merchant in the "Man of Laws' Tale" trades between the same city and Rome. The Tartars were already, before the fourteenth

[17] G. F. Warner, *Buke of John Maundevill* (Westminster, Roxburghe Club, 1889), is an admirable edition with the latest criticism.

century was over, almost as familiar in literature as the Romans, the Greeks or the Trojans.

The work of obtaining a reasonably full and accurate geographical knowledge of the whole of Asia except its extreme northeastern part had thus been accomplished long before the close of our period. Greater detail and greater accuracy were of course still to be obtained, but conditions for securing this became for the time less favorable. The great days of a single or a group of closely allied Tartar powers spreading over the eastern continent, with a certain receptiveness to foreign intercourse, trade and religion, were over.

Ukhagatu or Toghon Timour (1332-1368) was the last of the Mongol Emperors who reigned in Peking. Between 1360 and 1370, in a native movement arising in the commercial south the Mongols and all other foreigners were expelled from China; the native Ming dynasty took their place, the Celestial Kingdom closed its borders and withdrew into its own secluded life. The eastern Tartars retired to their original barbarous steppes, conflict broke out among the hereditary Khans, and central Asia became a land of a hundred warring tribes, till it was again unified for a moment under Tamerlane. Persia and Turkestan accepted Islam, and the Golden Horde gradually lost control of the lands they had occupied. But nothing could obliterate the widespread body of knowledge of the Asiatic continent now possessed by the people of Europe.[18]

[18] L. Halphen and Ph. Sagnac, *Peuples et Civilisations,* Vol. VII, *La Fin du Moyen Âge* (Paris, 1931), 176-87.

Chapter Ten

THE EASTERN FRONTIERS OF EUROPE

THE group of countries which stretched from the Baltic along the eastern confines of Europe nearly to the Black Sea and the Mediterranean—Poland, Bohemia, Hungary, Serbia, Bulgaria, to use the names which were to survive through several succeeding centuries—were during this period more than most countries of Europe in unstable equilibrium. Changes of boundaries, changes of dynasties, frequent regroupings among themselves and intrusions from outside gave a kaleidoscopic character to their history. Though they were Slav for the most part, it remained to the very end of the period uncertain whether their closer connections were to be with the Germanic countries to the west or with other Slavic regions to the east, or whether they were to form a distinct group of states partly within, partly without the European complex.

I. BOHEMIA, POLAND AND HUNGARY

Their history can be only glanced at here. That of the three westernmost, Poland, Bohemia and Hungary, had much in common. In each the old native dynasties died out and left the crown to the hazards of election through foreign and internal intrigue or to inheritance through distant female lines. This put upon the throne of Bohemia, John of Luxemburg, a royal knight errant who mingled in every conflict in Europe, losing his eyesight in a campaign against the heathens in Prussia and ultimately giving his life in battle for the King of France at Crécy. With equal illogicality it placed upon the throne of Hungary a descendant of the Angevin kings of Naples. These connections drew the interests of those two countries westward. Poland had for the longest time a purely native line, but even the last king of the Polish line was brought up at the half-Italian court of his Hungarian brother-in-law and was subject to much the same influences.

There was a time in the middle years of the fourteenth century when each of these countries had a sovereign of unusual abilities who occupied the throne for a considerable period and actively furthered the national interests. In Poland, Casimir the Great reigned from 1333 to 1370; Louis, also surnamed the Great, ruled Hungary from 1347 to 1382 and Poland after the death of Casimir in 1370; the Emperor Charles IV, son of King John, was King of Bohemia from 1346 to 1378. This condition of affairs held the possibility of a great period of development. The kings had the means of bringing into their countries the influence of a more advanced civilization, and they might, if they had worked in unison, have exercised a dominating influence over all eastern Europe.

There was, in fact, much advance in these three countries during this period. Some of the amelioration of conditions introduced by Charles into Bohemia we have already had occasion to mention. Prague was a literary and cultured center and Bohemia, before the desolation of the Hussite wars, a rich and prosperous country. The foundation of the University of Prague in 1348 had its counterpart in the establishment of a university at Cracow in Poland by Casimir in 1364. It was, for that matter, a period of university foundations east of the Rhine, Vienna being founded in 1365, Heidelberg in 1386, Cologne in 1388 and Leipzig in 1409. Louis of Hungary brought to Buda much French and Italian culture and made his court a brilliant center for the native aristocracy and for foreign visitors.

The economic basis for this advance in culture was a sound one. Bohemia was still a country of free peasants as well as of much local and foreign trade. On the bridge over the Moldau at Prague there was a dwelling-place for Venetian merchants, known as the *Walhenhof*, much like the *fondaco* in Venice for German merchants. The trading intercourse with the Baltic, with Russia and with the west and south was encouraged by Charles; he made plans for digging a canal to connect the upper waters of the Vistula and the Danube. Bohemia was especially rich in metals; the great silver mine at Kuttenberg was opened just at the beginning of this period. Its annual production in 1400 was said to be 50,000 pounds of bullion. The money for the diplomatic adventures of the Bohemian kings was largely drawn from this source.

Similarly the great salt deposits of Poland were opened up in the middle of the fourteenth century. They were granted as a government monopoly to a Genoese firm with headquarters at Cracow. The Italian banker, Fattinati, was the greatest capitalist in Poland at the close of that century. Polish trade extended eastward to the Black Sea region and Armenia, and much of the warlike policy of Casimir the Great and later of Jagellon was directed to the possession of these trading regions. The wide plains of Hungary were conducive to more primitive exploitation, but the mountainous province of Transylvania was, like Bohemia, a mining region, and its trade, like that of Poland, looked toward the Black Sea. King Sigismund of Hungary deliberately broke off relations with Venice when the Republic tried to exclude him from the Adriatic, and then entered into long negotiations with the Genoese by way of the Black Sea.

The aphorism that "westward the course of empire takes its way" has seldom been more completely belied than by the steady eastward advance of German and even Latin culture during this period. The inhabitants of the cities established by rulers of the Slavic countries or springing from less deliberate origins were almost entirely German; their charters were copied from German models and their civic life was similar to that of German cities further west. The names of the principal cities in far-off Transylvania, Hermannstadt, Cronstadt, Klausenburg, etc. give evidence of the nationality of their founders and inhabitants. Farther north the regions left desolate by the ravaging expeditions of the Mongols in the thirteenth century were filled in the fourteenth by men from the west invited in by the Polish kings.

Occasionally a ruler would annex lands already endowed with a culture superior to his own. Louis of Hungary, for instance, took part with Zara in her war with Venice and in a series of campaigns between 1348 and 1380 became for a while master of the whole Dalmatian coast. While he forced Venice to pay him tribute, the Italians exerted a powerful civilizing influence on his more backward dominion.[1]

But all this economic and cultural progress happened incidentally, so to speak. What we most hear of is the preoccupation of the Kings of Poland, Bohemia and Hungary with their inheritances. This was a natural outcome of the unsettledness of the dynasties. The establishment in a period of imperial confusion of Hapsburg heirs in Tyrol, Austria, Carinthia, Styria and Carniola, of the Bavarian house in its Rhenish possessions, and of the Hohenzollerns in their great northern mark of Brandenburg were all essentially results of the same interest. Marriage has been a familiar factor in diplomacy at all times, but it had its most frequent use in these elective monarchies. It was thus that Louis of Hungary, whose mother was a sister of Casimir of Poland, secured his election to the Polish throne. Charles, King of Bohemia, was especially fortunate in his family arrangements, to which he gave much attention. His older son, Wenzel, became King of Bohemia, his younger, Sigismund, King of Hungary and after his brother's death of Bohemia also. Charles, Wenzel and Sigismund were all successively elected emperor, due to the influence they derived largely from these, their eastern possessions.

It seems to have been a regular practice to marry a newly elected king to some representative of the old royal family, extinct in its male line, in the hope of giving him more prestige in the perpetual conflict between the crown and the great nobles, who were always inclined to wring privileges from the ruler as a condition of his election. John, elected King of Bohemia, married Elizabeth, a descendant of the old Premyslid line of that country. The King of Hungary married a sister of the King of Poland and thus prepared the way for his son's future election to the throne of that country. Even a regent of Bohemia, Zavich Falkenstein, married the widow of the late King to give dignity to his position.

A Polish marriage arrangement of this kind did much to give direction to the whole history of this eastern region during the next century. Louis the Great of Hungary and Poland had no

[1] K. Hampe, *Der Zug nach dem Osten* (Berlin, 1921), chaps. ii, iv—an excellent little book.

sons, but two daughters. In order to guarantee the succession to one of them he obtained in 1373 the agreement of the Polish nobility that their sex should be no bar to their inheritance. At the time of his death, in 1382, the elder daughter Mary was married to Sigismund, King of Hungary and Bohemia, who thus had hopes of gaining the Polish succession. The younger, Hedwig, was engaged to a Hapsburg prince. The great nobles of Poland, however, unwilling to have either a Bohemian, Hungarian or German king, succeeded in breaking off the engagement of Hedwig and bringing her under their control. In November 1384 she was crowned Queen of Poland and a few months later, February 18, 1386, was married to Jagellon, Grand Duke of Lithuania, the only remaining heathen country in Europe.

II. THE TEUTONIC KNIGHTS

The survival to this late date of heathenism in the midst of countries that were adherents of either the Roman Catholic or Greek Orthodox churches according to their conversion from either Rome or Constantinople, may need a word of explanation. A wild region of alternate forest, swamp and heath, stretching along the southeastern and eastern shores of the Baltic and up the river valleys of the Vistula, the Niemen and the Dwina, a region some 500 by 300 miles in extent, was, until the beginning of the thirteenth century, occupied by scattered Slavic tribes, unconverted to Christianity, unorganized politically and but little advanced in civilization. A few Scandinavian or German towns—Riga, Reval, Dorpat, Libau, Memel, Danzig—were planted on the coast, a bishopric was established at Riga and a local body, the Order of the Sword, was formed on the model of the Templars for its protection. But Prussia, Livonia, Kurland, Estonia and Lithuania remained wild and heathen and continued to be in frequent warfare with their more settled Slavic and German neighbors.

Into this region the crusading Order of the Teutonic Knights, like the Templars and the Hospitallers now without occupation, had been introduced in 1231. Within a century Prussia had been conquered and repopulated, and most of the districts to the north brought into a restless submission. This was accomplished partly by the hard fighting of the Knights, partly by the building of towns and fortresses, as the country was occupied, but most of all by the steady stream of German immigration into the newly established towns and into the districts whose native population had been slaughtered or driven eastward.[2] In 1309 the residence of the Grand Master of the Order was established in the great fortress of Marienburg, which remained their capital for 150 years. Thorn, Kulm, Elbing, Danzig and other cities were founded or seized, and Königsberg, "The King's City," was built in honor of the participation of Ottokar, King of Bohemia, in one of the campaigns. Most of these cities, like some of those of Poland, were members of the Hanseatic League.

Lithuania, however, separated from Prussia by a wide stretch of wilderness, remained unsubdued and unconverted, though border warfare was almost continuous.[3] It was, until 1280, when Kovno was founded, a country without cities. By that time, however, its scattered tribes, influenced largely by the attacks of the Teutonic Knights, had drawn together into a centralized state. After 1300 they began a career of expansion, which, partly by conquest, partly by marriages, carried their possessions up to the Baltic and far to the south and east. Under Olgard (1341-1372), the father of Jagellon, their conquests were carried southward to the Black Sea and eastward to the very borders of Russia. When the marriage of the Queen of Poland with the Grand Duke of Lithuania took place in 1386, the power of the combined state of Poland-Lithuania extended over more territory than was included in any other country in Europe. It might well seem that Poland-Lithuania was destined to have the future control of the Slavonic east.

It was part of the marriage agreement between the rulers of the two states that Jagellon should accept Christianity for himself and his country, where, as a matter of fact, there were already adherents of both the eastern and western churches and of Islam,

[2] K. Hampe, op. cit., chap. v; see further E. Caspar, *Hermann von Salza und die Gründung des Deutschordenstaates in Preussen* (Tübingen, 1924) which is excellent; also the well-illustrated account of Christian Krollmann, *Politische Geschichte des Deutschen Ordens in Preussen* (Königsberg, 1932).

[3] E. J. Harrison, *Lithuania Past and Present* (London, 1922), chap. iii, a good general account. Authoritative treatments may be found in Krollmann, op. cit., chaps. iv-vi; and especially in Waclau Sobieski, *Der Kampf um die Ostsee* (Leipzig, 1933), Book ii, which draws heavily on the Polish material.

as well as pagans. Jagellon was thereupon baptized, taking at the time the old Polish royal name of Ladislas. Bishoprics under the Roman obedience were established at Kovno and elsewhere. The queen interested herself until her death in 1399 in the spread of Christianity in her husband's dominions, and soon Lithuania became indistinguishable, so far as religion was concerned, from any other western country.

The prominence of Poland was favored by the decadence of the power of the Teutonic Knights. The religious basis for their existence as a crusading order had long been illusory and the conversion of the Lithuanians made it meaningless. They were now evidently, as they had long been in reality, simply a military government ruling over a large civil population and carrying on wars of conquest indiscriminately with their heathen and their Christian neighbors. There had been repeated conflicts with the Poles and now the formation of a united front by Poland and Lithuania precipitated a more decisive struggle. It was prepared for with deliberation on both sides and the largest armies were collected that had ever met in these regions. The Knights obtained contingents from Bohemia and Hungary; nevertheless they were defeated in the bloody battle of Tannenberg, or Grünewald, July 15, 1410, and left the Grandmaster and many of the Knights and their mercenaries dead on the field. They held out in their great castle of Marienburg for more than a year, but were in 1411 forced to submit to the dictated peace of Thorn. Their later history is one of gradual decline. In 1440 many of their own subjects turned against them. A number of nobles and twenty-one towns combined to form the "Prussian League." Shortly after the close of this period the League renounced the Order and offered the suzerainty of Prussia to the King of Poland. The long struggle until this contest ended with the victory of Poland need not be followed here.

III. THE BEGINNINGS OF RUSSIAN GREATNESS

It is to be observed that the Lithuanians took but small part in the Polish wars in the west. As a matter of fact the union between the two countries was by no means complete. Jagellon found it necessary, especially after his wife's death, when he became sole King of Poland, to spend much of his time in that country. On the other hand the desire for separateness by Lithuania had to be acknowledged by the appointment of his cousin Witold as Grand Duke of Lithuania. The new Grand Duke resumed the policy of conquest southward and eastward and soon came into conflict with the rising power of Russia.

Moscow, around which the reorganization of Russia was taking place, was simply one of those cities with its surrounding territory, under a ruling duke, which paid tribute to the Tartars of the Golden Horde. These remaining representatives of the old Mongols exercised their sway from their distant capital of Serai on the Volga. Whether from its favorable location for trade, from the early acknowledgment by the patriarch of Constantinople of its separate metropolitan, or from the grant by the Tartars of a superior title to its duke, by the middle of the fourteenth century Moscow was the leading state in Russia.[4] Its emergence into wider recognition may be dated from the accession of Dimitri, a boy of nine years of age, in 1359. His guardian and adviser was the able Archbishop Alexei, who used the title "Metropolitan of all Russia." In 1367 the city was encircled by stone walls and its fortress of the Kremlin was strengthened. Although Dimitri died at the age of thirty-nine, his time was one of conquest or at least of extension of the power of Moscow. In 1368, he was able to repel an attack of the rival city of Tver which had made an alliance with the Grand Duke of Lithuania.

More serious was the struggle with the Tartars. Believing that Lithuania was about to ally itself with the chiefs of the Golden Horde, he led an army southward and in 1380 defeated the Tartars in a great battle at Kulikovo on the Don River. He was afterwards known as Dimitri Donskoi, "conqueror of the Don." The immediate results of the battle were not great, since Dimitri's death occurred soon afterward and his son Vassili made peace with the Tartar government and married a Lithuanian princess. Nevertheless it was an important occurrence. The tradition that the Tartars

[4] The most important treatment of medieval Russia in a western tongue is the richly documented study of A. Eck, *Le Moyen Âge Russe* (Paris, 1933).

could not be defeated in battle was broken, and the ruler of Moscow stood forth as the representative of Russian nationality. The next two generations of Muscovite history show little advance, in either conquest or culture, and it is not till after the middle of the fifteenth century that a greater period begins.

IV. THE SERBIAN EMPIRE OF STEPHEN DUSHAN

In the middle years of the fourteenth century the Ottoman Turks crossed the Dardanelles as invaders. Eastern Europe was ill-fitted to resist them. Since the fall of Acre in 1291 the old crusading forces had disintegrated, except as they were represented by the small band of the Knights Hospitallers settled in the island of Rhodes. Cyprus, it is true, was still held somewhat firmly by a line of western princes, but the infinite subdivision of power among the islands and cities of the Aegean precluded any common action on their part for the defense of the eastern Mediterranean.[5] The differences of interest and policy between the Genoese and the Venetians led them to form conflicting alliances and prevented them from taking any joint action against a common enemy. The Eastern Empire, the old bulwark of Europe against Asia, was suffering that increasing decrepitude which can be best measured by the rapid steps of Ottoman advance. The only hope of resistance to invasion seemed to lie in the tier of Slavic states between the Danube and the borders of the Eastern Empire, the old kingdoms of Serbia and Bulgaria, with the Bosnians and Croatians in the north and the principalities of Wallachia and Moldavia, the modern Rumania, which were just now taking shape, on its lower course. The populations of these kingdoms and their dependent lands were large, their territories extensive and their rulers warlike. Back of them were the great Magyar and Slavic states whose history we have just reviewed.

For a while Serbia promised to become the centre of a great state under her king, Stephen Dushan.[6] Profiting by some ad-

[5] The details of this disintegration, so difficult to trace, are given in brief form in L. Halphen and Ph. Sagnac, *Peuples et Civilisations* (Paris, 1931), VII, 188-94.

[6] The best account of Dushan's reign may be found in C. Jireček, *Geschichte der Serben* (Gotha, 1911-1918), Book IV, chap. iii; but see also William Miller, "The Medieval Serbian Empire," *Quarterly Review*, CCXXVI (1916), 488-507; and A. A. Vasiliev, *History of the Byzantine Empire* (Madison, 1929), II, 302-15.

vances made by his grandfather and his father in drawing together certain units of the old Serbian empire around Uskub as a capital, and winning some new territory, Stephen Dushan entered upon his reign of twenty-five years (1331-1355) with vigor and apparently with a clear purpose. He captured or annexed, one after another, the ancient cities of Macedonia and Thrace, of Epirus and Thessaly that the weak hands of the Greeks could not hold, until his control in the south reached to the Aegean and gave him opportunity to enter into treaty relations with the remaining Frankish principalities of Greece. He gave protection to a fugitive Byzantine usurper and in return obtained from him a grant of the cities he had captured. He entered into diplomatic relations with Venice against Genoa, hoping to be able to obtain a seaport on the Adriatic. He exercised a dominating influence in Bulgaria, even beyond the reach of his conquests.

There is little doubt that Stephen had plans for the capture of Constantinople itself or for the building up of a rival empire which should inherit its prestige. He held a brilliant court; he used Byzantine titles in his administration; he took for himself the title "Tsar of the Serbs and the Greeks" and gave his son the lower title of "Kral," which was equivalent to king. He promulgated a new body of laws, the *Zakovik*, for his Greek and Serbian subjects; he reorganized the Serbian church, giving it a patriarch of its own, and he issued charters in the Greek language to convents and other church bodies. At one time he opposed the Ottoman advance, at another he planned to join with them in the conquest of Constantinople.

But all this proved to be a phantom empire. It had no adequate political organization or economic support. The curse of the East, the crumbling of authority when not persistently applied, allowed Stephen's empire to fall to pieces in less than a generation after his death. His sons and nephews seized various parts of his dominions, governors set up for themselves, cities resumed their former half-obedience to the Eastern Empire or to their local rulers, and in less than thirty years even the title of "Tsar" was forgotten. The whole story has little importance, except as a last episode in the history of Serbian independence, and as an indication of the hopeless disunion of southeastern Europe and of the powerlessness of the Eastern Empire to resist the attacks of the Turks which were now imminent.[7]

V. THE DECAY OF THE EASTERN EMPIRE

The greatness of the Empire had long been a memory only. Never since the Venetian conquest, during the Fourth Crusade, had it regained its medieval strength or glory. But during the fourteenth and early fifteenth centuries, its decline had become greatly accelerated.[8] The lamentations of contemporary chroniclers and moralists over the decaying virtues of the people are too familiar a strain to carry much conviction, but the plain story of narrowing territories, of decreasing population, of diminished income and smaller armed forces is incontrovertible evidence of a moribund state. Such was the Byzantine Empire during the hundred years in which the Osmanlis were pressing through its defenses into the Balkan peninsula and such was the process of weakening that made the fall of its capital in 1453 inevitable.

Its most serious affliction was, of course, the contraction of its territory. The conquests of Stephen Dushan were made largely at the expense of the Empire. The loss of Okhrida, Salonika, Seres and Kavala, of most of Epirus, Macedonia and Thrace was irreparable, for although the Serbian Empire of Stephen soon fell to pieces, its fragments were not generally returned to the Eastern Empire, but went into other hands. The loss of territory meant the loss of soldiers and the loss of taxes; the capture by the Turks, even before they entered Europe, of the imperial lands in Asia Minor deprived the government of its best recruiting grounds. The progressive loss or devastation of even those lands which remained longest to the Empire meant a decrease of population from which soldiers could be drawn, and a diminution of the number of prosperous landed proprietors who could pay taxes. The policy of the government had long been recklessly unwise. The proprietors, who secured the first claim on the product of the land, were granted such privileges that they paid little to the state, while the peasants

[7] Jireček, op. cit., Book IV, chap. iv.

[8] This process of decay is admirably, if briefly, told in Charles Diehl, *Byzance: Grandeur et Décadence* (Paris, 1920), especially Livre III, chaps. i-iv; vi-vii.

were so burdened as frequently to prefer flight to payment, or, if they remained, were ready to accept any change of rulers as a deliverance.[9]

Nothing, it might seem, could deprive Constantinople of the profits of its commerce. Its location was, under the trading conditions of the time, incomparable, and, as a matter of fact, the city was still one of the greatest ports of the world. But most of this commerce, so far as it was a source of taxation, had slipped out of the hands of the Byzantine government. A long succession of treaties had accorded to Venetians, Genoese and other trading states freedom from duties, or the possession of ports under their own control, or a monopoly of profitable lines of export and import. The Venetian colony at Constantinople was said at one time to number 10,000 persons. The Genoese were established at Pera across the harbor from the city, and at Galata on the Golden Horn. Pisa, Florence, Ancona, Ragusa, Barcelona, Marseilles, Montpellier and Narbonne, besides Venice and Genoa, each had in the late fourteenth century a flourishing commercial colony with various immunities in the city. The duties paid to the Genoese at Galata were at one time more than six times those paid in the harbor to the imperial government itself. Smuggling was constant and no government fleets or naval and police services were adequate to cope with it.[10]

Thus the two possible sources of income, the land and commerce, were equally unproductive. The government was never able to balance its budget and yet was driven to unwise economies. In 1423 Thessalonika was sold by its governor to the Venetians for 50,000 ducats. It was the second city in size and wealth in the empire, but he felt powerless to protect it. The imperial fleet was allowed to fall into neglect and insignificance.

The result of this paucity of lands, native population and money was that the Byzantine government fought its battles more and more with mercenaries. Soldiers by trade, as individuals and as

[9] Diehl, op. cit., 211-40.

[10] See Vasiliev, op. cit., II, 397-9; Christo M. Macri, *Des Byzantins et des Étrangers dans Constantinople au Moyen Âge* (Paris, 1928), 66-73; C. Diehl, *Une République Patricienne, Vénise* (Paris, 1915), contains an admirable account of Venetian activities in the Near East.

bands, were abundant in the fourteenth and fifteenth centuries, in eastern as in western Europe. Serbians, Bulgarians, Catalans, Germans and even Turks were available for hired service and were constantly made use of in the wars. But mercenaries were expensive, untrustworthy, disorderly and frequently as injurious to their employers as to the enemy. Over and over again such bands in Constantinople itself fought in the streets, pillaged shops, violated women and forced the government to grant outrageous demands.

All in all the Byzantine armies were very small; 2000, 8000, 10,000, 20,000, native and mercenary troops together, were as many as were apt to be taken out to fight rebels, Serbians, or the all-conquering Ottomans. To defend the capital in the agony of its last siege were only a few thousand Greeks with perhaps two thousand Venetians, Genoese and mercenaries. The old Empire of the East was once "a strong man armed" who kept his palace and his goods in peace, but the time was now fast approaching when "one stronger than he should come upon him and take from him all his armor wherein he trusted and divide his spoils."

VI. THE ENTRANCE OF THE OTTOMAN TURKS INTO EUROPE

The "stronger than he" was the Ottoman Turk. Nations have their entrances and their exits on the stage of history as truly as do actors on the mimic stage, and usually, as the stage directions of the old-fashioned tragedies say, they appear with "drums and trumpets." It was thus that the Osmanlis, destined to play a leading part during the next 600 years, entered southeastern Europe, in the middle of our period. At its close the Byzantine Empire, which had played its part for a still longer period, left the stage. The two series of events were inextricably connected. The Osmanlis, young, vigorous and warlike as they were, could not have broken through if the Greeks of Constantinople had been more than a degenerate and waning power. On the other hand the catastrophe of the Decline and Fall of the Roman Empire might have been long delayed if the Ottomans had not entered Europe from western Asia in the fourteenth century.

The early history of the Ottoman Turks, their obscure entrance upon a career of conquest from a focal point on the north-western slope of the great table-land of Asia Minor, and their advance under their first two emirs, Othman and Orkhan, to the Sea of Marmora and the Dardanelles is of great interest and has been the subject of much learned investigation and acute interpretation.[11] But it is no part of the history of Europe. That begins with their crossing of the Dardanelles in the middle of the fourteenth century.

While still in Asia Minor the Ottomans developed their characteristic military organization. The army was originally an irregular body of cavalry. As new land was acquired in the process of conquest it was granted out with the requirement of military service of a number of men proportioned to the size and value of the grant, a system much like the feudal military service prevalent in Europe. But the grants were usually not large and they were not hereditary, ultimate ownership remaining with the government. With the increase of territory royal domains were established for the sultan, and lands were set aside for the support of the mosques.

The need was soon felt for an infantry force and this was provided by the well known Janissaries, or "new troops." This was a chosen body, selected at first probably from favored prisoners. Later it was made up of a levy made every five years from the boys of conquered districts. They were converted to Islam, carefully trained and given many privileges until they were twenty-five years of age, when they became full members of this favored body. It was a famous fighting force, the main reliance of the sultan in battle, and seldom failing to attain victory.[12] As these levies were from conquered countries and since all countries conquered by the Ottomans, in Europe at least, were Christian, it was possible for men born Christian, to govern the Ottoman state sub ject only to the sultan's absolute power.[13]

[11] See the article by W. L. Langer and R. P. Blake, "The Rise of the Ottoman Turks and its Historical Background," *American Historical Review,* XXXVII (1932), 468-505. This article gives a bibliography of all recent study of the subject with comments and criticisms.

[12] Some members of the body were trained to civil duties and from their ranks were chosen the personal attendants of the sultan and government officials, even of the highest rank.

[13] See Hans Heinrich Schräder, "Der Osmanische Staat von seiner Entstehung bis zum Ausgang des siebzehnten Jahrhunderts," *Propyläen Weltgeschichte,* (volume V, Berlin, 1930), 513-29; there is a considerable literature on the Janissaries; see Langer and Blake, *loc. cit.,* 503-5.

There were in the Ottoman army, in addition to the regular cavalry and the Janissaries, irregular troops, both mounted and foot, which increased its numbers and sometimes its strength. Much use was made also of artillery, and there was an organized system of equipment, support and transportation. The Ottomans were, during the first two centuries of their career, primarily a military organization. The interest of the troops was preserved by permitting the seizure and sale into slavery of prisoners captured in battle, and there was of course the usual pillage of cities captured after sieges. Yet coins minted by the second ruler of the line of Othman still exist to prove how early those rulers acted as an independent and on the whole an enlightened dynasty. Their usual practice of permitting the peaceful inhabitants of conquered regions the practice of their own religion on condition of payment of a tax tended to a ready acceptance of their rule by the mass of the population, who must often have found little difference between their new masters and the old.

The Osmanlis entered Europe in the first place not as conquerors or as settlers but as mercenaries. From the beginning of the fourteenth century Turks from the emirates further south in Asia Minor—Aidin, Tavos, Karasin and Sarukhan—had become well known in the Aegean as merchants, as pirates, as invaders and as mercenaries, entering into paid alliance with contending cities or princes, or themselves making conquests. But these, although Turks, were not Osmanlis. It was not until 1345 that the nation that was to play so great a part became participants in this scene of struggle. John Cantacuzenos, who had been chancellor and principal adviser of the Byzantine Emperor Andronicus III, had on that monarch's death established himself in Thrace and usurped the crown. He was planning to seize Constantinople, then held by the widow of the late emperor and her young son.[14] He offered to Orkhan, chief of the Osmanlis, the hand of his daughter Theodora in return for the services of 6000 soldiers. The offer was accepted, the Ottoman troops crossed the Hellespont and took part in a cam-

[14] For internal events in the last years of the Empire see chap. ix in the second volume of the scholarly work by Vasiliev referred to above. The early conquests of the Turks are well treated in Nicolas Iorga, *Geschichte des Osmanischen Reiches* (Gotha, 1908-1913), I; and by Herbert A. Gibbons, *The Foundation of the Ottoman Empire, 1300-1403* (Oxford, 1916).

paign that carried them to Adrianople, to the Black Sea and, as allies of the usurper, into Constantinople itself. There Cantacuzenos and his wife were crowned joint rulers with the old empress and her son; a daughter of the usurper was married to the young emperor and the agreement with Orkhan was reluctantly carried out.

Thus the ruler of the Osmanlis became allied by marriage to both the usurping and the legitimate imperial houses. This alliance soon involved new demands. Twenty thousand Ottoman troops were asked for and sent into Macedonia to help in dislodging from the coast cities the Serbians who were for the time a more serious threat to the western possessions of the empire than the Ottomans to the eastern. Still a third time Cantacuzenos, now engaged in civil war with the young emperor, sought the help of the Ottomans, robbing the churches of Constantinople of their plate in order to obtain the money Orkhan demanded. As mercenaries also in the war between Genoa and Venice that broke out in 1351 Orkhan's troops sold their help to the Genoese colonies at Pera and on the Sea of Marmora.

Having thus been taught the way into Europe, its wealth and attractions and at the same time its disunion and weakness, the Osmanlis soon made the most natural use of their knowledge and military power. In the year 1354 Soleiman, son of Orkhan, under his father's orders took a body of troops across the Hellespont not as mercenaries but as invaders. He occupied the fortress of Tzympe, near the Aegean end of the straits, and the next year seized the city of Gallipoli. Turkish settlers from Asia Minor followed the soldiers, colonizing the European coast of the Sea of Marmora, pushing on eastward almost to within sight of Constantinople.

The next few years brought the inevitable break between the Ottoman sultan and the Greek emperor. A campaign followed in which the invaders took by assault Demotika and Rodosto, thus cutting off Constantinople from the western possessions of the empire. They then captured Adrianople, which was always afterward, and still is their military headquarters. This rapid progress of the Osmanlis in Thrace and Macedonia and the helplessness of the Greeks of Constantinople brought about in 1363 the recognition of Murad I, the second successor of Othman, by the emperor as his suzerain, the acknowledgment of the Turkish conquests made up to that time and a promise to perform military service in the Ottoman army against the Asiatic enemies of the sultan. Ten years later the emperor was forced to agree to pay an annual tribute and to put his son in the hands of the sultan as a hostage. This unnatural and troubled relationship was alternately held to, broken and renewed for almost a century.

VII. THE CONQUEST OF SERBIA, BULGARIA AND GREECE

In the meantime the wave of Ottoman conquest spread westward, northward and southward. The lands beyond Thrace and Macedonia—that is to say, Serbia, Bosnia, Bulgaria, Wallachia and Moldavia—the vast Balkan peninsula, stretching away to the north and west to Hungary and the borders of Poland and the Holy Roman Empire, with their fertile stretches of country and large populations, as well as Dalmatia and Greece with their rich and populous cities and outlets upon the sea, offered an irresistible attraction to the invader. The Ottoman leaders had already, in the days when they were mercenaries in the service of the emperor and of the Republic of Genoa, come into contact with the Serbians, and had defeated them in a battle on the Maritza River in 1352. Now they were brought into a more independent but no less hostile relationship with them.

Three princes from among the descendants of Stephen Dushan, one of whom retained the title of "kral," or king, gathered the fragments of the race together and, in the hope of warding off invasion, themselves entered the territory of which the Turks were already masters. They were met and overwhelmingly defeated in 1371 in a second battle on the Maritza River. Two of the three princes were killed on the field of battle and the Ottomans followed up their victory by a conquering expedition through Macedonia and southern Serbia. The strategic valley of the Vardar, the route to the north, became Turkish territory; the land was as usual either parcelled out to Osmanli soldiers or set apart for the use of the sultan and the support of religion.

The towns Drama and Seres were filled with a Turkish population and Christian churches were replaced by Mohammedan mosques. Turkish troops pushed from here far to the west, indeed to within sight of the Adriatic, but these were as yet raids, not conquests. The capture of Sofia and Nish, far up in ancient Serbia, of Monastir on the border of Albania and, after a long siege, of the old city of Salonika were more permanent. The principal ruler left in Serbia, Lazar, became, like the emperor, a vassal of the sultan, bound to pay him tribute and to furnish him with military assistance. Such dependence was in no way meaningless; over and over again in the conflicts by which southeastern Europe came under Turkish control some of the hardest fighting was done by European and nominally Christian troops fighting under the Moslem banner.

This was true of the great battle which in 1389 destroyed the remains of Serbian independence. It was preceded by a momentary victory. Murad had been called to Anatolia by disorders in his Asian dominions; the Ottomans had so often pushed their expeditions up into the heart of Serbia and western Bulgaria that it was realized that if they were to be resisted at all it must be soon. Leadership was found in an ambitious Bosnian prince, Turtko, who had extended his control along the shores of the Adriatic and obtained momentary recognition from Venice of his title of "King of Serbia, Bosnia and the whole seacoast." His ambitious title did not prevent him from joining forces with Lazar, who claimed to be the head of all Serbian chieftains, but only used the title of prince, and in 1388 the two leaders defeated the Osmanli in three successive battles.

These unexpected victories drew together an alliance of Bosnians, Serbians, Bulgarians, Wallachians and Albanians, but it was only to enter into a fatal struggle the next year. The Sultan Murad pacified Asia Minor, brought together all his forces, summoned to their duties as dependent allies the south Serbian and Albanian princes, and on June 11, 1389, fought a great battle on the plain of Kossovo. It was the culminating conflict and an irretrievable disaster for the Serbians and their allies. It is the subject of legend and folk-song in the Balkans still and was accompanied by enough tragedy to justify its long remembrance.[15] The Sultan Murad was assassinated during or after the battle by a faithless ally, a deserter or a wounded soldier. When the Ottoman soldiers heard of it they killed all the common prisoners as they captured them; Lazar and all other noble prisoners were executed after the battle by order of Bayezid, successor to Murad. The new sultan at the same time ordered his brother, who had led a body of the victorious troops, to be brought to his tent and strangled in his presence. There was to be no question of the succession. The custom in the family of Othman of which this was the initiation, that the oldest of a family of brothers should put to death on his accession all brothers and half brothers who might dispute his inheritance survived until 1603 when, on the death of Mohammed III, Achmet I allowed his brother Mustapha to live.

During the period when the Eastern Empire was being restricted and humiliated and Serbia was being conquered, the Osmanlis were pressing into Bulgaria. When in 1365 the Bulgarian Tsar Alexander died, conflicts immediately broke out among his sons. Aid given to one of them by the Hungarians precipitated a struggle between adherents of the Greek and the Catholic churches. The seizure and holding for ransom of the Byzantine ruler by a Bulgarian chieftain gave additional opportunity for invaders to fish in troubled waters. On the appeal of one of the contestants the Ottoman army advanced as allies into the fertile regions that lay just to the south of the Balkan range; in another campaign it passed beyond the mountains and for the first time saw the Danube, so long to be the river of their conflicts and their pride.

As in their first entrance into Europe they learned as allies what they soon utilized as invaders. In 1369 the most powerful of the Bulgarian princes was forced to make a treaty in which he acknowledged Murad as his suzerain and gave him his sister Mara as a wife. Only two years later one of the other Bulgarian princes took the same oath of dependence; the sultan gave him back his principal city, but he held it only as a vassal and all Bulgaria became an Ottoman dependency. Local legend still makes

[15] The best account of the battle is in Jireček, *Geschichte der Serben,* Book V, chap. i; see also Harold Temperley, *A History of Serbia* (London, 1917).

the last of the independent tsars, a ghostly inhabitant of the Rhodope mountains, ride as a headless horseman from time to time down into the plain.[16]

In 1389 the Bulgarians shared in the rising and the disaster of Kossovo. In 1393 an Ottoman army after successes in Serbia marched into Bulgaria, besieged, captured and sacked its old capital and carried much of its population into captivity; seized and garrisoned the line of fortresses along the Danube, drove the last of its princes into exile and forced his son to become a Moslem and a soldier in the Turkish army. Moslem immigrants from the south entered the country, many of the inhabitants accepted Mohammedanism and Bulgaria became for the next four and a half centuries merely an outlying province of the Ottoman empire.[17]

There was evidently no local resistance adequate to the task of blocking the Ottoman advance; there was, however, always the possibility of reinforcements from the west. The Crusades had been wars of united Christian Europe against the Moslems of Asia. Now that Asiatic Mohammedanism was represented by a new and vigorous race which was carrying its religion in turn into Europe, the spirit of the Crusades might fairly enough be invoked to resume its early work. Over and over again the eastern emperors in the fourteenth and fifteenth centuries appealed for such help and in a few cases it was sent, but always to end only in catastrophe.

The emperor had always one offer to make that was of great attraction to the pope and to the western church generally, avid as it was of extension and determined to attain the unity of all Christendom. This was the union of the two church organizations, the Holy Roman Catholic and the Holy Orthodox Catholic. Such union was offered repeatedly by the emperors of the east as an inducement for obtaining help from the west. Influenced by this hope the pope as regularly urged upon the rulers of western states the rescue of their fellow Christians from the infidel. The usurping emperor John Cantacuzenos appealed to the pope to launch

[16] The standard treatment of this period is W. N. Slatarski, *Geschichte der Bulgaren* (Leipzig, 1918), which reaches to 1396.

[17] Cf. Alois Hajek, *Bulgarien unter der Türkenherrschaft,* (Stuttgart, 1925), one of the few dispassionate, scholarly studies of Turkish rule over Christian lands.

a crusade in his defense against the Turks. On Good Friday of 1363, the pope at Avignon gave the cross to several princes who volunteered for a new crusade. In 1369 the Emperor John V went on his knees before the pope and formally abjured all the errors of the Greek church. In the next three years the administration of two popes, Urban V and Gregory XI, saw a series of negotiations for union in return for help.[18]

From 1399 to 1402 the Emperor Manuel II made a number of visits to the west, which took him to Venice, to Paris, to London and elsewhere. He was treated with great distinction and his visits to Paris, where he was lodged in the Louvre, have left many intimate memorials.[19] But he was given little support. The long negotiations at the Council of Basel in 1435 and at Ferrara and Florence in 1438 and 1439, the gorgeous ceremonial, the endless discussions, the formal union and its rejection by the Greeks at home have been touched on in the chapter on the church councils. All these efforts were hollow and futile. The need of the Greeks was doubtless desperate, but there was no real willingness on their part to make the concessions the pope demanded. Petrarch in a letter to the pope contrasting the Turks with the Greeks says, with Latin pride, "The former, it is true, are our enemies, but the schismatics are worse than enemies. The former fear us more than they hate us, but the latter both fear and hate us with their whole soul."

On the other hand, papal appeals to European sovereigns came to nothing. Quite other problems were interesting the kings of France and England, the German emperor and the popes themselves in these years of the Black Death, of the bitter campaigns of the Hundred Years war, of the wars between Venice and Genoa and of the Great Schism and the church councils. The only direct responses to Greek appeals were the half buccaneering journey, in 1366, of the Count of Savoy who, with a fleet of galleys and

[18] This whole problem is well handled by W. Norden, *Das Papsttum und Byzanz, die Trennung der beiden Mächte und das Problem ihrer Wiedervereinigung bis 1453* (Berlin, 1903); see also N. Iorga, *Philippe de Mézières et la Croisade au XIVe Siècle* (Paris, 1896).

[19] G. Schlumberger, "Un empereur de Byzance à Paris et à Londres" *Revue des Deux Mondes,* (Dec. 15, 1915); A. N. Vasiliev, *History of the Byzantine Empire,* II, 330-3.

1500 soldiers, sailed through the Dardanelles and the Hellespont and into the Black Sea, ravaged the Bulgarian coast, intervened in a dispute in the family of the emperor and obtained from him a reluctant consent to favor the union of the churches; the chivalrous expedition to Constantinople of Marshal Boucicault thirty years later with his little body of French troops and a few galleys sent by the pope himself.[20]

But there were other incentives to resistance to the Turks. The progress of the Ottomans raised serious apprehension in the minds of the Venetians and Genoese for their commercial interests in the region of their Aegean and Euxine possessions. The grain supply from Russia and Anatolia, on which the cities of Italy so largely depended, was also endangered. For a while it seemed that their naval powers might be used jointly to cut off the advance of the Turks across the waters which these commercial powers could so easily control. But they fell back on a policy first of inaction then of commercial alliance with the conquerors of the eastern Mediterranean. In 1365 Ragusa, in 1387 Genoa and in 1388 Venice made treaties with the Ottoman government, paying a subsidy that became practically tribute. It is true, the Italian cities broke these treaties repeatedly; on the other hand the help they gave in resistance to the Ottomans, even though these bade fair to control their field of trade, was always half-hearted.[21]

It was rather from those northeastern states of Europe whose boundaries the Ottomans were now approaching—Hungary, Poland, Bohemia and even the German empire—that action might be expected. It was scarcely more than a century since the Tartars had swept through eastern Europe, ravaged much of Hungary and Poland, and made their way into the heart of Silesia. And now the lands to the south of them were being overrun with a new body of Asiatic conquerors. When the news of the Turkish seizure of the northern strip of the possessions of the Eastern Empire spread abroad, Casimir the Great of Poland invited to

[20] J. Delaville le Roulx, *La France en Orient au XIVe Siècle. Expéditions du Maréchal Boucicaut* (Paris, 1886).

[21] M. Silberschmidt, *Das orientalische Problem zur Zeit der Entstehung des Türkischen Reiches* (Leipzig, 1923), deals with these relationships in great detail for the period 1381-1400, making extensive use of Venetian sources.

his capital at Cracow with the object of arranging joint resistance a number of European sovereigns and princes. The German Emperor Charles IV, the kings of Hungary, Denmark and Cyprus were there. An army of Hungarians, Serbs, Bosnians and Wallachians, said to have numbered 20,000, was formed and in 1364 started out with the object of recapturing Adrianople and restoring it to the Eastern Empire. But they were surprised on their way by the Turks and cut to pieces.

The Danube, after the crushing of Bulgaria and Serbia, was as much a Turkish as a Hungarian or Slavic boundary, and it was along its line that the greatest attempt of the west to succor the east was made. In 1394 Sigismund, King of Hungary, sent letters to Venice and in 1395 to the kings of France and England, the emperor and other reigning princes, asking for volunteers in a great campaign against the Ottomans. The response to this invitation reflects the temporary cessation of the Hundred Years war and the restlessness of the unoccupied and undisciplined chivalry of Europe, as well as the rising dread of the Turks. In the spring of 1396 there gathered at Buda nobles and their attendants from all parts of Germany, France, England and The Netherlands, making up in all perhaps 100,000 men. From France alone came about a thousand knights and nobles of the highest rank, accompanied by several thousand attendants, mercenaries and women. They were under the command of John of Nevers, son of the Duke of Burgundy and grandson of King John of France.

The story of the assemblage of the host loses nothing in the telling by Froissart and other chroniclers who have described this, perhaps the last of the tournaments on a grand scale which took the place of scientifically waged warfare in this age. The French marched across Transylvania and Wallachia and so into northern Bulgaria; the Hungarians and others made their way down the Danube and through Serbia, the crusaders pillaging the countries through which they passed quite as ruthlessly as ever did the Ottoman overlords of those countries. Gathering under the walls of Nicopolis on the right bank of the Danube, the most recent conquest of the Ottomans, they besieged it for two weeks but did not assault the city, uncertain whether they should go further to seek the Turkish sultan and his army or await his coming.[22]

Bayezid did not leave them long in uncertainty. Abandoning the siege of Constantinople in which he was engaged, he summoned his Christian allies to send their quotas and after two weeks moved over roads familiar to him from earlier campaigns to face the crusaders in the plain before Nicopolis. The French repeated the worst tactics of Crécy and Poitiers. Refusing to submit to any formulated plan of attack or defense, the French knights with many of those of England and Germany and their followers, recklessly keen for glory, galloped against the Turks and to their own destruction. They broke, it is true, the first line of the enemy, made up of irregular troops, and massacred their opponents and prisoners indiscriminately, on the ground that they were unbelievers. But they were after this first onslaught now for the first time facing the veteran and disciplined army of the Turkish sultan. There could be only one result; numbers of the proudest nobles of France were killed, the rest were forced to surrender to the overwhelming numbers of fresh and well-handled troops of Bayezid, or take flight as best they could. Sigismund himself, with the Grand Master of the Knights of St. John and a few others, deserted his army and succeeded in getting aboard one of the galleys which had come up the Danube as allies of the crusaders. He went with them down the river, through the Black Sea, the Bosporus and the Dardanelles and so through the Mediterranean and back home where we have already had occasion in this work to observe his somewhat dubious career as King of Hungary and later of Bohemia, as emperor, as opponent of the Hussites, and as convener of the Council of Constance.

The Serbians, loyal to their Moslem overlord, fought victoriously with him against their own coreligionists. The main body of the western army fled in utter confusion; many were killed in flight; many were drowned in the river; they suffered intensely from

[22] The story of this crusade has recently been retold, most admirably and with the use of much Oriental source material, by Aziz Suryal Atiya, *The Crusade of Nicopolis* (London, 1934); see also Silberschmidt, op. cit., whose detailed treatment does not appear to have been used by Atiya. G. Beckmann, *Der Kampf Kaiser Sigmunds gegen die Werdende Weltmacht der Osmanen, 1392-1437* (Gotha, 1902), and E. Kling, *Die Schlacht bei Nicopolis* (Berlin, 1906) are still of interest.

the elements and were slaughtered by the outraged peasantry as they crossed the Carpathian mountains to the relative safety of Hungary. In anger and retaliation for the massacre of prisoners by the French knights, the sultan ordered a general execution of all prisoners taken in the battle. By the interposition of a French knight who could speak Turkish, and in the expectation of a rich ransom, Bayezid was induced to spare the Count of Nevers, Marshal Boucicault and some twenty others. But they were all forced to stand beside the sultan and watch the execution of their friends and companions. The massacre went on through a whole day. When the sun set those who had not yet been put to death were turned over to the soldiers to be sold as slaves. Johannes Schiltberger, a German captive, who was in the battle and was spared because of his youth, and whose later travels have given us light on European geographical knowledge of the time, estimated the number put to death that day as 10,000.

The few nobles reserved for ransom were taken to Brusa. They stopped at Gallipoli and watched from the shore the Venetian galley with Sigismund aboard pass amidst the jeers of the Turks. They were allowed a certain amount of liberty while the ransom of 20,000 pieces of gold which Bayezid required was being obtained by two of their number who were sent to seek it in Paris and Constantinople. Eventually, within a year, through the mediation of certain Genoese and Venetian bankers who negotiated with the Ottomans, the ransom was paid and those of the prisoners who were still living returned to their homes. The Count of Nevers, John, surnamed the Fearless because of his recklessness at Nicopolis, later the Duke of Burgundy, lived to lead one of the parties in the fatal civil wars of France, to instigate the murder of his royal cousin, and himself to be assassinated on the bridge at Montereaux.

The great Ottoman victory at Nicopolis in 1396 was followed by frontier raids far into Hungary and Wallachia, the ravaging of fields, burning of towns and carrying off of thousands of the population to be sold as slaves in the older parts of the now well established Ottoman lands. But these like the former campaigns in Greece were rather raids than actual acquisitions of new territory. On the other hand, the conquest of Greece was now completed. Under the sultan himself and the generals he left behind after his withdrawal, the peninsula was conquered and pillaged and somewhat later made into a Turkish province.

After Nicopolis and the punitive expeditions that had succeeded it the sultan resumed the siege of Constantinople which had been intermittently in progress for some years. In 1402 he summoned it to surrender on pain of massacre of the entire population if they continued their resistance. He was apparently planning a final assault when he was forced, strong as he was, to change all his plans and to gather all his forces to oppose a great danger from the east.

The conquests of Timur the Lame, the "Tamerlane" of tradition and literature, belong to the history of Asia rather than of Europe, but here and for a moment they touch. This petty chieftain, sprung from old Turkish stock but claiming to be a descendant of the Mongol conquerors, during the last half of the fourteenth century, in a succession of campaigns of unbroken success accompanied by incredible cruelties, had passed through and conquered much of Central Asia, India, Persia, Mesopotamia, Syria and Georgia, and by the end of the century had reached the eastern borderland of recent Ottoman conquest.[23] The cities and principalities of northern Anatolia were conquered and reconquered alternately by the two powers. Bayezid in the extension of his dominions eastward seized and put to death certain local rulers who had already acknowledged Timur; the latter returned and recaptured these districts, burying alive, it was said, 4000 Christian soldiers, subjects of Bayezid, and committing other indescribable atrocities. Threatening messages were exchanged; the two rulers collected their forces; Bayezid abandoned the siege of Constantinople in which he was engaged, marched eastward, and July 20, 1402, a decisive battle was fought near Angora in Asia Minor. There was great slaughter, the Ottomans were defeated and the sultan captured and held in confinement by Timur until he died, still a prisoner, a year later. Timur carried his con-

[23] See *Encyclopedia of Islam*, edited by M. T. Houtsma and others, (Leyden and London, 1930) "Timur"; Harold Lamb, *Tamerlane* (New York, 1930) is better than most popular biographies.

quests to the very boundaries of Europe but then turned back. He was preparing for an invasion of China when he died suddenly in 1405. His empire like so many others in the east soon broke up into fragments.

Constantinople was saved for the time. Wars of succession broke out among the descendants of Bayezid and for a quarter of a century and more the Ottoman boundaries drew back rather than advanced. Then a conquering sultan, Murad II, again took the offensive, won back most of what had been lost and laid siege to Belgrade, the farthest advanced post of the Hungarians on the Danube.

This renewal of warfare saw the rise of two leaders who, appealing for popular support, won victories that suggest both by their contemporaneous date and their similar circumstances the efforts of the national party to drive the English invaders from France. An Albanian soldier, George Castriota, reared at Constantinople, forced by the conquest of his country to serve in the Ottoman army, and there by his bravery winning the cognomen of Skander-beg, that is "Alexander the Great," when opportunity offered returned to his natural allegiance, spurred his countrymen to rebellion and drove the invaders repeatedly out of Albania. Similarly John Hunyadi, a knight of Transylvania who had risen by his abilities to be governor of that province, so roused the people and organized their defense that they defeated the Ottoman invaders in two successive battles and drove them across the Danube. When the new king of Hungary and Poland, Ladislas III, encouraged by a Turkish discomfiture in 1443, formed an army for an advance southward, Hunyadi and his troops were its main support and aid in a successful battle at Nish and in the recapture of Sofia. These Christian successes drove the Ottoman sultan to sign a ten years' truce, to abandon many of his recent conquests and to withdraw for the time to his Asiatic dominions.

Faithlessly and unwisely the Hungarian king and Hunyadi, under the urgency of Cardinal Cesarini, who had come from the pope to give to the expedition the dignity of a crusade, broke the truce and pushed on through Bulgaria to the Black Sea at Varna. The sultan returned and November 10, 1444, overwhelmed the Christian forces in a battle in which King Ladislas was killed. He is known in Hungarian history as Ladislas Varnenczyk, "the martyr of Varna."[24]

The tide was already turning in favor of the Ottomans. The sultan followed up his advantage; even Hunyadi, who, after the death of the king was made regent of Hungary, was defeated in a second battle of Kossovo, October 1448. Only Skander-beg gained some success in Albania. The northern and western boundaries of Ottoman conquest were to remain uncertain, advancing and retreating, for a century. But the definite inclusion of the Turks as a European power was now to be consummated by the capture of Constantinople.

VIII. THE FALL OF CONSTANTINOPLE

Constantinople had long stood as an outlying bastion of Christendom, separated from it by settled Ottoman provinces. Its dependent possessions had been gnawed away until it stood isolated, back of its walls, looking out on the Bosporus and the Golden Horn, awaiting the end. Three times the Turks had beleaguered the great walled city. In 1396 it was saved by the diversion of Nicopolis, and scarcely had the siege been resumed when the sultan was summoned away to Angora and to his death; again in 1422 it had been brought apparently to the verge of surrender when a formidable insurrection in Asia Minor caused Sultan Murad II to raise the siege.

Now, however, the young Sultan Mohammed II, son of Murad, girt with the sword of Othman at Adrianople in 1451, his dominions relatively secure, his forces overwhelming in numbers and his income adequate, determined to carry out the plans he had made since he was a boy for the siege and capture of Constantinople. His preparations were deliberate and extensive. He reduced to submission or entered into truces with all his enemies, built a castle to dominate the Bosporus above the city, cast cannon more numerous and larger than had ever been used before, amassed an infinite store of powder, balls, bows, arrows and all kinds of

[24] See the excellent monograph of L. Kupelweiser, *Die Kämpfe Ungarns mit den Osmanen bis zur Schlacht bei Mohacs* (Vienna, 1899).

siege material, destroyed all the villages in the vicinity of the city to cut off its food supply, gathered an army of 15,000 men under the walls of the city, and early in April, 1453, formally demanded its surrender.[25]

The emperor who, like the founder of the city 1100 years before, was a Constantine (the Eleventh), rejected the terms and entered upon the defense of the city with a courage, judgment and devotion that have given an interest and dignity to the last struggle of the empire that had often been sadly lacking to it in intervening centuries.[26] His forces for defense were quite inadequate. Some 5000 native troops were strengthened by the presence of 3000 foreigners, mostly Venetians and Genoese from the galleys in the harbor and recent additions of mercenaries. A well-trained soldier, the Genoese Giustiniani, was second in command under the emperor. The harbor, the Golden Horn, was defended by a chain stretched across its mouth, which held against all attacks from Turkish vessels. But in the midst of the siege the sultan's engineers were successful in building a wooden track across a mile of land from the straits to the upper end of the Horn, and dragged a fleet of sixty or eighty boats across so as to take the Greeks in the rear. Week after week of attack and defense of the walls and of the ships in the harbor went by. Some reinforcements were brought in and at one time the Turks seem to have considered abandoning the siege.

The ancient walls encircling the city, thirteen miles in length and in the more exposed portions forty feet high, built on the land-ward side in a triple series with a wide moat, were still, as they had always been, the principal and usually an adequate protection of the city. But now they had to endure battering by cannon of unprecedented power and persistency, and they gradually crumbled. Assaults were made on the 18th of April, on the 7th and 12th and 21st of May, but they were successfully driven

[25] The standard accounts of this famous siege are those of Edwin Pears, *The Destruction of the Greek Empire and the Story of the Capture of Constantinople by the Turks* (New York, 1903), and of Gustave Schlumberger, *Le Siège, la Prise et le Sac de Constantinople par les Turcs* (sixth edition, Paris, 1922); the famous chapter lxviii of Gibbons' *Decline and Fall of the Roman Empire* should be read, if only for its literary charm and its long repute.

[26] See Chedomil Mijatovich, *Constantine, the Last Emperor of the Greeks* (London, 1892), a very competent biography.

back with much loss to the besiegers, and the breaches in the walls were partially repaired. A vigor and a unity were exhibited in defense of the city which had never existed in the days of its prosperity.

Greeks and Romans even worshipped together on May 28, in St. Sophia, on the eve of what it was understood would be the sultan's greatest assault. It came the next day and was the final catastrophe for the city, the emperor and the empire. At midnight the main Turkish army broke through the outer walls at several points, but was driven back; at dawn 12,000 Janissaries and choice detachments of archers and other infantry, under the protection of the cannon and with the personal encouragement of the sultan, rushed forward and with wild cries of *Allah! Allah!* finally surmounted the walls and temporary stockades, cut down their opponents and made their way into the city. The emperor died fighting. Somewhere under the piles of dead his body lay, but it was never recognized. At ten o'clock the next morning, or possibly the day after, the sultan entered in triumph and the city was handed over to the soldiers for a three days' sack. The Empire of the East had fallen. Constantinople, the city of the Caesars, now became the capital of the sultans, who fixed there their dwelling-place. From Istambul, as it came now to be called, the Ottomans ruled over the whole of southeastern Europe.

Chapter Eleven

RECAPITULATION

1. THE UNITY OF HISTORY

THE most marked characteristic of the history of Europe, considered as a whole, during the period whose events have now been sketched was its uniformity. Notwithstanding a multiplicity of detail, the main movements in this history appear as a single story. What happened in one country happened, in a somewhat different form, in others. Evidences are numberless. Medieval feudalism was dying out alike in all countries of Europe. Town life was encroaching on rural life from Castile to Poland, from Italy to Sweden. Capitalism was at work in all countries. Centralization within larger or smaller boundaries was everywhere in progress. A common language, spoken and written, was coming into use in every considerable stretch of territory. These and a score of other instances of parallel development indicate that the history of Europe was a single current, not a series of separate national, racial, or regional streams. The division of history, during this period at least, into a number of parallel histories of separate countries has convenience but no great degree of actuality to justify it.

The reasons for this uniformity are sometimes obvious. In the year 1351, for instance, the English parliament and the cortes of Castile, as has been stated, both passed statutes requiring workmen to accept labor when it was offered to them, and established obligatory rates of wages. In the same year the French government issued a detailed *ordonnance* for the same purpose, and various other governments within that year or shortly before or afterward adopted similar statutes concerning laborers. This was an evident reaction to the "Black Death" which during the years from 1348 to 1352 swept in turn through almost every town and rural district in Europe. Its germs carried, as we now know, by the vermin of rats, the disease appeared in port after port and rapidly spread inland. It made its way westward and northward from the Near East to the utmost limits of European commerce. The great mortality—the bubonic plague has still the highest death rate of all diseases—caused a shortage of labor and this led to almost universal demands by the workmen for higher wages. This demand was met by the government and by the employing classes in their representative assemblies by laws making labor compulsory and restricting wages to their former rate. The cause was, in this case, common to all Europe; it was natural that the effect should be the same everywhere.

The curious simultaneity with which representative assemblies came into existence is not so easily explained. The beginning of regular participation of representatives of the cities in the cortes of Castile and Leon in 1250, in Catalonia in 1285, and in Aragon at practically the same time, the summons of the Rhenish towns to the German diet in 1255, the entrance of the classes which were to become the commons into the parliament of England in 1265, and the first appearance of the Third Estate in France in 1302 all occurred, it will be observed, in the same half-century. The correspondence of dates is the more striking from the fact that a similar development took place in several other countries at about the same time and that local bodies of estates also were making their appearance. This is a parallelism the reason for which is not obvious, but is perhaps discoverable.

Copying by one country from another is not a satisfactory explanation, since in each country there was a preceding period of embryonic growth which cannot have been imitated. Nor does any testimony to such imitation exist. That Henry III and Edward I of England, William of Holland, Philip IV of France, and the Ferdinands and Pedros of Spain or their advisers, intentionally adopted the same measures is highly improbable. The new practice was apparently connected with the growth of a well-to-do middle class of which the governments had good reason to take cognizance. This in turn was closely connected with the growth of towns, and this again with the extension of trade. Political institutions have a development that is closely analogous to organic evolution. The typical medieval monarchy may have gone through a normal series of changes in which the summons of a third estate to its counsels was a natural stage.

Coincidences extended far beyond the common dates of origin, to the forms of summons, to organization, to experiments in taxation, to the development of powers and to the subjects of legislation. The wording is almost identical in the royal writs convoking the nobles and prelates to the English parliament, in the analogous summons of the French estates general and in the orders convoking the cortes of Castile or the German imperial diet. In all these the king sends greetings to his "beloved and faithful," declares his intention of holding a "deliberation," "convocation," "colloquy," "discussion," "council," or "parliament" at a certain place and time, explains the reasons for the summons and orders the recipient to lay aside all other matters and attend the meeting. In the summons to the third estate, the writ was sent in England to the sheriff of each county, in France to the corresponding official, the *seneschal*, or *bailli* of each administrative division of the country.

There was an evident tendency in all countries of central and northern Europe for the assemblies to divide into four estates rather than the usual three. The petty noblesse of France, the knights and gentry of England, the lesser counts, lords, and knights of the Empire, the *hidalgos* or *caballeros* of Spain had interests different from those of the great princes, nobles, and barons, their feudal and social superiors. In some countries, as in Aragon, this was duly recognized and the four *brazos* of the cortes became there a traditional division. In Moravia four estates were recognized, the lesser nobles making, as in Aragon, a class intervening between the great nobles and the cities. In France, the large part played by the king's officials in selecting those who were to come or send representatives to the estates, made it possible to give the lesser nobility the place with the barons to which they socially belonged.

In England, on the other hand, certain unifying influences overcame separatist tendencies and put knights and burgesses together in the house of commons. In Germany the position of the nobility was anomalous; the electoral and other great princes were so powerful that all the other nobles great and small, fell into one class below them. In Hungary the lesser nobility formed the third estate, since there were practically no cities to be represented. Other variations occurred or seemed at one time likely to occur, but the grouping of the estates into three remained almost universal. The prestige of the number three probably had much to do with making it the regular number of estates; the doctrine of the Trinity has had some curious reactions in history.

It was claimed in all of these assemblies, and early acknowledged by the king, that he must ask for the money which was to be raised by taxation. This meant all payments beyond the most primitive and long established and customary dues to the crown. This might be a mere form, but in some countries it was early reduced to law, as in the English "Confirmation of the Charters" of 1297. The answer to such a request from the king was usually conditional; at one time on supervision of the collection and expenditure of the fund by the body that gave it, at another on the redress of some pressing grievance, at still another on a favorable reply to the proposal of some piece of legislation. Laws were always enacted by the monarch, but they were very generally initiated by the aggressive third estate in the form of such a proposal. The whole system of estates,—parliament, cortes,—whatever its denomination, was in its origin a monarchical device to attain ends of interest primarily to the ruler; but after the institution had taken shape, after use had given it security of position, and after the power of numbers, organization, and money had disclosed itself, these assemblages regularly used their powers to serve their own ends and in some countries to become rivals of the king in the government of the state.

In all countries alike, parliaments exerted some control over the passage of laws. The uniformity of legislation which so often placed upon the statute books of different countries laws so nearly identical in their provisions and even in their wording was quite natural. The nations had the same problems and naturally met them in the same way. The church, for instance, was an institution common to all western Europe, and the encroachments of the papacy upon local ecclesiastical communities in its efforts to increase its income and its power were equally universal. It is not a matter of surprise, therefore, to find the cortes of Castile and the parliament of England passing in the same year, without any evidence of communication, statutes against provisors and against intrusive local ecclesiastical jurisdiction; nor to find similar legislation in other countries at practically the same time.

The adoption of the same devices by the crown in different countries to obtain grants from the assemblies was equally natural, since needs were similar and ingenuity naturally discovered similar methods of meeting them. One finds the English commons and the French third estate making exactly the same provisions, much to the disapproval of the crown, for the appointment under their own control of collectors and auditors to see that their grants were used for the purpose for which they were intended.

The simultaneous decay of parliamentary institutions in practically all the countries of Europe during the fifteenth century has been mentioned before. As they arose, so they declined contemporaneously. As the century progressed it became evident that the powers of kings and their councils were increasing, the activity and authority of parliaments were declining. This was true of France, of England, and of the Spanish monarchies. Kings like Louis XI in France, Edward IV and Henry VII in England, Ferdinand in Aragon, and Isabella in Castile, whose reigns filled so much of the later fifteenth century, carried on stronger royal governments than their predecessors and brooked little interference from their estates. But this was later than our period. Autocratic monarchy is a sixteenth , even a seventeenth-century phenomenon; nevertheless its beginnings were already visible in the fifteenth. It consisted largely in the abolition, suspension, or depression of the systems of estates. Parliaments, cortes, estates-general were the bridge over which the medieval monarchs passed to the control of the centralized, popularly supported, governments of their respective countries. Only here and there, as in England, was the bridge left standing. The decline of parliamentary powers was so universal that it must have had a common cause, though the search for that cause does not belong here.

The settlement, enfranchisement, and growth of cities has already been spoken of as a general European movement. Their origin, due to somewhat different causes in different regions, was followed, nevertheless, by a very similar development in their form of government and degree of independence. This similarity, so noticeable in the charters of cities in all countries—in the *fueros* of Spanish cities, in the statements of immunities of French communes, in the charters of the cities of England, Flanders, Germany, and even of those of Scandinavia and eastern Europe, is no doubt partly attributable to copying, partly to the background of Roman law and municipal institutions common to so much of Europe, but for the most part it was a response to the needs of the situation. Cities were founded or grew up earlier in the center, south, and west of Europe than in the north and east. The extension of German population and influence northward and eastward by the foundation of cities beyond the old Roman province and through the Slavic regions is one of the great constructive processes of medieval history. After 1250 cities were numerous, were possessed of many civic rights and, despite difference of origin and history, of remarkable uniformity in their institutions. The same statements hold true of organizations within the cities. The regulations of the gilds of Venice, Florence, Paris, Cologne, Vienna, York, and many other cities read much alike. There was a general type of city and gild life.

The city leagues are an instance of similar usages that arose, doubtless, from similar needs. The *hermandades* of Spain, the Rhenish and Swabian leagues of Germany, and the less long-lived unions of towns in Italy, France and other countries were presumably all intended to gain strength by combination, to resist injuries and to attain advantages not secured to them by the existing governments of their countries. If sometimes these leagues obtained an actually independent existence, as was true of the Swiss cities and their surrounding cantons and of the Hanseatic League, this was simply the logical outcome of the circumstances that led to their combination.

The wide spread of heresy, which was one of the marks of the period, is probably explicable on general grounds. It is well known that religious dissent is contagious, and it may have been carried far and wide at this period by direct contact, without the hypothesis of any recondite means of its propagation. This is demonstrably true of the extension of English Lollardy to Bohemia. Nevertheless, a curious current of independent radical thinking flowed below the surface of these centuries, appearing in a score of forms, from the critical attitude of the University of Paris and of such thinkers as Marsiglio of Padua and Raymond Lull to the communism of John Ball and the criticism of private property of Wyclif. "It will never go well in England till all things be in common and no one have more than another" is no very different doctrine from "dominion is founded in grace."

The general habit of preaching has been frequently observed as a characteristic of this period common to all Europe. Savonarola calling on the people to repent in the market place of Florence, John Ball preaching in the churchyards, a Lollard priest speaking from his pile of millstones by the wayside, Bohemian reformers preaching in the parish churches and the Bethlehem chapel, the Dauphin, Stephen Marcel, and the King of Navarre preaching political sermons to the people of Paris in the midst of the rising of 1356, are only a few of the instances of the voice of the pulpit that was to be heard at every turn. Its influence on the life and literature of early times has just been brought to the attention of the reading world with singular force.[1] Its universality and the obscurity of the reasons for its existence at this particular time belong with those of heresy, radicalism, and revolution.

A few conspicuous instances of popular insurrections in the fourteenth century have already been described. There were many others. The Dutch and Rhenish and Hanse towns had their risings. From Danzig and Venice to Thessalonica (where the "zealots" and the populace rose in 1342 and massacred great numbers of the upper classes), the unstable equilibrium of social classes was from time to time overthrown. The risings of the populace in the Swiss cities, Zurich in 1336, Luzern in 1343, that gave its first accessions to the League of the Forest Cantons were contemporaneous with those of France and Italy. Was this proclivity of the lower classes to violence due to some general cause or were its manifestations in so many different places at the same time merely a matter of coincidence? An answer to such a speculation would lead more deeply into a philosophy of history than can perhaps be justified here.

[1] G. R. Owst, *Preaching in Medieval England* (Cambridge, 1926), and *Literature and Pulpit in Medieval England* (Cambridge, 1935).

II. THE IDEA OF NATIONALITY

Of all the developments common to Europe in this period there was none more striking or more influential than the growth of the sentiment of nationalism. We have met it in so many countries that it can be fairly supposed to have existed in all. Whatever else the expression nationalism includes, it involves a certain degree of unity within the national boundaries and a certain degree of separateness of feeling and interest from all outside them. It was perhaps especially manifest in England. At the very beginning of our period it showed itself in the opposition to the pope of Robert Grosseteste, Bishop of Lincoln, and the national protests which he initiated in 1247 against papal exactions. These were exactly contemporary with the baronial opposition to the Provençals, Savoyards and Poitevins who filled the court of Henry III. If these actions signalized the opposition of Englishmen to foreign influence, the summons of representatives of the shires and the towns into consultation with the nobles and the prelates in 1265 was a step toward the attainment of internal unity. In the summons of Edward I to the parliament of 1295 both ideals were expressed. The king appealed to the national spirit of the people by calling to their attention the French threat to "conquer this kingdom" and to "destroy the English language altogether from the earth"; and at the same time he summoned a specially complete representation of all classes from all parts of the kingdom to take united action to defeat that purpose.

The whole history of the Hundred Years' War is a commentary on this spirit. The long series of English invasions were advocated in successive appeals to English patriotism. National feeling grew with what it fed on until in the fifteenth century Henry V was able to count on a determined and passionate support by England, though his claim to the French throne was of the most tenuous character. On the other hand, hardly perceptible at first in France, it became stronger and stronger with the progress of the war. The English alliances with French nobles and cities in Brittany, Guienne, and Burgundy successively melted away under the solvent action of the growing French sentiment of patriotism. When the Treaty of Brétigny was abrogated in 1360 more than a hundred towns formerly in English occupation opened their gates to the French armies. Even the cynical Duke of Burgundy could not withstand the pressure of patriotism, and at the Treaty of Arras in 1435 withdrew his support from the English. The effective appeal of Joan of Arc to that spirit has already been sufficiently insisted upon. The ordinance of 1438 providing for a standing army in France was not so much a device to increase the power of the king as it was a nationalistic effort to drive out the English.

At almost exactly the same time, at the far end of Europe, the appeals of John Hunyadi and Scanderbeg to the national spirit in Hungary and Albania, respectively, brought about the few victories of the time against the oncoming Turks. The east of Europe was rich in evidences of the growth of nationalism. The Bohemian nobles, as early as 1310, asserted their national rights against the foreign King John of Luxemburg, and forced him to leave the government in the hands of a Bohemian noble during his frequent absences. In the University of Prague, founded in 1348, the native element soon asserted its supremacy by excluding students of other nationalities from participation in its government. The Hussite wars were in the main national wars,—Bohemia for the Bohemians,—Slavic Ziska and Prokop against the German Emperor. Poland in the fourteenth century rebelled against foreign influences, even those most closely connected with its culture. The records of the city of Cracow were ordered to be kept in Polish in place of German. Indeed, the whole growth of national and vernacular literatures was to a certain degree an assertion of nationalism and was, perhaps more than any other influence, conducive to its increasing strength. The Teutonic Knights were doomed to disappear because in a time of nationalism they were an order, not a nation.

Through the whole foregoing narrative has run the thread of increasing national self-consciousness; to quote its many forms would be mere repetition. Those states, like England, France and the Spanish monarchies, which were already largely centralized became more so. One of the leagues of counties and cities of Germany grew in the century between 1291 and 1389 into the new state of Switzerland. Another group of provinces attained a momentary unity as the independent duchy of Burgundy. Denmark, Sweden and Norway in the Union of Kalmar of 1397 obtained what promised but unfortunately failed to be a permanent Scandinavian nationality.

No one characteristic can alone satisfactorily differentiate one period from another. History is complex and a vast number of changes are always concurrently in progress. But if an attempt were made to choose that aspect of thought that most clearly marked the difference between the Europe of 1250 and that of 1450, it would probably be the growth of the national spirit. It was not, of course, that robust, assertive, highly organized, legally supported and sentimentally defended system of national exclusiveness that the world has become accustomed to in later times. On the other hand, a search for the origins of modern nationalism leads back to, but hardly beyond, this period. It was in its soil that the roots of the plant of the national spirit were embedded.

III. THE CONTINUITY OF HISTORY

Some analogies of the time were certainly fortuitous. Why should four unusually long reigns of unusually enlightened kings, James I of Aragon (1213-76), Henry III of England (1216-72), Louis IX of France (1226-70) and Alfonso X of Castile (1252-84) have been so nearly exactly contemporaneous? Why should five native lines of sovereigns, well established in their respective kingdoms for centuries, all run out within the same century, as was true of the descendants of Malcolm Canmore of Scotland in 1286, the Arpadians of Hungary in 1290, the Premyslids of Bohemia in 1306, the Capetians of France in 1329, and the Piasts of Poland in 1370? In all the variety of fifteenth-century literature why should there be two poems, one written in Venice, the other in England, one in 1420 the other in 1438, alike in subject and length, both descriptive of the commerce of their respective lands, both by unknown authors? It is evident that these and many other parallelisms that strike the speculative reader are mere coincidences, though often strange enough to be startling.

A much greater number of contingencies, on the other hand, irresistibly suggest a general development, a more logical and consistent movement of human history than appears on the surface. The stately and continuous march of events that gives its meaning, if meaning it has, to the apparently incoherent mass of historical events may only occasionally and with difficulty be recognizable, but in the history of Europe during this period it seems more than usually apparent. Similarity is inherent in the homogeneity of the human race. Why should there be diversity when so short a period of time and so small a section of the world are under consideration as are dealt with in this volume? The five or six generations of men that lived between 1250 and 1450 are so few compared with the multitudes who have lived through the uncounted ages; the little stretch of Europe is such a small theater of operations compared with the continents through which the human hordes have passed or in which they have temporarily settled, that the wonder is not that in it we should find uniformity, but that there should be discoverable so much difference.

Anthropology, psychology, a study of the evolution of institutions all stress what is common to all humanity. It is the particular interest of history to recognize individual differences without disregarding the general movements common to all or large parts of mankind. Thus the continuity of history is seldom more manifest than at those times which we are apt to call periods of transition.

It seems now, as we look back on this period, that an intelligent observer living in the middle of the fifteenth century might have perceived much that was going to happen. There were bound to be great national or dynastic wars. The centralized monarchies, provided with armies or levies for them by the legislation of their estates, supported by an aroused national spirit and freed from the threat of baronial revolt, were in a position to gratify their ambitions or to use territorial disputes as occasions for war. It would almost have been possible to prophesy that Italy would be the principal theater of war, for that country more than any other in Europe was deficient in national spirit, either for resistance or aggression, and it was an old theater of warfare. The east of Europe would surely be more influential. The Turks were pushing irresistibly forward. Russia was a cloud on the horizon that would soon overspread the sky.

A split in the Church was bound to come. No one could gauge the force of popular and royal dissatisfaction with the ecclesiastical system and measure the power of the national governments without realizing that if reforms were proposed the Church would be powerless in the hands of the state. There could hardly fail to be a great extension of exploration and commerce. Capital, equipment, knowledge, enterprise, royal patronage were all ready for an advance. The rapid progress of art and a new march of knowledge had already begun. In the very last year of our period the invention of printing gave the world its most valuable means of disseminating knowledge and ideas. A much larger proportion of the population would participate in all intellectual life. The most conspicuous characteristic of this period was its assurance that it was introductory to a new era.

Bibliographical Notes

(Revised as of November, 1957)

GENERAL WORKS

I. J. Paetow, *Guide to the Study of Medieval History,* rev. ed. (New York, 1931), is still valuable for all medieval and early modern history and, along with L. Halphen, *Initiation aux études d'histoire du moyen âge,* rev. ed. (Paris, 1952), will fill out some deficiencies in this bibliography. Also of aid are the two volumes of the series Clio, *Introduction aux études historiques,* nos. IV and V by J. Calmette, *Le monde féodale,* rev. ed. (Paris, 1951), and *L'élaboration du monde moderne,* rev. ed. (Paris, 1942), respectively. Special sections in these last are devoted to sources.

The period 1250–1450 has fortunately had its diverse elements brought together into at least the formal unity of a single volume in several excellent series. This is true of the *Cambridge Medieval History*, of which vol. VII, *The Decline of Empire and Papacy* (Cambridge, 1932), covers almost exactly the limits of this book, although certain chapters in vol. IV, pt. 1 (Cambridge, 1927), and in vol. VI (Cambridge, 1929), also deal with the period. The bibliography is abundant, if somewhat undiscriminating. Vol. VII, *La fin du moyen âge, 1285–1453* (Paris, 1931), of the series *Peuples et civilisations,* L. Halphen and P. Sagnac, eds., is distinguished by the unusually fresh and interesting chapters by H. Pirenne and A. Renaudet on economic and on religious and cultural history respectively, and by its excellent and well-classified bibliography. The great German work, *Propyläen Weltgeschichte*, of which vol. IV (Berlin, 1932) covers this area, is brilliantly written and handsomely illustrated, with useful tables of events, though lacking a bibliography. In addition, a new, completely rewritten edition has appeared (Berlin, 1945) and another is in process. However, recent literature will be taken into account in the new series *Historia Mundi,* vol. VI of which covers this period and is scheduled to appear in the winter of 1957–58. Excellent surveys of the time are vol. VI and vol. VII, pt. I, of the *Histoire générale,* G. Glotz, ed.; *L'Europe occidentale de 1270 à 1380* (Paris, 1940–41), by A. Coville and R. Fawtier, and *La France et l'Angleterre en conflit* (Paris, 1937), by J. Calmette and E. Deprez. Many works, though nominally on an earlier period, extend into this one, which is seldom clearly distinguished from the Middle Ages as a whole.

Cultural history may be studied in G. Grupp, *Kulturgeschichte des Mittelalters,* 6 vols. (Paderborn, 1921–25), and in the recent sketch by J. Hashagen, *Kulturgeschichte des Mittelalters; eine Einführung* (Hamburg, 1950). H. Pirenne et al., *La civilisation au moyen âge, du XIe au milieu du XIVe siècle* (Paris, 1933), in the above-mentioned Glotz history, and the more recent E. Perroy, *Le moyen âge; l'expansion de l'orient et la naissance de la civilisation occidentale*, vol. III, in M. Crouzet, ed., *Histoire générale des civilisations,* are also valuable, with the latter placing the subject in an unusually broad frame of reference. In English one may consult C. Crump and E. Jacob, eds., *The Legacy of the Middle Ages* (Oxford, 1951), and any one of several textbook-type publications such as that of H. Lucas, *A Short History of Civilization*, 2nd ed. (New York, 1953), none of which is completely satisfactory.

H. O. Taylor, *The Medieval Mind*, 2 vols. (Cambridge, 1949), is a basic treatment of the thought of the period, and may now be supplemented by F. Artz, *The Mind of the Middle Ages, A.D. 200–1500, an Historical Survey,* 2nd ed. (New York, 1953), and J. Huizinga, *The Waning of the Middle Ages* (New York, 1956, Anchor Books, A42), the latter an especially brilliant and provocative study which may now be supplemented by the writings of R. Stadelmann, *Vom Geist des ausgehenden Mittelalters* (Halle, 1929), W. Penckert, *Die grosse Wende, Das apokalyptische Saeculum und Luther* (Hamburg, 1948), and especially H. Heimpel, "Das Wesen des Spätmittelalters," in *Archiv für Kulturgeschichte* (1953).

Some single-volume but mature histories of the period are K. Kaser, *Das späte Mittelalter* (Gotha, 1921), vol. V of *Weltgeschichte in gemeinverständlicher Darstellung*, L. Hartmann, ed.; F. Baethgen, *Europa im Spätmittelalter: Grundzüge seiner politischen Entwicklung* (Berlin, 1951); and W. Waugh, *History of Europe from 1378 to 1494*, 3rd ed. (London, 1949).

Among important special studies may be mentioned J. Russell, "Medieval Population," *Social Forces,* vol. XV (1937); H. Lucas, "The Great European Famine of 1315–1317," *Speculum,* vol. V (1930); J. Nohl, *The Black Death* (New York, 1926); G. Coulton, *The Black Death* (London, 1929), with bibliography; Y. Renouard, "La peste noire de 1348–1350," *Revue de Paris* (Mar., 1950).

Some of the more recent textbooks on the age are those by J. Strayer and D. Monro, *The Middle Ages, 395–1500* (New York, 1942); S. Painter, *A History of the Middle Ages* (New York, 1953); and J. Thompson and E. Johnson, *An Introduction to Medieval Europe, 300–1500,* (New York, 1937). A handy selection of sources is to be found in J. Ross and M. McLaughlin, eds., *The Portable Medieval Reader* (New York, 1949), while a more extensive list of translated works is provided in C. Farrar and A. Evans, *Bibliography of English Translations from Medieval Sources* (New York, 1946). An excellent companion to the study of history in general is W. Langer, ed., *An Encyclopedia of World History, Ancient, Medieval and Modern, Chronologically Arranged,* rev. ed. (Boston, 1952). A recent atlas, often of great value, is R. Muir, *Historical Atlas* (New York, 1956).

HISTORIES OF SEPARATE COUNTRIES

Notwithstanding the inchoate state of the nationalities of Europe at this time, much of the history of the period is to be found in national histories. Some of the best of these, several of them with broad outlook, are the following: E. Lavisse, ed., *Histoire de France depuis les origines jusqu'à la Révolution,* vol. III, pt. 2, *Saint Louis, Philippe le Bel, les derniers Capétiens directs,* by C. Langlois (Paris, 1901), and vol. IV, pt. 1, *Les premiers Valois et la Guerre de Cent Ans,* by A. Coville (Paris, 1902). A lucid summary of the period is that by E. Perroy in *Histoire de France pour tous les français* (Paris, 1950), and a brief work in English is that of J. Merriott, *A Short History of France* (London, 1942). A more extensive and still valuable narrative is that of J. Moreton MacDonald, *A History of France,* 3 vols. (London, 1915). Social and cultural history is treated in L. Parras, ed., *Histoire du peuple français,* 4 vols. (Paris, 1951–53), and in J. Evans, *Life in Medieval France* (London, 1957). Both of the last named are furnished with excellent illustrations.

The best recent treatment of English history is to be found in G. Clark, ed., *The Oxford History of England,* although the volumes covering the period at hand have not appeared. But the volume by F. Powicke, *The Thirteenth Century, 1216–1307* (Oxford, 1953), covers the first part of the era and the narrative may be picked up there in the excellent work by V. Green, *The Later Plantagenets: A Survey of English History between 1307 and 1485* (New York, 1955). Also valid as a detailed political treatment are vol. III, *1216–1377,* by T. Tout (London, 1905), and vol. IV, *1377–1485,* by C. Oman (London, 1906), of *A Political History of England in Twelve Volumes,* edited by W. Hunt and R. Poole. A good text is W. Lunt, *A History of England* (New York, 1957). A social and cultural treatment is that of G. Coulton, *Medieval Panorama; the English Scene from the Conquest to the Reformation* (New York, 1955, Meridian Books, MG2), although it ought to be noted that the author looks on the darker side of the picture. Works on the period of the

Hundred Years War, the Black Death, and the Peasants' Rebellion will be noted in the bibliographies of later chapters.

Some brief treatments of Germany in English are those of V. Valentin, *The German People* (New York, 1946), and G. Barraclough, *The Origins of Germany,* rev. ed. (New York, 1947). More intensive study of the history of Germany may best be approached by consulting B. Gebhardt, *Handbuch der deutschen Geschichte,* vol. I, 8th rev. ed. (Stuttgart, 1954). A multi-volume work dealing with the era is that of E. Michael, *Geschichte des deutschen Volkes, vom 13 Jahrhundert bis zum Ausgang des Mittelalters,* 6 vols. (Freiburg, 1897–1915), while K. Lamprecht, *Deutsche Geschichte,* 12 vols. (Berlin, 1920–22), is a brilliant work that aroused much controversy. The part dealing most nearly with this period is vol. IV, pts. 11–13 (Berlin, 1894). H. Heimpel, "Deutschland im Spätmittelalter," *Handbuch der deutschen Geschichte,* ed. O. Brandt, A. Meyer, Constance L. Just, 3 vols. (1936–52), and R. Andreas, *Deutschland vor der Reformation,* 5th ed. (Stuttgart, 1948), are both studies of great merit. Cultural histories are those of G. Steinhausen, *Kulturgeschichte der Deutschen im Mittelalter,* 3rd rev. ed. (Leipzig, 1921), and F. Zoepfl, *Deutsche Kulturgeschichte,* 2 vols. (Freiburg, 1928), and F. Lütge, *Deutsche Sozial- und Wirtschaftsgeschichte* (Berlin, 1952).

The most available history of Spain for this period remains R. Merriman, *The Rise of the Spanish Empire,* vol. I, *The Middle Ages* (New York, 1918); however, a good text is provided by R. Altamira y Crevea, *A History of Spain from the Beginnings to the Present Day,* Eng. tr. of 2nd rev. (New York, 1949). An excellent work with extensive bibliographies is P. Aguado-Bleye, *Manual de historia de España,* 3 vols. (Madrid, 1954–56), and this is also true of A. Ballesteros y Beretta, *Historia de España y su influencia en la historia universal,* 11 vols. 2nd ed. (Madrid, 1943–56). Another recent, less detailed work is that of L. de Valdeavellano, *Historia de España,* vol. I, *De los origenes a la baja edad media* (Madrid, 1952). The small book by J. Font Ruíz, *Instituciones medievales españolas, la organización politica, ecónomica y social de los reinos cristianos de la reconquista* (Madrid, 1949), is of great value for that side of the development. Cultural history is treated in R. Altamira y Crevea, *A History of Spanish Civilization,* Eng. tr. (London, 1930), and in G. Litschauer, *Spanische Kulturgeschichte,* 2 vols. (Vienna, 1939), the latter with a good bibliography.

H. Pirenne, *Histoire de Belgique,* 4 vols. (Brussels, 1948–52), is the standard history of Belgium, and this Renaissance du Livre edition has excellent illustrations; the work of G. Dumont, *Histoire des Belges*, 3 vols. (Brussels, 1954–56), is a shorter, more recent work. The work of P. Blok, *A History of the People of the Netherlands*, Eng. tr., 5 vols. (New York, 1898–1912), is the most satisfactory English account of the history of the Low Countries as a whole, while vol. II, *De volle Middeleeuwen, 925–1305* (Utrecht, 1950), and vol. III, *De late Middeleeuwen, 1305–1477* (Utrecht, 1951), of the 12-volume *Allgemene Geschiedenis der Nederlanden* is an excellent recent compilation by eminent Dutch and Belgian historians.

One of the better histories of Italy in this period is the *Storia politica d'Italia scritta da una società di professori*, with the volumes by F. Gianani, *I communi, 1000–1300* (Milan, 1909), and by P. Orsi, *Signorie e principati, 1300–1530* (Milan, 1901), covering the age at hand. More up to date is the series *Storia d'Italia*, with vol. IV, *L'Italia communale, dal secolo XI alla metà del secolo XIV* (Milan, 1940), by L. Salvatorelli, and vol. V, *L'Italia nell'età dei principati, dal 1343 al 1516* (Milan, 1949), by N. Valeri. The one-volume history by L. Salvatorelli, *A Concise History of Italy from Prehistoric Times to Our Own Day*, Eng. tr. (New York, 1940), is a good manual. Recommended histories of the individual towns are those of R. Davidsohn, *Geschichte von Florenz*, 4 vols. (Berlin, 1896–1927); F. Schevill, *A History of Florence from the Founding of the City through the Renaissance* (New York, 1936); D. Bueno de Mesquita, *Giangaleazzo Visconti, Duke of Milan, 1351–1402* (New York, 1941), which takes a wider view than mere biography; A. Visconti, *Storia di Milano*, 2nd ed. (Milan, 1952); H. Kretschmayr, *Geschichte von Venedig*, 4 vols. (Gotha, 1905–34); R. Cessi, *Storia della Repubblica di Venezia*, 2 vols. (Milan, 1949); and R. Gregorovius, *Geschichte der Stadt Rom im Mittelalter*, 8 vols. in 4 (Dresden, 1926), Eng. tr., 2nd rev. ed., London, 1900–1906.

The lack of attention to the history of the Scandinavian countries and of Switzerland in this volume, due to limitations of space, may be partially corrected by the following references: The most recent work on the former has been done by L. Musset in *Les peuples scandinaves au moyen âge* (Paris, 1951) and in his article "Influences réciproques du monde scandinave et de l'Occident dans la domaine de la civilisation au moyen âge," *Journal of World History* (July, 1953). Various national histories are E. Bull et al., *Det Norske Folks Liv og Historie gjennem Tiderne*, vols. I-IV (Oslo, 1929–35); M. Gerhardt, *Norwegische Geschichte* (Hamburg, 1942), excellent bibliography; K. Larsen, *A History of Norway* (New York, 1948); S. Tunberg et al., *Sveriges Historia till vara dager*, vols. II and III (Stockholm, 1926-44); I. Anderson, *A History of Sweden*, Eng. tr. (London, 1956); V. La Cour and M. Mackeprang, *Schultz' Danmarks Historie,* vols. I and II (Copenhagen, 1941), good illustrations; L. Krabbe, *Histoire de Danemark des origines jusqu'à 1945* (Copenhagen, 1950). For Switzerland, additional bibliography may be found in H. Nabholz et al. *Geschichte der Schweiz*, 2 vols. (Zurich, 1932–38), while a brief survey is that of E. Bonjour et al., *A Short History of Switzerland* (Oxford, 1952). For Burgundy at its height, see J. Calmette, *Les grands ducs du Bourgogne* (Paris, 1949), a good survey; O. Cartellieri, *Geschichte der Herzöge von Burgund, 1363–1477,* of which only vol. I, *Philip der Kühne* (Leipzig, 1910), was ever completed; and by the same author, *The Court of Burgundy*; *Studies in the History of Civilization*, Eng. tr. (New York, 1929).

Bibliographies for the other states of Europe will be given under later chapters: for Bohemia in connection with the heresies and the Hussite wars; for Poland, Hungary, the Balkan states, the Eastern Empire and Turkey under the chapter on the eastern frontiers of Europe.

Chapters One and Two

THE EXTENSION OF COMMERCE AND THE GROWTH OF CAPITALISM

The increasing interest in economic and social history is shown by the larger space given to these topics in general works and by the publication of large works and numerous monographic studies on various phases of the subject. The most recent views are to be found in the *Cambridge Economic History of Europe from the Decline of the Roman Empire* (Cambridge, 1944–), of which the first two volumes deal with the Middle Ages and vol. II, M. Postan and E. Rich, eds., *Trade and Industry in the Middle Ages* (Cambridge, 1952), with the specific topic of these chapters. Also helpful is I. Kulischer, *Allgemeine Wirtschaftsgeschichte des Mittelalters und der Neuzeit*, new ed. (Munich, 1954), and the sketch of F. Rörig, *Mittlelalterliche Weltwirtschaft* (Jena, 1933). P. Boissonnade, *Life and Work in Medieval Europe*, Eng. tr. (New York, 1950), is a good general treatment of commerce, banking, land tenure, etc., while J. Thompson, *Economic and Social History of the Later Middle Ages, 1300–1500* (New York, 1931), is still a mine of information. The views of H. Pirenne may be found in his *Economic and Social History of Medieval Europe*, Eng. tr. (New York, 1956, Harvest Books, 14), and more at length in his *Histoire économique de l'Occident médiéval* (Bruges, 1951). A. Dopsch,

The Economic and Social Foundations of European Civilization, Eng. tr. (New York, 1937), must also be dealt with. Representative of the textbook approach are H. Heaton, *Economic History of Europe* (New York, 1936), and S. Clough and C. Cole *Economic History of Europe*, rev. ed. (Boston, 1946). More specifically on this period are W. Abel, *Die Wüstungen des ausgehenden Mittelalters*, 2nd rev. ed. (Stuttgart, 1955), on the depression aspects of the age; E. Perroy, "À l'origine d'une économie contracté: Les crises du XIVe siècle," *Annales* (Apr.-June, 1949); M. Mollat et al., "L'économie européenne aux deux derniers siècles du moyen âge," in *Relazioni del X Congresso Internazionale di Scienze Storiche*, vol. III (1955), and F. Lütge, "Das 14. und 15. Jahrhundert in der Wirschaftsgeschichte," in *Jahrbucher für Nationalökonomie und Statistik* (May, 1950). M. Arnould et al., *Vingt années d'histoire économique et sociale* (Paris, 1953), is a useful bibliography.

Various works have also appeared on individual countries. Some representative ones are A. Doren, *Italienische Wirtschaftsgeschichte* (Jena, 1934), the first and only volume of which covers the Middle Ages; G. Luzzatto, *Storia economica d'Italia* (Rome, 1949); J. Clapham, *A Concise Economic History of Britain from the Earliest Times to 1750* (Cambridge, 1949); H. Bechtel, *Wirtschaftsgeschichte Deutschlands*, 3 vols. (Munich, 1951–56); R. Doehard, *L'expansion économique belge au moyen âge* (Brussels, 1946); H. Sée, *Histoire économique de la France*, vol. I (Paris, 1939); J. Vicens Vives, *Apuntes del curso de historia económica de España*, vol. I (Barcelona, 1956). The rise of the towns will be dealt with in the following section.

Dealing more strictly with commercial history are works such as those by A. Segre, *Manuale di storia del commercie*, 2 vols., 2nd rev. ed. (Turin, 1923), and by J. Lacour-Gayet, *Histoire de commerce*, 5 vols. (Paris, 1950). An important general bibliography may be found in A. Sapori, "Il commercio internazionale nel medioevo," *Revista storica italiana* (Sept., 1938). In this field also many more local works have appeared: F. Carli, *Storia del commercio italiano*, 2 vols. (Milan, 1934–36); A. Sapori, *Les marchands italiens au moyen âge* (Paris, 1952), with a good bibliography; E. Levasseur, *Histoire du commerce de la France*, 2 vols. (Paris, 1910); L. Salzman, *English Trade in the Middle Ages* (Oxford, 1931); and on the important Eastern trade, the classic study of W. Heyd, *Histoire du commerce du Levant au moyen âge* (Leipzig, 1923), is still of value. More recent treatments may be had in R. Lopez and I. Raymond, *Medieval Trade in the Mediterranean World* (New York, 1955), in J. Heers, "Il commercio nel Mediterraneo alla fine del secolo XIVe nei primi anni del secolo XV°," *Archivio storico italiano* (1955, no. II), and in G. Bratianu, "La Mer Noire, plaque tournant du trafic international à la fin du moyen âge," *Revue historique du sud-est européen*, vol. XXI (1944).

An important center of trade during the period was the Baltic Sea, controlled by the Hansa. A sketch of this organization is found in D. Schaefer, *Die deutsche Hanse,* 4th ed. (Leipzig, 1943), while a more intensive study is that of E. Daenell, *Die Blütezeit der deutschen Hanse,* 2 vols. (Berlin, 1905–06). K. Pagel, *Die Hanse* (Brunswick, 1952), is an excellent one-volume history. F. Rörig's article "Les raisons intellectuelles d'une suprématie commerciale; la Hanse," *Annales d'histoire économique et sociale* (Oct., 1930), is a philosophical analysis based upon his excellent work, *Hansische Beiträge zur deutschen Wirtschaftsgeschichte* (Breslau, 1928). Documentary sources are published in K. Hohlbaum et al., *Hansisches Urkundenbuch,* 10 vols. (Halle and Leipzig, 1876–1907), and in *Hanserecesse*, 23 vols. (Leipzig, 1870–1910), on the earlier and later periods respectively. Further bibliography is listed in W. Vogel, "La Hanse d'après les publications récentes," *Revue historique* (Jan., 1937).

Many monographs have been published on various local phases and individual factories of the Hansa. A few such are A. Agatz, *Der Hansische Baienhandel* (Heidelberg, 1904); F. Schulz, *Die Hanse und England von Edward III bis zu Heinrich VIII* (Berlin, 1911); K. Bahr, *Handel und Verkehr der deutschen Hanse in Flandern während des vierzehntsen Jahrhunderts* (Leipzig, 1911); R. Häpke, *Der deutsche Kaufmann in den Niederlanden* (Leipzig, 1911); J. A. Gode, *The Hanseatic Control of Norwegian Commerce during the Late Middle Ages* (New York, 1950); and A. Winckler, *Die deutsche Hanse in Russland* (Berlin, 1886). Many more could be cited.

Venetian relations with the North may be traced realistically, if unsystematically, by following its history through the *Calendars of State Papers, Venetian*, vol. I (London, 1864), with its valuable *Introduction* by the editor, R. Brown. Other select publications on this topic are H. Rawlinson, "The Flanders Galleys," *The Mariner's Mirror* (Apr., 1926); and A. Ruddock, "Italian Trading Fleets in Medieval England," *History* (Sept., 1944); and W. Stieda, *Hansische-Venetianische Handelsbeziehungen im 15. Jahrhundert* (Rostock, 1894). Valuable information may also be drawn from the works of F. Lane: "Venetian Shipping during the Commercial Revolution," *American Historical Review* (Jan., 1933), and *Venetian Ships and Shipping of the Renaissance* (Baltimore, 1934).

Only a few of the ever-growing number of monographs on other specific phases of commercial history may be mentioned here: M. Maowist, "Polish-Flemish Trade in the Middle Ages," *Baltic and Scandinavian Countries* (Jan., 1938); E. Sabbé, "Les relations économiques entre Angleterre et le continent au haut moyen âge," *Moyen âge*, nos. 3-4 (1950); R. Häpke, *Brugges Entwickelung zum mittelalterlichen Weltmarkt* (Berlin, 1908); M. Mollat, *Le commerce maritime normand à la fin du moyen âge, étude d'histoire économique et sociale* (Paris, 1952); F. Reynaud, *Histoire du commerce de Marseilles*, 2 vols. (Paris, 1951); P. Wolff, *Commerce et marchands de Toulouse* (Paris, 1954); E. Friedmann, *Der mittelalterliche Welthandel von Florenz in seiner geographischen Ausdehnung* (Vienna, 1912).

The important fairs have had several extensive treatments. The basic work is that of G. Bouquelot, *Les foires de Champagne*, 2 vols. (Paris, 1938), but important contributions have been made also by E. Chapin, *Les villes des foires de Champagne des origines au début du XIVe siècle* (Paris, 1937); S. Poignant, *La foire de Lille* (Lille, 1932), really a comparative study on the organization of all the Flemish fairs; and R. Bautier, "Les principales étapes du développement des foires de Champagne," *Académie des inscriptions et belles-lettres; comptes rendus des séances* (Apr.-June, 1952).

One of the most important aspects of economic activity was the manufacture and marketing of wool cloth. Two basic works on this subject are H. Laurent, *Un grand commerce d'exportation au moyen âge: la draperie des Pays-Bas en France et en les pays méditerranéens, XIIe au XVe siècle* (Paris, 1935), and G. Espinas, *La draperie dans la Flandre française au moyen âge*, 2 vols. (Paris, 1923). Another article of interest is E. Coornaert, "Draperies rurales, draperies urbaines: l'évolution de l'industrie flamande au moyen âge et au XVIe siècle," *Revue belge de philologie et d'histoire*, XXVIII, no. 1 (1950). More specialized is G. Bigwood, "Un marché des matières premières; laines d'Angleterre et marchands italiens vers la fin du XIIIe siècle," *Annales d'histoire économique et sociale* (Apr. 1930). Political repercussions of the wool business are treated in E. Power, *The Wool Trade in English Medieval History* (New York, 1941); G. Bigwood, "La politique de la laine en France sous les règnes de Philippe le Bel et de ses fils," *Revue belge de philologie et d'histoire* (Jan., 1936); and H. Smit, *Bronnen tot de Geschiedenis van den Handel met England, Schotland en Ierland* (The Hague, 1928–42), which contains much documentary material on the wool trade with the Low Countries to 1485.

The trade in salt, mentioned in a great number of sources, is fully treated in H. Hauser, "Le sel dans l'histoire," *Revue économique internationale* (Aug., 1927); A. Bridbury, *England and the Salt Trade in the Later Middle Ages* (Oxford, 1955); E. Kriechbaum, "Alte Salztrassen zwischen den Alpen und Böhmen," *Deutsche Archive für Landes und Volksforschungen,* vol. II, no 2; and H. von Srbik, *Studien zur Geschichte des Oesterreichischen Salzwesens* (Innsbruck, 1917).

The wine trade is the subject of articles by H. Pirenne, "Un grand commerce d'exportation au moyen âge; les vins de France," *Annales d'histoire économique et sociale* (May, 1933), and H. von Werveke, "Le commerce des vins français au moyen âge," *Revue belge de philologie et d'histoire,* vol. XII, no. 4 (1933); and of books by A. L. Simon, *The History of the Wine Trade in England* (London, 1906), and H. Hartmeyer, *Der Weinhandel im Gebiete der Hanse im Mittelalter* (Jena, 1905). A more specialized study is that of M. James, "The Fluctuations of the Anglo-Gascon Wine Trade during the 14th Century," *Economic History Review*, vol. IV, no. 2 (1951).

There are a number of works on the subject of commercial law. A. Desjardins, *Introduction historique à l'étude du droit commercial maritime* (Paris, 1890), and L. Goldschmidt, *Universalgeschichte des Handelsrechts,* vol. I (Stuttgart, 1891), remain good general surveys. Two of the widely used codes are described in T. Tisselbach, "Der Ursprung der Rôles d'Oléron und des Seerechts von Damme," *Hansische Geschichtsblätter,* vol. XII (1906), and in W. Ashburner, *The Rhodian Sea Law* (Oxford, 1909). The working of these laws is discussed in A. Sayous, "Les méthodes commerciales de Barcelone au XVe siècle, d'après des documents inédits de ses archives," *Revue historique du droit français et étranger* (June, 1937); C. Gross, *Select Cases Concerning the Law Merchant, Selden Society* (London, 1908–32), and "The Court of the Piepowder," *Quarterly Journal of Economics,* Vol. XX (1906); and R. Marsden, *Select Pleas in the Court of Admiralty, Selden Society,* 2 vols. (London, 1894–97). On England, F. Sanborne, *Origins of the Early English Maritime and Commercial Law* (New York, 1930), may be consulted.

Research on the financial history of this period has led tc the production of a vast number of monographs, partial guidance to which may be found in M. Postan, "Medieval Capitalism," *Economic History Review* (Apr., 1933). Works on the beginnings of capitalism are G. Espinas, *Les origines du capitalisme,* 4 vols. (Paris, 1933–46); F. Nussbaum, *A History of the Economic Insti-*

tutions of Modern Europe: An Introduction to "Der Moderne Kapitalismus" of Werner Sombart (New York, 1933), and A. Sayous, "Le capitalisme commerciale et financier dans les pays de la Méditerranée occidentale, depuis la première Croisade jusqu'à la fin du moyen âge," *Vierteljahrschrift für Sozial-und Wirtschaftsgeschichte,* vol. XXIX, no. 3 (1936); J. Strieder, "Origin and Evolution of Early European Capitalism," *Journal of Economic and Business History,* vol. II (1929); and J. Halperin, "Les transformations économiques du XIIe au XIIIe siècles," *Revue d'histoire économique,* nos. 1 and 2 (1950). More specific studies are those of A. Fanfani, *Le origini del spirito capitalistico in Italia* (Milan, 1932), an excellent analysis of the economic theory of the time, and his "La préparation intellectualle et professionelle à l'activité économique en Italie du XIVe au XVIe siècle," *Moyen âge,* nos. 3–4 (1951); R. Haynes, *Zur Entstehung des Kapitalismus in Venedig* (Stuttgart, 1905); R. Lopez, "Aux origines du capitalisme gênois," *Annales d'histoire économique et sociale* (Sept., 1937); and A. Zycha, "Ueber die Anfänge der kapitalistischen Ständebildung in Deutschland," *Vierteljahrschrift für Sozial-und Wirtschaftsgeschichte,* Vol. XXXI, nos. 2 and 3 (1938). More purely financial is R. Ehrenburg, *Capital and Finance in the Age of the Renaissance* (New York, 1928), an abridged translation of his *Das Zeitalter der Fugger: Geldkapital und Creditverkehr im 16. Jahrhundert* (Jena, 1896).

There is so much that is personal in the activities of the merchants and bankers of the period that it has led to a new type of biography, based on ledgers, contracts, accounts and business letters, rather than private correspondence, diplomatic documents or contemporary chronicles. A few such business biographies are the following: E. Carus-Wilson, *Medieval Merchant Venturers* (London, 1954); Y. Renouard, *Les hommes d'affaires italiens du moyen âge* (Paris, 1949); O. Meltzing, *Das Bankhaus der Medici und seine Vorläufer* (Jena, 1906); A. Sapori, *La crisi della compagnie mercantili dei Bardi e dei Peruzzi* (Florence, 1926), and his *Le marchand italien au moyen âge* (Paris, 1952) with extensive bibliography; A. Beardwood, *Alien Merchants in England, 1350–1377, their Legal and Economic Position* (Cambridge, 1931); F. Lane, *Andrea Barbarigo: Merchant of Venice, 1418–1499* (Baltimore, 1944); G. Luzzatto, "Les noblesses: les activités économiques du patriciat venétien, X[e]-XIVe siècles," *Annales d'histoire économique et sociale* (Nov., 1937); I. Origo, *A Merchant of Prato, Francesco di Marco Datino, 1335–1410* (New York, 1957); J. Lestocquoy, *Les dynasties bourgeoises d'Arras du XIe au XVe siècle* (Arras, 1945); H. Bennett, *The Pastons and their England*, 2nd ed. (Cambridge, 1951); S. Thrupp, *The Merchant Class of Medieval London, 1300–1500* (Chicago, 1948); M. Mollat, ed., *Les affaires de Jacques Coeur, Journal du procureur Dauvet, procès-verbaux de séquêtre et d'ajudication*, 2 vols. (Paris, 1952); and J. Strieder, *Jacob Fugger the Rich, Merchant and Banker of Augsburg* (New York, 1931).

In spite of the fact that banking was quite embryonic during this period, it has received a good deal of attention, as shown in the following works: A. Stockden, "Medieval Money and Banking," *Journal of Economic History* (May, 1945); M. W. Hall, "Early Banking in Genoa," *Economic History Review*, vol. VI (1935); A Usher, *The Early History of Deposit Banking in Mediterranean Europe*, vol. I (Cambridge, U.S.A., 1943); and R. de Roover, *Money, Banking and Credit in Medieval Bruges* (Cambridge, U.S.A., 1948).

The literature on the forms and value of money is traditionally unsatisfactory, with the science of numismatics better represented than the study of value, either absolutely or in prices of the time. A handbook for the former is A. Engel and R. Serrure, *Traité de numismatique de moyen âge*, 3 vols. (Paris, 1891–1905); and a brief treatment may be had in K. Lange, *Münzkunde des Mittelalters* (Leipzig, 1942), which goes into some of the technicalities of the minting process. In the field of values, some aid may be had from E. Dotti, *Tariffa di monete mediovali e moderne italiane secondo l'ordine sequito dal "Corpus Nummorum Italicorum,"* vols. I-V (Rome, 1913–15), and in the treatments of E. Hamilton, *Money, Prices and Wages in Valencia, Aragon and Navarre, 1351–1500* (Cambridge, U.S.A., 1936); E. Perroy, "Wages and Labour in France in the Later Middle Ages," *Economic History Review* (Dec., 1955); J. Saltmarsh, "Plague and Economic Decline in England in the Later Middle Ages," *Cambridge Historical Journal*, vol. VII (1941); J. Schreiner, "Prices and Wages in England in the Later Middle Ages," *Scandinavian Economic History Review*, vol. II, no. 2 (1954). Of more general nature are the works of M. Bloch, *Esquisse d'une histoire monétaire de l'Europe* (Paris, 1954), and C. Cipolla, *Money, Prices and Civilization in the Mediterranean World, 5th to 17th Centuries* (Princeton, 1956).

Chapter Three

RISE OF THE MIDDLE CLASS

In a bibliography of this period cities may be mentioned in several connections, not only economic, but political, cultural, and artistic. The history of their rise and increasing importance holds a large place in the general histories of the period already mentioned and in those of the various countries. Some separate works on the history of towns have also been mentioned in connection with commerce and industry; to list those of importance for the rise of representative institutions would introduce the whole subject of local and regional history. Such lists, more or less complete, can be found in the general works. More specifically on town history is the work of H. Pirenne, *Medieval Cities, their Origins and the Revival of Trade,* new ed. (New York, 1956, Anchor Books, A82), which treats them from the economic point of view. Other general works are R. Rörig, *Die europäische Stadt und die Kultur des Bürgertums im Mittelalter,* 2nd ed. (Gottingen, 1955), and C. Petit-Dutaillis, "L'évolution de l'idée de commune au moyen âge: vieillesse et mort des communes françaises," *Académie des inscriptions et belles-lettres, comptes rendus* (Nov., 1939).

On national groups the following may be mentioned: A. Luchaire, *Les communes françaises à l'époque des Capétiens directs,* new ed. (Paris, 1911), which treats the narrow sense of the word, i.e., those towns granted formal charters of liberties; C. Petit-Dutaillis, *Les communes françaises, caractères et évolution des origines au XVIIIe siécle* (Paris, 1947), widens the term to include all citizen organizations of the name, chartered or not; F. Lot, "L'évolution des communes françaises," *Revue historique* (Jan., 1949); C. Stephenson, *Borough and Town* (Cambridge, U.S.A., 1933), uses views of Pirenne; J. Tait, *The Medieval English Borough: Studies on its Origins and Constitutional History* (Manchester, 1936), differs from the last named; H. Pirenne, *Les anciennes démocraties des Pays-Bas* (Paris, 1910); G. Espinas, *La vie urbaine de Douai au moyen âge,* 4 vols. (Paris, 1931), a model comparative study of Flemish conditions; C. Verlinden, "L'histoire urbaine dans la péninsule ibérique," *Revue belge de philologie et d'histoire* (July, 1936); R. Corande, *Sevilla fortaleza y mercado* (Madrid, 1925); W. F. Butler, *The Lombard Communes* (New York, 1906); J. Luchaire, *Les démocraties* *italiennes* (Paris, 1915); D. Waley, *Medieval Orvieto: The Political History of an Italian City-State, 1157–1334* (New York, 1952).

A good general introduction to the medieval estates is found in vol. VII of the *Cambridge Medieval History,* and the most recent accounts in the national histories. On the theory of representation, common to all parliaments, see the important article by G. Post, "Plena Potestas and Consent in Medieval Assemblies: A Study in Roman Canonical Procedures and the Rise of Representation, 1150–1325," *Traditio,* vol. I (1943), and H. Cam, "Medieval Representation in Theory and Practice," *Studies Presented to the International Commission for the Study of Representative and Parliamentary Institutions,* vol. XVII, printed in *Speculum* (Apr., 1954). The entire series of essays may be consulted with profit.

For the cortes of Spain the accounts of R. Merriman in his *Rise of the Spanish Empire* and in "The Cortes of the Spanish Kingdoms in the Later Middle Ages," *American Historical Review* (Apr., 1911), are two of the few in English. The fullest account of the cortes of Castile is M. Colmeiro, *Cortes de los antiguos reinos de Léon y de Castilla,* 2 vols. (Madrid, 1883–84). This is an introduction to the great series of records of the cortes with the same title, 5 vols. (Madrid, 1896–1922). There is a similar series, *Cortes de los antiguos reinos de Aragon y da Valencia y Principado de Cataluna,* 26 vols. (Madrid, 1896–1922), which unfortunately has no introduction. There is, however, a work on the subject, J. Coroleu y Inglada and D. J. Pella y Forgas, *Cortes catalaños,* 2nd ed. (Barcelona, 1876). There is much material on the early cortes of Aragon in V. de la Fuente, *Estudios criticos sobre la historia y el derecho de Aragon,* 3 vols. (Madrid, 1884–85). More titles may be gleaned from the invaluable work of J. Vicens Vives, *Bibliografía histórica de España e Hispanoamerica,* vol. I, 1953–54, and from its quarterly supplement, *Indice histórico español,* as to this topic, as well as to Spanish history in general.

The best accounts of the French estates, though not the fullest, are to be found in the larger histories previously referred to. More special accounts are H. Hervieu, *Récherches sur les premiers états généraux pendant la première moitié du XIVe siècle* (Paris, 1879); G. Picot, *Histoire des états généraux,* 2nd ed., 4 vols. (Paris, 1888); A. Desjardins, *Etats généraux, 1355–1614* (Paris, 1871); and R. Jellifier, *Histoire des états généraux* (Paris, 1885), a convenient brief study. A recent publication on two specific sessions of the estates is that of J. Strayer and C. Taylor, *Studies in Early French Taxation*

(Cambridge, U.S.A., 1939). Other important articles are those by C. Taylor: "Some New Texts on the Assembly of 1302," *Speculum* (Jan., 1936), and "Assemblies of the Towns in 1316," *ibid.* (July, 1939). This subject is also treated in general works on French public law, such as J. Ellul, *Histoire des institutions,* 2 vols. (Paris, 1956); E. Cheron, *Histoire générale du droit français, public et privé,* 2 vols. (Paris, 1926–29); F. Olivier-Martin, *Histoire du droit français des origines à la Révolution* (Paris, 1945). There is also an extensive literature on the history of the principal provincial estates which cannot be given here. The stormy period between 1355 and 1358 will be dealt with in the next section.

A great mass of books and articles treat the development of the English parliament, and only a small part of these may be included here. Interpretative guides to the material may be found in H. Cam, "Recent Books in England on the Parliamentary Institutions of the British Isles in the Middle Ages," *Bulletin of the International Committee of Historical Sciences,* vol. IX, pt. 4 (1937), and in R. S. Hoyt, "Recent Publications in the United States and Canada on the History of Representative Institutions before the French Revolution," *Speculum* (Apr., 1954). All later writing on the English parliament goes back to the great work of W. Stubbs, *Constitutional History of England,* 3 vols. (Oxford, 1847–78), and many later editions, which ought to be used with C. Petit-Dutaillis, *Studies and Notes Supplementary to Stubbs' Constitutional History,* Eng. tr. (Manchester, 1930). Also illuminating is H. Cam, "Stubbs Seventy Years After," *Cambridge Historical Journal,* vol. IX, no. 2 (1948). The judicial aspects of parliamentary development were first broached by F. Maitland in his Introduction to the *Memoranda de Parliamento* (London, 1893), and elaborated by C. McIlwain, *The High Court of Parliament* (New Haven, 1910). Dr. Pasquet, *Essays on the Origins of the House of Commons,* Eng. tr. (Cambridge, 1921), and J. Jolliffe, *Constitutional History of England,* 3rd ed. (London, 1947), are balanced works. New interpretations enter into F. Thompson, *A Short History of Parliament, 1295–1399* (Minneapolis, 1953), and into G. Haskins, *The Growth of English Representative Government* (Philadelphia, 1948). A criticism of some of the recent work is to be found in B. Wilkinson, *The Constitutional History of England, 1216–1399,* 2 vols. (New York, 1948–1952), which includes translations of many sources. Also important is the section on Parliament in J. Willard and W. Morris, eds., *The English Government at Work, 1327–1336,* 3 vols. (1940–50), and in H. Richardson and G. Sayles, "The Parliaments of Edward III,"

Bulletin of the Institute of Historical Research (Nov., 1930, and June, 1931). On the Lancastrian era various views may be found in H. Gray, *The Influence of Commons on Early Legislation* (Cambridge, 1932); S. Chrimes, *English Constitutional Ideas in the Fifteenth Century* (Cambridge, 1936); G. Lapsley, *Crown, Community and Parliament in the Later Middle Ages* (Oxford, 1951); and G. Haskins, "Parliament in the Later Middle Ages," *American Historical Review,* vol. LII, no. 4 (1947). As aforesaid, studies on specific events are exceedingly numerous, and R. Fawtier, "Parlement d'Angleterre et états-généraux de France," *Académie des inscriptions et belles-lettres, comptes rendus* (July-Oct., 1953), is an interesting comparative study.

The German Reichstag is discussed in R. Schröder, *Lehrbuch der deutschen Rechtsgeschichte,* 7th ed. (Leipzig, 1932), and A. Meister, *Deutsche Verfassungsgeschichte,* 3rd ed. (Leipzig, 1922); and in special monographs such as A. Valen, *Der deutsche Reichstag unter König Wenzel* (Leipzig, 1892); E. Zickel, *Der deutsche Reichstag unter König Rupprecht von der Pfalz* (Frankfurt, 1908); and H. Wendt, *Der deutsche Reichstag unter König Sigmund, 1410–1431* (Breslau, 1890).

An interesting study of representative government, with stress on Poland and Eastern Europe, is S. Kutrzeba, "Origines et caractère du parlementarisme au moyen âge," *Proceedings of the Fifth International Historical Congress* (1923).

Chapter Four

INSURRECTIONS OF THE LOWER CLASSES

The history of popular risings of this period is imbedded for the most part in the histories of the various countries, where they form episodes in the general narrative. They fill a large part also in the contemporary chronicles whose accounts are in some cases the only source of knowledge of these movements. Some general works are G. Franz, *Die agrarischen Unruhen des ausgehenden Mittelalters* (Marburg, 1930); M. Aragoneses, *Los movimentos y luchas sociales en la baja edad media* (Madrid, 1949); R. Turner, "Economic Discontent in Medieval Western Europe," *Journal of Economic History,* Supplement, VIII (1948); B. Jarrett, *Social Theories of the Middle Ages, 1200–1500,* new ed. (New York, 1942). N. Cohn, *In Pursuit of the Millennium* (London, 1957), reviews of a large number of social disturbances with special reference to their Messianic aspects. For the rising of the Pastoreaux, see Elis Berger, *Histoire de Blanche de Castille, Reine de France,* Bibliothèque de l'École française d'Athènes et de Rome, Fasc. 70 (Paris, 1895). For the Sicilian Vespers the standard works are M. Amari, *La Guerra del Vespero Siciliano,* new ed., 3 vols. (Mazara, 1947, Eng. tr. London, 1950); and L. Cadier, *L'administration du royaume de Sicile sous Charles I et Charles II d'Anjou* (Paris, 1891). This rising is usually treated as an incident in the wars between the house of Anjou and the kings of Aragon, on which there is a large literature, of which C. Cartellieri, *Peter von Aragon und die sicilianischen Vesper* (Heidelberg, 1904), is an example.

The Flemish risings fill a particularly large place in the history of the Netherlands and even of France, because they were so much a part of the long struggle between Flanders and its overlords, the kings of France. They are described with especial fullness in several works of H. Pirenne, in *Le soulèvement de la Flandre maritime de 1323–1328* (Brussels, 1900), and in those on Belgium already cited. The rising with which the name of Jacques van Artevelde is connected is most fully described in H. Lucas, *The Low Countries and the Hundred Years War, 1326–1347* (Ann Arbor, 1929), although the author minimizes the extent to which this was an insurrection of the common people. The rising known as that of Philip van Artevelde is hardly treated apart from the history of the time except in the small work of W. Ashley, *James and Philip van Artevelde* (London, 1883). The standard work on the great rural French rising is S. Luce, *Histoire de la Jacquerie,* 2nd ed. (Paris, 1894), with many documents. The Parisian rising under Étienne Marcel is treated in Yves le Tebore, *Étienne Marcel et le Paris des marchands au XIV siècle* (Paris, 1927). Also of interest is the article by A. Funk, "Robert Le Coq and Étienne Marcel," *Speculum* (Oct., 1944). M. Boudet, *La Jacquerie des Tuchins, 1363–1384* (Paris, 1895), refers to a peasants' rising in the south. The Rouen rising of 1382 is described in G. Lecarpentier, "La Harelle, révolte rouennais de 1382," *Moyen âge,* 2nd series, vol. VII (1903).

Conditions at Rome that led to the rising under Rienzi are well described in A. de Bouard, *Le régime politique et les institutions de Rome au moyen âge, 1252–1374* (Paris, 1920). The events of the rising are narrated in I. Origo, *Tribune of Rome: A Biography of Cola di Rienzo* (London, 1938), and in P. Piur, *Cola di Rienzo* (Vienna, 1931).

Conditions in Florence that made that city a center of revolutions are described in the excellent volume by E. Staley, *The Guilds of Florence* (London, 1906), and in A. Doren, *Das Florentiner Zunftwesen vom XIV bis zum XVI Jahrhundert* (Stuttgart, 1908); and in the detailed work of G. Salvemini, *Magnati e popolani in Firenze dal 1280 al 1295* (Florence, 1899). There is no adequate account of the rising of the Ciompi in any other language than Italian, though it is mentioned in all the general histories. The background is provided in M. Becker and G. Brucker, "The Arti Minori in Florentine Politics, 1342–1378," *Medieval Studies,* vol. XVIII (1956); a recent Italian work is G. Scaramella, *Firenze allo scoppio del tumulto dei Ciompi* (Pisa, 1914). There are also individual treatments of other of the Italian risings.

Histories of some German popular risings are enumerated in the general bibliographies mentioned above and in G. Schmoller, No. 47 of the *Sitzungen der Preussischen Academie der Wissenschaften* (1903).

The background for the Peasants' Rising of 1381 in England is given in R. Hilton, "Peasant Movements in England before 1381," *Economic History Review* (Feb., 1949). A brief account is found in the works of G. Trevelyan, *England in the Age of Wyclif,* new ed. (London, 1925), and in his *The Peasants' Rising and the Lollards* (London, 1899), done in conjunction with E. Powell. More studied are A. Réville, *Le soulèvement des travailleurs anglais en 1381* (Paris, 1898), with a particularly valuable introduction by C. Petit-Dutaillis; P. Lindsay and R. Groves, *The Peasants' Revolt of 1381* (London, 1950); and R. Hilton, *The English Rising of 1381* (London, 1950). A large literature also exists on the revolt in local areas; and G. Kriehn, "Studies in the Sources of the Social Revolt in 1381," *American Historical Review* (Jan. and Apr., 1902), seeks to discover the causes of the insurrection.

Chapter Five

THE HUNDRED YEARS WAR

Narrative histories of England and France during the fourteenth and the first half of the fifteenth century are largely occupied with the war. Taking for granted, therefore, that the histories already named and the contemporary chronicler, J. Froissart, *Chronicles of England, France, Spain and the adjoining Countries* (time-honored Johnes tr.), will be looked to as the main sources of information, more specialized works may be named.

The war as a whole is admirably treated in E. Perroy, *The Hundred Years War,* Eng. tr. (New York, 1951); and the origins are dealt with in H. Lucas, *The Low Countries and the Hundred Years War* (Ann Arbor, 1929);

in E. Deprez, *Les préliminaires de la Guerre de Cent Ans; la Papauté, la France et l'Angleterre, 1328–1342* (Paris, 1902); in G. Templeman, "Edward III and the Beginning of the Hundred Years War," *Transactions of the Royal Historical Society,* 5th series, vol. II (1952); and in G. Cuttino, "Historical Revision: The Causes of the Hundred Years War," *Speculum* (July, 1956). The diplomatic and legal entanglements of the commencement of the struggle may be studied in the following: J. de Sturler, "Les relations politiques de l'Angleterre et du Brabant, 1272–1326," *Revue belge de philologie et d'histoire,* vol. XI, nos. 3-4 (1932); and P. Chaplin, "English Arguments concerning the Feudal Status of Aquitaine in the Fourteenth Century," *Bulletin of the Institute of Historical Research* (May-Nov., 1948).

On the military side, the books *The Crécy War* and *The Agincourt War* (both Fairlawn, N. J., 1956), by Lieut.-Col. A. H. Burne, are valuable as the works of an experienced professional soldier who has been at the scenes of the various conflicts. On more general matters see the little book by C. Oman, *The Art of War in the Middle Ages, A.D. 378–1515* (Utica, 1953), also F. Lot, *L'art militaire et les armées au moyen âge,* 2 vols. (Paris, 1946); J. Verbruggen, "La tactique militaire des armées de chevaliers," *Revue du Nord* (Aug.-Sept., 1947), and, on the important change from feudal to mercenary groups, B. Lyon, *From Fief to Indenture* (Cambridge, U.S.A., 1957). On specific campaigns there are J. Viard, "La campagne de juillet-août, 1346, et la bataille de Crécy," *Moyen âge* (Jan.-Apr., 1926), and "Le siège de Calais," *ibid.* (May-Dec., 1929); R. Newhall, *The English Conquest of Normandy, 1416–1424* (New Haven, 1924); J. Moisant, *Le Prince Noire en Aquitaine* (Paris, 1894); J. Tourneur-Aumont, "L'originalité militaire de Du Guesclin," *Moyen âge* (Mar., 1938); and H. Barande, *Orléans et Jeanne d'Arc, étude critique et stratégique du siège d'Orléans* (Paris, 1910).

A general work on diplomatic relations is that of P. Renouvin, ed., *Histoire des relations internationales,* of which vol. I, *Le moyen âge,* by F. Ganshof (Paris, 1953), is excellent. More specifically dealing with the situation at hand are A. Larson, "English Embassies during the Hundred Years War," *English Historical Review* (July, 1940); E. Cosneau, *Les Grands traités de la Guerre de Cent Ans,* 2 vols. (Paris, 1897–99); E. Perroy, "Charles V et le traité de Brétigny," *Moyen âge* (Sept.-Dec., 1928); and J. Dickinson, *The Congress of Arras, 1435: a Study in Medieval Diplomacy* (New York, 1955).

On the Spanish phase of the Anglo-French conflict, see R. Russell, *The English Intervention in Spain and Portugal in the Time of Edward III and*

Richard II (New York, 1955); and F. Suarez, *Intervención de Castilla en la guerra de los Cien Años* (Valladolid, 1950). On the resumption of the direct clash the narrative is taken up by J. Calmette, *Chute et relèvement de la France sous Charles VI et Charles VII* (Paris, 1945), and by E. Jacob, *Henry V and the Invasion of France* (New York, 1947). On the internal dissensions of France some recent views are those of J. d'Avout, *La querelle des Armagnacs et des Bourguignons* (Paris, 1943). And on the final resurgence of the French crown centered around Jeanne d'Arc the following are only a few out of a great many works: F. Lowell, *Joan of Arc* (Boston, 1897); J. Quicherat, *Procès de condamnation et réhabilitation de Jeanne d'Arc,* 5 vols. (Paris, 1841–49), full material for a study of her life; P. Champion, *Procès de condamnation de Jeanne d'Arc,* 2 vols. (Paris, 1920), a simpler account of the trial; G. Hanotaux, *Jeanne d'Arc,* new ed. (Paris, 1938), is of value; J. Cordier, *Jeanne d'Arc, sa personalité, son rôle* (Paris, 1948), does much to smash the mythical picture; and S. Stolpe, *The Maid of Orleans,* Eng. tr. (London, 1956), is a more traditional interpretation, using Cordier's book. For a psychological study see B. Hilliger, *Jeanne d'Arc, eine Seelenstudie,* 4th ed. (Freiburg im Breisgau, 1949).

On the effects of the war on France there are a number of good books: H. Deniflé, *La désolation des églises, monastères et hôpitaux en France pendant la Guerre de Cent Ans,* 2 vols. (Paris, 1897–99), and A. Tuetey, *Les écorcheurs sous Charles VII,* 2 vols. (Montbéliard, 1874), give an idea of the war damage in a physical sense; life in general is portrayed in S. Luce, *La France pendant la Guerre de Cent Ans* (Paris, 1890), and in the contemporary *Journal d'un bourgeois de Paris,* new ed. (Paris, 1926–27). On specific phases, see P. Cambier, *La vie économique en France à la fin de la Guerre de Cent Ans* (Paris, 1942), and R. Fawtier, "La crise d'une société durant la Guerre de Cent Ans," *Revue historique* (Jan., 1950). G. Grosjean, *La sentiment national dans la Guerre de Cent Ans* (Paris, 1928), and F. Lot, "La naissance et le développement d'un sentiment national," *Revue historique* (Apr.-June, 1950), deal with that nebulous question.

Chapters Six and Seven

THE DECLINE OF THE CHURCH

No field of human interest has been marked by more writing than the ecclesiastical, and no period, probably, has given rise to more of such writing than the two centuries covered by this volume. Moreover, controversy has been so rampant that there are few generally accepted "standard" works. This list, therefore, can only include such as are reasonably available and well known, and are directed toward the special aspects of the subject mentioned in the text.

The most recent general treatment of church history is the monumental work of M. Fliche and V. Martin, *Histoire de l'église des origines jusqu'à nos jours,* 24 vols. (Paris, 1934), still in process of publication. Recent text-type books are those of W. Walker, *A History of the Christian Church,* new ed. (New York, 1954), and K. Latourette, *A History of Christianity* (New York, 1953). Still important is the classic work of L. von Pastor, *History of the Popes from the Close of the Middle Ages,* 24 vols., Eng. tr. (London, 1930), with much valuable material on the relations between the Church and the early Renaissance; and A. Hauck, *Kirchengeschichte Deutschlands,* vol. 5, 8th ed. (Berlin, 1954). G. Schnürer, *Kirche und Kultur im Mittelalter,* 3 vols., 2nd ed. (Paderborn, 1927–30), is a basic study of the cultural aspect of the church organization, while E. Troeltsch, *The Social Teaching of the Christian Churches,* 2 vols., Eng. tr. (New York, 1931), is invaluable. H. Lea, *History of the Inquisition in the Middle Ages,* 3 vols., new ed. (New York, 1956), is a basic treatment of that institution. A good setting for the events of the period is given in G. Coulton, *Five Centuries of Religion,* 4 vols. (New York, 1923–30), and in H. Daniel-Rops, *Cathedral and Crusade; Studies of the Medieval Church, 1050–1350* (London, 1957), which is the English translation of volume III of the author's eight-volume *Histoire de l'église du Christ.* On England, see W. Capes, *The English Church in the Fourteenth and Fifteenth Centuries* (London, 1909), and, more recently, J. R. Moorman, *Church Life in England in the Thirteenth Century* (New York, 1945), and W. Pantin, *The English Church in the Fourteenth Century* (New York, 1955). On certain general problems, see G. Constant, "L'état de l'église au commencement du XIV° et XV° siècle d'après deux écrits du temps," *Revue d'histoire ecclésiastique* (Oct., 1937); G. de Lagarde, *La naissance de l'esprit laïque au déclin du moyen âge,* 6 vols. (Paris, 1948), and J. Strayer, "The Laicization of French and English Society in the Thirteenth Century," *Speculum* (Jan., 1940).

The struggle between Boniface VIII and the kings of France and England is described in all the narrative histories, and generally in the over-all treatments mentioned above. More detailed is G. Digard, *Philippe le Bel et le*

Saint Siège de 1285 à 1304, 2 vols. (Paris, 1936). Some of the fundamental questions arising from the contest are treated in the following: O. Gierke, *Political Theories of the Middle Ages,* Eng. tr., new ed. (Cambridge, 1951); R. W. and A. J. Carlyle, *A History of Medieval Political Theory in the West,* vol. V, new ed., (New York, 1953); C. McIlwain, *The Growth of Political Thought in the West from the Greeks to the End of the Middle Ages* (New York, 1932); J. Figgis, *Studies in Political Thought from Gerson to Grotius* (Cambridge, 1931); and F. Hearnshaw, *The Social and Political Ideas of some great Medieval Thinkers,* new ed. (New York, 1950). More specifically on the question are J. Leclerq, "La renonciation de Celestin V et l'opinion théologique en France du vivant Boniface VIII," *Revue de l'histoire de l'église de France* (June, 1939); M. Seidelmayer, "Papst Bonifaz VIII. und der Kirchenstaat," *Historisches Jahrbuch,* vol. LX, no. 1-2; L. Rongione, "Two Swords," *Historical Bulletin* (Jan., 1944); J. Rivière, *Le problème de l'église et de état au temps de Philippe le Bel* (Paris, 1926); and R. Scholz, *Die Publizistik zur Zeit Philips des Schönen und Bonifaz VIII* (Stuttgart, 1903). There are also various articles on the characters and positions of the participants: J. Strayer, "Philip the Fair—A Constitutional King," *American Historical Review* (Oct., 1956); L. Hommel, "Philippe-le-Beau, ou le Prince national," *Revue belge* (May, 1955); R. Scholz, "Zur Beurtheilung Bonifaz VIII und seines Caracters," *Historische Vierteljahrschrift* (Oct., 1906); and M. Melville, "Guillaume de Nogaret et Philippe le Bel," *Revue d'histoire de l'église de France* (Jan.-June, 1950), a recent continuation of the dispute over the legality of the Anagni incident.

For the attack on the Templars, omitted from this volume for considerations of space, see E. S. Martin, *The Trial of the Templars* (London, 1928), and H. Finke, *Papsttum und Untergang des Tempelordens* (Munich, 1907). For their financial activities, see J. Piquet, *Des banquiers au moyen âge, les Templiers* (Paris, 1937). Also in connection with the reign of Clement V and the Captivity consult G. Mollat, *Les papes d'Avignon,* 9th rev. ed. (Paris, 1950), a small but scholarly book with a valuable bibliography. E. Kraack, *Rom oder Avignon?* (Marburg, 1929), is an analysis of the causes of the sojourn in France, while R. Brun, *Avignon au temps des papes* (Paris, 1928), investigates the cultural milieu of the court.

The financial system of the popes at Avignon is described in A. Flick, *The Decline of the Medieval Church,* 2 vols. (London, 1930); also in L. Nina, *Le finanze pontificale nel medio aevo,* 2 vols. (Milan, 1929–30); C. Bauer,

"Die Epochen der Papstfinanz," *Historische Zeitschrift,* vol. CXXXVIII, no. 3 (1928); W. E. Lunt, *Papal Revenues in the Middle Ages,* 2 vols. (New York, 1934), and *Financial Relations of the Papacy with England to 1327* (Cambridge, 1939); C. Samaran and G. Mollat, *La fiscalité pontificale en France au XIVe siècle* (Paris, 1905); and E. Hennig, *Die päpstlichen Zehnten aus Deutschland in Zeitalter des Avignonischen Papsttums und während des grossen Schismas* (Halle, 1909).

For the return to Rome and the Great Schism, the following books will prove of use: L. Mirot, *La politique pontificale et le retour du Saint Siège à Rome* (Paris, 1899); J. Kirsch, *Die Rückkehr der Päpste Urban V und Gregor XI von Avignon nach Rom* (Paderborn, 1898); N. Valois, *La France et le Grand Schisme d'Occident,* 4 vols. (Paris, 1896–1902), who favors the Avignonese line; L. Salambrier, *Le Grand Schisme d'Occident,* 5th ed. (Paris, 1921, Eng. tr. London, 1907), who is oriented toward Rome; and G. J. Jordan, *The Inner History of the Great Schism of the West* (London, 1930), a treatment of the various methods proposed and finally used to re-establish unity in the Church. On the origins of the split, see W. Ullman, *The Origins of the Great Schism* (London, 1948).

The standard work on the councils is C. J. von Hefele, *Histoire des conciles,* tr. and rev. by H. Leclerq, 8 vols. (Paris, 1907–21); and N. Valois, *Le crise religieuse du XVe siècle; le pape et le concile, 1418–1450,* 2 vols. (Paris, 1909), serves as a sequel to his work mentioned above. On the theory underlying the movement, see B. Tierney, *Foundations of the Conciliar Theory: the Contribution of the Medieval Canonists from Gratian to the Great Schism* (New York, 1955). Other articles of interest are H. Jedin, "Nouvelles données sur l'histoire des conciles généraux," *Journal of World History* (July, 1953), and H. Finke, "Die Nation in den spätmittelalterlichen Konzilien," *Historisches Jahrbuch,* vol. LVII, nos. 2 and 3. The political implications of the movement may be touched upon in E. Göller, *König Sigismunds Kirchenpolitik vom Tode Bonifaz VIII bis zur Berufung des Konstanzer Konzils, 1404–1413* (Freiburg, 1901).

The various mystic and heretical sects are of great importance during this period. A. Evans, "Social Aspects of Medieval Heresy," in *Persecution and Liberty,* essays presented to G. L. Burr (New York, 1931), touches an important aspect. G. Volpe, *Movimente religiosi e sette ereticali nella sooietà medievale italiana* (Todi, 1917), and E. Gebhart, *L'Italie mystique* (Paris, 1908), are general studies of the Italian situation. J. Döllinger, *Prophecy and the Pro-*

phetic Spirit in the Christian Era (London, 1873); H. Grundmann, *Studien über Joachim von Floris* (Leipzig, 1927), and "Neue Forschungen über Joachim von Fiore," *Münstersche Forschungen,* vol. 1 (1950); and M. Bloomfield and M. Reeves, "The Penetration of Joachim into Northern Europe," *Speculum* (Oct., 1954), deal with that personage. Writings on the more important mystic groups are D. Douie, *The Nature and the Effect of the Heresy of the Fraticelli* (Manchester, 1932); D. Muzzey, *The Spiritual Franciscans* (New York, 1907); H. G. Beck, "The Discussion over Franciscan Poverty, 1226–1318," *American Ecclesiastical Review* (Nov.-Dec., 1943); A. Hyma, *The Brethren of the Common Life* (Grand Rapids, 1950); E. Jacob, "The Brethren of the Common Life," *Bulletin of the John Rylands Library* (Apr., 1940), and "Gerard Groote and the Beginning of the 'New Devotion' in the Low Countries," *Journal of Ecclesiastical History* (Jan., 1952); R. Post, *De moderne Devotie; Geert Groote en zijn stichtingen* (Amsterdam, 1950); E. McDonnell, *The Beguines and Beghards in Medieval Culture* (New Brunswick, N. J., 1954); and D. Phillips, *Beguines in Medieval Strasburg: A Study of the Social Aspect of Beguine Life* (Stanford, 1941). A good idea of mystic thought may be gained by reading some representative writings such as those of Meister Eckhart: *Meister Eckhart, A Modern Translation* (New York, 1941); or of Thomas a Kempis, *The Imitation of Christ,* in many translations and editions.

A remarkably compact and satisfactory analysis of the teachings of Ockham and Marsiglio and of the controversy to which their writings led is given in the small book by R. Poole, *Illustrations of the History of Medieval Thought,* 2nd rev. ed. (New York, 1920). The works of Ockham have begun to be edited and published in J. Sikes et al., *Guillelmi de Ockham Opera Politica,* vol. I- (Manchester, 1940–); while various recent works on him are A. Maier, "Zu einigen Problemen der Ockhamforschung," *Archivum Franciscanum Historicum* (Jan., 1953); A. Pegis, "Some Recent Interpretations of Ockham," *Speculum* (July, 1948); C. Bayley, "The Political Philosophy of William of Ockham," *Journal of the History of Ideas* (Jan., 1949); and J. Morrall, "William of Ockham as a Political Thinker," *Cambridge Historical Journal* (Sept., 1952). The most recent works on Marsiglio are those of A. Giwirth, *Marsilius of Padua: the Defender of the Peace,* 2 vols. (New York, 1951–56), of which the second volume is a translation of the *Defensor Pacis,* and "John of Jandun and the 'Defensor Pacis,' " *Speculum* (Apr., 1948). Other works of value are E. Emerton, *The 'Defensor Pacis' of Marsiglio of Padua,* new edition (New York, 1950); C. Previté-Orton, *The 'Defensor Pacis' of Marsilius of Padua* (London, 1935); F. Battaglia, *Marsilio da Padova e la filosofia politica del medio evo* (Florence, 1928); M. Tooley, "The Authorship of the Defensor Pacis," *Transactions of the Royal Historical Society,* vol. IX (1926); J. Sullivan, "Marsiglio of Padua and William of Ockham," *American Historical Review* (Apr. and July, 1897); and R. Scholz, *Marsilius von Padua, Defensor Pacis,* 2 vols. (Hannover, 1932–33).

There is an especially full bibliography of Wyclif literature in the *Cambridge Medieval History,* and his astonishingly numerous writings are published in various forms, the most extensive group, especially the Latin works, by the Wyclif Society, 32 vols. (London, 1883–1913). The most satisfactory life is still the old work of G. Lechler, *Johann von Wiclif und die Vorgeschichte der Reformation,* 2 vols. (Leipzig, 1873), abridged English translation as *John Wycliffe and his English Precursors* (London, 1884). Brief treatments are those of R. Poole, *Wycliffe and Movements for Reform in the Fourteenth Century* (London, 1911) and R. Vaughan, *The Life and Opinions of John de Wycliffe* (London, 1928), while more ponderous is H. B. Workman, *John Wyclif; A Study of the English Medieval Church,* 2 vols. (London, 1901–02). Selected translations of his works as well as of many others may be had in M. Spinka, *Advocates of Reform: from Wyclif to Erasmus* (Philadelphia, 1953).

J. Gairdner, *Lollardy and the Reformation in England,* 4 vols. (London, 1908–13), is in the main a study of the question whether the Lollard movement of the fourteenth and fifteenth centuries persisted into the sixteenth; and the chapters in G. Trevelyan, *England in the Age of Wycliffe,* mentioned above, are of much interest, as is the little book by W. Summers, *The Lollards of the Chiltern Hills* (London, 1906). On the English translation of the Bible, see M. Deansley, *The Lollard Bible and other Medieval Biblical Versions* (Cambridge, 1920); J. Forshall and F. Madden, eds., *The Holy Bible . . . in the Earlier English Versions made by John Wycliffe and his Followers,* 4 vols. (Oxford, 1850); and H. Bett, "Wyclif's New Testament," *London Quarterly Review* (July, 1943).

The connection between English Lollardy and the Hussite movement in Bohemia makes it necessary to introduce here the titles of some works on Bohemian history. J. Loserth, *Hus und Wiclif,* 2nd rev. ed. (Munich, 1925, Eng. tr. of 1st ed. London, 1884), lays great stress on the dependence of Hus on Wyclif. This influence is minimized by V. Novotny and V. Kybal, *Mistr. Jan Hus,* 2 vols. in 5 (Prague, 1919–31), made available in part to a non-

Czech audience by the reviews of J. Šušta, "Histoire de la Tchécoslovaquie," *Revue historique* (July-Aug.-Sept.-Oct., 1925). Other works on the origins of the movement are V. Novotny, "Les origines du mouvement Hussite en Bohême," *Revue de l'histoire des religions* (Jan.-Apr., 1924), and V. Kybal, "Étude sur les origines du mouvement Hussite en Bohême, Mathias de Janov," *Revue historique* (Jan.-Feb., 1910). Also on this subject are articles by K. Krofta, "L'aspect national et social du mouvement Hussite," *Le monde slave* (March, 1928); S. Thomson, "Cultural Relations of Bohemia with Western Europe before the White Mountain," *Bulletin of the Polish Institute of Arts and Sciences in America* (Jan., 1944); O. Odložilík, "Wycliffe's Influence upon Central and Eastern Europe," *Slavonic Review* (March, 1929); and M. Spinka, "Paul Kravar and the Lollard Hussite Relations," *Church History* (March, 1956). On the persons of the Czech reformers, see R. Betts, "Jerome of Prague," *University of Birmingham Historical Journal,* vol. I, no. 1 (1947), and "Jan Hus," *History* (Sept., 1939), while the work of M. Spinka, *John Hus and the Czech Reform* (Chicago, 1941), uses most of the recent Czech literature on the subject. Some of the writings of Hus may be had in F. Strunz, *Johannes Huss, sein Leben und seine Werke* (Munich, 1927).

On the successors of Hus the classic work is E. Denis, *Huss et les Guerres Hussites* (Paris, 1930), and F. Heymann, *John Žižka and the Hussite Revolution* (Princeton, 1955), which incorporates much of the work done since the appearance of the former; also J. Waskovich, "Juan Žižka y la Crisis Checoeslovaca en el siglo XV," *Revista de estudios eslavos* (March, 1947). Fervently nationalistic is the work of F. Palacký, *Geschichte von Böhmen,* 5 vols. (Prague, 1836–67), while just as anti-Czech are A. Bachmann, *Geschichte Böhmens,* 2 vols. (Gotha, 1899–1905), and B. Bretholz *Geschichte Böhmens,* 2 vols. (Reichenberg, 1921–22). These last, along with the *Jan Žižka* of J. Pekař, 3 vols. (Prague, 1927–30), have modified the traditional conceptions of the Hussite wars. For a brief picture see F. Lutzow, *Bohemia, an Historical Sketch* (London, 1939). Also of interest is the article of R. Betts, "Social and Constitutional Developments in Bohemia in the Hussite Period," *Past and Present* (Apr., 1955).

Works of some value on the Council of Basel are F. Lazarus, *Das Basler Konzil* (Berlin, 1912), and J. Toussaint, *Les relations diplomatiques de Philippe le Bon avec le concile de Bâle, 1431–49* (Louvain, 1942), but in the main reference must be had to the general works listed above.

Chapter Eight

THE BEGINNINGS OF MODERN LANGUAGE, LITERATURE, AND ART

The dates which begin and close this volume do not furnish so clear a division in the intellectual and artistic spheres as in some others. This is especially true of its close. The great modern movements in art and learning which began in Italy in the late thirteenth and early fourteenth centuries were in full progress of development as this work closes in 1453. A new era had already begun but had not yet reached its prime. Much of the vast mass of writing on these aspects of history, therefore, applies more to a later period than to this one. In general the reader may be referred to the excellent chapters on literature and art in the general works in the introductory sections, especially to the various cultural histories.

The establishment of the modern vernacular languages, however, had already taken place before the middle of the fifteenth century. F. Snell, *The Fourteenth Century* (Edinburgh, 1923), is an interesting comparative study of European literature against the political and social background. Language and literature are seldom completely distinguished, so the larger works on early modern literature should be consulted, among which may be suggested, for France, J. Bédier and P. Hazard, *Littérature française,* 2 vols., rev. ed. (Paris, 1948–49), and L. Cazamian, *A History of French Literature* (Oxford, 1955); for Spain, J. Fitzmaurice-Kelly, *History of Spanish Literature* (London, 1917); for Germany, G. Ehrismann, *Geschichte der deutschen Literatur bis zum ausgang des Mittelalters,* 3 vols. (Munich, 1918–35), with rich bibliographical notes, and H. Gumbel, *Deutsche Kultur von der Mystik bis zur Gegenreformation* (Potsdam, 1936–39), and particularly J. Nadler, *Literaturgeschichte des deutschen Volkes,* 4 vols. (Berlin, 1938–41); for England, A. Ward and A. Waller, *The Cambridge History of English Literature,* vol. II, new ed. (Cambridge, 1949), text only; and H. Craig, *A History of English Literature* (Oxford, 1950); for Italy, F. de Sanctis, *History of Italian Literature,* vol. I, Eng. tr. from edition of B. Croce (Bari, 1912), and more recently, A. Pompeati-Lucchini, *Storia della letturatura italiana,* 5 vols. (Turin, 1944–). One of the best pictures of the literature of the age in general can be gained from the selections in C. Jones, *Medieval Literature in Translation* (New York, 1950).

Among specific works on the history of languages, one of the best is F. Brunot, *Histoire de la langue française des origines à 1890*, 9 vols. (Paris, 1905–35). A. Tilley, ed., *Medieval France, a Companion to French Studies* (New York, 1922), contains chapters by eminent authorities on many aspects of French literature; and the collections of C. Langlois, *La vie en France au moyen âge*, new ed. (Paris, 1926–28), are invaluable for abstracts of literature reflecting the life from the twelfth to the fourteenth centuries. A. C. Baugh, *A History of the English Language* (New York, 1935), is good; and some interesting phases of the question are treated in E. Curtius, *European Literature and the Latin Middle Ages*, Eng. tr. (New York, 1953).

G. Volpi, *Il Trecento* (Milan, 1898), is one of the best general accounts of Italian literature in the fourteenth century, and E. Underhill, *Jacopone da Todi, Poet and Mystic, 1228–1306* (London, 1919), is a study of the beginning of modern thought and literature in Italy. A good bibliography of Dante is U. Cosmo, *A Handbook to Dante Studies* (Oxford, 1950). Some biographies of Dante are P. Toynbee, *Dante Alighieri, his Life and Works*, 6th ed. (London, 1924), and F. Schneider, *Dante, sein Leben und sein Werk*, 4th rev. ed. (Weimar, 1947). Of the great mass of articles on the poet some of the more illuminating are those on his political ideas: R. Montano, "La *Monarchia* e il pensiero politico di Dante," *Delta* (Oct.-Dec., 1952), and B. Carter, "Dante's Political Ideas," *Review of Politics* (July, 1943).

H. Hauvette, *Boccaccio, étude biographique et littéraire* (Paris, 1915), is an excellent work, with a full bibliography. See also E. Rodocanachi, *Boccace: poète, conteur, moraliste, homme politique* (Paris, 1908); and, in English, E. Hutton, *Giovanni Boccaccio, a Biographical Study* (London, 1910).

For Petrarch a bibliography of recent works is given in E. Wilkins, "Recent Petrarch Publications," *Studies in the Renaissance*, W. Peery, ed., vol. I (1954). Still basic are the works of G. Körting, *Petrarchs Leben und Werke* (Leipzig, 1878), and P. de Nolhac, *Pétrarque et l'humanisme*, 2nd ed., 2 vols. (Paris, 1907), which exists in an abridged translation as *Petrarch and the Ancient World* (Boston, 1908). Other biographies are E. Wilkins, *Studies in the Life and Works of Petrarch* (Cambridge, U.S.A., 1955), and J. Robinson and R. Rolfe, *Petrarch, the First Modern Scholar and Man of Letters*, 2nd ed. (New York, 1925). On his political beliefs, see R. Mattei, *Il sentimento politico del Petrarca* (Florence, 1944); M. Cosenza, ed., *Francesco Petrarch and the Revolution of Cola di Rienzo* (Chicago, 1913); and C. Bayley, "Petrarch, Charles IV, and the 'Renovatio Imperii,' " *Speculum* (July, 1943).

Humanism as a study of ancient literature is treated in such extended works as G. Voigt, *Die Wiederbelebung des Classischen Altherthums, oder das erste Jahrhundert des Humanismus*, 2 vols., 3rd ed. (Berlin, 1893); J. Burckhardt, *The Civilization of the Renaissance in Italy*, Eng. tr., 4th rev. ed. (London, 1951); and P. Mounier, *Le quattrocento, étude sur l'histoire littéraire du XVe siècle*, 2 vols., 2nd ed. (Paris, 1918); however, there are pros and cons for the influence of the classics on Renaissance culture. Some books on the transitional period are the following: R. Weiss, *The Dawn of Humanism in Italy* (London, 1947); G. Toffanin, *The History of Humanism*, Eng. tr. (New York, 1954); H. Baron, *The Crisis of the Early Italian Renaissance*, 2 vols. (Princeton, 1955); B. Ullman, "Some Aspects of the Origin of Italian Humanism," *Philological Quarterly* (July, 1941); E. Garin, *L'umanesimo italiano: Filosofia e vita civile nel rinascimento* (Bari, 1952); for political theory, E. Emerton, *Humanism and Tyranny* (Cambridge, 1925); K. Brandi, *Das Werden der Renaissance* (Göttingen, 1908); R. Hefels, "Zum Begriff der Renaissance," *Historisches Jahrbuch*, vol. XLIX, no. 3 (1929), and W. Ferguson, *The Renaissance in Historical Thought* (Boston, 1948).

Some of the later authors connected with the movement have been separately treated: L. Mohler, *Kardinal Bessarion als Theologe, Humanist und Staatsmann*, 2 vols. (Paderborn, 1923–27), and R. Sabbadini, *Le scoperti dei codici latini e greci ne' secoli XIV e XV* (Florence, 1905), and L. Loomis, "The Greek Renaissance in Italy," *American Historical Review* (Jan., 1908), all on the renewed study of Greek; also E. Walser, *Poggius Florentinus, Leben und Werke* (Leipzig, 1914); C. Colman, *The Treatise of Lorenzo Valla on the Donation of Constantine* (New Haven, 1922); C. Ady, *Pius II: the Humanist Pope* (London, 1913); W. Woodward, *Vittorino da Feltre and Other Humanists* (Cambridge, 1905).

The philosophy of this period is admirably presented in the works of M. de Wulf, *Philosophy and Civilization in the Middle Ages* (New York, 1953), and his *History of Medieval Philosophy*, Eng. tr. from the 6th ed., 2 vols. (New York, 1935–38), vol. I of a new definitive edition appeared (New York, 1952) with the others yet to come; and in E. Gilson, *La philosophie au moyen âge*, 2 vols., 3rd rev. ed. (Paris, 1947). A more general picture may be had in C. Brinton, *Ideas and Men: The Story of Western Thought* (New York, 1951), and F. Artz, *The Mind of the Middle Ages* (New York, 1953). On the important question of the place of Greek thought in the Middle Ages see C. Buhler, "Greek Philosophers in the Literature of the later Middle Ages,"

Speculum (Oct., 1957); H. Kantorowicz, "Plato in the Middle Ages," *Philosophic Review* (May, 1942); and R. Klibansky, *The Continuity of the Platonic Tradition during the Middle Ages* (London, 1939).

Some surveys of the art of the period may be had in W. Lethaby, *Medieval Art, from the Peace of the Church to the Eve of the Renaissance, 312–1350,* rev. ed. (London, 1949); and in F. Adama von Scheltema, *Die Kunst des Mittelalters* (Stuttgart, 1953). A more detailed study is that of A. Michel, *Histoire de l'art depuis les premiers temps chrétiens jusqu'à nos jours* (Paris, 1926–). E. Mâle, *L'art religieux à la fin du moyen âge* (Paris, 1908), is still of great interest. On England and France, see J. Evans, *English Art, 1307–1461* (New York, 1949), vol. V of the *Oxford History of English Art;* and her *Art in Medieval France, 987–1498* (Oxford, 1948); while also of interest is L. Dimier and L. Réaux, *Histoire de la peinture française* (Paris, 1925), and H. Bouchot, *Les primitifs français* (Paris, 1904). Space does not here permit any but a very selective listing of the vast mass of materials on the history of Italian art. Some of the better known and more general are H. Wölfflin, *Classic Art: an Introduction to the Italian Renaissance* (New York, 1952), and A. Venturi, *Storia dell'arte italiana* (Milan, 1904–39), and M. Dvořák, *Geschichte der italienischen Kunst im Zeitalter der Renaissance,* 2 vols. (Munich, 1927–29), although the latter extends beyond the age at hand. W. Stammler, *Der Totentanz: Enstehung und Bedentung* (Munich, 1948), and H. Rosenfeld, *Der Mittelalterliche Totentanz* (Munster, 1954), are among the most important treatments of that theme.

There are also studies on the various disciplines of the Italian art world. On painting, see F. Mather, *A History of Italian Painting,* new ed. (New York, 1948); F. Berenson, *The Italian Painters of the Renaissance* (New York, 1957, Meridian Books); R. Marle, *The Development of the Italian Schools of Painting,* 2 vols. (The Hague, 1923–29); L. Hautecouet, *Les primitifs italiens* (Paris, 1931); F. Antal, *Florentine Painting and its Social Background* (London, 1948); M. Meiss, *Painting in Florence and Siena after the Black Death* (Princeton, 1951); G. Edgell, *A History of Sienese Painting* (New York, 1932). On the various artists of the transition period, see J. Mesnil, *Masaccio et les débuts de la Renaissance* (The Hague, 1927); W. Bode, *Florentine Sculptors of the Renaissance* (London, 1928); M. Cruttwell, *Verrochio* (London, 1911) and *Donatello* (London, 1911); M. Zimmerman, *Giotto und die Kunst Italiens im Mittelalter* (Leipzig, 1899); I. Supino, *Giotto,* 2 vols. (Florence, 1927); A. Schmarsow, *Hubert and Jan van Eyck* (Leipzig, 1924); and of course G. Vasari,

Lives of the Most Eminent Painters, Sculptors and Architects, in many editions and translations—not always trustworthy, but still a classic.

On architectture there is also a rich selection of works: A. Porter, *Medieval Architecture,* 2 vols., 2nd ed. (New Haven, 1912); W. Anderson, *The Architecture of the Renaissance in Italy,* 5th rev. ed. (London, 1927); G. Scott, *The Architecture of Humanism* (New York, 1954, Anchor Books, A33); R. Wittkower, *Architectural Principles in the Age of Humanism,* 2nd ed., (London, 1952); and the interesting article of R. Lopez, "Economie et architecture mediévales," *Bulletin of the Institute of Historical Research* (May, 1953).

Chapter Nine

THE REVELATION OF THE EAST

So little advance was made in exploration westward and southward before 1453 that its few tentative steps have been left to be described in the next volume of this series, this chapter recounting only exploration to the eastward. It may be remarked, however, that whatever was known of these other areas may be traced in the general works on the subject. These are C. Beazley, *The Dawn of Modern Geography,* 3 vols. (Oxford, 1897–1906); P. Sykes, *A History of Exploration from the Earliest Times to the Present,* 3rd ed. (New York, 1950); R. Hennig, *Terrae Incognitae: eine Zusammenstellung und kritische Bewertung der wichtigsten vorcolumbischen Entdeckungsreisen an der Hand der darüber vorliegenden Originalberichte,* 4 vols. (Leiden, 1939); and E. Zechlin, *Maritime Weltgeschichte* (Hamburg, 1947). Also illuminating is the article by E. Taylor, "Ideas of the Shape and Habitability of the Earth Prior to the Great Age of Discovery," *History* (June, 1937).

The journeys and observations of Marco Polo which began the opening up of the Far East to western knowledge are described in the standard work of Sir Henry Yule, *The Book of Ser Marco Polo the Venetian,* rev. ed. by H. Cordier, 2 vols. (London, 1929), best used in conjunction with H. Cordier, *Ser Marco Polo; Notes and Addenda to Sir Henry Yule's Edition* (New York, 1920). Of course, many other editions exist of the narrative proper, and a good biography of Polo is that of H. Hart, *Venetian Adventurer: being an Account of the Life and Times of the Book of Messer Marco Polo* (Stanford, 1942). For translations of other contemporary narratives see the Cordier revision of Yule's *Cathay and the Way Thither*, 3 vols. (London, 1913–16). Separate translations and annotated editions of these works are C. Beazley, ed., *Texts and Versions of John de Plano Carpini and William de Rubruquis*, Hakluyt Soc., extra series (London, 1903); G. Pulle, ed., *Viaggio ai Tartari*, Italian translation of G. di Plano Carpini (Milan, 1956); H. Matrod, *Notes sur le voyage de Fr. Jean de Plan-Carpin* (Paris, 1912), and *Le voyage de Fr. Guillaume de Rubrouck* (Paris, 1909); V. Langmantel, *Hans Schiltbergers Reisebuch* (Tübingen, 1885), and H. Cordier, ed., *Les merveilles d'Asie* of Jourdain Catalan de Sévérac (Paris, 1925).

The papal policy toward the Mongols is given in great detail in G. Soranzo, *Il Papato, l'Europa Cristiana e i Tartari; un secolo di penetrazione occidentale in Asia* (Milan, 1930). On the Mongol conquest itself, see M. Prawdin, *The Mongol Empire, its Rise and Legacy* (New York, 1940), R. Grousset, *Histoire de l'Asie*, 3 vols., new ed. (Paris, 1944), and his *L'Asie orientale des origines au XVe siècle* (Paris, 1941). Also of great value is vol. VII of the *Peuples et civilisations* series, and the scholarly works of B. Spuler, *Die Goldene Horde: die Mongolen in Russland, 1225–1502* (Leipzig, 1943), vol. 2 of E. Haenisch and H. Schaed, eds., *Das Mongolischen Weltreich; Quellen und Forschungen*, and his *Geschichte der islamischen Lander*, II, *Die Mongolenzeit* (*Handbuch der Orientalistik*, VI, Leiden, 1953).

The missionary journeys of the Franciscans and Dominicans are described, in addition to their own narratives, in the following works: A. Moule, *Christians in China before the Year 1553* (London, 1930); P. Schlager, *Mongolenfahrten der Franziskaner* (Trier, 1911); and P. Altaner, *Die Dominikanermissionen des 13ten Jahrhunderts* (Habelschwerdt, 1924).

What is apparently a definite disproof of the veracity of the most popular work of travel of this period is given in F. Warner, *The Buke of John Maundeville*, pub. for the Roxburghe Club (Westminster, 1889).

Chapter Ten

THE EASTERN FRONTIERS OF EUROPE

Some references for the history of Bohemia have been given under chapters VI and VII of this bibliography, and for the advance of the Mongols under chapter IX. It remains to mention a few of the leading works on the early modern history of the group of countries that lie along the eastern boundary of Europe, of the declining Eastern Empire and the rising state of the Ottoman Turks. Histories of these countries in English are few and those written in the native languages are largely unavailable to scholars of other nations. This leaves for the most part only a literature in German and French to be listed here. References to works in Czech, Hungarian, and Polish may be found in some fullness in the bibliographies of the general works in the introductory section, but must in the main be sought in journals devoted to the history of Eastern Europe.

For the general history of the area C. Diehl et al., *L'Europe orientale de 1081 à 1453* (Paris, 1945), vol. IX, pt. 1, in the Glotz *Histoire générale*, is useful. Some other helpful works are O. Halecki, *Borderlands of Civilization: a History of East Central Europe* (New York, 1952); the series of *Dumbarton Oaks Papers* on Slavic and East European history.

K. Hampe, *Der Żug nach dem Osten,* 3rd ed. (Leipzig, 1935), is still an admirable account of German expansion to the East, while another work is R. Kötzschke and W. Ebert, *Geschichte der ostdeutschen Kolonisation,* 2nd ed. (Leipzig, 1944). For the Teutonic Order, see the excellent work of E. Casper, *Hermann von Salza und die Gründung des Deutschordenstaates in Preussen* (Tübingen, 1924). Indispensable for the student of the Order is the collection of E. Joachim and W. Hubatsch, eds., *Regesta Historico-Diplomatica Ordonis S. Mariae Theutonicorum, 1198–1529,* vol. I, parts I and II (Göttingen, 1948–). Also of use are the works of C. Krollmann, *The Teutonic Order in Prussia,* Eng. tr. (Elbing, 1938), and P. Tumler, *Der Deutsch Orden im Werden, Wachsen und Wirken bis 1400* (Montreal, 1955), with a recent bibliography.

For Poland and neighboring lands, T. Schiemann, *Russland, Polen und Livland bis ins 17 Jahrhundert,* 2 vols. (Berlin, 1886–87), is still good. See also *The Cambridge History of Poland*, 2 vols. (Cambridge, 1951), and O. Halecki, *A History of Poland* (New York, 1956); and the interesting articles of P. Skivarczynski, "The Problem of Feudalism in Poland up to the beginning of the Sixteenth Century," *Slavic and East European Review* (June, 1956), and of C. Backvis, "Rapports entre la Pologne et l'Occident, tout particulièrement l'Empire Germanique," *Revue belge de philologie et d'histoire,* vol. XXXI, no. 1 (1953), on those two important phases of that country's history.

For Hungary, see E. Sayous, *Histoire générale des Hongrois* (Paris, 1900); G. Bratianu, "Byzance et la Hongrie," *Revue historique du sud-est européen,* vol. XXII (1945); C. Dawson, "Hungarian Middle Ages," *The Hungarian Quarterly* (Winter, 1939–40); and P. Kosary, *A History of Hungary* (New

York, 1941). For Serbia, Bulgaria, and Rumania, see C. Jireček, *Geschichte der Serben,* 2 vols. (Gotha, 1911–18), his *Geschichte der Bulgaren* (Vienna, 1876), and his *Staat und Gesellschaft im mittelalterlichen Serbien* (Vienna, 1912); H. Temperley, *A History of Serbia* (London, 1917); N. Iorga, *Geschichte des rumänischen Volkes* (Gotha, 1905); and R. W. Seton-Watson, *History of the Roumanians* (Cambridge, 1934). The book of L. Eisenmann, *La civilisation serbe au moyen âge* (Paris, 1930), is a translation of that part of the abovementioned work of Jireček which deals with Serbian culture in the thirteenth and fourteenth centuries. V. N. Slatarski, *Geschichte der Bulgaren* (Leipzig, 1918), is the work of a leading Bulgarian authority, and serves as a correction to Jiriček in many respects for the period prior to 1396. See also E. Haumont, *La formation de la Yougoslavie* (Paris, 1930), and A. Gegaj, *L'Albanie et l'invasion turque au XVe siècle* (Paris, 1937). There is, of course, much concerning the history of these states in works on the Eastern Empire and the advance of the Ottomans.

For Russia, see the text of M. Florinsky, *Russia: a History and an Interpretation,* 2 vols. (New York, 1953). A good account in English is the great and original work of V. Kliuchevskii, *A History of Russia,* 5 vols., Eng. tr. (London, 1911–31). Consult also the excellent account of K. Stählin, *Geschichte Russlands,* 5 vols. (Leipzig, 1923–39), and the recent studies of G. Vernadsky and M. Karpovich, *A History of Russia, vol. III, The Mongols and Russia* (New Haven, 1953), and A. Eck, *Le moyen âge russe* (Paris, 1933), which brings together a mass of monographic writing in Russian and other languages.

For the Eastern Empire in its later days, A. Vasiliev, *History of the Byzantine Empire,* 2nd rev. ed. (Madison, 1952), is convenient and scholarly, with a good bibliography. Authoritative is the recent study of G. Ostrogorskii, *History of the Byzantine State* (Oxford, 1956). Still of value are L. Brehier, *Le monde byzantin,* 3 vols. (Paris, 1947–50), the latter in the series *L'évolution de l'humanité,* H. Berr ed.; and the recently translated work of C. Diehl, *Byzantium: Greatness and Decline* (New Brunswick, N.J., 1957). Also of interest is the article of P. Charanis, "Economic Factors in the Decline of the Byzantine Empire," *Journal of Economic History* (Fall, 1953). On the relations of the East with the West and the Crusades, see M. Silberschmidt, *Das orientalische Problem zur Zeit der Entstehung des Türkischen Reiches* (Leipzig, 1923); W. Norden, *Das Papsttum und Byzanz, die Trennung der beiden Mächte und das Problem ihrer Wiedervereinigung bis 1453* (Berlin, 1903); N. Iorga, *Philippe de Mézières et la Croisade au XVe siècle* (Paris, 1896); O. Halecki, *The Crusade of Varna: Discussion of Controversial Problems* (New York, 1943); F. Pall, "Les croisades en Orient au bas moyen âge," *Revue historique du sud-est européen* (Feb., 1942); and A. Suryal Atiya, *The Crusade in the Later Middle Ages* (London, 1938), and *The Crusade of Nicopolis* (London, 1934), an excellent study of that disaster.

The process of decay of the old Eastern Empire facilitated the rise of the Ottoman Turks. For their history the basic works are still J. v. Hammer-Purgstall, *Geschichte des osmanischen Reiches,* 2nd ed., 4 vols. (Budapest, 1834–36), and J. Zinkeisen, *Geschichte des osmanischen Reiches in Europa,* 7 vols. (Gotha, 1840–63), both of which rest on extensive manuscript and archival sources and have served as the basis for shorter works like E. Creasy, *History of the Ottoman Turks,* rev. ed., 2 vols. (London, 1878), A. de La Jonquière, *Histoire de l'empire ottoman,* rev. ed., 2 vols. (Paris, 1914), and Lord Eversley and V. Chirol, *The Turkish Empire,* 2nd ed. (London, 1923). A later comprehensive history is that of N. Iorga, *Geschichte des osmanischen Reiches,* 5 vols. (Gotha, 1908–1913). The baffling problem of the origins of the Ottoman state has been studied in detail by H. Gibbons, *The Foundation of the Ottoman Empire, 1300–1403* (Oxford, 1916); W. Langer and R. Blake, "The Rise of the Ottoman Turks and Its Historical Background," *American Historical Review,* XXXVII (April, 1932); Mehmed Fuad Köprülü, *Origines de l'empire ottoman* (Paris, 1935); P. Wittek, *The Rise of the Ottoman Empire* (London, 1938); and G. Arnakis, *The Early Ottomans* (in Greek, with English summary, Athens, 1947). Important monographic studies are A. Alderson, *The Structure of the Ottoman Dynasty* (Oxford, 1956); D. Vaughan, *Europe and the Turk, 1350–1700* (Liverpool, 1954); F. Hasluck, *Christianity and Islam under the Sultans* (Oxford, 1929); H. Inalcik, "Ottoman Methods of Conquest," *Studia Islamica,* II (1954); P. Wittek, "De la défaite d'Ankara a la prise de Constantinople," *Revue d'études islamiques* (1938); G. Roloff, "Die Schlacht bei Angora, 1402," *Historische Zeitschrift,* CLXI (1939); G. Beckmann, *Der Kampf Kaiser Sigmunds gegen die werdende Weltmacht der Osmanen, 1392–1437* (Gotha, 1902); and L. Kupelweiser, *Die Kämpfe Ungarns mit den Osmanen bis zur Schlacht bei Mohacs* (Vienna, 1899).

The best secondary accounts of the siege and fall of Constantinople in 1453 are still those of E. Pears, *The Destruction of the Greek Empire and the Story of the Capture of Constantinople by the Turks* (New York, 1903), and G. Schlumberger, *Le siège, la prise et le sac de Constantinople par les Turcs,* 6th ed. (Paris, 1923). See also the essay of G. Jäschke, "Die Eroberung Konstantinopels in Jahre 1453 und ihre Bedeutung für Geschichte und Gegenwart," *Die Welt als Geschichte* (1953). For biographies of the two contestants, see C. Mijatovich, *Constantine, the Last Emperor of the Greeks* (London, 1882), and the imposing study of F. Babinger, *Mehmed der Eroberer und seine Zeit* (Munich, 1953, French tr. Paris, 1954).

INDEX

73 12 11 10 9

Revised January, 1970

harper torchbooks

American Studies: General

HENRY ADAMS Degradation of the Democratic Dogma. ‡ *Introduction by Charles Hirschfeld.* TB/1450

LOUIS D. BRANDEIS: Other People's Money, *and How the Bankers Use It. Ed. with Intro. by Richard M. Abrams* TB/3081

HENRY STEELE COMMAGER, Ed.: The Struggle for Racial Equality TB/1300

CARL N. DEGLER: Out of Our Past: *The Forces that Shaped Modern America* CN/2

CARL N. DEGLER, Ed.: Pivotal Interpretations of American History Vol. I TB/1240; Vol. II TB/1241

A. S. EISENSTADT, Ed.: The Craft of American History: *Selected Essays* Vol. I TB/1255; Vol. II TB/1256

LAWRENCE H. FUCHS, Ed.: American Ethnic Politics TB/1368

MARCUS LEE HANSEN: The Atlantic Migration: 1607-1860. *Edited by Arthur M. Schlesinger. Introduction by Oscar Handlin* TB/1052

MARCUS LEE HANSEN: The Immigrant in American History. *Edited with a Foreword by Arthur M. Schlesinger* TB/1120

ROBERT L. HEILBRONER: The Limits of American Capitalism TB/1305

JOHN HIGHAM, Ed.: The Reconstruction of American History TB/1068

ROBERT H. JACKSON: The Supreme Court in the American System of Government TB/1106

JOHN F. KENNEDY: A Nation of Immigrants. *Illus. Revised and Enlarged. Introduction by Robert F. Kennedy* TB/1118

LEONARD W. LEVY, Ed.: American Constitutional Law: *Historical Essays* TB/1285

LEONARD W. LEVY, Ed.: Judicial Review and the Supreme Court TB/1296

LEONARD W. LEVY: The Law of the Commonwealth and Chief Justice Shaw: *The Evolution of American Law, 1830-1860* TB/1309

GORDON K. LEWIS: Puerto Rico: *Freedom and Power in the Caribbean. Abridged edition* TB/1371

RICHARD B. MORRIS: Fair Trial: *Fourteen Who Stood Accused, from Anne Hutchinson to Alger Hiss* TB/1335

GUNNAR MYRDAL: An American Dilemma: *The Negro Problem and Modern Democracy. Introduction by the Author.* Vol. I TB/1443; Vol. II TB/1444

GILBERT OSOFSKY, Ed.: The Burden of Race: *A Documentary History of Negro-White Relations in America* TB/1405

CONYERS READ, Ed.: The Constitution Reconsidered. *Revised Edition. Preface by Richrd B. Morris* TB/1384

ARNOLD ROSE: The Negro in America: *The Condensed Version of Gunnar Myrdal's* An American Dilemma. *Second Edition* TB/3048

JOHN E. SMITH: Themes in American Philosophy: *Purpose, Experience and Community* TB/1466

WILLIAM R. TAYLOR: Cavalier and Yankee: *The Old South and American National Character* TB/1474

American Studies: Colonial

BERNARD BAILYN: The New England Merchants in the Seventeenth Century TB/1149

ROBERT E. BROWN: Middle-Class Democracy and Revolution in Massachusetts, 1691–1780. *New Introduction by Author* TB/1413

JOSEPH CHARLES: The Origins of the American Party System TB/1049

HENRY STEELE COMMAGER & ELMO GIORDANETTI, Eds.: Was America a Mistake? *An Eighteenth Century Controversy* TB/1329

WESLEY FRANK CRAVEN: The Colonies in Transition: 1660-1712† TB/3084

CHARLES GIBSON: Spain in America † TB/3077

CHARLES GIBSON, Ed.: The Spanish Tradition in America + HR/1351

LAWRENCE HENRY GIPSON: The Coming of the Revolution: 1763-1775. † *Illus.* TB/3007

JACK P. GREENE, Ed.: Great Britain and the American Colonies: 1606-1763. + *Introduction by the Author* HR/1477

AUBREY C. LAND, Ed.: Bases of the Plantation Society + HR/1429

JOHN LANKFORD, Ed.: Captain John Smith's America: *Selections* from his Writings ‡ TB/3078

LEONARD W. LEVY: Freedom of Speech and Press in Early American History: *Legacy of Suppression* TB/1109

PERRY MILLER: Errand Into the Wilderness TB/1139

PERRY MILLER T. H. JOHNSON, Eds.: The Puritans: *A Sourcebook of Their Writings* Vol. I TB/1093; Vol. II TB/1094

† The New American Nation Series, edited by Henry Steele Commager and Richard B. Morris.
‡ American Perspectives series, edited by Bernard Wishy and William E. Leuchtenburg.
a History of Europe series, edited by J. H. Plumb.
§ The Library of Religion and Culture, edited by Benjamin Nelson.
‖ Researches in the Social, Cultural, and Behavioral Sciences, edited by Benjamin Nelson.
Σ Harper Modern Science Series, edited by James A. Newman.
° Not for sale in Canada.
+ Documentary History of the United States series, edited by Richard B. Morris.
# Documentary History of Western Civilization series, edited by Eugene C. Black and Leonard W. Levy.
Λ The Economic History of the United States series, edited by Henry David et al.
¶ European Perspectives series, edited by Eugene C. Black.
** Contemporary Essays series, edited by Leonard W. Levy.
* The Stratum Series, edited by John Hale.

EDMUND S. MORGAN: The Puritan Family: *Religion and Domestic Relations in Seventeenth Century New England* TB/1227

RICHARD B. MORRIS: Government and Labor in Early America TB/1244

WALLACE NOTESTEIN: The English People on the Eve of Colonization: 1603-1630. † *Illus.* TB/3006

FRANCIS PARKMAN: The Seven Years War: *A Narrative Taken from* Montcalm and Wolfe, The Conspiracy of Pontiac, *and* A Half-Century of Conflict. *Edited by John H. McCallum* TB/3083

LOUIS B. WRIGHT: The Cultural Life of the American Colonies: 1607-1763. † *Illus.* TB/3005

YVES F. ZOLTVANY, Ed.: The French Tradition in America + HR/1425

American Studies: The Revolution to 1860

JOHN R. ALDEN: The American Revolution: 1775-1783. † *Illus.* TB/3011

MAX BELOFF, Ed.: The Debate on the American Revolution, 1761-1783: *A Sourcebook* TB/1225

RAY A. BILLINGTON: The Far Western Frontier: 1830-1860. † *Illus.* TB/3012

STUART BRUCHEY: The Roots of American Economic Growth, 1607-1861: *An Essay in Social Causation. New Introduction by the Author.* TB/1350

WHITNEY R. CROSS: The Burned-Over District: *The Social and Intellectual History of Enthusiastic Religion in Western New York, 1800-1850* TB/1242

NOBLE E. CUNNINGHAM, JR., Ed.: The Early Republic, 1789-1828 + HR/1394

GEORGE DANGERFIELD: The Awakening of American Nationalism, 1815-1828. † *Illus.* TB/3061

CLEMENT EATON: The Freedom-of-Thought Struggle in the Old South. *Revised and Enlarged. Illus.* TB/1150

CLEMENT EATON: The Growth of Southern Civilization, 1790-1860. † *Illus.* TB/3040

ROBERT H. FERRELL, Ed.: Foundations of American Diplomacy, 1775-1872 HR/1393

LOUIS FILLER: The Crusade against Slavery: 1830-1860. † *Illus.* TB/3029

DAVID H. FISCHER: The Revolution of American Conservatism: *The Federalist Party in the Era of Jeffersonian Democracy* TB/1449

WILLIAM W. FREEHLING, Ed.: The Nullification Era: *A Documentary Record* ‡ TB/3079

WILLIM W. FREEHLING: Prelude to Civil War: *The Nullification Controversy in South Carolina, 1816-1836* TB/1359

PAUL W. GATES: The Farmer's Age: *Agriculture, 1815-1860* Δ TB/1398

FELIX GILBERT: The Beginnings of American Foreign Policy: *To the Farewell Address* TB/1200

ALEXANDER HAMILTON: The Reports of Alexander Hamilton. ‡ *Edited by Jacob E. Cooke* TB/3060

THOMAS JEFFERSON: Notes on the State of Virginia. ‡ *Edited by Thomas P. Abernethy* TB/3052

FORREST MCDONALD, Ed.: Confederation and Constitution, 1781-1789 + HR/1396

BERNARD MAYO: Myths and Men: *Patrick Henry, George Washington, Thomas Jefferson* TB/1108

JOHN C. MILLER: Alexander Hamilton and the Growth of the New Nation TB/3057

JOHN C. MILLER: The Federalist Era: 1789-1801. † *Illus.* TB/3027

RICHARD B. MORRIS, Ed.: Alexander Hamilton and the Founding of the Nation. *New Introduction by the Editor* TB/1448

RICHARD B. MORRIS: The American Revolution Reconsidered TB/1363

CURTIS P. NETTELS: The Emergence of a National Economy, 1775-1815 Δ TB/1438

DOUGLASS C. NORTH & ROBERT PAUL THOMAS, Eds.: *The Growth of the American Economy to 1860* + HR/1352

R. B. NYE: The Cultural Life of the New Nation: 1776-1830. † *Illus.* TB/3026

GILBERT OSOFSKY, Ed.: Puttin' On Ole Massa: *The Slave Narratives of Henry Bibb, William Wells Brown, and Solomon Northup* ‡ TB/1432

JAMES PARTON: The Presidency of Andrew Jackson. *From Volume III of the* Life of Andrew Jackson. *Ed. with Intro. by Robert V. Remini* TB/3080

FRANCIS S. PHILBRICK: The Rise of the West, 1754-1830. † *Illus.* TB/3067

MARSHALL SMELSER: The Democratic Republic, 1801-1815 † TB/1406

TIMOTHY L. SMITH: Revivalism and Social Reform: *American Protestantism on the Eve of the Civil War* TB/1229

JACK M. SOSIN, Ed.: The Opening of the West + HR/1424

GEORGE ROGERS TAYLOR: The Transportation Revolution, 1815-1860 Δ TB/1347

A. F. TYLER: Freedom's Ferment: *Phases of American Social History from the Revolution to the Outbreak of the Civil War. Illus.* TB/1074

GLYNDON G. VAN DEUSEN: The Jacksonian Era: 1828-1848. † *Illus.* TB/3028

LOUIS B. WRIGHT: Culture on the Moving Frontier TB/1053

American Studies: The Civil War to 1900

W. R. BROCK: An American Crisis: *Congress and Reconstruction, 1865-67* ° TB/1283

T. C. COCHRAN & WILLIAM MILLER: The Age of Enterprise: *A Social History of Industrial America* TB/1054

W. A. DUNNING: Reconstruction, Political and Economic: 1865-1877 TB/1073

HAROLD U. FAULKNER: Politics, Reform and Expansion: 1890-1900. † *Illus.* TB/3020

GEORGE M. FREDRICKSON: The Inner Civil War: *Northern Intellectuals and the Crisis of the Union* TB/1358

JOHN A. GARRATY: The New Commonwealth, 1877-1890 † TB/1410

JOHN A. GARRATY, Ed.: The Transformation of American Society, 1870-1890 + HR/1395

HELEN HUNT JACKSON: A Century of Dishonor: *The Early Crusade for Indian Reform.* † *Edited by Andrew F. Rolle* TB/3063

ALBERT D. KIRWAN: Revolt of the Rednecks: *Mississippi Politics, 1876-1925* TB/1199

ARTHUR MANN: Yankee Reforms in the Urban Age: *Social Reform in Boston, 1800-1900* TB/1247

ARNOLD M. PAUL: Conservative Crisis and the Rule of Law: *Attitudes of Bar and Bench, 1887-1895. New Introduction by Author* TB/1415

JAMES S. PIKE: The Prostrate State: *South Carolina under Negro Government.* ‡ *Intro. by Robert F. Durden* TB/3085

WHITELAW REID: After the War: *A Tour of the Southern States, 1865-1866.* ‡ *Edited by C. Vann Woodward* TB/3066

FRED A. SHANNON: The Farmer's Last Frontier: *Agriculture, 1860-1897* TB/1348

VERNON LANE WHARTON: The Negro in Mississippi, 1865-1890 TB/1178

American Studies: The Twentieth Century

RICHARD M. ABRAMS, Ed.: The Issues of the Populist and Progressive Eras, 1892-1912 + HR/1428

RAY STANNARD BAKER: Following the Color Line: *American Negro Citizenship in Progressive Era. ‡ Edited by Dewey W. Grantham, Jr. Illus.* TB/3053

RANDOLPH S. BOURNE: War and the Intellectuals: *Collected Essays, 1915-1919. ‡ Edited by Carl Resek* TB/3043

A. RUSSELL BUCHANAN: The United States and World War II. † *Illus.* Vol. I TB/3044; Vol. II TB/3045

THOMAS C. COCHRAN: The American Business System: *A Historical Perspective, 1900-1955* TB/1080

FOSTER RHEA DULLES: America's Rise to World Power: 1898-1954. † *Illus.* TB/3021

JEAN-BAPTISTE DUROSELLE: From Wilson to Roosevelt: *Foreign Policy of the United States, 1913-1945. Trans. by Nancy Lyman Roelker* TB/1370

HAROLD U. FAULKNER: The Decline of Laissez Faire, 1897-1917 TB/1397

JOHN D. HICKS: Republican Ascendancy: 1921-1933. † *Illus.* TB/3041

ROBERT HUNTER: Poverty: *Social Conscience in the Progressive Era. ‡ Edited by Peter d'A. Jones* TB/3065

WILLIAM E. LEUCHTENBURG: Franklin D. Roosevelt and the New Deal: 1932-1940. † *Illus.* TB/3025

WILLIAM E. LEUCHTENBURG, Ed.: The New Deal: *A Documentary History* + HR/1354

ARTHUR S. LINK: Woodrow Wilson and the Progressive Era: 1910-1917. † *Illus.* TB/3023

BROADUS MITCHELL: Depression Decade: *From New Era through New Deal, 1929-1941* ^ TB/1439

GEORGE E. MOWRY: The Era of Theodore Roosevelt and the Birth of Modern America: 1900-1912. † *Illus.* TB/3022

WILLIAM PRESTON, JR.: Aliens and Dissenters: *Federal Suppression of Radicals, 1903-1933* TB/1287

WALTER RAUSCHENBUSCH: Christianity and the Social Crisis. ‡ *Edited by Robert D. Cross* TB/3059

GEORGE SOULE: Prosperity Decade: *From War to Depression, 1917-1929* Δ TB/1349

GEORGE B. TINDALL, Ed.: A Populist Reader: *Selections from the Works of American Populist Leaders* TB/3069

TWELVE SOUTHERNERS: I'll Take My Stand: *The South and the Agrarian Tradition. Intro. by Louis D. Rubin, Jr.; Biographical Essays by Virginia Rock* TB/1072

Art, Art History, Aesthetics

CREIGHTON GILBERT, Ed.: Renaissance Art ** *Illus.* TB/1465

EMILE MALE: The Gothic Image: *Religious Art in France of the Thirteenth Century. § 190* illus. TB/344

MILLARD MEISS: Painting in Florence and Siena After the Black Death: *The Arts, Religion and Society in the Mid-Fourteenth Century. 169 illus.* TB/1148

ERWIN PANOFSKY: Renaissance and Renascences in Western Art. *Illus.* TB/1447

ERWIN PANOFSKY: Studies in Iconology: *Humanistic Themes in the Art of the Renaissance. 180 illus.* TB/1077

JEAN SEZNEC: The Survival of the Pagan Gods: *The Mythological Tradition and Its Place in Renaissance Humanism and Art. 108 illus.* TB/2004

OTTO VON SIMSON: The Gothic Cathedral: *Origins of Gothic Architecture and the Medieval Concept of Order. 58 illus.* TB/2018

HEINRICH ZIMMER: Myths and Symbols in Indian Art and Civilization. *70 illus.* TB/2005

Asian Studies

WOLFGANG FRANKE: China and the West: *The Cultural Encounter, 13th to 20th Centuries. Trans. by R. A. Wilson* TB/1326

L. CARRINGTON GOODRICH: A Short History of the Chinese People. *Illus.* TB/3015

DAN N. JACOBS, Ed.: The New Communist Manifesto and Related Documents. *3rd revised edn.* TB/1078

DAN N. JACOBS & HANS H. BAERWALD, Eds.: Chinese Communism: *Selected Documents* TB/3031

BENJAMIN I. SCHWARTZ: Chinese Communism and the Rise of Mao TB/1308

BENJAMIN I. SCHWARTZ: In Search of Wealth and Power: *Yen Fu and the West* TB/1422

Economics & Economic History

C. E. BLACK: The Dynamics of Modernization: *A Study in Comparative History* TB/1321

STUART BRUCHEY: The Roots of American Economic Growth, 1607-1861: *An Essay in Social Causation. New Introduction by the Author.* TB/1350

GILBERT BURCK & EDITORS OF *Fortune:* The Computer Age: *And its Potential for Management* TB/1179

JOHN ELLIOTT CAIRNES: The Slave Power. ‡ *Edited with Introduction by Harold D. Woodman* TB/1433

SHEPARD B. CLOUGH, THOMAS MOODIE & CAROL MOODIE, Eds.: Economic History of Europe: *Twentieth Century #* HR/1388

THOMAS C. COCHRAN: The American Business System: *A Historical Perspective, 1900-1955* TB/1180

ROBERT A. DAHL & CHARLES E. LINDBLOM: Politics, Economics, and Welfare: *Planning and Politico-Economic Systems Resolved into Basic Social Processes* TB/3037

PETER F. DRUCKER: The New Society: *The Anatomy of Industrial Order* TB/1082

HAROLD U. FAULKNER: The Decline of Laissez Faire, 1897-1917 Δ TB/1397

PAUL W. GATES: The Farmer's Age: *Agriculture, 1815-1860* Δ TB/1398

WILLIAM GREENLEAF, Ed.: American Economic Development Since 1860 + HR/1353

J. L. & BARBARA HAMMOND: The Rise of Modern Industry. || *Introduction by R. M. Hartwell* TB/1417

ROBERT L. HEILBRONER: The Future as History: *The Historic Currents of Our Time and the Direction in Which They Are Taking America* TB/1386

ROBERT L. HEILBRONER: The Great Ascent: *The Struggle for Economic Development in Our Time* TB/3030

FRANK H. KNIGHT: The Economic Organization TB/1214

DAVID S. LANDES: Bankers and Pashas: *International Finance and Economic Imperialism in Egypt. New Preface by the Author* TB/1412

ROBERT LATOUCHE: The Birth of Western Economy: *Economic Aspects of the Dark Ages* TB/1290

W. ARTHUR LEWIS: Economic Survey, 1919-1939 TB/1446

W. ARTHUR LEWIS: The Principles of Economic Planning. *New Introduction by the Author°* TB/1436

ROBERT GREEN MC CLOSKEY: American Conservatism in the Age of Enterprise TB/1137

PAUL MANTOUX: The Industrial Revolution in the Eighteenth Century: *An Outline of the Beginnings of the Modern Factory System in England°* TB/1079

WILLIAM MILLER, Ed.: Men in Business: *Essays on the Historical Role of the Entrepreneur* TB/1081

GUNNAR MYRDAL: An International Economy. *New Introduction by the Author* TB/1445

RICHARD S. WECKSTEIN, Ed.: Expansion of World Trade and the Growth of National Economies ** TB/1373

Historiography and History of Ideas

HERSCHEL BAKER: The Image of Man: *A Study of the Idea of Human Dignity in Classical Antiquity, the Middle Ages, and the Renaissance* TB/1047

J. BRONOWSKI & BRUCE MAZLISH: The Western Intellectual Tradition: *From Leonardo to Hegel* TB/3001

EDMUND BURKE: On Revolution. Ed. by Robert A. Smith TB/1401

WILHELM DILTHEY: Pattern and Meaning in History: *Thoughts on History and Society.° Edited with an Intro. by H. P. Rickman* TB/1075

ALEXANDER GRAY: The Socialist Tradition: *Moses to Lenin °* TB/1375

J. H. HEXTER: More's Utopia: *The Biography of an Idea. Epilogue by the Author* TB/1195

H. STUART HUGHES: History as Art and as Science: *Twin Vistas on the Past* TB/1207

ARTHUR O. LOVEJOY: The Great Chain of Being: *A Study of the History of an Idea* TB/1009

JOSE ORTEGA Y GASSET: The Modern Theme. *Introduction by Jose Ferrater Mora* TB/1038

RICHARD H. POPKIN: The History of Scepticism from Erasmus to Descartes. *Revised Edition* TB/1391

G. J. RENIER: History: *Its Purpose and Method* TB/1209

MASSIMO SALVADORI, Ed.: Modern Socialism # HR/1374

BRUNO SNELL: The Discovery of the Mind: *The Greek Origins of European Thought* TB/1018

W. WARREN WAGER, ed.: European Intellectual History Since Darwin and Marx TB/1297

W. H. WALSH: Philosophy of History: In *Introduction* TB/1020

History: General

HANS KOHN: The Age of Nationalism: *The First Era of Global History* TB/1380

BERNARD LEWIS: The Arabs in History TB/1029

BERNARD LEWIS: The Middle East and the West ° TB/1274

History: Ancient

A. ANDREWS: The Greek Tyrants TB/1103

ERNST LUDWIG EHRLICH: A Concise History of Israel: *From the Earliest Times to the Destruction of the Temple in A.D. 70°* TB/128

THEODOR H. GASTER: Thespis: *Ritual Myth and Drama in the Ancient Near East* TB/1281

MICHAEL GRANT: Ancient History ° TB/1190

A. H. M. JONES, Ed.: A History of Rome through the Fifgth Century # *Vol. I: The Republic* HR/1364
Vol. II The Empire: HR/1460

SAMUEL NOAH KRAMER: Sumerian Mythology TB/1055

NAPHTALI LEWIS & MEYER REINHOLD, Eds.: Roman Civilization *Vol. I: The Republic* TB/1231
Vol. II: The Empire TB/1232

History: Medieval

MARSHALL W. BALDWIN, Ed.: Christianity Through the 13th Century # HR/1468

MARC BLOCH: Land and Work in Medieval Europe. *Translated by J. E. Anderson* TB/1452

HELEN CAM: England Before Elizabeth TB/1026

NORMAN COHN: The Pursuit of the Millennium: *Revolutionary Messianism in Medieval and Reformation Europe* TB/1037

G. G. COULTON: Medieval Village, Manor, and Monastery HR/1022

HEINRICH FICHTENAU: The Carolingian Empire: *The Age of Charlemagne. Translated with an Introduction by Peter Munz* TB/1142

GALBERT OF BRUGES: The Murder of Charles the Good: *A Contemporary Record of Revolutionary Change in 12th Century Flanders. Translated with an Introduction by James Bruce Ross* TB/1311

F. L. GANSHOF: Feudalism TB/1058

F. L. GANSHOF: The Middle Ages: *A History of International Relations. Translated by Rêmy Hall* TB/1411

DENYS HAY: The Medieval Centuries ° TB/1192

DAVID HERLIHY, Ed.: Medieval Culture and Socitey # HR/1340

J. M. HUSSEY: The Byzantine World TB/1057

ROBERT LATOUCHE: The Birth of Western Economy: *Economic Aspects of the Dark Ages °* TB/1290

HENRY CHARLES LEA: The Inquisition of the Middle Ages. || *Introduction by Walter Ullmann* TB/1456

FERDINARD LOT: The End of the Ancient World and the Beginnings of the Middle Ages. *Introduction by Glanville Downey* TB/1044

H. R. LOYN: The Norman Conquest TB/1457

GUIBERT DE NOGENT: Self and Society in Medieval France: *The Memoirs of Guilbert de Nogent.* || Edited by John F. Benton TB/1471

MARSILIUS OF PADUA: The Defender of Peace. *The* Defensor Pacis. *Translated with an Introduction by Alan Gewirth* TB/1310

CHARLES PETET-DUTAILLIS: The Feudal Monarchy in France and England: *From the Tenth to the Thirteenth Century °* TB/1165

STEVEN RUNCIMAN: A History of the Crusades Vol. I: *The First Crusade and the Foundation of the Kingdom of Jerusalem. Illus.* TB/1143
Vol. II: *The Kingdom of Jerusalem and the Frankish East 1100-1187. Illus.* TB/1243
Vol. III: *The Kingdom of Acre and the Later Crusades. Illus.* TB/1298

J. M. WALLACE-HADRILL: The Barbarian West: *The Early Middle Ages, A.D. 400-1000* TB/1061

History: Renaissance & Reformation

JACOB BURCKHARDT: The Civilization of the Renaissance in Italy. *Introduction by Benjamin Nelson and Charles Trinkaus. Illus.* Vol. I TB/40; Vol. II TB/41

JOHN CALVIN & JACOPO SADOLETO: A Reformation Debate. *Edited by John C. Olin* TB/1239

FEDERICO CHABOD: Machiavelli and the Renaissance TB/1193

THOMAS CROMWELL: Thomas Cromwell. *Selected Letters on Church and Commonwealth, 1523-1540.* ¶ *Ed. with an Intro. by Arthur J. Slavin* TB/1462

R. TREVOR DAVIES: The Golden Century of Spain, 1501-1621 ° TB/1194

J. H. ELLIOTT: Europe Divided, 1559-1598 *a* ° TB/1414

G. R. ELTON: Reformation Europe, 1517-1559 ° *a* TB/1270

DESIDERIUS ERASMUS: Christian Humanism and the Reformation: *Selected Writings. Edited and Translated by John C. Olin* TB/1166

DESIDERIUS ERASMUS: Erasmus and His Age: *Selected Letters. Edited with an Introduction by Hans J. Hillerbrand. Translated by Marcus A. Haworth* TB/1461

WALLACE K. FERGUSON et al.: Facets of the Renaissance TB/1098

WALLACE K. FERGUSON et al.: The Renaissance: *Six Essays. Illus.* TB/1084

FRANCESCO GUICCIARDINI: History of Florence. *Translated with an Introduction and Notes by Mario Domandi* TB/1470

WERNER L. GUNDERSHEIMER, Ed.: French Humanism, 1470-1600. * *Illus.* TB/1473

MARIE BOAS HALL, Ed.: Nature and Nature's Laws: *Documents of the Scientific Revolution #* HR/1420

HANS J. HILLERBRAND, Ed., The Protestant Reformation HR/1342

JOHAN HUIZINGA: Erasmus and the Age of Reformation. *Illus.* TB/19

JOEL HURSTFIELD: The Elizabethan Nation TB/1312

JOEL HURSTFIELD, Ed.: The Reformation Crisis TB/1267

PAUL OSKAR KRISTELLER: Renaissance Thought: *The Classic, Scholastic, and Humanist Strains* TB/1048

PAUL OSKAR KRISTELLER: Renaissance Thought II: *Papers on Humanism and the Arts* TB/1163

PAUL O. KRISTELLER & PHILIP P. WIENER, Eds.: Renaissance Essays TB/1392

DAVID LITTLE: Religion, Order and Law: *A Study in Pre-Revolutionary England.* § *Preface by R. Bellah* TB/1418

NICCOLO MACHIAVELLI: History of Florence and of the Affairs of Italy: *From the Earliest Times to the Death of Lorenzo the Magnificent. Introduction by Felix Gilbert* TB/1027

ALFRED VON MARTIN: Sociology of the Renaissance. ° *Introduction by W. K. Ferguson* TB/1099

GARRETT MATTINGLY et al.: Renaissance Profiles. *Edited by J. H. Plumb* TB/1162

J. E. NEALE: The Age of Catherine de Medici ° TB/1085

J. H. PARRY: The Establishment of the European Hegemony: 1415-1715: *Trade and Exploration in the Age of the Renaissance* TB/1045

J. H. PARRY, Ed.: The European Reconnaissance: *Selected Documents #* HR/1345

BUONACCORSO PITTI & GREGORIO DATI: Two Memoirs of Renaissance Florence: *The Diaries of Buonaccorso Pitti and Gregorio Dati. Edited with Intro. by Gene Brucker. Trans. by Julia Martines* TB/1333

J. H. PLUMB: The Italian Renaissance: *A Concise Survey of Its History and Culture* TB/1161

A. F. POLLARD: Henry VIII. *Introduction by A. G. Dickens.* ° TB/1249

RICHARD H. POPKIN: The History of Scepticism from Erasmus to Descartes TB/1391

PAOLO ROSSI: Philosophy, Technology, and the Arts, in the Early Modern Era 1400-1700. || *Edited by Benjamin Nelson. Translated by Salvator Attanasio* TB/1458

FERDINAND SCHEVILL: The Medici. *Illus.* TB/1010

FERDINAND SCHEVILL: Medieval and Renaissance Florence. *Illus. Vol. I: Medieval Florence* TB/1090 *Vol. II: The Coming of Humanism and the Age of the Medici* TB/1091

R. H. TAWNEY: The Agrarian Problem in the Sixteenth Century. *Intro. by Lawrence Stone* TB/1315

H. R. TREVOR-ROPER: The European Witch-craze of the Sixteenth and Seventeenth Centuries and Other Essays ° TB/1416

VESPASIANO: Rennaissance Princes, Popes, and *XVth Century: The Vespasiano Memoirs. Introduction by Myron P. Gilmore. Illus.* TB/1111

History: Modern European

RENE ALBRECHT-CARRIE, Ed.: The Concert of Europe # HR/1341

MAX BELOFF: The Age of Absolutism, 1660-1815 TB/1062

OTTO VON BISMARCK: Reflections and Reminiscences. *Ed. with Intro. by Theodore S. Hamerow* ¶ TB/1357

EUGENE C. BLACK, Ed.: British Politics in the Nineteenth Century # HR/1427

EUGENE C. BLACK, Ed.: European Political History, 1815-1870: *Aspects of Liberalism* ¶ TB/1331

ASA BRIGGS: The Making of Modern England, 1783-1867: *The Age of Improvement* ° TB/1203

ALAN BULLOCK: Hitler, A Study in Tyranny. ° *Revised Edition. Illus.* TB/1123

EDMUND BURKE: On Revolution. *Ed. by Robert A. Smith* TB/1401

E. R. CARR: International Relations Between the Two World Wars. 1919-1939 ° TB/1279

E. H. CARR: The Twenty Years' Crisis, 1919-1939: *An Introduction to the Study of International Relations* ° TB/1122

GORDON A. CRAIG: From Bismarck to Adenauer: *Aspects of German Statecraft. Revised Edition* TB/1171

LESTER G. CROCKER, Ed.: The Age of Enlightenment # HR/1423

DENIS DIDEROT: The Encyclopedia: *Selections. Edited and Translated with Introduction by Stephen Gendzier* TB/1299

JACQUES DROZ: Europe between Revolutions, 1815-1848. ° *a Trans. by Robert Baldick* TB/1346

JOHANN GOTTLIEB FICHTE: Addresses to the German Nation. *Ed. with Intro. by George A. Kelly* ¶ TB/1366

ROBERT & ELBORG FORSTER, Eds.: European Society in the Eighteenth Century # HR/1404

C. C. GILLISPIE: Genesis and Geology: *The Decades before Darwin* § TB/51

ALBERT GOODWIN, Ed.: The European Nobility in the Enghteenth Century TB/1313

ALBERT GOODWIN: The French Revolution TB/1064

ALBERT GUERARD: France in the Classical Age: *The Life and Death of an Ideal* TB/1183

JOHN B. HALSTED, Ed.: Romanticism # HR/1387

J. H. HEXTER: Reappraisals in History: *New Views on History and Society in Early Modern Europe* ° TB/1100

STANLEY HOFFMANN et al.: In Search of France: *The Economy, Society and Political System In the Twentieth Century* TB/1219

H. STUART HUGHES: The Obstructed Path: *French Social Thought in the Years of Desperation* TB/1451

JOHAN HUIZINGA: Dutch Civilisation in the 17th Century and Other Essays TB/1453

LIONAL KOCHAN: The Struggle for Germany: *1914-45* TB/1304

HANS KOHN: The Mind of Germany: *The Education of a Nation* TB/1204

HANS KOHN, Ed.: The Mind of Modern Russia: *Historical and Political Thought of Russia's Great Age* TB/1065

WALTER LAQUEUR & GEORGE L. MOSSE, Eds.: Education and Social Structure in the 20th Century. ° *Volume 6 of the* Journal of Contemporary History TB/1339

WALTER LAQUEUR & GEORGE L. MOSSE, Ed.: International Fascism, 1920-1945. ° *Volume 1 of the* Journal of Contemporary History TB/1276

WALTER LAQUEUR & GEORGE L. MOSSE, Eds.: Literature and Politics in the 20th Century. ° *Volume 5 of the* Journal of Contemporary History. TB/1328

WALTER LAQUEUR & GEORGE L. MOSSE, Eds.: The New History: *Trends in Historical Research and Writing Since World War II.* ° *Volume 4 of the* Journal of Contemporary History TB/1327

WALTER LAQUEUR & GEORGE L. MOSSE, Eds.: 1914: *The Coming of the First World War.* ° *Volume3 of the* Journal of Contemporary *History* TB/1306

C. A. MACARTNEY, Ed.: The Habsburg and Hohenzollern Dynasties in the Seventeenth and Eighteenth Centuries # HR/1400

JOHN MCMANNERS: European History, 1789-1914: *Men, Machines and Freedom* TB/1419

PAUL MANTOUX: The Industrial Revolution in the Eighteenth Century: *An Outline of the Beginnings of the Modern Factory System in England* TB/1079

FRANK E. MANUEL: The Prophets of Paris: *Turgot, Condorcet, Saint-Simon, Fourier, and Comte* TB/1218

KINGSLEY MARTIN: French Liberal Thought in the Eighteenth Century: *A Study of Political Ideas from Bayle to Condorcet* TB/1114

NAPOLEON III: Napoleonic Ideas: *Des Idées Napoléoniennes, par le Prince Napoléon-Louis Bonaparte. Ed. by Brison D. Gooch* ¶ TB/1336

FRANZ NEUMANN: Behemoth: *The Structure and Practice of National Socialism, 1933-1944* TB/1289

DAVID OGG: Europe of the Ancien Régime, 1715-1783 ° *a* TB/1271

GEORGE RUDE: Revolutionary Europe, 1783-1815 ° *a* TB/1272

MASSIMO SALVADORI, Ed.: Modern Socialism # TB/1374

HUGH SETON-WATSON: Eastern Europe Between the Wars, 1918-1941 TB/1330

DENIS MACK SMITH, Ed.: The Making of Italy, 1796-1870 # HR/1356

ALBERT SOREL: Europe Under the Old Regime. *Translated by Francis H. Herrick* TB/1121

ROLAND N. STROMBERG, Ed.: Realism, Naturalism, and Symbolism: *Modes of Thought and Expression in Europe, 1848-1914* # HR/1355

A. J. P. TAYLOR: From Napoleon to Lenin: *Historical Essays* ° TB/1268

A. J. P. TAYLOR: The Habsburg Monarchy, 1809-1918: *A History of the Austrian Empire and Austria-Hungary* ° TB/1187

J. M. THOMPSON: European History, 1494-1789 TB/1431

DAVID THOMSON, Ed.: France: Empire and Republic, 1850-1940 # HR/1387

ALEXIS DE TOCQUEVILLE & GUSTAVE DE BEAUMONT: Tocqueville and Beaumont on Social Reform. *Ed. and trans. with Intro. by Seymour Drescher* TB/1343

G. M. TREVELYAN: British History in the Nineteenth Century and After: 1792-1919 ° TB/1251

H. R. TREVOR-ROPER: Historical Essays TB/1269

W. WARREN WAGAR, Ed.: Science, Faith, and MAN: *European Thought Since 1914* # HR/1362

MACK WALKER, Ed.: Metternich's Europe, 1813-1848 # HR/1361

ELIZABETH WISKEMANN: Europe of the Dictators, 1919-1945 ° *a* TB/1273

JOHN B. WOLF: France: 1814-1919: *The Rise of a Liberal-Democratic Society* TB/3019

Literature & Literary Criticism

JACQUES BARZUN: The House of Intellect TB/1051

W. J. BATE: From Classic to Romantic: *Premises of Taste in Eighteenth Century England* TB/1036

VAN WYCK BROOKS: Van Wyck Brooks: The Early Years: *A Selection from his Works, 1908-1921 Ed. with Intro. by Claire Sprague* TB/3082

ERNST R. CURTIUS: European Literature and the Latin Middle Ages. *Trans. by Willard Trask* TB/2015

RICHMOND LATTIMORE, Translator: The Odyssey of Homer TB/1389

SAMUEL PEPYS: The Diary of Samual Pepys. ° *Edited by O. F. Morshead. 60 illus. by Ernest Shepard* TB/1007

ROBERT PREYER, Ed.: Victorian Literature ** TB/1302

ALBION W. TOURGEE: A Fool's Errand: *A Novel of the South during Reconstruction. Intro. by George Fredrickson* TB/3074

BASIL WILEY: Nineteenth Century Studies: *Coleridge to Matthew Arnold* ° TB/1261

Philosophy

HENRI BERGSON: Time and Free Will: *An Essay on the Immediate Data of Consciousness* ° TB/1021

LUDWIG BINSWANGER: Being-in-the-World: *Selected Papers. Trans. with Intro. by Jacob Needleman* TB/1365

H. J. BLACKHAM: Six Existentialist Thinkers: *Kierkegaard, Nietzsche, Jaspers, Marcel, Heidegger, Sartre* ° TB/1002

J. M. BOCHENSKI: The Methods of Contemporary Thought. *Trans. by Peter Caws* TB/1377

CRANE BRINTON: Nietzsche. *Preface, Bibliography, and Epilogue by the Author* TB/1197

ERNST CASSIRER: Rousseau, Kant and Goethe. *Intro. by Peter Gay* TB/1092
FREDERICK COPLESTON, S. J.: Medieval Philosophy TB/376
F. M. CORNFORD: From Religion to Philosophy: *A Study in the Origins of Western Speculation* § TB/20
WILFRID DESAN: The Tragic Finale: *An Essay on the Philosophy of Jean-Paul Sartre* TB/1030
MARVIN FARBER: The Aims of Phenomenology: *The Motives, Methods, and Impact of Husserl's Thought* TB/1291
MARVIN FARBER: Basic Issues of Philosophy: *Experience, Reality, and Human Values* TB/1344
MARVIN FARBERS: Phenomenology and Existence: *Towards a Philosophy within Nature* TB/1295
PAUL FRIEDLANDER: `Plato: *An Introduction* TB/2017
MICHAEL GELVEN: A Commentary on Heidegger's "Being and Time" TB/1464
J. GLENN GRAY: Hegel and Greek Thought TB/1409
W. K. C. GUTHRIE: The Greek Philosophers: *From Thales to Aristotle* ° TB/1008
G. W. F. HEGEL: On Art, Religion Philosophy: *Introductory Lectures to the Realm of Absolute Spirit.* || *Edited with an Introduction by J. Glenn Gray* TB/1463
G. W. F. HEGEL: Phenomenology of Mind. ° || *Introduction by George Lichtheim* TB/1303
MARTIN HEIDEGGER: Discourse on Thinking. *Translated with a Preface by John M. Anderson and E. Hans Freund. Introduction by John M. Anderson* TB/1459
F. H. HEINEMANN: Existentialism and the Modern Predicament TB/28
WERER HEISENBERG: Physics and Philosophy: *The Revolution in Modern Science. Intro. by F. S. C. Northrop* TB/549
EDMUND HUSSERL: Phenomenology and the Crisis of Philosophy. § *Translated with an Introduction by Quentin Lauer* TB/1170
IMMANUEL KANT: Groundwork of the Metaphysic of Morals. *Translated and Analyzed by H. J. Paton* TB/1159
IMMANUEL KANT: Lectures on Ethics. § *Introduction by Lewis White Beck* TB/105
WALTER KAUFMANN, Ed.: Religion From Tolstoy to Camus: *Basic Writings on Religious Truth and Morals* TB/123
QUENTIN LAUER: Phenomenology: *Its Genesis and Prospect. Preface by Aron Gurwitsch* TB/1169
MAURICE MANDELBAUM: The Problem of Historical Knowledge: *An Answer to Relativism* TB/1198
H. J. PATON: The Categorical Imperative: *A Study in Kant's Moral Philosophy* TB/1325
MICHAEL POLANYI: Personal Knowledge: *Towards a Post-Critical Philosophy* TB/1158
KARL R. POPPER: Conjectures and Refutations: *The Growth of Scientific Knowledge* TB/1376
WILLARD VAN ORMAN QUINE: Elementary Logic *Revised Edition* TB/577
WILLARD VAN ORMAN QUINE: From a Logical Point of View: *Logico-Philosophical Essays* TB/566
JOHN E. SMITH: Themes in American Philosophy: *Purpose, Experience and Community* TB/1466
MORTON WHITE: Foundations of Historical Knowledge TB/1440
WILHELM WINDELBAND: A History of Philosophy *Vol. I: Greek, Roman, Medieval* TB/38 *Vol. II: Renaissance, Enlightenment, Modern* TB/39
LUDWIG WITTGENSTEIN: The Blue and Brown Books ° TB/1211
LUDWIG WITTGENSTEIN: Notebooks, 1914-1916 TB/1441

Political Science & Government

C. E. BLACK: The Dynamics of Modernization: *A Study in Comparative History* TB/1321
DENIS W. BROGAN: Politics in America. *New Introduction by the Author* TB/1469
CRANE BRINTON: English Political Thought in the Nineteenth Century TB/1071
ROBERT CONQUEST: Power and Policy in the USSR: *The Study of Soviet Dynastics* ° TB/1307
ROBERT A. DAHL & CHARLES E. LINDBLOM: Politics, Economics, and Welfare: *Planning and Politico-Economic Systems Resolved into Basic Social Processes* TB/1277
HANS KOHN: Political Ideologies of the 20th Century TB/1277
ROY C. MACRIDIS, Ed.: Political Parties: *Contemporary Trends and Ideas* ** TB/1322
ROBERT GREEN MC CLOSKEY: American Conservatism in the Age of Enterprise, 1865-1910 TB/1137
MARSILIUS OF PADUA: The Defender of Peace. *The* Defensor Pacis. *Translated with an Introduction by Alan Gewirth* TB/1310
KINGSLEY MARTIN: French Liberal Thought in the Eighteenth Century: *A Study of Political Ideas from Bayle to Condorcet* TB/1114
BARRINGTON MOORE, JR.:Political Power and Social Theory: *Seven Studies* || TB/1221
BARRINGTON MOORE, JR.: Soviet Politics—The Dilemma of Power: *The Role of Ideas in Social Change* || TB/1222
BARRINGTON MOORE, JR.: Terror and Progress—USSR: *Some Sources of Change and Stability*
JOHN B. MORRALL: Political Thought in Medieval Times TB/1076
KARL R. POPPER: The Open Society and Its Enemies *Vol. I: The Spell of Plato* TB/1101 *Vol. II: The High Tide of Prophecy: Hegel, Marx, and the Aftermath* TB/1102
CONYERS READ, Ed.: The Constitution Reconsidered. *Revised Edition, Preface by Richard B. Morris* TB/1384
JOHN P. ROCHE, Ed.: Origins of American Political Thought: *Selected Readings* TB/1301
JOHN P. ROCHE, Ed.: American Political Thought: *From Jefferson to Progressivism* TB/1332
HENRI DE SAINT-SIMON: Social Organization, The Science of Man, and Other Writings. || *Edited and Translated with an Introduction by Felix Markham* TB/1152
CHARLES SCHOTTLAND, Ed.: The Welfare State ** TB/1323
JOSEPH A. SCHUMPETER: Capitalism, Socialism and Democracy TB/3008

Psychology

ALFRED ADLER: The Individual Psychology of Alfred Adler: *A Systematic Presentation in Selections from His Writings. Edited by Heinz L. & Rowena R. Ansbacher* TB/1154
LUDWIG BINSWANGER: Being-in-the-World: *Selected Papers.* || *Trans. with Intro. by Jacob Needleman* TB/1365
HADLEY CANTRIL: The Invasion from Mars: *A Study in the Psychology of Panic* || TB/1282
MIRCEA ELIADE: Cosmos and History: *The Myth of the Eternal Return* § TB/2050
MIRCEA ELIADE: Myth and Reality TB/1369

MIRCEA ELIADE: Myths, Dreams and Mysteries: *The Encounter Between Contemporary Faiths and Archaic Realities* § TB/1320
MIRCEA ELIADE: Rites and Symbols of Initiation: *The Mysteries of Birth and Rebirth* § TB/1236
HERBERT FINGARETTE: The Self in Transformation: *Psychoanalysis, Philosophy and the Life of the Spirit* || TB/1177
SIGMUND FREUD: On Creativity and the Unconscious: *Papers on the Psychology of Art, Literature, Love, Religion. § Intro. by Benjamin Nelson* TB/45
J. GLENN GRAY: The Warriors: *Reflections on Men in Battle. Introduction by Hannah Arendt* TB/1294
WILLIAM JAMES: Psychology: *The Briefer Course. Edited with an Intro. by Gordon Allport* TB/1034
C. G. JUNG: Psychological Reflections. *Ed. by J. Jacobi* TB/2001
KARL MENNINGER, M.D.: Theory of Psychoanalytic Technique TB/1144
JOHN H. SCHAAR: Escape from Authority: *The Perspectives of Erich Fromm* TB/1155
MUZAFER SHERIF: The Psychology of Social Norms. *Introduction by Gardner Murphy* TB/3072
HELLMUT WILHELM: Change: *Eight Lectures on the* I Ching TB/2019

Religion: Ancient and Classical, Biblical and Judaic Traditions

W. F. ALBRIGHT: The Biblical Period from Abraham to Ezra TB/102
SALO W. BARON: Modern Nationalism and Religion TB/818
C. K. BARRETT, Ed.: The New Testament Background: *Selected Documents* TB/86
MARTIN BUBER: Eclipse of God: *Studies in the Relation Between Religion and Philosophy* TB/12
MARTIN BUBER: Hasidism and Modern Man. *Edited and Translated by Maurice Friedman* TB/839
MARTIN BUBER: The Knowledge of Man. *Edited with an Introduction by Maurice Friedman. Translated by Maurice Friedman and Ronald Gregor Smith* TB/135
MARTIN BUBER: Moses. *The Revelation and the Covenant* TB/837
MARTIN BUBER: The Origin and Meaning of Hasidism. *Edited and Translated by Maurice Friedman* TB/835
MARTIN BUBER: The Prophetic Faith TB/73
MARTIN BUBER: Two Types of Faith: *Interpenetration of Judaism and Christianity* ° TB/75
MALCOLM L. DIAMOND: Martin Buber: *Jewish Existentialist* TB/840
M. S. ENSLIN: Christian Beginnings TB/5
M. S. ENSLIN: The Literature of the Christian Movement TB/6
ERNST LUDWIG EHRLICH: A Concise History of Israel: *From the Earliest Times to the Destruction of the Temple in A.D. 70* ° TB/128
HENRI FRANKFORT: Ancient Egyptian Religion: *An Interpretation* TB/77
ABRAHAM HESCHEL: The Earth Is the Lord's & The Sabbath. *Two Essays* TB/828
ABRAHAM HESCHEL: God in Search of Man: *A Philosophy of Judaism* TB/807
ABRAHAM HESCHEL: Man Is not Alone: *A Philosophy of Religion* TB/838
ABRAHAM HESCHEL: The Prophets: *An Introduction* TB/1421
T. J. MEEK: Hebrew Origins TB/69
JAMES MUILENBURG: The Way of Israel: *Biblical Faith and Ethics* TB/133
H. J. ROSE: Religion in Greece and Rome TB/55
H. H. ROWLEY: The Growth of the Old Testament TB/107
D. WINTON THOMAS, Ed.: Documents from Old Testament Times TB/85

Religion: General Christianity

ROLAND H. BAINTON: Christendom: *A Short History of Christianity and Its Impact on Western Civilization. Illus.* Vol. I TB/131; Vol. II TB/132
JOHN T. MCNEILL: Modern Christian Movements. *Revised Edition* TB/1402
ERNST TROELTSCH: The Social Teaching of the Christian Churches. *Intro. by H. Richard Niebuhr* Vol. TB/71; Vol. II TB/72

Religion: Early Christianity Through Reformation

ANSELM OF CANTERBURY: Truth, Freedom, and Evil: *Three Philosophical Dialogues. Edited and Translated by Jasper Hopkins and Herbert Richardson* TB/317
MARSHALL W. BALDWIN, Ed.: Christianity through the 13th Century # HR/1468
W. D. DAVIES: Paul and Rabbinic Judaism: *Some Rabbinic Elements in Pauline Theology. Revised Edition* ° TB/146
ADOLF DEISSMAN: Paul: *A Study in Social and Religious History* TB/15
JOHANNES ECKHART: Meister Eckhart: *A Modern Translation by R. Blakney* TB/8
EDGAR J. GOODSPEED: A Life of Jesus TB/1
ROBERT M. GRANT: Gnosticism and Early Christianity TB/136
WILLIAM HALLER: The Rise of Puritanism TB/22
GERHART B. LADNER: The Idea of Reform: *Its Impact on the Christian Thought and Action in the Age of the Fathers* TB/149
ARTHUR DARBY NOCK: Early Gentile Christianity and Its Hellenistic Background TB/111
ARTHUR DARBY NOCK: St. Paul ° TR/104
GORDON RUPP: Luther's Progress to the Diet of Worms ° TB/120

Religion: The Protestant Tradition

KARL BARTH: Church Dogmatics: *A Selection. Intro. by H. Gollwitzer. Ed. by G. W. Bromiley* TB/95
KARL BARTH: Dogmatics in Outline TB/56
KARL BARTH: The Word of God and the Word of Man TB/13
HERBERT BRAUN, et al.: God and Christ: *Existence and Province. Volume 5 of* Journal for Theology and the Church, *edited by Robert W. Funk and Gerhard Ebeling* TB/255
WHITNEY R. CROSS: The Burned-Over District: *The Social and Intellectual History of Enthusiastic Religion in Western New York, 1800-1850* TB/1242
NELS F. S. FERRE: Swedish Contributions to Modern Theology. *New Chapter by William A. Johnson* TB/147
WILLIAM R. HUTCHISON, Ed.: American Protestant Thought: *The Liberal Era* ‡ TB/1385
ERNST KASEMANN, et al.: Distinctive Protestant and Catholic Themes Reconsidered. *Volume 3 of Journal for Theology and the Church,*

edited by Robert W. Funk and Gerhard Ebeling TB/253

SOREN KIERKEGAARD: On Authority and Revelation: *The Book on Adler, or a Cycle of Ethico-Religious Essays. Introduction by F. Sontag* TB/139

SOREN KIERKEGAARD: Crisis in the Life of an Actress, *and Other Essays on Drama. Translated with an Introduction by Stephen Crites* TB/145

SOREN KIERKEGAARD: Edifying Discourses. *Edited with an Intro. by Paul Holmer* TB/32

SOREN KIERKEGAARD: The Journals of Kierkegaard. ° *Edited with an Intro. by Alexander Dru* TB/52

SOREN KIERKEGAARD: The Point of View for My Work as an Author: *A Report to History.* § *Preface by Benjamin Nelson* TB/88

SOREN KIERKEGAARD: The Present Age. § *Translated and edited by Alexander Dru. Introduction by Walter Kaufmann* TB/94

SOREN KIERKEGAARD: Purity of Heart. *Trans. by Douglas Steere* TB/4

SOREN KIERKEGAARD: Repetition: *An Essay in Experimental Psychology* § TB/117

SOREN KIERKEGAARD: Works of Love: *Some Christian Reflections in the Form of Discourses* TB/122

WILLIAM G. MCLOUGHLIN, Ed.: The American Evangelicals: 1800-1900: *An Anthology* TB/1382

WOLFHART PANNENBERG, et al.: History and Hermeneutic. *Volume 4 of* Journal for Theology and the Church, *edited by Robert W. Funk and Gerhard Ebeling* TB/254

JAMES M. ROBINSON, et al.: The Bultmann School of Biblical Interpretation: New Directions? *Volume 1 of* Journal for Theology and the Church, *edited by Robert W. Funk and Gerhard Ebeling* TB/251

F. SCHLEIERMACHER: The Christian Faith. *Introduction by Richard R. Niebuhr.* Vol. I TB/108; Vol. II TB/109

F. SCHLEIERMACHER: On Religion: *Speeches to Its Cultured Despisers. Intro. by Rudolf Otto* TB/36

TIMOTHY L. SMITH: Revivalism and Social Reform: *American Protestantism on the Eve of the Civil War* TB/1229

PAUL TILLICH: Dynamics of Faith TB/42

PAUL TILLICH: Morality and Beyond TB/142

EVELYN UNDERHILL: Worship TB/10

Religion: The Roman & Eastern Christian Traditions

A. ROBERT CAPONIGRI, Ed.: Modern Catholic Thinkers II: *The Church and the Political Order* TB/307

G. P. FEDOTOV: The Russian Religious Mind: *Kievan Christianity, the tenth to the thirteenth Centuries* TB/370

GABRIEL MARCEL: Being and Having: *An Existential Diary. Introduction by James Collins* TB/310

GABRIEL MARCEL: Homo Viator: *Introduction to a Metaphysic of Hope* TB/397

Religion: Oriental Religions

TOR ANDRAE: Mohammed: *The Man and His Faith* § TB/62

EDWARD CONZE: Buddhism: *Its Essence and Development.* ° *Foreword by Arthur Waley* TB/58

EDWARD CONZE: Buddhist Meditation TB/1442

EDWARD CONZE et al, Editors: Buddhist Texts through the Ages TB/113

ANANDA COOMARASWAMY: Buddha and the Gospel of Buddhism TB/119

H. G. CREEL: Confucius and the Chinese Way TB/63

FRANKLIN EDGERTON, Trans. & Ed.: The Bhagavad Gita TB/115

SWAMI NIKHILANANDA, Trans. & Ed.: The Upanishads TB/114

D. T. SUZUKI: On Indian Mahayana Buddhism. ° *Ed. with Intro. by Edward Conze.* TB/1403

Religion: Philosophy, Culture, and Society

NICOLAS BERDYAEV: The Destiny of Man TB/61

RUDOLF BULTMANN: History and Eschatology: *The Presence of Eternity* ° TB/91

RUDOLF BULTMANN AND FIVE CRITICS: Kerygma and Myth: *A Theological Debate* TB/80

RUDOLF BULTMANN and KARL KUNDSIN: Form Criticism: *Two Essays on New Testament Research. Trans. by F. C. Grant* TB/96

WILLIAM A. CLEBSCH & CHARLES R. JAEKLE: Pastoral Care in Historical Perspective: *An Essay with Exhibits* TB/148

FREDERICK FERRE: Language, Logic and God. *New Preface by the Author* TB/1407

LUDWIG FEUERBACH: The Essence of Christianity. § *Introduction by Karl Barth. Foreword by H. Richard Niebuhr* TB/11

ADOLF HARNACK: What Is Christianity? § *Introduction by Rudolf Bultmann* TB/17

KYLE HASELDEN: The Racial Problem in Christian Perspective TB/116

MARTIN HEIDEGGER: Discourse on Thinking. *Translated with a Preface by John M. Anderson and E. Hans Freund. Introduction by John M. Anderson* TB/1459

IMMANUEL KANT: Religion Within the Limits of Reason Alone. § *Introduction by Theodore M. Greene and John Silber* TB/FG

WALTER KAUFMANN, Ed.: Religion from Tolstoy to Camus: *Basic Writings on Religious Truth and Morals. Enlarged Edition* TB/123

H. RICHARD NIERUHR: Christ and Culture TB/3

H. RICHARD NIEBUHR: The Kingdom of God in America TB/49

ANDERS NYGREN: Agape and Eros. *Translated by Philip S. Watson* ° TB/1430

JOHN H. RANDALL, JR.: The Meaning of Religion for Man. *Revised with New Intro. by the Author* TB/1379

WALTER RAUSCHENBUSCHS Christianity and the Social Crisis. ‡ *Edited by Robert D. Cross* TB/3059

Science and Mathematics

JOHN TYLER BONNER: The Ideas of Biology. Σ *Illus.* TB/570

W. E. LE GROS CLARK: The Antecedents of Man: *An Introduction to the Evolution of the Primates.* ° *Illus.* TB/559

ROBERT E. COKER: Streams, Lakes, Ponds. *Illus.* TB/586

ROBERT E. COKER: This Great and Wide Sea: *An Introduction to Oceanography and Marine Biology. Illus.* TB/551

W. H. DOWDESWELL: Animal Ecology. *61 illus.* TB/543

C. V. DURELL: Readable Relativity. *Foreword by Freeman J. Dyson* TB/530
GEORGE GAMOW: Biography of Physics. Σ *Illus.* TB/567
F. K. HARE: The Restless Atmosphere TB/560
J. R. PIERCE: Symbols, Signals and Noise: *The Nature and Process of Communication* Σ TB/574
WILLARD VAN ORMAN QUINE: Mathematical Logic TB/558

Science: History

MARIE BOAS: The Scientific Renaissance, 1450-1630 ° TB/583
STEPHEN TOULMIN & JUNE GOODFIELD: The Architecture of Matter: *The Physics, Chemistry and Physiology of Matter, Both Animate and Inanimate, as it has Evolved since the Beginnings of Science* TB/584
STEPHEN TOULMIN & JUNE GOODFIELD: The Discovery TB/576
STEPHEN TOULMIN & JUNE GOODFIELD: The Fabric of the Heavens: *The Development of Astronomy and Dynamics* TB/579

Science: Philosophy

J. M. BOCHENSKI: The Methods of Contemporary Thought. *Tr. by Peter Caws* TB/1377
J. BRONOWSKI: Science and Human Values. *Revised and Enlarged. Illus.* TB/505
WERNER HEISENBERG: Physics and Philosophy: *The Revolution in Modern Science. Introduction by F. S. C. Northrop* TB/549
KARL R. POPPER: Conjectures and Refutations: *The Growth of Scientific Knowledge* TB/1376
KARL R. POPPER: The Logic of Scientific Discovery TB/1376
STEPHEN TOULMIN: Foresight and Understanding: *An Enquiry into the Aims of Science. Foreword by Jacques Barzun* TB/564
STEPHEN TOULMIN: The Philosophy of Science: *An Introduction* TB/513

Sociology and Anthropology

REINHARD BENDIX: Work and Authority in Industry: *Ideologies of Management in the Course of Industrialization* TB/3035
BERNARD BERELSON, Ed.: The Behavioral Sciences Today TB/1127
JOSEPH B. CASAGRANDE, Ed.: In the Company of Man: *Twenty Portraits of Anthropological Informants. Illus.* TB/3047
KENNETH B. CLARK: Dark Ghetto: *Dilemmas of Social Power. Foreword by Gunnar Myrdal* TB/1317
KENNETH CLARK & JEANNETTE HOPKINS: A Relevant War Against Poverty: *A Study of Community Action Programs and Observable Social Change* TB/1480
LEWIS COSER, Ed.: Political Sociology TB/1293
ROSE L. COSER, Ed.: Life Cycle and Achievement in America ** TB/1434
ALLISON DAVIS & JOHN DOLLARD: Children of Bondage: *The Personality Development of Negro Youth in the Urban South* || TB/3049
PETER F. DRUCKER: The New Society: *The Anatomy of Industrial Order* TB/1082
CORA DU BOIS: The People of Alor. *With a Preface by the Author*
Vol. I *Illus.* TB/1042; Vol. II TB/1043
EMILE DURKHEIM et al.: Essays on Sociology and Philosophy: *with Appraisals of Durkheim's Life and Thought.* || *Edited by Kurt H. Wolff* TB/1151
LEON FESTINGER, HENRY W. RIECKEN, STANLEY SCHACHTER: When Prophecy Fails: *A Social and Psychological Study of a Modern Group that Predicted the Destruction of the World* || TB/1132
CHARLES Y. GLOCK & RODNEY STARK: Christian Beliefs and Anti-Semitism. *Introduction by the Authors* TB/1454
ALVIN W. GOULDNER: The Hellenic World TB/1479
ALVIN W. GOULDNER: Wildcat Strike: *A Study in Worker-Management Relationships* || TB/1176
CESAR GRANA: Modernity and Its Discontents: *French Society and the French Man of Letters in the Nineteenth Century* TB/1318
L. S. B. LEAKEY: Adam's Ancestors: *The Evolution of Man and His Culture. Illus.* TB/1019
KURT LEWIN: Field Theory in Social Science: *Selected Theoretical Papers.* || *Edited by Dorwin Cartwright* TB/1135
RITCHIE P. LOWRY: Who's Running This Town? *Community Leadership and Social Change* TB/1383
R. M. MACIVER: Social Causation TB/1153
GARY T. MARX: Protest and Prejudice: *A Study of Belief in the Black Community* TB/1435
ROBERT K. MERTON, LEONARD BROOM, LEONARD S. COTTRELL, JR., Editors: Sociology Today: *Problems and Prospects* ||
Vol. I TB/1173; Vol. II TB/1174
GILBERT OSOFSKY, Ed.: The Burden of Race: A Documentary History of Negro-White Relations in America TB/1405
GILBERT OSOFSKY: Harlem: The Making of a Ghetto: *Negro New York 1890-1930* TB/1381
TALCOTT PARSONS & EDWARD A. SHILS, Editors: Toward a General Theory of Action: *Theoretical Foundations for the Social Sciences* TB/1083
PHILIP RIEFF: The Triumph of the Therapeutic: *Uses of Faith After Freud* TB/1360
JOHN H. ROHRER & MUNRO S. EDMONSON, Eds.: The Eighth Generation Grows Up: *Cultures and Personalities of New Orleans Negroes* || TB/3050
ARNOLD ROSE: The Negro in America: *The Condensed Version of Gunnar Myrdal's* An American Dilemma. *Second Edition* TB/3048
GEORGE ROSEN: Madness in Society: *Chapters in the Historical Sociology of Mental Illness.* || *Preface by Benjamin Nelson* TB/1337
PHILIP SELZNICK: TVA and the Grass Roots: *A Study in the Sociology of Formal Organization* TB/1230
PITIRIM A. SOROKIN: Contemporary Sociological Theories: *Through the First Quarter of the Twentieth Century* TB/3046
MAURICE R. STEIN: The Eclipse of Community: *An Interpretation of American Studies* TB/1128
EDWARD A. TIRYAKIAN, Ed.: Sociological Theory, Values and Sociocultural Change: *Essays in Honor of Pitirim A. Sorokin* ° TB/1316
FERDINAND TONNIES: Community and Society: *Gemeinschaft und Gesellschaft. Translated and Edited by Charles P. Loomis* TB/1116
SAMUEL E. WALLACE: Skid Row as a Way of Life TB/1367
W. LLOYD WARNER: Social Class in America: *The Evaluation of Status* TB/1013
FLORIAN ZNANIECKI: The Social Role of the Man of Knowledge. *Introduction by Lewis A. Coser* TB/1372